BONES OF CONTENTION

BONES OF CONTENTION

THE LIVING ARCHIVE OF VASIL LEVSKI AND THE MAKING OF BULGARIA'S NATIONAL HERO

Maria Todorova

Central European University Press
Budapest–New York

©2009 by Maria Todorova

Paperback edition published in 2011 by

CENTRAL EUROPEAN UNIVERSITY PRESS

An imprint of the
Central European University Share Company
Nádor utca 11, H-1051 Budapest, Hungary
Tel: +36-1-327-3138 or 327-3000
Fax: +36-1-327-3183
E-mail: ceupress@ceu.hu
Website: www.ceupress.hu

400 West 59th Street, New York NY 10019, USA
Tel: +1-212-547-6932
Fax: +1-646-557-2416
E-mail: mgreenwald@sorosny.org

All rights reserved. No part of this publication may be reproduced,
stored in a retrieval system, or transmitted,
in any form or by any means, without the permission
of the Publisher.

ISBN 978-615-5053-09-2 Paperback

LIBRARY OF CONGRESS CATALOGING-IN-PUBLICATION DATA

Todorova, Mariia Nikolaeva.
  Bones of contention : the living archive of Vasil Levski and the making of Bulgaria's national hero / Maria Todorova.
   p. cm.
  Includes bibliographical references and index.
  ISBN 978-6155053092 (pbk.)
  1. Levski, Vasil Ivanov, 1837–1873—Tomb. 2. Levski, Vasil Ivanov, 1837–1873—Death and burial. 3. Dead—Political aspects—Bulgaria. 4. Levski, Vasil Ivanov, 1837–1873—Public opinion. 5. Heroes—Bulgaria. 6. Bulgaria—Historiography. 7. Nationalism—Bulgaria. 8. Canonization—Political aspects—Bulgaria. 9. Memory—Social aspects—Bulgaria. 10. Public opinion—Bulgaria. I. Title.

DR83.2.L4T63 2011
949.9'015092--dc22

2010045604

Printed in the USA

*To the memory of my father,
who is part of this story*

Table of Contents

PREFACE TO THE PAPERBACK EDITION IX

INTRODUCTION XI

PART I.
Bones of Contention or Professionals, Dilettantes, and Who Owns History 1
1. A "Social Drama" at the Bulgarian Academy of Sciences ... 7
2. From Breach to Crisis 27
3. No Redress, or Where Are Levski's Bones? 47
4. A Socialist Public Sphere? 59
5. "Professionals" and "Dilettantes" 75
6. Recognizing the Schism, or What Is Worse: Bad Professionals or Good Nationalists? 91

PART II.
The Apostle of Freedom, or What Makes a Hero? 109
1. What Is a Hero and Are Heroes Born? 117
2. The "Making" of Vasil Levski 129
3. A Banner for All Causes: Appropriating the Hero 149
4. Contesting the Hero 167
5. The Literary and Visual Hypostases of the Hero 179
6. From Hero for All to Dissident and Back 187

PART III.
The National Hero as Secular Saint: The Canonization of Levski 209
1. The Split, or How a Bicephalous Organism Functions 217
2. The Canonization and Its Implications 225
3. Levski and the Bulgarian Church: Memory and Narration .. 241

4. The Orchestration of a Grassroots Cultus	261
5. Commemoration, Ritual, and the Sacred	271
6. Heroes and Saints: the Dialectics of Reincarnation	291
CONCLUSION	307
REFERENCES	317
INDEX	325

Preface to the Paperback Edition

I have been extremely fortunate with my publisher, in fact spoilt by it, and realize that this is a very luxurious and rare kind of luck. Therefore, I want to begin this brief preface with my warmest thanks to Central European University Press for their unflinching support throughout the double process of publishing my manuscript. Without the immense generosity of the press, neither the hardback, not the paperback would have seen the light of day.

This paperback may be unique in the history of its genre. It is nearly half the size of the hardback and at a considerably lower price, yet the entire argument and practically the whole main text have remained intact. The questions that beg an answer are: How was this achieved? Why was it not done in the first place?

Had I done the abridgement two years ago, when the voluminous hardback was on the agenda, the book still would have had the title *Bones of Contention*, and it still would have been about the making of a great hero of a small nation throughout the nineteenth and twentieth centuries, with all the accompanying problematic about nationalism, socialism, post-socialism, saint a hero worship, memory, ritual, and the place of the historical profession. What would have been omitted would be the "living archive," a notion that encompasses both the classical archive, as well as the unconventional sources that have been accumulated and are being created as we speak, including this book itself.

Why did this matter so much to me? The obvious but also too conventional answer is that I wanted to support my research in the greatest possible detail, to make it foolproof. I also wanted to challenge the practice of seeing detailed and voluminous works in English that afforded such apparatus only on events and personalities from usually the history of countries pertaining to the privileged zone of Western Civ, whereas works on Eastern Europe or other world regions that are not deemed significant enough form the current hegemonic point of view, are supposed to be condensed to the essentials of their argument. But there was a further and more substantial motivation. What mattered to me was the parallel documenting of an archive and also of my own past, as the past of a particular generation that lived through late socialism. All of this was possible only by resorting to detailed and dense description, much of it in footnotes. I have always been an inveterate and unabashed lover of footnotes, and once CEU Press agreed to take the manuscript in its entirety, they went for the best possible and most meaningful, but certainly also most luxurious, in terms of space, referencing system: footnotes at each page. The one thing we economized on in the hardback was a separate bibliography because this would have bloated the volume further and, in many ways, would have been a mere repetition to the detailed reference illustrations at each instance in the text.

The living archive, admittedly, is interesting to a much more narrow readership, but I thought that it deserved it. Once the hardback was out, this was achieved. Other readers, no less attentive and critical, but not so much immersed in the detail or vested in the specialized knowledge, would be reassured about the quality of the main argument by the supporting apparatus, but most likely would only glance through it, if at all. It is for this majority that the present cuts were made. This was not such a painful process as it seems at first glance, although quite time-consuming. Most of it was at the expense of the footnotes that have vanished and there are at present only references to a bibliography at the end of the paperback. Obviously, this bibliography is much shorter than the cumulative but unpublished bibliographical entries mentioned in the hardback. Most of the Bulgarian archival and bibliographical detail is gone. Furthermore, I used the possibility to make some corrections and further trim the prose and condense the argument.

The resulting paperback can now stand on its own, as a separate book. Its reference to the hardback is not mechanical. It can be seen as a companion to the hardback (or vice versa), rather than the soft-covered and cheap mirror version of its older sibling. The "living archive" is still in the title, because, even if it is not on the pages of the paperback, it can be reached by readers with real in-depth interest without any difficulty in the hardback.

Introduction

This book is about documenting and analyzing the living archive around the figure of Vasil Levski, arguably the major and only uncontested hero of the Bulgarian national pantheon. In the course of working on the problem, it became clear that this cannot be a finite task. The processes described, although with a chronological depth of almost two centuries, are still very much in the making, and the living archive expands not only in size but constantly adding surprising new forms. While archives continue to occupy an almost sacral place both in the public imagination (as repositories of truth) as well as in legitimizing the historical profession (as the centerpiece and major tool of the historians' work), they have become themselves objects of sophisticated scrutiny. It has been long (although not broadly) recognized that archives are neither neutral institutions in struggles for power, nor does their content impart unbiased objectivity on interpretive applications. They are loci of dynamic encounters not only between scholars and historical "traces," between the present and the past, but sites of contestation between institution builders both at the time of their genesis and in the course of their preservation. In the past several decades the notion of the archive itself has opened up to include materials that have not been conventionally covered under this rubric: oral testimony, novels, the press, material artifacts, art. This study is both an attempt to create a personal archive of Levskiana (from the plethora of existing archives), to describe and analyze it and, at the same time, to unpack its meaning and transparently detail its making.

The project itself started as an investigation of nationalism, turned into one on communism and postcommunism, and remained, above all, an experiment in writing a living archive. My interest in Levski began as an offshoot of an attempt to make sense of what has been called Balkan nationalism but consists of very different phenomena in terms of their genealogy, typology, articulation and intensity. I had been specially interested in the metaphoric glue (shorthand for cohesive processes or ideologies) that keeps nations together, in a word, in national symbology, and had been thinking of a comparative history of the national symbols of Greeks, Turks, Bulgarians, Romanians, Albanians, Serbs and the other South Slavs. All of this was building on a loose hypothesis that there exists a correlation between the cultural articulation of nationalism and its practical goals and strength. The more I looked into this metaphoric glue—analyzing the phases of nation building, the history of educational institutions and communications systems, the history of language and language reforms, the development of the polity, in a word, at the different aspects of constructing "the imagined community,"—the more my interest shifted from the nature and functions of the glue to its "brand names." That is, it shifted to the question of why one type of glue is preferred over another, and what this can tell us about the specific characteristics of separate nationalisms. It is a question that has interested other observers, and various scholars have suggested various answers within diverse explanatory frameworks. Here is one from a very different period:

> The most suggestive antithesis between the Greek soul and the Bulgarian soul rings out in the popular poetry developed in Greece and Bulgaria during the Turkish occupation. During this dark age, the popular muse of the Greeks, as that of the Serbs also, sang of the ancient glories and the exalted deeds of heroes who frequently turned against the Turkish tyrant; by contrast, Bulgarian popular poetry cannot offer us a single historical or heroic poem: it can only take in certain Bacchic or amorous poems; or, indeed, in the absence of any other sort of hero, it exalts the *haidouts*, otherwise known as brigands, who have absolutely no connection with the Serbian *hajduks* or the Greek *klefts*. The latter are national heroes, after a historical model; the Bulgarian *haidouts* are common-law criminals, devoid of personality and lacking even the virile audacity of ordinary brigands (Colocotronis 1918: 129).

This merciless verdict, written almost a century ago, at the height of the Greek–Bulgarian animus at the end of the First World War is not merely an illustration of the *Zeitgeist*, obsessed as it was with the national soul and character, as well as with the collective (un)conscious, and mostly with the virtues of one's own national psyche. It points to the weight allotted by nationalists to the heroes of the nation as the tangible embodiment of its soul, next to language as its intangible quintessence. National heroes are a recognized cornerstone of the symbolic repertoire of nationalism:

> While definitions of grandeur and glory vary, every nationalism requires a touchstone of virtue and heroism, to guide and give meaning to the tasks of regeneration. The future of the ethnic community can only derive meaning and achieve its form from the pristine 'golden age' when men were 'heroes.' Heroes provide models of virtuous conduct, their deeds of valor inspire faith and courage in their oppressed and decadent descendants (Smith 1999: 65).

At the same time, they are not necessarily the central pillar of its symbolic order. In a Balkan context—the first larger comparative circle, in which Bulgarian nationalism can be understood—the national imaginary has diverse foci. In the Serbian national imagination, alongside the attention to heroes, the special focus is on an epic and a battle; in the Greek, on the classical past and the notion of direct continuity; in the Romanian, for all the controversies over "the ideal prince," it is on events and their commemoration (the 1848 revolutions or the 1919 unification). In the Bulgarian case, however, *pace* Colocotronis's verdict, there is a clear orientation to national heroes. What emerges is not only the centrality of heroic figures in general but the ubiquity of one particular national hero: Vasil Levski. In this sense, one can posit a distinct particularity of Bulgarian nationalism (that itself underscores Bulgarian history in the past two centuries): an unusual concentration of competing and contesting discourses and appropriations on the same figure. If a parallel instance has to be found, it would point out mostly in the direction of Joan of Arc in French history and self-perception, or Abraham Lincoln in the American one, all chronological, factual, and structural differences notwithstanding. The other obvious parallel is Giuseppe Garibaldi who was hailed as "a popular hero, a saint, a second Christ," and among the Sicilian peasantry his red shirt was reputed to repel bullets. One is told that "historians judge him to have been the only great democratic leader of truly humble origins in the 19th century, and that surely this fact goes a long way to explain his extraordinary fame and the cult surrounding him" (*The Times Literary*

Supplement, June 17, 2005, 8). This book is, among other things, about another great democratic leader of humble origins who apparently has escaped the gaze of the self-appointed tribunal of historians who are gate-keepers to the assembly of 19th-century heroes.

It is my belief that the choice of Levski as the pinnacle of the Bulgarian national pantheon explains much about the specific characteristics of Bulgarian nationalism. In a larger framework, the Levski problem is intimately involved with the question of historical heroes and the nature of hero worship in general, the relation between chronometric and mythopoetized time, as well as the link between masculinity and gender, and heroism. I am particularly interested in how the hero-creating process depends on the historical context, what its specificities are within differing socio-political frameworks, and in particular the link between sainthood and heroism.

This is a historical study of the posthumous fate of the major figure of the Bulgarian national pantheon in the course of over a hundred and fifty years. By concentrating on the symbology of nationalism and the mechanisms of hero worship, I am trying to understand the particular role of cultural processes and artifacts in the formation of national identity. The study takes as its narrative focus the life, death and, especially, the posthumous fate of what has arguably become the sole truly uncontested Bulgarian hero: Vasil Levski (1835–1873). The saga of Levski's posthumous fate not only parallels the development of modern Bulgaria, it is its embodiment. The tribulations of the hero are an allegory of the evolution of Bulgarian nationalism. In the Bulgarian pantheon of national heroes, Levski, an early and arguably the greatest martyr of the 19th-century national revolution, became the only unifying and uncontested figure, accepted by a whole range of mutually incompatible parties, institutions, movements and ideologies. He has been evoked as the ultimate authority and has been on every banner: believer and atheist, republican and monarchist, conservative and radical. His hero worship does not necessarily unite the nation, but precisely these efforts at appropriation for opposing causes underlie the claim for his unique and truly national status. The analysis of Levski's consecutive and simultaneous appropriations by different social platforms, political parties, secular and religious institutions, ideologies, professional groups, and individuals, demonstrates how boundaries within the framework of the nation are negotiated around accepted national symbols.

By exploring the vicissitudes of his heroicization, glorification, consecutive appropriations by different, often opposing political forces, reinterpretation, commemoration and, finally, canonization, the book seeks to engage in several broad theoretical debates, and provide the basis for subsequent regional comparative research. I hope that such analysis would allow us to arrive at more nuanced conclusions about the lately much-debated character of Balkan nationalism as well as about the manifestations of nationalism in general, apart from the historical specificity of a particular case. The impressive literature on nationalism has emphasized its extraordinary intensity, passion and conviction in general. It is only natural that most research has chosen to concentrate on the cases of particularly forceful and persistent nationalisms, looking for correlations with religious myth, or belief in the mission of "chosen peoples." In contrast, instances of nationalism not characterized by a virulent form (to differentiate it from simply national identity), have not attracted enough scholarly attention. By concentrating on a relatively "weak" case, I hope to provide a historical explanation for its causes and manifestations.

On a further level, the Levski story engages organically with a variety of other general theoretical questions. Most broadly, it offers insights into the problem of history and memory, with its concomitant aspects: the question of public, social or collective memory as treated by historians; the nature of national memory in comparison to other types of memory; the variability of memory over time and social space; alternative memories; memory's techniques like commemorations, the mechanism of creating and transmitting memory. The reevaluation of the role played by memory in recent works has followed two main directions as far as the historical discipline is concerned. The bulk of the scholarly production is concentrated on commemoration. The other direction, which encompasses the whole genre of "invention of tradition," interprets the ways in which history is remembered and transmitted as an important indicator of power relationships. With very few exceptions, historians do not squarely deal with the relationship between memory and history, or the exact mechanisms of constructing and transmitting memory. It is one of the goals of the present study to address these problems by using the Levski case.

In the past several decades Levski's figure was embroiled in a number of disputes in Bulgarian social life, of which two assumed the characteristics of what Victor Turner defines as social drama, and became a metaphor for professional and political rivalry, an illustration of the great fight over "who owns history." One was the dispute over the unknown remains of Levski that involved archaeologists, historians, architects and one of the most popular writers, Nikolai Khaitov. In the 1950s, during archeological excavations accompanying the building of socialist high rises, graves were discovered in the sanctuary of an early modern church, and this resonated with rumors since at least the 1930s about the reburial of Levski's remains in this particular place. The reburial controversy and the search for Levski's bones, whence the title of my book—*Bones of Contention*—had a meaning different from the reburial mania which swept over the post-communist space. The narrative of the dispute between the archaeologists and the writer offers a privileged glimpse into the world of Bulgarian intellectual life, specifically Bulgarian academia under communism. It also allows one to question some of the established theoretical premises with which East European communism was axiomatically approached, more concretely the application of the categories of civil society and public sphere.

By choosing to describe an episode of late communism in Eastern Europe and thus recreating some of the atmosphere in a particular setting, I am not trying to whitewash all the shortcomings, failures or crimes of the communist regimes. I am acutely aware that any "historicization" confronts the past at the same time as it complicates it, and a very fine line runs between complication, understanding and apologia. I don't believe that *tout comprendre c'est tout pardonner*. Nevertheless, up until now the literature criminalizing the whole socialist period has been so preponderant that it needs a counterbalance, of course one that is aware of the trappings of its own approach. If Bulgaria in the late communist period emerges in this account as an almost completely normal socialist state with its own completely normal intellectual and public debates, so much the better. It will show a country with its own reflections and longstanding traditions, instead of the usual standard, generic and boring narratives of triumphant collapse of communism, rebirth of civil society, and democracy galore.

It is my sense that the reburial controversy had serious consequences for the understanding of social processes as well as for historiography. The reburial debate is one of these rare instances when the material offers the historian a unique opportunity to experiment with it and approximate the role of the judge. Carlo Ginzburg, Natalie Zemon Davis and Partha Chatarjee are among the historians who have fortuitously concentrated on trial cases in order to raise questions about the nature of historical truth. While the reburial controversy did not assume formal legal dimensions, the attempts at resolution acquired the underpinnings of a formal investigation, and this gives the historian the luxury not only of reconstituting the factual and intellectual environment of the event but also of trying to adjudicate the case itself.

The other scandal was the quarrel between the two patriarchates of the newly split Bulgarian Orthodox Church, in which the secessionist church resorted to a legitimizing tool very different from its usual political argumentation: the canonization of Levski in 1996. This story opens a window toward the climate during the ongoing post-communist decades, specifically the reactions over the phenomena some call by the generic name of globalization. It also offers an opportunity to approach politics as a form of cultural interaction, to enchant it with a richer sense of what it might consist of or, as Clifford Geertz would define it, "to elaborate a poetics of power, not a mechanics." This work is thus an effort to think through problematic issues of the uses of history, its relations to memory, nation-building, ritual and the quest for a dignified individual identity over the *longue durée* of several and opposing political regimes.

The diachronic span of the narrative brings it to the present, and this forcefully poses the problems of personal memory, lived experience and participant observation. How can one write a scholarly account, if one is, in some cases, an observer and even a participant with or without a stake? While I am addressing the issue in the relevant places, suffice it to state here that I strongly oppose the stereotype that only outsiders (ethnic, social, kin, or ones not belonging to the same time period) can be "objective" or at least impartial. This may seem superfluous were this a purely anthropological study meant to be consumed within the confines of a discipline that has overcome such issues quite some time ago. It is, however, still an argument within the historical profession.

I feel like the narrator in Nabokov's *The Real Life of Sebastian Knight* who explains his conception of investigating his half-brother's life:

As I planned my book it became evident that I would have to undertake an immense amount of research, bringing up his life bit by bit and soldering the fragments with my inner knowledge of his character. Inner knowledge? Yes, this was a thing I possessed, I felt it in every nerve. And the more I pondered on it, the more I perceived that I had yet another tool in my hand: when I imagined actions of his which I had heard of only after his death, I knew for certain that in such or such a case I should have acted as he had (1959: 33).

"Personal memory," "inner knowledge," "lived experience": these are all categories that have been delegitimized in scholarly research (except if they are the object of this research) as mired by affect, and affect by some pedantic definition is opposed to thought and cognition. Yet, it is precisely the organic link between affect and cognition that I am striving for in this book. I would like to endow my analysis with what some authors have called affective specificity. "Inner knowledge," I claim, offers access to facets that are unreachable through other means. It allows the elevation of particular aspects of the story so as to tune them to the basic "key" of a period or conjuncture.

The tonality is something that is heard as a totality, and it is my aim to make it heard as a melody, rather than to decompose it to its particulars. I am in no ways rejecting the rigors of the profession, and preaching what has become lately fashionable in some historical circles, namely that there is no difference between history and art, particularly fiction, and that both depend solely on comparable rhetoric, history merely making an utopian claim to truth. I will address some of these issues further in the book but suffice it to say that "inner knowledge" and "personal experience" in no way challenge the formal claim of history to knowledge. What they do afford, however, is a more honest, hence more visible, approach to the strategies employed. After all, if the historian is a professional remembrancer, and if the historian's central role is in preserving and presenting social alternatives, it would be a loss not to follow these unusual but privileged pathways guided by insight.

All of this also explains my choice of genre, which is a collection of, at times, fractured narratives rather than a totality of structured explanation. These fractured narratives are not mere facets of an existing whole, but frames that systematize the seeming chaos of life. Too often the existing sources impose limits on the elaboration of these frames and it is the "personal memory," "inner knowledge," and "lived experience" of the narrator that creates the coherent whole.

Working on this story opened episodes deeply buried in my own memory. I vividly remembered the little gestures on Levski's behalf during the 1980s when laying flowers at his monument was interpreted in our circle as a kind of semi-dissident symbol. Looking back those twenty years ago brings forth a self-critical chuckle. It reminds me of the anecdote of a well-known Bulgarian Social-Democrat in the interwar period who celebrated Labor Day, May 1, by creeping under his bed, covering himself with a blanket and singing the *International* in his mind. Nonetheless, the self-congratulatory feeling of justified and fulfilled opposition is still recognizable. Following the reburial controversy and then rereading it, I also remembered how, as a child, I myself once found a human skull in the vicinity of the National Library, where workers were digging in order to install the new water-supply system. I triumphantly carried what I was convinced was Levski's skull to my school, and presented it to the director. To her credit, she was quite sanguine and never tried to disabuse me of my patriotic discovery, although I am sure she immediately but tactfully disposed of it.

I was clearly carried away by the narrative of Levski's case and, for the first time in my professional life, I genuinely understood what has been affirmed as the historian's deepest motive: to tell a story because, when all is said and done, it is a very good yarn. Besides, I was aching to get again to an archive, talk to people, spin a narrative, embroider side-stories. I also wanted to do something purely Bulgarian for a change. When Georges Bizet wrote *Carmen* in 1875, his father told him he would never write anything better. Bizet died the same year at age 36. My father didn't tell me this after I had written *Imagining the Balkans*, although a few years ago, when he heard I had been awarded a John Simon Guggenheim and a NHC fellowship for this project, he exclaimed bemused: "Someone is giving you money for *that?*" My mother tactfully never did but would have told me, I think, that I should write something better. I didn't die the same year, so here is the result. It may not be better but it is completely different.

Despite my love for it, this could not become an opera, although at times I was playing with the idea of an oratorio. In the end, the structure most closely resembles the sonata form. The introduction—

allegretto (molto moderato)—with an emphasis on personal memory is followed by three main sections. Part I, the *exposition,* is about the sites of production of historical knowledge, their claims and competition. It has two themes in different keys: a dominant one, in a major key, what the politically incorrect 19th century called the "male theme" (the narrative of the archeological excavations and the social scandal over the different interpretations), and a subordinate one, the "female theme" in a minor key (the analysis of motives, the questioning of categories and similar destabilizing topics). Part II, the *development,* is, very broadly, about the uses and abuses of history. It is a diachronic survey of the different appropriations of the hero over roughly a century and a half. It is one of considerable tonal instability, as it moves through a number of keys and pitches: poetry and literature, historiography, journalism, memoirs, textbooks, archival documentation, the press, paintings, monuments. It also prepares the "double return" to Part III, the *recapitulation,* about the meaning of ritual and heroes in contemporary society. Here, the main theme of the exposition—the social scandal—is recapitulated but restated in a different narrative: the formal canonization of the hero. Its orchestration involves instruments from anthropology, history, journalism, political science, and sociology. A brief *coda* brings the long piece to a close by suggesting the usefulness of the category "weak nationalism." This adds a new melody and potentially threatens to become a fourth part, but handling a symphony was not part of the original design.

Research on this study took a number of years as it was always somehow a side-effect of other, seemingly more important issues. Analysis of the material and an early writing stage began during my stint as fellow of the National Humanities Center (2000–2001) and the Vienna-based *Institut für die Wissenschaften vom Menschen* (2001), both of which provided a wonderful creative atmosphere. After a personal interval, I resumed work on the manuscript in the paradisiacal environment of the *Wissenschaftskolleg zu Berlin* where I was a fellow in 2004–2005. It is there that this work took on its present shape and was almost completed. My heartfelt gratitude goes to my fellow friends and colleagues, as well as to the scientific and administrative staff of WIKO, who have influenced this work in more ways than they suspect. The numerous debts to a host of individual friends and colleagues that I have incurred in the course of writing for ideas, suggestions, stories, and other help are acknowledged, with gratitude, in the appropriate places in the text. Last, but not least, I am deeply appreciative and indebted to the Central European University Press which, at a moment of dominant corporate and market thinking, took the risk with a sizeable manuscript and didn't even fuss about the footnotes. With their decision, they also allowed me to finally let go. Lastly, I am dedicating this book to my last memories of my father. Age and illness slowed him down until he quietly passed away in 2003, but they made his humanity all the more apparent.

July 18, 2007 (on Levski's 170th birthday)
Champaign, Illinois

PART I

BONES OF CONTENTION, OR PROFESSIONALS, DILETTANTES, AND WHO OWNS HISTORY

It was late December, 1985 when my old friend Diana Gergova called me over the phone, and asked to meet her urgently. We had been inseparable since the 1960s in high school, and later as history students at the University of Sofia. At the time of the call, I was associate professor of Balkan history at the University of Sofia, and Diana was research fellow at the Archeological Institute at the Bulgarian Academy of Sciences, and acted as party secretary. She immediately came to the point: my father, at that moment vice president of the Bulgarian Academy of Sciences, had been requested to mediate over a long-standing dispute between the Archeological Institute (further AI) and one of the most popular writers—Nikolai Khaitov—which had gone out of control. Diana was soliciting my help in persuading my father to "objectively" look into the case and not succumb to pressure: after all, we all had heard about Khaitov's "connections" high up. Among some intellectual circles, in particular, Khaitov had acquired a bad name because it was rumored that he was appropriating the labor of his collaborators, that he had stolen the private archives of old scholars and writers, and was using them indiscriminately without acknowledgment, that he meddled in spheres that should only be within the perimeter of specialists, in a word, that he was poking his nose too much in other people's affairs. It was also said that he made a lot of money from his publications and used it to buy off collaborators, and that he had created a virtual publishing and propaganda empire. To complete the picture, it was affirmed that he had intellectually burnt out: after his wonderful short stories of decades ago that made his name, he was producing only journalistic writing, and as for the short stories themselves, there were those "reliable" rumors that were questioning his authorship. Like most of my contemporaries, I adored Khaitov's *Divi razkazi* (*Wild Stories*). I did not pay much attention to the rumors: the same accusations about appropriated work had been hurled on so many writers, not least upon Shakespeare. As for the political insinuations, I even refused to give an ear to them: this was an age-old game that could be broken only by refusing to play it. But my lights went up, and red they were, when Diana told me that Khaitov's new line was to accuse Bulgarian historians of any degree of vice situated in the range between lack of patriotism and national apostasy. More concretely, he was revisiting the 1956 excavations in the center of Sofia, specifically in and around the church "Sv. Petka Samardzhiiska," and flatly accusing the archeologists that they had, willingly or unintentionally, destroyed the remains of Bulgaria's greatest hero—Vasil Levski—who had been reburied in the church in 1873.

December 1985 was the end of the first year of the deplorable renaming campaign of the Bulgarian Turks, known by the pompous name of "revival process" (*vŭzroditelen protses*). I was teaching Ottoman history, and was known least of all for any national zeal. Next day, I duly marched into my father's study, proudly reminded him that I had never asked for favors nor had I lobbied excessively on anyone's behalf, and told him to be on the alert against nationalist excesses on the part of Khaitov. He said he would. A few weeks later, in January 1986, he called me over the phone, and asked that I stop by. When I came, he handed two thick files without a single comment: the materials that the two sides had deposited before the discussion that was to take place at the academy. And this is where my story about the bones of Levski starts.

There are several goals I would like to pursue in this part. Through a narrative of the dispute between the archeologists and the writer Khaitov, I want to offer a glimpse into the world of Bulgarian intellectual life, specifically academia under communism. This is not meant to provide any kind of generalizable narrative with the pretension of representativeness. Yet, so many (if only cursory) generalizations have been advanced about the monotony and placidity of intellectual life under communism, and particularly about Bulgarian intellectual life (or rather lack thereof), that it would be instructive to offer a "thick description" of *wie es eigentlich gewesen ist* in one particular case. It is not a case chosen to extol any kind of great or dissident achievement but precisely its ordinariness and comic, even ludicrous overtones are closer to the general atmosphere of late socialism. This brings me to a further goal: by taking a close look at the contestants' arguments, I want to explore to what extent or even whether the real issue in the controversy was over ideology, either communist or nationalist, although the dispute was clad in the discursive conventions of both ideologies. The crux of the matter was a fight centered on the monopoly over historical knowledge, in a word, over who owns history, to use Natalie Zemon Davis's felicitous phrase (Davis 1996). This is something that reaches far beyond the concrete case that played itself out in the framework of Bulgarian academe. It cannot be understood by looking simply at the characteristics of the communist system, although surely, some systemic features account for certain specificities. The question is a fundamental and structural one about the production of historical knowledge in any contemporary society. Michel-Rolph Trouillot rightly insists that "the fact that history is also produced outside of academia has largely been ignored in theories of history. Beyond a broad—and relatively recent—agreement on the situatedness of the professional historian, there is little concrete exploration of activities that occur elsewhere but impact significantly on the object of study." As he shows, "the production of historical narratives involves the uneven contribution of competing groups and individuals who have unequal access to the means for such production" (Trouillot 1995: ixi, 21).

Mediated by the narrative of my story, I would also like to give an idea of the climate during the post-communist years, specifically the reactions over phenomena some call by the generic name of globalization. It is always the case, as Steven Feierman has perceptively written about the place of microhistory in an African setting, that "there is a danger that it will come to be viewed as one more piece of charming and exotic local color. Yet microhistories at their best challenge the categories of analysis underlying larger and more general historical narratives" (1999: 206). Indeed, Jacques Revel's comment on the work of Carlo Ginzburg and other Italian historians who concentrate on small-scale events, communities, or individuals, affirms that "the change in the scale of observation revealed not just familiar objects in miniature but different configurations of the social" (Revel 1995:46.) There are a host of amazing continuities between the pre- and post-1989 periods that are usually divided by a presumed deep chasm. Of course, the real challenge is not to create dichotomies but rather emphasize both continuity and rupture, but the post-1989 literature has generally erred more in the direction of rupture. A revision of the perspective will allow to question the universal applicability of strict periodizations coming exclusively from the realm of political history. Analyzing the agents' behavior may also offer unexpected conclusions about the character of civil society, whose existence has been so axiomatically brushed off from any depiction of real existing socialism. On the other hand, one may be less sanguine about the positive effect of embroidered case studies. After all, "the heavier the burden of the concrete, the more likely it is to be bypassed by theory." (Trouillot 1995: 22).

Finally, why start with a personal story? It is not merely to play with open cards and fend off accusations of a personal *parti pris*, something that will probably happen anyway. Rather, I would like to experiment with the genre of writing, and attempt to produce a convincing scholarly historical account that stretches the borders of conventional narrative by resorting at times to what some might disparagingly refer to as personalized journalistic prose. The distinction between history as a lived event and history as an account of this event has been at the center of a long controversy over what actually is history. Oral history and contemporary history, developed as imaginative fields, accepted as not being oxymorons, only after the Second World War. I do not claim to have mastered Bourdieu's art of participant objectification but I am trying.

1. A "Social Drama" at the Bulgarian Academy of Sciences

Social dramas, as Victor Turner describes them, are "in large measure political processes, that is, they involve competition for scarce ends—power, dignity, prestige, honor, purity—by particular means and by the utilization of resources that are also scarce—goods, territory, money, men and women. Ends, means, and resources are caught up in an interdependent feedback process" (Turner 1981: 148). Significant is Turner's insistence that they are not merely a representation (oral or written) of discord or conflict in society, and as such only a story with its discernible inaugural, transitional, and terminal motifs. These "dramas of living" are universal processual forms, "public episodes of tensional irruption" that "constitute isolable and minutely describable units of social process" (ibid.: 33). They represent "a spontaneous unit of social process and a fact of everyone's experience in every human society." Because they are universal, they can take on different forms: in most societies they are agonistic, with clear-cut profiles of contestants and argument; in some cultures, elaborate codes of etiquette are able to mute the abrasiveness of the conflict; in others direct confrontation can be avoided and conflict would be low-key (ibid.: 148). And, of course, social dramas occur among groups of individuals tied by real or common history, and shared values or interests. Yet, all cases can be aptly studied as having four phases: "breach, crisis, redress, and *either* reintegration *or* recognition of the schism (ibid.: 145).

In February, 1986, when the debates at the Bulgarian Academy of Sciences (further BAN) took place, the "scandal" had matured to the point where it had reached the phase of redress. The discussion in BAN had been indirectly initiated by the archeologists who sought a venue to popularize their views in their sincere conviction that they were being silenced. The story, as far as my father (henceforth referred to both as "my father" and Nikolai Todorov), was concerned, began in the following way. In late November, 1985, he was summoned to the office of Academician Angel Balevski, the president of the BAN. Balevski turned to Todorov in his capacity as vice president, responsible for the social sciences and humanities, as well as the academy's publishing house. He was asked to head a new commission to delve into the disputes around Levski's grave, and pronounce himself on the AI's demand that the discussion of Khaitov's book at the Medieval Section of the institute in September, 1985, be published by the academy. He had no previous knowledge of the Levski dispute. In the 1950s he was a graduate student in Moscow, and had missed the details around the excavations and the archeological controversy. At the end of the 1970s, when the affair flared up again, he was Ambassador to Greece (1979–1983), and had missed the historians' commission under the leadership of Academician Dimitîr Kosev (hence Balevski's demand for a "new" commission). After getting acquainted with the materials deposited by the AI, Todorov became convinced that if published as is, they would intellectually discredit the institute (*BAN volume*: 341). He deemed it premature to create a new commission, since not even the whole existing archeological documentation about the excavations had been assembled, systematized or even offered by the AI. He therefore suggested to Balevski that, instead, a discussion should be organized with the direct participants in the excavations; that all existing documentation should be gathered and systematized; and that, subsequent to the scholarly debates, all materials together with the critical assessment of the documentation, should be printed by the publishing house of the academy (ibid.: 5–6).

In the following weeks the two sides were asked to deposit materials to which both had access. The debates took place in three meetings on February 10, 12, and 27, 1986, and were duly recorded. There were eighteen participants in the meetings, including Todorov. These were the two members of the 1956 excavation team: the leader Stamen Mikhailov, and Georgi Dzhingov, who kept the diary. Magdalina Stancheva from the Museum of the City of Sofia was not directly involved, but had had access to the excavations; the architect Stefan Boiadzhiev had been engaged in conservation works since 1956. These four were witnesses to the events of 1956. The working group from the AI consisted of the director of the institute Dimitîr Angelov, Velizar Velkov, Dimitîr Ovcharov, Ivan Sotirov, and Diana Gergova. The Khaitov team was made up of Khaitov himself, the architects Georgi

Kolev and Nikola Mushanov, the artist Mikhail Benchev and Dr. Spas Razboinikov. Present were also three representatives of the Ministry of Culture. Before taking a closer look at the redressive dispute itself, let us reconstruct its prehistory, especially the events that produced the breach and crisis in the "social drama."

Vasil Levski, caught by the Ottoman police on December 27, 1872 near the northern Bulgarian town of Lovech, was taken to Sofia where he stood trial in January, 1873. Sentenced to death, he was hanged on February 18, 1873. While there is consensus on the date and the time of his hanging (a couple of hours before dawn), all other details entail different versions: how long did he hang from the gallows, where did his confession take place, who was the confessor, was there a funeral service (*opelo*) after he was taken down, did the Bulgarian community receive his body, where was he buried and by whom, and was he eventually reburied? All these questions have not only factual value but, as we shall see further, deep moral and political implications. The most widespread belief and the only still current textbook account holds that Levski was betrayed by one of the Lovech Committee members—Pop Krîstiu—a priest. It also holds that Levski was buried close to the gallows, but that the exact location is unknown.

The reason for the varying and often controversial versions was that they were all based on subsequent memoirs, put down in written form and published several decades after the event, mostly as a result of the nationwide campaign to gather recollections about Levski, initiated on the eve of the centennial anniversary of his birth (1937) and the 65th anniversary of his hanging (1938). Even the single recollection from a much earlier period, that of his confessor, came only over a decade after Levski's execution. With very few exceptions, all recollections were indirect: they were stories told by someone who had heard a witness (usually a relative or friend) speak of the events. The few representing direct witness accounts belonged to individuals who had been children or adolescents at the time, and who had seen the body on the gallows, either because their teacher had taken them there or because they lived nearby. The only two accounts by mature witnesses and actual participants in the events belonged to two priests, and they were, in fact, mutually exclusive. One was the recollection of Pop Todor who was widely accepted as Levski's confessor, and which dated from the 1880s. The other belonged to Pop Khristo

Nikolov (Takiia) who claimed that he had administered the confession. (Undzhiev 1947: 716–7, 1075).

This poses the question of what constitutes legitimate historical evidence. Are memoirs unreliable, and should they be dismissed altogether as a means to reconstruct factuality, to be used only as an illustration of the popular imagination? Nikolai Genchev in his popular and influential book on Levski distinguishes between two types of memoirs: the first, that he calls the "graveseekers' memoirs," are "sclerotic and biased, espoused by crafty treasure-hunters"; the second type he defines as "the folk memoiristic tradition which is calm and evenhanded. It does not stain other graves. For this tradition it is sufficient that Levski's legacy has been fulfilled." He then passes his verdict on the utility of these two types of sources: "For history and national psychology both types are important. One could wish success to the first, while hoping to calm down its hysteria. The second one could be studied and utilized as a reliable measure for the spiritual proclivities of the Bulgarians" (Genchev 1987: 206–7). Aside from the fact that this classification is illogical (after all, why should the "sclerotic" or "hysterical" members of the nation be excluded from an overview of its proclivities?), its primary purpose is to delegitimize some of the recollections that do not square with Genchev's own views. Still, Genchev is right in emphasizing the unique quality and distinguishing characteristic of oral sources: they "tell us less about events, than about their meaning" (Portelli 1998: 67). Yet what is discernible in his verdict is the typical patronizing attitude of the traditional archival (or generally textual) historian toward oral sources, and the implicit dismissal of the contribution they can also make to facticity.

Ivan Undzhiev, Levski's first scholarly biographer whose work is unsurpassed until this day, and a more patient and meticulous researcher, was not so quick to dismiss: "Despite all their weaknesses, the memoirs should not be pushed aside altogether. The recollection is always something subjective, and an event like this cannot be easily encompassed in all its totality. Whatever small part of the truth they contain, these rare recollections about the Apostle's last minutes cannot be ignored" (Undzhiev 1947: 719). He knew what he was talking about. Although he always thought of himself as a mainstream historian, a traditional biographer, he was to a great extent an oral historian *avant la lettre*. He never subscribed to "the dominant prejudice which sees factual credibility as a monopoly of written documents," well aware that a lot of written documents are either the uncontrolled transmission of unidentified oral sources or often the controlled (and therefore inexact) transmission of identified ones (Portelli 1998: 68). Faced with the extreme dearth of documentary sources on the period and on his hero, Undzhiev's biography of Levski was in large measure based on oral accounts, many collected for the specific purposes of producing an official scholarly biography. At the end of his over 1,100-page biography, Undzhiev did not focus on a detailed critical analysis of the memoirs relating to the execution and burial of Levski, comparing the recollections in all their specific points, and reconstructing a more or less reliable narrative, but was satisfied with mostly narrating them at length (Undzhiev 1947: 713–9, 1070–84). He attributed the amount of contradictory information partly to the fact that the recollections had been assembled late, sharing the view that memory fades with time, and that fresh memories are more reliable. That some memories fade with time is undeniable but contradictions between testimonies hardly have to do with this, as freshly assembled but mutually exclusive witness accounts on big events and the courtroom practice persuades us every day. It seems that the belief in the inferior quality of oral sources, when or because they are distant from events and undergo the distortion of faulty memory, is yet another prejudice. The very same charge applies to written sources. Besides, oral narrators utilize certain aids to memory that preserve the sharpness of the recollection: numerous repetitions of the storytelling, frequent discussions with members of the community, recourse to formalized narrative. In addition, oral sources can compensate the temporal distance with an immediate personal involvement (Portelli 1998: 68–69). There is, therefore, no clear-cut correlation between the reliability and authenticity of the source and its temporal closeness to the event it describes. More poignantly, Undzhiev (1947: 718, 1076) in an oft cited passage pointed to the central and sore point of the Bulgarians' national discourse, their comparatively weak national feeling:

> The circumstance that the grave of the Apostle remained unknown can be explained neither by the conditions of the oppressive realities nor by the events that absorbed our attention after the liberation. A significant amount of guilt lies also with the weak historical con-

sciousness of the people, something that could not be otherwise within the continuous misery of bondage.

A recent scholarly contribution to the debate pays close attention to the body of recollections, and subjects them to critical assessment for the sake of opting for the most reliable factual line. Ivan Petev acknowledges the controversies but refuses to disqualify the sources; their comparatively late appearance he attributes not to orchestration and imagination but to the fact that they were not sought out for a long time. In the classical tradition of critical historiography he maintains, however, that "while this is no easy task, scrutinized in the light of the logic of events, these memoirs permit the contemporary researcher to discover what specific information they pass on, and to what extent it conforms to the historical facts" (Petev 1993: 151–2). He may be accused of trying to prove a thesis, and sometimes his argument is forced, but, on the whole, he is convincing in laying out a scrupulously argued hypothesis. A historian and professor at the Theological Academy in Sofia, he identifies the main controversial tropes around Levski's end and how they are treated in the different memoirs. Summarized, they relate to the following questions: Was Levski betrayed or not? If he was, was it Pop Krîstiu or was he an innocent victim of slander? When was the confession administered and by whom? How long did the body hang from the gallows? Did the Bulgarian community demand the body for burial or was this orchestrated by the Ottoman authorities? Was a priest present and was there a proper funeral service? Where did the burial take place: in the Bulgarian cemetery on the western side of town or in the so-called mixed "criminal" cemetery on the eastern outskirts? Was it near or away from the place of execution? Was there a reburial and if so, by whom and where?

These are not questions satisfying mere factual curiosity, albeit about the greatest national hero. The problem of Levski's betrayal touches upon a sore point that has been periodically taken up by writers or scholars: that not only was the nation immature and unworthy of its hero but it actually gave him away. Specifying the traitor as Pop Krîstiu put the blemish straight upon the church as an institution. The type of Levski's burial and eventual reburial as well as the scrutiny into the confession and funeral service would shed light on whether the Bulgarian community behaved as abject cowards, or whether there were enough patriotic individuals who, in the face of extremely adverse circumstances, had found the courage to honor the hero's remains and thus his legacy. These are clearly issues very central to the national identity. Petev well summarizes the moral stakes that make these questions resonate with a very broad audience in the country: "It has to be emphasized, to the credit of all Bulgarians, that Hierodeacon Ignatii Vasil Levski, as a great son of Bulgaria and a treasured child of the church, was not forsaken in his last moments by his loyal friends and followers" (Petev 1993: 151).

Most professional historians, on the other hand, from Undzhiev on have shared the dominant vision of the events, and have considered the obsession with these factual details an unnecessary footnote deflating from the only important issue: Levski's revolutionary ideology, practice, and legacy. According to them, this is the sole aspect worthy of scholarly attention. The rest can be food for the popular imagination or for the writer's pen but it has no place within a legitimate scholarly discourse. Insofar, then, as there was always present what can be called a revisionist view, it was never represented by mainstream figures, and was more often than not absent from the public eye. Petev's book, although written by a professional historian outside the usual central institutions of creating historical discourse, is one of the very few scholarly representatives of the dissenting variety, whose chief exponent had become Nikolai Khaitov.

Let us briefly follow Petev on the issues that constitute the backbone of the revisionist thesis. In his case, there is an additional motive, not encountered in the argumentation of the other "revisionists." This is the attempt (quite successful) to prove Levski's unflinching religious belief, visible already in the title of the book, introducing the protagonist as "Hierodeacon Ignatii Vasil Levski." Mostly, I choose to introduce the revisionist thesis through his book because it is written in what can be easily described as the acceptable academic genre and language, in a manner that illustrates the best of the traditions and conventions of historical critical analysis. Khaitov's polemic digressions and his frequent *ad hominem* attacks, on the other hand, as well as his occasional penchant to "silence" evidence not in his favor might detract from appreciating his otherwise very powerful and logical line of reasoning. At the same time, it was precisely his style that brought an otherwise lingering but not so passionate conflict to a crisis point, and it is on this aspect that I will lay the emphasis when analyzing Khaitov's particular role.

Two thirds of Petev's book is devoted to Pop Krîstiu's alleged guilt, a question that has evoked strong passions since at least the 1920s. Although hardly accepted as the dominant version, the view of the priest's innocence is making unexpected but significant strides into mainstream territory. Petev's last section deals with Levski's execution and burial. The recollections differ widely even over how long the body was hanging from the gallows for public display: from a few hours to one, two, even three days. Most concur that the corpse was removed in the evening of the same day when the burial took place, and Petev accepts it as the most plausible version (1993: 140–1). This, at first glance, minor detail became quite important during the BAN debate about the state of the corpse, particularly when discussing the medical expertise. On how Levski was buried, the contemporaries' recollections varied from assertions that his body was arbitrarily "thrown away" by his executioners in an unknown place, to different versions of how he received a regular Christian burial in the hands of his community. Some point out that the terror was so great, the arrests among the Bulgarians so extensive, that no one dared even come by the gallows, let alone dare bury the corpse. Others are specific about the burial, the most widespread version being that the governor of the Sofia district, Mazhar Pasha, after having inspected the dead body, ordered it to be handed to the priest Pop Todor. Petev scrupulously points out that none of the recollections explicitly addresses whether the Bulgarian community itself asked for the corpse, but judging from the existing Ottoman penal legislation and judicial traditions, he concludes that the body was delivered to the Bulgarians for burial (1993: 137–140).

The question of Levski's last confession is central for Petev who is set on proving that "raised in a religious family, educated in the light of evangelical commands, Vasil Levski remained a real Christian throughout his whole life." The memoirs are not unanimous, some denying that a confession took place at all or insisting that Levski rejected the last sacrament. While Petev's opinion that "there is no doubt that Levski had a confession and received the last sacrament" may be worded too categorically, it is a perfectly plausible conclusion, supported by the majority of sources (Petev 1993: 121–3). As for the identity of the confessor, he proves without reasonable doubt that this was Pop

Todor, the only witness and participant in the events to leave an early (though not verbatim) testimony (ibid.: 124–8). Petev is equally convincing about the time and place of the confession: it had occurred at the gallows, immediately before the hanging took place (while an alternative version has it that it had taken place in the prison cell). Again, this is not an exotic minor detail: it has consequences about discovering the real identity of the priests who carried out the funeral as well as definitively refuting an ongoing popular belief that Levski had attempted to commit suicide while in prison (ibid.: 129–136).

A key issue that has bedeviled most Levskologists is where the body was buried. Most accounts suggest it was close to the gallows, specifying the nearby cemetery for criminals on the eastern outskirts of town, the area where Levski's monument was erected. This was also the presumption of the commission created at the Sofia municipality, which initiated the building of the monument in 1878, the year of Bulgaria's liberation. The Russian governor of Sofia—P. V. Alabin—wrote in October, 1878 to the St. Petersburg Slavic Committee that the remains of Levski would be transferred from the criminal graveyard and buried under the monument. The commission accordingly issued a decree ordering the finding of reliable witnesses who could show Levski's grave (SGODA, Fond 1k, op.3, a.e.178, 6–7). None of the existing detailed documentary sources around the building of the monument suggest that the remains of Levski were discovered, let alone buried under the monument. Nevertheless, after a great amount of memoirs were published in 1937, a commission from the Department of Museums and Monuments at the General Staff undertook to probe in the foundations of the monument but the partial drilling in 1938–1939 did not produce any results (*BAN volume:* 133–135).

There is a detailed body of recollections pointing to the Bulgarian cemetery in the western outskirts of town. Here is where Petev provides an exemplary analysis. He carefully examines the descriptions of the funerary procession, and concludes that it is unlikely for it to have crossed the whole town in the evening hours. Never dismissing the good faith in which the recollections were given, he suggests that the Bulgarians, unsure of what would happen till the last moment, might have prepared a grave in the Bulgarian cemetery on the morning of the execution, as one of the testaments asserts (Petev 1993: 146–8). He reflects on why the criminal cemetery was the most likely option, not simply because these recollections are more probable but because this version corresponds better to the behavior and motives of the Ottoman authorities (ibid.: 148–9). The story of Levski's burial in the cemetery on the eastern outskirts of town has been widely accepted also by mainstream historians. Petev, however, is the first one to give equal and exhaustive attention to all evidence, and to convincingly argue his thesis.

Petev is particularly good in his detective work with establishing the identity of the priests who administered the confession and the funeral service. This is not an issue that has direct bearing on the controversy, except that it gives indirectly greater veracity to the quality of Petev's other findings. Finally, Petev adds his read on the reburial issue. He has not much new to say, mostly endorsing the memoirs of Maria Poppavlova who was the first to mention that Levski's remains were reburied in the "Sv. Petka" church. Her recollections, first published in 1937 have been reprinted many times, since they are at the foundation of the later controversy. It is still worth reproducing them here. Maria Poppavlova-Lazarova had been the daughter of a Sofia priest and the widow of Iliia Lazarov, a survivor of the famous Botev *cheta* of 1876, who had died in 1902. She herself died in 1936 at age 86, and had shared her story with a family friend. This is how he reproduces her testimony (it is to be emphasized again that most of the recollections of this and earlier periods were transmitted as second hand accounts):

> Grandmother Maria described the hanging and burial of Deacon Levski in the following details. The day of Levski's hanging had been cold and windy. No Bulgarian dared to be at the hanging except two or three representatives of the guilds, ordered to be present. Levski hung from the gallows 1–2 days, and during that time only youngsters had the courage to come by the gallows. The Apostle's body was buried by Pop Todor close to the gallows. Until this moment grandmother Maria was speaking calmly but when I asked her where Levski's body was today, she seems to have transposed herself into this dark era, when such questions are answered only under oath that she would not be betrayed to the Turkish authorities. And in all her sincerity and decency she added that the body of Deacon Levski had been dug out by the then sexton of the church

"Sv. Parashkeva" on "Maria Luisa" Street, and buried in the altar of the same church. This heroic deed had been accomplished by the late Khristo Khambarkov-Gîskata, who was in touch with the members of the Sofia Revolutionary Committee (Stanchev 1937).

The assertion that Levski's body hung from the gallows so long was implausible when juxtaposed to other testimonies. But one cannot help hearing Khaitov's later exclamation: "Just imagine that on the next day after the publication of the paper—on March 7, 1937—someone had dug into the altar of 'Sv. Petka' and had come upon the skeleton in the northern part of the altar which was dug out in May, 1956 during the 'rescue' archeological excavations! Would there have been the slightest hesitation where the grave with Levski's bones was?" And he adds even more effectively: "If I would give you a phone call, dear readers, saying that in front of your doorstep, under the mat, I have put two gold coins wrapped in paper, and you would check and find them, will you doubt my message?" (Khaitov 1987: 55 and personal communication).

Petev himself used this and other memoirs to establish the identity of the two priests and of the two "servants" who helped take down the body. He concluded that these were the above-mentioned Khristo Khambarkov-Gîskata, as well as Maria Poppavlova-Lazarova's own husband Iliia Lazarov whom she does not mention in her testimony. The reason was, Petev guesses (not very convincingly), her modesty not to speak of the heroic deed of her spouse. The person who does speak of Lazarov is their daughter Anastasiia Ilieva Bokova who was interviewed at age 75 in 1956 at the time of the excavations by Professor Khristo Giaurov. Her testimony, alongside the one by her mother, has been scrutinized and either celebrated or completely dismissed. In some points, it corroborates the mother's; in others it differs from it (Giaurov 1959: 138. 242).

> I was born in Sofia. My mother was from Sofia. My father came from a peasant household in Lokorsko village. He died at around 50, in 1902. Shortly before his death he shared with our mother and us, his children the following: 'Remember, you should know this, because it may some day become useful for history to know where and how Vasil Levski was buried.' Here are a few details as I heard them from my father. After Levski's hanging, late in the evening, my father

and Khristo Khambarkov (the churchwarden of 'Sv. Paraskeva' who lived in a house in Sofia, Sredna Gora Street, near the pub 'The Grey Horse'), went to the place where Vasil Levski had been hanged with fezzes on their heads and with a wooden wine vessel (*bîklitsa*). The weather was cold and icy. There was noone around except the guards, the fields were desolate. They started treating the guards. Following the custom, they drank first from the vessel. They drank but did not swallow. The guards also drank. They repeated this several times until they emptied the vessel. The wine had its effect soon, since there was some kind of sedative in it; I don't know exactly what. The guards got drunk and fell asleep. The moment was opportune. My father and grandfather Khristo took the corpse off the gallows and put it in an earlier prepared sack. My father carried it on his back, while grandfather Khristo led the way with the lantern. My father was a strong and healthy peasant, and was a true rebel all his life. With difficulty and not entirely fearless they reached the old church "Sv. Paraskeva Samardzhiiska." Pop Krîstiu whose family name I don't remember, expected them. The priest administered the funeral service and then they buried him in the altar of the church, to the left.

There are obvious folkloric elements, especially around the soporific wine potion. Likewise, the identification of the left northern side of the altar as the burial place can be suspected to have been, maybe unwittingly, suggested by Giaurov, since it postdated the discovery of the skeleton. The 1983 historians' commission dismissed this statement, as it did the testimony of Dr. Petîr Dimkov, a popular doctor and author of best-selling books on herbal treatment who corroborated the information in 1982 (Khaitov 1987: 219; 2002: 56). It professed that "no researcher who has worked with historical sources would use such testimony for the solution of a scientific problem" (*BAN volume*: 138). One is not expected to treat any memory automatically as factual proof but a careful historian would weigh the credibility of the testifier against his evidence. No one, given Dimkov's social status, would accuse him of conscious confabulation or falsification. His story is evidence of a comparatively wide-spread belief in Levski's reburial in the church. In a word, his "memory" cannot prove the fact of Levski's reburial, but it proves that such a belief was widely held at the time. Dimkov's testimony is interesting not so much for the reported facts but for the manner in which they were reported. At the end of his interview, he says he urged his informants—his father, Maria Poppavlova, and Vasil Bozhilov—to write down what they knew, but they all responded: "Come on, who would be dealing with Levski now?" (Khaitov 2002: 56). Dimkov's brief interview does not specify the exact time of these reactions: judging from his brief text they could have been uttered both in the 1930s and in the 1950s. This is no reason to dismiss his recollections. They can be characterized by what is defined by cognitive scientists as gist, memory of meaning or content accuracy. This is different from the technical accuracy of episodic memory and corresponds to "recalling or recognizing the meaning or content of what has been experienced." As distinguished from technical accuracy stressesing verbatim memory, "content accuracy stresses memory for concepts and ideas, the meaningful, semantic content of the material" (Ashcraft 1993: 325).

What this semantic memory gives is the overall atmosphere, where it was felt that dealing with an issue such as Levski's grave was insignificant. The phrase "Come on, who would be dealing with Levski now?" should not be read as evidence of neglect. Levski, pace Khaitov's accusations, was never purged from his central place in the Bulgarian pantheon once he was established there at the beginning of the 20th century. The phrase can be taken as an illustration of a particular *Zeitgeist* and interpreted in the framework of a relatively weak nationalism or at least one less vocal and demonstrable, less obsessed with its symbolic repertoire. This tallies well with both Undzhiev's mid-century conclusions about the lack of interest in Levski's grave in the 1870s, as well as my own impressions in the last decades of the 20th century. My circle of friends with no immediate stake in the dispute thought the whole issue was overblown, insignificant, and did not merit the sensationalist attention conferred on it. If the phrase is indeed the emanation of a *Zeitgeist*, it is one that has had and is having a continuous lifespan.

Researchers less squeamish than the 1983 historical commission, like Petev or Khaitov and others before them, did try to seek out the reliable information from the existing accounts taken from memory. After all, isn't work on mediaeval sources often confronted by the same caveats? Mikhailov's attempt to dismiss both the mother and the daughter's accounts on the ground that they did not tally, entirely misses the point that the mother's 1937 testimony predated the discovery of the skeleton by two decades. In addition, these were not lonely accounts. The rumor about Levski's reburial in the church was widespread at least since the beginning of the 20th century, because it is recorded as "old knowledge" by the early 1920s. Does all this mean that there should not be "the slightest hesitation where the grave with Levski's bones was" as Khaitov would have it? Hardly, but this is explored in the next section. For now, this is the general version of the revisionists' view. In its separate points, it had been argued since the 1920s but received systematic articulation only in the late 20th century. Petev's reasoning is in no way a definitive proof. This is unfeasible given the state of the information and the impossibility to sustain it with material evidence. It is simply one hypothesis amongst others, but a plausible one. If Petev occasionally errs on the side of categorical statements — "there is no doubt," "it can be considered proven"— this is not a sin of logic but of style, typical of much scholarly writing not enamored of conditional grammatical forms like "it seems probable, plausible, feasible," deemed a display weakness and hesitation rather than intellectual discretion. With few exceptions, I prefer to introduce the revisionists' version through Petev's short book rather than Khaitov's extensive, earlier and more detailed one. This is mostly because the seductiveness of Khaitov's prose is so powerful that one tends to raise one's guard, and as a result becomes immune to the seductiveness of his logic. In addition, Khaitov occasionally commits the sins of omission or excessive polemic twists, whereas Petev, conforming to the expected rules of scholarly exposition, lays bare the logic of the argument. Most importantly, it is my belief that Petev's book or any other like his would not have generated the tension that triggered off the social drama. It would have been consumed as an internal dispute within academe or not even reached the stage of dispute. True, we are not to know for sure because it appeared much later, after the crisis had reached and passed its culmination.

Almost all issues of contention had already been in place in the previous decades, and this is the manner in which they fared. The controversy about Pop Krîstiu had been publicly and forcefully voiced already in the mid-1920s, and with time a considerable historiography built around the problem. It had its surges and ebbs but never really threatened to overflow the banks of more or less civilized, even though impassioned, scholarly discourse. The same is true of the questions around the execution and burial. They would flare up with differing degrees of intensity, usually around one of Levski's bigger anniversaries. They would produce dramas in their own right but not a social drama. The 100th anniversary of Levski's birth resulted not only in the first massive publication of recollections in 1937, but also in the formation of a citizens' committee with the express aim to discover Levski's remains. The committee authored three reports, maintaining it had discovered the grave and the bones (Undzhiev 1947: 1081–4). The claim was based partly on the recollections of the 82-year-old Atanasa Ianeva, partly on the witness account of a watchmaker who asserted Levski's skeleton had been dug up during the construction of a house in 1923. Ianeva, eighteen at the time of the execution, remembered that Levski had been buried in the cemetery close to the gallows. A few days later, she attended a funeral in the same cemetery, and her godfather showed her Levski's grave. Over 60 years later, and despite the drastic changes in the landscape that had transformed the cemetery in the outskirts of town in one of the densely populated town quarters, she still believed she could identify the place, and pointed it out to the members of the commission.

In 1923, when a judge was building a house, his neighbor's wife observed the laborers and saw them unearth a skeleton. Her husband shared this information with his old landlord, and was told that Levski had been buried there. He took the skull and preserved it for 13 years. In 1936, he put it in a paper box and buried it across from his house. In 1937, alerting the citizens committee, the Archeological Museum, and the municipality, and in the presence of their representatives, he dug the skull out. It was impossible to link it to Levski, since it had been quite damaged. In addition, the doctor who was sent to examine the skull, concluded that it belonged to a 14–15-year-old boy. The judge himself wrote that he had been present at the "discovery," and that there was no talk at the time about Levski. There had been no preserved skeleton, and he gave the skull to his neighbor who asked for it. The judge was furious with the intimation that he may have hidden such momentous information, and threatened to sue for slander (Undzhiev 1947: 1083–4). What is remarkable about this story is how much it reminds of the 1956 events—the coupling of a memoir with an excavation—yet how fundamentally different the outcome was.

The 1937 "discovery" ended in complete fiasco: there was the generally accepted demise of the theory, and the only genuinely dramatic element was the unrealized threat of a slander suit. The 1956 skeleton, on the other hand, proved much more resilient, and by the 1980s had provided the basis for the real social drama. How and why did this happen?

In April, 1956, the AI ordered the beginning of excavations in and around the church "Sv. Petka Samardzhiiska." The excavations had been prompted by plans for the restructuring of the capital's center. They began on May 8, and a week later, on May 17, the newspaper *Trud* (N.118/2995) published an editorial on its first page under the title "Research around the church 'Sv. Paraskeva' in the 'Center.' Are Levski's bones going to be discovered?" The article disclosed the widespread belief that the remains of Levski had been reburied in the church, either in its western part near the narthex or in its eastern part in the sanctuary. It did not, however, mention the 1937 memoirs of Maria Poppavlova-Lazarova published in *Mir*.

Figure 1. Excavations at the northern side of the "Sv.Petka Samardzhiiska" church in May 1956. Note the crowd of onlookers behind the fence.
Source: Nikolai Khaitov, *Grobît na Vasil Levski: Sbornik s istoricheski i arkheologicheski dokumenti i svidetelstva*, Sofia: Goreks Pres, 2002, 142, fig. 24.

On May 30, 1956 the archeologists discovered a well preserved skeleton in the sanctuary, to the left side of the altar stone which became known as Skeleton No. 95 and was dutifully recorded it in the diary (*BAN volume*: 27–8). The excavations were visited the very same day by Professor Giaurov from the Theological Academy who informed the leader of the excavations Stamen Mikhailov that these might be Levski's bones, and offered him the memoirs collection he had compiled in support of this view. Mikhailov was unimpressed. The fact that the lower limbs of the skeleton were positioned beneath the

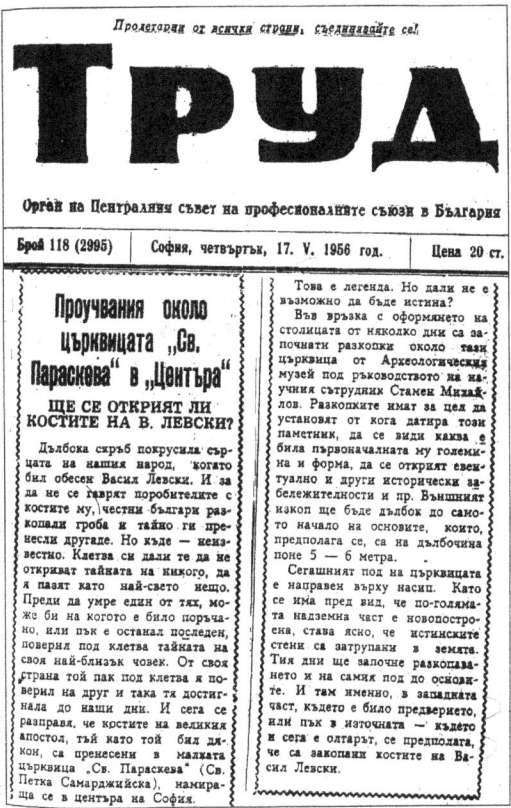

Figure 2. Article in *Trud*, No. 118 (2995), 17 May 1956. "Research around the church 'Sv. Paraskeva' in the 'Center'. Are Levski's bones going to be discovered?"

sanctuary wall was an irrefutable argument in favor of an early burial, before the construction of the church at the end of the 14th century. Giaurov continued to collect relevant information, in the course of which he interviewed Anastasiia Bokova, and at the end of July handed copies of his manuscript "Written documents about Levski's grave" to several institutions and individuals, among them the AI, as well as the "Botev-Levski" Institute, whose director was Ivan Undzhiev. He insisted that the bones should be examined by specialists. His article (Giaurov 1959) was published in the journal of the Theological Academy but there was no follow up. When the dispute flared up again in the 1980s Giaurov was long dead but his motives were commented on and they bear mentioning here. The posthumous critique of Giaurov emphasized his credulity concerning the recollections but he had simply asked for professional expertise on the bones. There was another attempt to shed suspicion on Giaurov's motives, namely that he had tried to save the church from demolition, as if the two motives—finding Levski's grave and saving the church from destruction—were mutually exclusive (*BAN volume*: 150, 374–6; Khaitov 1987: 211).

It was not only Giaurov's activities that drew attention to the issue. The article in *Trud* had alerted the public, and people of all walks of life were showing keen interest. While he didn't reflect it in his diary, Dzhingov had taken a photograph and reminisced later:

Figure 3. Photograph of Skeleton No. 95. A view of the apsidal foundations and the niche holding the legs of Skeleton No. 95 below the knees.
Source: Nikolai Todorov, ed., *Arkheologicheski danni po spora za groba na Vasil Levski v tsîrkvata "Sv. Petka Smardzhiiska." Dokumenti i stanovishta*, Sofia: Izdatelstvo na BAN, 1988, 79.

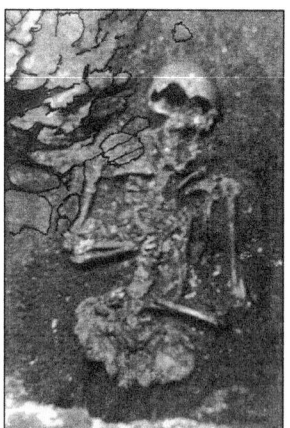 

Figure 4. Photographs of Skeleton No. 95.
Source: Todorov, ed., *Arkheologicheski danni po spora za groba na Vasil Levski*, 77.

The interest was great... People were crowding at the fence to watch the excavations when we discovered the skeletons. Professor Giaurov was showing keen interest. When we discovered the skeleton on May 30, Giaurov saw it... Everyone was talking, everyone was talking. And even more. Sava Ganovski came, in his capacity as vice president of the Academy, and saw the church and specifically said we should be careful. Therefore, we made the photographs, therefore we called the museum artist to make a sketch. And Petîr Boev arrived, didn't he? (*BAN volume*: 267).

In 1959, Mikhailov published a study of the frescoes of "Sv. Petka Samardzhiiska." Two years later, his publication on the excavations appeared (Mihailov 1959, 1961). Already the respective size of the two publications—a mere twelve pages for the excavations to the nearly forty pages dedicated to the frescoes bespoke the real interests of the author. Nonetheless, these articles came to be accepted as the definitive scholarly view on the problem, and nothing challenged it in the next two decades. Yet, "the definitive scholarly view on the problem" took the form of a single paragraph and a footnote in the second publication, in which Mikhailov refuted the Levski link by indicating *inter alia* that No. 95 may have been a female skeleton.

2. From Breach to Crisis

In 1979, 23 years after the excavations, a journal article appeared that revived Giaurov's thesis (Bobchev 1979). What was remarkable was that one of the authors was a direct participant in the excavations—Sava Bobchev. An architect and research associate of the AI, he had been commissioned in 1956 as deputy to Mikhailov, charged with the architectural sketches of the excavations. Immediately following this publication, and in the same vein of reasoning, was a newspaper article in *Puls* (December 18, 1979), authored by a legal historian, a historian of the revival period, and an artist. This marked the real beginning of the social drama: "[It] first manifests itself as the breach of a norm, the infraction of a rule of morality, law, custom, or etiquette, in some public arena. The breach is seen as the expression of a deeper division of interests and loyalties than appears on the surface. The incident of breach may be deliberately, even calculatedly, contrived by a person or party disposed to demonstrate or challenge entrenched authority… Once visible, it can hardly be revoked" (Turner 1981: 146). The breach was occasioned by the fact that the dominant thesis was challenged from within the scholarly community, indeed from within the same institution. True, there had been an alternative opinion gestating over all these years. It was even articulated by a scholar—Giaurov—and was published in 1959. In these days, however, a publication in a theological journal did not carry the necessary scholarly, let alone ideological clout, and it was widely believed that Giaurov's real motive had been to save the church form destruction. In addition, Giaurov passed away in 1966. The others who harbored doubts, and had spoken up in 1956, were keeping silent.

Or so it seemed when the scandal broke loose in the 1980s, and the archeologists accusingly pointed to this fact in order to undermine the opposing thesis. Bobchev came out in the public eye in 1979, but he had not kept his beliefs to himself at the time. As he stated during the round table of *Rabotnichesko delo* in February, 1981, "the discovery occurred by chance but the coincidence is remarkable." At the time he remarked to Mikhailov that this seemed to be something special, a secret, it had to be duly documented and the position of the skeleton exactly described. "Stamen Mikhailov objected that this had nothing to do with archeology and there are others who can deal with it... According to me, [he] very boldly and unilaterally decided that the whole story was fabricated. I didn't think so." As a subordinate, Bobchev did not press further. When a few days later Giaurov insisted they had discovered Levski's bones, the bones had already disappeared. "Nobody further inquired how this could happen, why it happened. Nobody." (*BAN volume*: 121–32). In Bobchev's private diary kept during the excavations, he added a postscript in 1959 stating his belief about the discovery, and his private sketches depicting Skeleton No. 95 bear the note "Here rests Vasil Levski" (ibid.: 61–75).

Bobchev adds that he later tried to write in the press but was told his opinion could not be published since it would implicate the newspaper as taking sides. Finally, a friend in the magazine *Sofia* printed his opinion, but Mikhailov immediately sent a disclaimer accusing Bobchev of disinformation (ibid.: 125). This is an important detail, in view of the archeologists' complaints that their opinions were not published at all or not in the same range as Khaitov's. It is also an accurate illustration on publishing policies under an authoritarian communist regime. The idea that one could publish just anything never crossed anyone's mind, of course. Yet not persevering because censorship was ubiquitous more often than not a convenient excuse for inertia. What

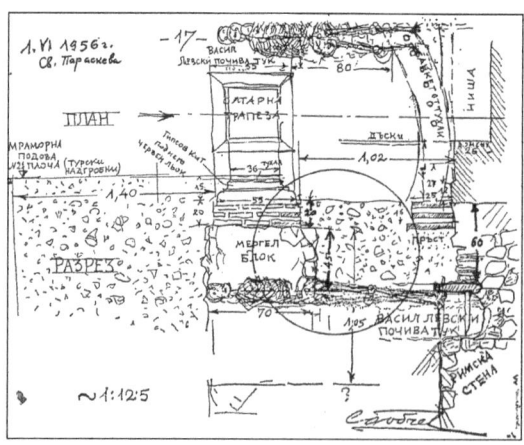

Figure 5. Bobchev's sketch of 1 June 1956. The text under the skeleton's legs says "Vasil Levski rests here." Source: Todorov, ed., *Arkheologicheski danni po spora za groba na Vasil Levski*, 67.

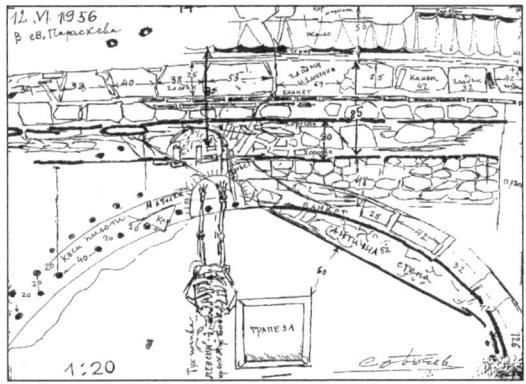

Figure 6. Bobchev's sketch of 12 June 1956. The text around the skull reads: "Here rests Levski despite Dr. Boev."
Source: Todorov, ed., *Arkheologicheski danni po spora za groba na Vasil Levski*, 65.

often was the ultimate criterion for publishability was not ideological correctness, especially not in the later communist decades, but either personal connections in the party/state bureaucracy or perceived connections that made editors malleable to influence or sycophantic even without pressure. This does not mean that editors had no real grounds to fear retribution for moves they had taken, and that had angered the authorities or just someone in a high position.[1] What it means is that there were no strict and clear censorship rules on what was or was not ideologically permissible. What was exhausting about cultural politics under state socialism was the almost complete arbitrariness of the system where "dangerous" pieces could suddenly appear without impunity, and trivial ones be suppressed with an uproar. This is one additional detail that distinguished a totalitarian from an authoritarian system of the clientelist type.

Bobchev was obviously trying to find an opening and express his views all throughout the period following the excavations, in a word

---

[1] The most celebrated case is the publication of the future post-communist president Zheliu Zhelev's book *Fascism* (Zhelev 1982) which resulted in the sacking of the editor-in-chief, and reprimand for his internal reviewers, but without any professional consequences for Zhelev, who worked at the Institute of Culture, except for the constant psychological dread of arbitrary repercussions. The other consequence was that he was propelled into immediate fame and the book became a bestseller. Suppression and censorship—as the communist authorities failed to learn until the very end—were the best advertising device in a publishing system without proper market mechanisms.

to occasion what can be described as the breach. The opportune moment came in the 1970s. The architect Nikola Mushanov from the Institute for the Preservation of Cultural Monuments had been appointed as the conservationist of "Sv. Petka Samardzhiiska" in 1969. In 1976, preparing the site on the eve of the 11th Party Congress, his colleague Bobchev visited him and told him about the legend concerning Levski's grave. At first Mushanov did not take him seriously and was in a hurry to finish the conservation before the opening of the party congress ten days later. Later, however, he reported to the Committee for Art and Culture. A commission was set up in 1978 with Professor Doino Doinov (a historian, and vice-chairman of the committee), Bobchev, Stancheva, and a few others (*BAN volume*: 131, 297). We have two sets of recollections about its work: one belonging to Mushanov, the other to Stancheva. Luckily, they come from two highly respected professionals and articulate individuals, who ended up representing the two opposing views in the 1980s.

According to Mushanov's statement at the round table of *Rabotnichesko delo* in 1981, Doinov decided that the Medieval Section of the AI should be invited to reassess the materials in light of Bobchev's thesis, and he asked the section "Revival Period" at the Institute for History about all existing materials pertaining to Levski's burial. There was no follow up to this decision; it seems the invitation never even reached the institutes. Having familiarized himself with the arguments, Mushanov took a careful position, trying to accommodate both the lack of material proofs and the persistence of beliefs: "My thesis is that… we have the right to speak of a legend, we are entitled to say that the church is linked with a folk legend or saga about Levski's grave. I think that this gives us enough ground to mark this place of the church in some appropriate way, stating that according to Bulgarian folk legends Levski has been buried here… Beyond this the facts absolutely do not allow us to say: 'it was here.'" Mushanov reasoned that it would be good to impart some additional meaning to this church in the center of the capital, which was nice but rather poor, and whose frescoes were not that extraordinary from an artistic viewpoint. He shared his view with Doinov and, "as far as I know, he took the question to L. Zhivkova, and she has a positive attitude towards the problem: to mark the place in exactly this way" (*BAN volume*: 131). The journalist Eduard Baltadzhian who co-authored the 1979 article with Bobchev and was also present, corroborates this information: "At the meeting, Comrade Karadzhova said the following on behalf of L. Zhivkova: 'Quite apart from whether the scholars and the forum will come to a conclusive result about the real whereabouts of Levski's grave, if it is clear from the discussions that the thesis originating from Professor Giaurov's inquiry is taking precedence [vzima preves], then we would agree to place such a plaque which would have an educational and patriotic effect on the young generation'" (ibid.: 132).

Stancheva was working at the Museum of the City of Sofia since 1952, and had regularly visited the excavations in 1956. She was included in the several commissions dealing with the problem of Levski's grave, among them the Commission of the Committee of Art and Culture. In view of the fact that Stancheva and Mushanov ended up defending different versions of the thesis, it is important to hear her side of the story about the 1978 meetings:

> I participated in two commissions about the fate of this grave. The first was a meeting under the leadership of Doino Doinov, which took place in the church itself. It was convened with an order of L. Zhivkova. Present at this meeting were architect Mushanov and his wife... Prof. Bobchev was also there. He was pleading the cause that this was Levski's grave. However, everyone present—historians of the Revival Period and archeologists—said that there are no proofs, and it would be therefore improper to mislead people and disingenuous to create a place for worship in this church. At this meeting architect Mushanov's wife, Zlatka Kirova, and others too, voiced the following opinion: 'And why not? After all, why shouldn't there be a place where people could feel at peace and fulfilled, and where they could say: there, it is acknowledged that [the grave] is here, the legend can be validated...' She did not say this with any malicious intention or desire to misinform. However, my personal opinion is unequivocal: history, archeology and all the sciences which deal with similar problems will lose their authority, if they link a place to an event or to an individual based on such an approach without convincing and exact proofs. I firmly believe that people can be moved only by the authentic, and I therefore have always objected to some

of the methods used for restoration and conservation in our country (*BAN volume*, 150).

She further added she had nothing against monuments and mausoleums, and the seeking of graves, but only if they really existed: "I do not believe that the Bulgarian people are thinking now in a less sacred manner about Levski than if a place existed which would be considered to be the resting place of his bones" (ibid.: 150). These are important statements, because they complicate the parameters of the whole dispute. By the mid-1980s the stakes were so high and the tone so acrimonious that the conflict was articulated, depending on the side, as the unbridgeable dichotomy between rigorous experts and demagogic dilettantes, or between sloppy, unpatriotic professionals and alert public intellectuals. This was not yet the case at the end of the 1970s. What emerges from Mushanov's and Stancheva's statements, both reasonable in their own right, is a different approach, indeed a different philosophy on how monuments of the past should be preserved. Where Mushanov and his wife believed in creatively enhancing the restored objects aesthetically and intellectually, Stancheva shared the view that only absolute authenticity (or rather the way she understood it) was scientifically and pedagogically defensible. One could object to her somewhat purist naiveté that people are stirred only by "real" things. Pilgrimages to the Holy Land or to Christian shrines with imaginary relics should have disabused her of her enlightenment illusions about human nature. But what lurks behind her statement is the ethos of a whole generation that desired to transform the existing traditional, often superstitious worldview, into one based on a scientific attitude. She was not moved merely and not even primarily (as would seem a few years later) by the urge to defend the profession from the encroachment of dilettantes. It was the defense of a particular *Weltanschauung* and of a professional philosophy, whether or not one may want to agree with it.

It was during the same period that the restoration of Tsarevets, the residential hill of the medieval kings and patriarchs in Tîrnovo, was taking place. Only the foundations and fragments of the fortification walls were in place. There are no authentic reliable sources, illustrative or textual, about the exact appearance even of the towers, let alone of the buildings. Yet, the view prevailed that a plausible construction

Figure 7. The "Sv.Petka Samardzhiiska" church after the restoration (present view).
Source: Khaitov, *Grobît na Vasil Levski*, 74, fig. 1.

is more valuable than an unimaginative reconstruction. As a consequence, not only the entire fortification walls were erected but also an imposing building like the patriarchal church. Today Tsarevets presents quite a spectacular view but without a firm scholarly foundation, according to a number of opinions. The contrary opinion, still within academia, counters that there is a scholarly basis even if it is based on existing medieval sources by analogy. This clash of different philosophies of restoration is nothing unique to Bulgaria or the communist world. It is constantly encountered in all societies around the world, as the controversies over Williamsburg and Jamestown in the United States attest.

Yet what is typical for Bulgaria is the timing of when this approach became prevalent. The 1970s in the cultural sphere are indelibly linked to the name of Liudmila Zhivkova, the daughter of Todor Zhivkov. A historian of the modern Balkans and an art historian, in 1971 she had become Deputy Chair of the Committee for Friendship and Cultural Ties with Foreign Countries, and a year later Deputy Chair of the Committee for Art and Culture. Four years later, she already headed the committee, in 1976 became member of the Central

Committee of the Bulgarian Communist Party, and in 1979 Politburo member charged with science, culture and the arts. Under her aegis, the highly fanfared celebrations of the founding of the first Bulgarian state, heralded as the oldest European state existing under its original name, took place. During her less than a decade-long cultural rule, and with the posture of a communist Maecenas, an enormous number of monuments were erected all over the country. Her ear was thus attuned to the appeal of a story like the discovery of Levski's grave. In other words, the atmosphere created under her leadership provided the favorable conditions for the explosion of the breach. When Bobchev attributed the publication of his article in 1979 to a friend in the editorial office of the journal *Sofia*, he was only partly right. His editor friend was not feeling threatened or even insecure with approving the publication given the overall atmosphere at the time.

The question was attracting growing public attention, and in July, 1980 the Bulgarian national television showed a documentary—"Legend about Levski"—in prime time. All participants of the excavations were interviewed. Milhailov reiterated his thesis, and added that at the time he did not pay attention to this question because he was totally convinced that it had been an earlier funeral, and that the Levski legend was a mystification. Bobchev expounded at equal length on his view. As an architect, he asserted, it was impossible not to destroy or at least dislocate the skeleton during the construction of the site, given the small depth of the burial. Among the other interviewees, the professor of anthropology Boev cuts the most comic figure. Apart from the fact that his memory was failing him, his statement that "Levski, as is well known, was of the Nordic race, and these skeletons were of the Mediterranean race" is an apt illustration of scientific discourse he was shaped by in the interwar period (*BAN volume*: 120). One would suspect that such argumentation, still carrying clout in the 1950s, would have become obsolete by the 1980s. Even in 1981, however, during the roundtable discussions, the young film director Iuri Zhirov, countered Boev by maintaining that Levski was of the Thracian, not Nordic type (ibid.: 127). The most striking feature of this 1980 documentary is that, all in all, it leaves the impression of a certain parity in the voiced opinions. Both sides stood firmly by their views and there was no real exchange of opinions, but the effect on the viwer is that two valid hypotheses await their scholarly scrutiny. There were also no *ad hominem* attacks yet.

The atmosphere had become much tenser at the next round of the public discussion, the round table of the party newspaper *Rabotnichesko delo* in February, 1981. It was presided by Iordan Iotov, editor-in-chief, member of the Central Committee, and subsequently Politburo member. In his opening words, he evoked the eve of the 1,300th anniversary of the founding of the Bulgarian state which fell on the same year, and defined the roundtable as a forum to review the stage of the research on Levski's grave. In terms of substantive arguments, there was nothing new that either side added. For the first time, however, one had the feeling that, at least emotionally, the scales were slightly tipped in favor of the reburial argument. One of the historians present, spelled his concern which closely approximated an accusation: "The guilt of our colleagues, the archeologists who were leading the excavations in 1956 is not in denying that the skeleton they discovered belongs to Levski but in their negligence as Bulgarian scholars, and having lost the bone materials. Especially when they themselves publicly admitted that the issue was spoken of at the time" (*BAN volume*: 123). This, alas, is the conclusion that any unbiased observer of the conflict is bound to reach, even if one totally rejects the reburial hypothesis.

Serious as this verdict was, it never went beyond the personal professional responsibility of the archeologists involved directly with the excavations, especially Mikhailov. Another charge was spelled out, however, by a journalist at the roundtable going far beyond accusations of negligence. It had the ominous sound of a general denunciation of the profession as lacking in patriotism. Contemplating the reasons for Mikhailov's and Boev's attitude, he exclaimed: "To me, the explanation lies only in the lack of an emotional attitude toward Bulgarian history often encountered among Bulgarian historians... I am not the only one to have reached this conclusion. The Hungarian scholar Péter Juhász is also amazed at Bulgarian nihilism" (*BAN volume*: 130). This vilification was a solitary note, but it signaled the existence of a discourse that was successfully revived a few years later with great bravado by Khaitov.

At this point it was not picked by anyone, least of all by the chairman Iotov. His interventions are the ones that signaled the official attitude to the problem. His statement represents a cross between wishful patriotic thinking and unlimited belief in the "people," and a strict devotion to scientific methods, the predictable attitude of a genuine utopian communist:

I would distinguish several levels when approaching this problem: after Levski's hanging, would the Bulgarian people take their greatest son from the gallows? It seems to me, the answer is yes... Looking at the 1956 excavations, there are a number of unclear archeological circumstances... This generates discussions with arguments pro and con. Anthropology, on the other hand, besides dealing with physical appearance, anthropological types, age, and gender, can also contribute to the identification of the buried individual through the method of plastic reconstruction. This involves a graphic sketch and a plastic portrait. It is something widely used in criminology. I have therefore a simple rational suggestion, and I think it is in line with our times: give us the bones. Then this whole dispute will become superfluous (*BAN volume*: 131, 297).

His concluding remarks were reassuring without any hint of recrimination against the archeologists: "What is the truth? We assembled here not to establish the truth at this stage of the research, being aware that this is a matter for science to decide, but to activate the scholarly inquiry, to approach if not reach the truth.... My impression is that not enough efforts are directed to finding the bones, as if this is a precluded question. Maybe more efforts should be put in this direction because if we find them the problem will be solved" (ibid.: 132).

A year later, in 1982, Bobchev died. A more momentous death had occurred in July, 1981, when Zhivkova unexpectedly passed away. She was not personally involved in the dispute but, judging from the existing exchanges, she had cast a favorable eye on the efforts of the "grave seekers." By the time of the roundtable in 1981, the reburial thesis was, at least morally, gradually taking the upper hand. One can only presume, but my presumption is that had Zhivkova been alive, the suggested plaque commemorating the legend about Levski's reburial would probably have been placed at the "Sv. Petka Samardzhiiska" church. It surely would have met the silent disapproval of many, but it is equally sure that it would not have encountered any open protest. Zhivkova's death changed the constellation of power or, at the very least, its perception by the outside world. The new head of the Committee of Culture Georgi Iordanov together with the president of BAN invited a committee of experts headed by the doyen of the historical profession—Academician Dimitîr Kosev—to prepare a report on the current state of the dispute and the historians' position. This commission consisted of eight historians specializing on the 19th century, two archeologists, and two architects. The report, completed in July, 1983, is hardly a complement to the analytical capacities of professional historians, even if one disregards its uncritical dependence on Boev's dubious anthropological statements. There was one mitigating circumstance: the commission did not have all existing materials at its disposal, nor did it know about their existence. It had neither seen Bobchev's sketches nor the official diary of the excavations, known informally as Dzhingov's diary. For all practical purposes, in its work it stepped entirely on Mikhailov's 1961 publications, since the other piece of evidence at their disposal—the short Bobchev diary—consisted simply of entries about the workers' payments. This circumstance made even someone as uncompromising as Khaitov spare the Kosev Commission his unrelenting pen (*BAN volume*: 173). Quite apart from one's opinion on the quality of the report, it gave its scholarly imprimatur to Mikhailov's thesis, in the hope of tilting back public opinion to what it considered the proper scientific position.

To summarize, since the end of the 1950s a breach occurred starting the social drama that came to be known as the affair around Levski's grave. It played itself out as a challenge to the entrenched authority of a scholarly consensus. Voiced by a challenger, albeit a scholar himself, outside the mainstream academic infrastructure, at the time it was not experienced as a breach; moreover, it never really caught the public eye in the next couple of decades. However, beneath the seeming quiet, there were deeper divisions waiting for an opportune moment to come to the surface. This moment came at the end of the 1970s, and was facilitated by the atmosphere accompanying the patriotic and cultural upsurge on the eve of the 1,300th anniversary of the foundation of the Bulgarian state. Once it came into the public eye, a mounting crisis followed, yet it kept short of an explosion. The Kosev Commission was the latest attempt to contain the crisis within the academic profession, by giving the dominant thesis another shot of legitimacy. The shot was too feeble and came too late. Nevertheless, a temporary truce set in, a kind of consensus of divided spheres where the scholars were dealing with general ideas and the scientifically provable truth, and writers and journalists with some factual details, which feed

Figure 8. Nikolai Khaitov, 1919–2002.

the popular imagination, but were not really considered to be of major significance. And, of course, it was the scholarly sphere that was the dominant one. Or so it seemed for a very brief period.

This precarious equilibrium was broken with the interference in the conflict of Khaitov, widely believed to be one of the two Bulgarian writers, alongside Iordan Radichkov, with, if not the greatest, then certainly the most idiosyncratic talent. Khaitov closely and actively watched the developments of the conflict but had not participated in any of the public fora in the early 1980s. When he came out with his detailed account of the controversy and strong endorsement of the reburial thesis (Khaitov 1985), all hell broke loose: the breach had turned into a crisis. This time the challenge did not come from within academe, but from a different field that was not under the control of the scholarly sphere, and which had usually been perceived by scholars as privileged vis-à-vis the positions of power. The so-called artistic intelligentsia—especially some actors, artists and a number of writers—were thought to be and often really were on intimate footing with the higher ups. In addition, the new challenge was articulated in a forceful and effective prose, popular enough to reach a broad readership and strongly polemic: even friends of Khaitov would never describe him as shy, let alone easily intimidated by authority.

The entry of Khaitov on the scene effected the "momentous juncture or turning point in the relations between components of a social field—at which seeming peace becomes overt conflict and covert antagonisms become visible. Sides are taken, factions are formed, and unless the conflict can be sealed off quickly within a limited area of social interaction, there is a tendency for the breach to widen and spread until it coincides with some dominant cleavage in the widest set of social relations to which the parties in conflict belong" (Turner 1981: 146) As Turner insists, the crisis is the turning point "when a true state of affairs is revealed, when it is least easy to don masks or pretend that there is nothing rotten in the village" (Turner 1974: 39).

Immediately upon publishing his book, Khaitov sent it to the then Chairman of the Committee of Culture—Georgi Iordanov. His accompanying letter stated that after long years of discussions, sufficient facts had been gathered in support of the thesis that Levski had been reburied in the "Sv. Petka" church. His book was presenting a summary of these facts. Khaitov appealed to Iordanov to consider the possibility, after due discussion, of "announcing the church 'Sv. Petka Samarzhiiska' in Sofia to be the grave of the Apostle of Freedom Vasil Levski" (*BAN volume*: 140). The Committee of Culture forwarded Khaitov's letter and book to the director of the AI, asking for a written opinion "in line with the archeological facts." A second letter followed, this time by the president of BAN Balevski. It was sent in response to the numerous citizens' letters which, in the aftermath of Khaitov's television interview of August 24, 1985, were asking about BAN's official position. It ordered the Scientific Council of the institute to come up with a written verdict by September 30, which would be published in the mass media.

These two letters led to the September 14, 1985 discussion at the Medieval Section of the AI, and then, on October 2, at the Scientific Council. Despite later insinuations on the part of the archeologists that they were faced with a *fait accompli* and that party pressure had been exerted on them to waste their time with discussing dubious theories, they were actually given ample room to defend their standpoint. It doesn't need much familiarity with how a one-party system operates, to know that had it been a precluded issue, the church would have been immediately turned into Levski's commemorative grave, with or without the archeologists' consent. In the present circumstances, it was clear that in the higher party echelons there were those who sided with one or the other opinion, but that the issue itself was not worthy of clumsy authoritarian dictates. This was, after all, the 1980s, not the 1950s, and democratic discussion could be tolerated as long as it did not question immediate state/party politics. Besides, the burning question of the day was the renaming process, and the last thing the authorities wished to foment, was additional intellectual discontent. Hence, the whole issue was handed to BAN for resolution.

The completely new element in the equation was the involvement of the mass media: the press, radio and television. Added to Khaitov's immense popularity, it made sure that the discussion, unlike previously, could not be confined within professional circles. Khaitov himself took ample advantage of the new outlets. Energetic and basking in his stature as a public figure, he undertook numerous public lectures and book promotions in Sofia and all over the country. The result was the barrage of citizen's letters to the academy. Some archeologists were quick to dismiss these letters as organized pressure on the local level by the Khaitov propaganda machine, but they could not so easily dismiss the immediate sting to their professional efforts.

Excavations in Bulgaria were financed partly by the institute, from the state budget allocated to the academy, and partly with the support of local administrative and party authorities (*BAN volume:* 290; Bailey 1998: 96). Many archeologists depended on and cultivated good relations with these authorities on the district, city and village level. These secured the local infrastructure—labor, living quarters, food—and guaranteed the successful outcome of the excavations. Local moneys allocated for archeological digs were under the rubric of cultural and patriotic needs. One of the archeologists' complaints, never spelled out in writing, but that I heard in numerous personal conversations, was that the great popularity of Khaitov's book among this middle and lower echelon of state and party employees, had cast the archeologists in a negative light, either as unprofessional or unpatriotic. This had resulted in the alarming withdrawal of local funds from many archeological sites. After the debates, the memorandum of the AI of June 6, 1986 tacitly recognized this by mentioning the heavy repercussions from the general distrust towards the archeological discipline fomented by Khaitov's book (*BAN volume*: 468). There was, thus, more at stake, than simply countering some irresponsible nationalist's accusations or defending the professional ethos from dilettantish onslaughts.

The "debate" at the AI was so pitiful from the point of view of substantive arguments, that it bears mention only because it led directly to the important discussions at the academy. It is, however, extremely important in view of the rhetoric used by both sides, especially the archeologists' attempt to undermine any legitimacy Khaitov may have claimed as an expert. The discussion was also important for showing that any hope for a compromise was completely deflated by this meeting. The atmosphere was overheated, at times scandalous and chaotic, *ad hominem* attacks were not spared, and it was clear that the crisis was getting out of hand. What this debate demonstrated (quite apart from the language and emotions) was that the archeologists had not taken Khaitov seriously. Most of their interventions did not address the substance of his arguments but focused on the assault by a dilettante against a profession. The final opinion of the AI, following the discussion of September 14 and the meeting of the Scientific Council on October 2, was summarized in the report of Dimitîr Ovcharov from October 4.

Briefly, this report summarized the substantive part of the archeologists' objections about a late burial and thus, a possible reburial. It bears enumerating them since all were subsequently dismissed: a) Skeleton No. 95 was not the only altar burial; its depth was coeval with other burials in the altar and other parts of the church; there were no precedents of sanctuary burials; there was no need to dig into the sanctuary wall to lay the lower limbs, when three meters would be enough to lay the body entirely within the sanctuary space; b) architect Boiadzhiev's sketches convincingly destroy the thesis of a hole in the wall; instead he postulates that there was a later natural destruction of the last row of the constructed wall whereas the ancient foundation beneath was intact; c) the discovery of the two holes through the limbs near the knees conclusively show that the bones must have been broken; Khaitov's interpretation of the issue is a falsification, "meant to mislead the reader;" d) the position of the hands in a situation of *rigor mortis* exclude the reburial; e) the fact that this burial was without a coffin is no reason to assume a later or irregular burial: there are numerous medieval funerals without coffins; f) Boev's anthropological expertise is definitive about the type and age of the skeleton being over 50, whereas Levski was 36 at the time of his death. Much of the report, however, dealt with Khaitov's "rude and ironic-sarcastic remarks, which [he] addresses in his book against the archeologists in general, and the AI in particular. This to a great extent inflicts harm upon the authority of the whole archeological science." In conclusion, Ovcharov insisted that the scholarly view should be publicized through the TV, roundtables, and the press; it should be published separately by BAN, and recommended not to place a commemorative plaque because this "would be in complete defiance of scholarly research and observations" (*BAN volume*: 189–90). The report was sent to Balevski, with a copy to Khaitov, who did not waste time to respond and deposit his own response.

It was brilliant: the archeologists had offered him plenty with which to exercise his mind and pen (*BAN volume*: 191–96). Part of it addressed the substantive objections. Khaitov dismissed the assertion that the altar burials were coeval; on the contrary, he demonstrated that the diary of the excavations, which the archeologists insisted on being the only authentic source, had documented different depths. He also exposed the numerous fallacies in dating the different burials. He challenged Boiadzhiev's sketches with the few existing photographs taken at the time of the excavations, and subsequently Boiadzhiev himself had them withdrawn from the discussion (ibid.: 311). Basing himself on the newly released photographs by the archeologists themselves, Khaitov convincingly showed that the lower limbs could not have been broken. His comments about *rigor mortis*, referring the archeologists to the standard textbook on forensic medicine was to the point, and the other two objections only demonstrated that Ovcharov had not read Khaitov's book. Khaitov was at his best, however, when he countered Ovcharov's allegations of arrogance and damage for the archeological discipline:

> I will not discuss with Ovcharov whether my book is beneficial or harmful to the whole archeological science. I have never and nowhere written nor spoken about the "authority of the whole archeological science" because I am aware no less than Ovcharov that the archeological science is not Prof. Mikhailov, nor Ovcharov, nor the two of them taken together, not even the whole section of medieval archeology. Archeology is a system of research methods and accumulated knowledge, and to accuse it is like accusing chemistry, physics, or mathematics. It is quite another issue that one or another archeologist can make mistakes... These mistakes affect the authority of the one who has made them, not the authority of the science or its institution. It is unacceptable that the ones who have committed a mistake hide behind the authority of this institution, nor is it acceptable for them to boast with its achievements. In science everyone is responsible for

one's mistakes, and Ovcharov, should not attempt to identify the archeological science or the Archeological Institution with Mikhailov. (*BAN volume*: 192–3).

He was stinging in his riposte to Stancheva's comment that he had behaved like an investigator and that there was pressing need to rehabilitate archeology from his onslaughts: "I wonder how she expected me to behave: on my feet, silent, hat down? The search for scientific truth is a kind of investigation, and if Stancheva did not know that, it is time she learned it. Instead of worrying about 'rehabilitating archeology,' she should think about the rehabilitation of those representatives who enact outrages in its name" (*BAN volume*: 193). Khaitov compared the archeologists' intolerance to critique with what was going on in other sectors of society: "We read every day not only sharp, but even devastating critiques in the press against managers, general directors, vice-ministers. Lessons are drawn, punishments are passed and nobody would even think of taking this form of public criticism for something strange or offensive. Only the archeologists are of the opinion that no one should meddle in their work" (ibid.: 195).

It was these two documents—Ovcharov's report and Khaitov's response—that Balevski passed on to Todorov in late November, charging him with making a decision about a BAN-sponsored publication. And it was after getting acquainted with the stenogram of the discussions and the institute's report that Todorov became convinced that a publication would irreparably damage the reputation of the institute. Eager to save it from public embarrassment, and hopeful that a better prepared discussion might yield points of consensus, he agreed to organize such a meeting and publish all records in a documentary volume at the publishing house of BAN. The debates were contentious, but their most important aspect was that the two sides were talking to one another for the first time. In the course of these, often very technical exchanges, neither side changed its initial version, but there were corrections in the argumentation of both. At the end of the meeting, Todorov summarized: "We have not reached the stage where we can say that one of these theses is able to entirely displace the other... We cannot come up with a categorical statement from this meeting" (*BAN volume*: 379). His proposal that the deliberations be published, was supported by everyone. The director Angelov declared:

We are a country in which scholarship has an important role, it receives great attention... Obviously scholarship has to be free, different opinions can be articulated... I am very happy this will be solved properly, both sides will be heard *auditor et altera pars*, as the Latins would say... I completely support this project proposed by Acad. Todorov for a possible publication...This will be a very serious work. This is scholarship, after all: hearing several standpoints (ibid.: 378).

After the conclusion of the debates, the parties were invited to deposit their final statements. The AI had done so on the eve of the last meeting (February 25), and had reiterated all its previous opinions (ibid.: 380–1). The opponents deposited their statement on March 1, 1986. For his final report, Todorov was waiting on the expert opinion of the Research Institute of Criminology at the Interior Ministry, asked to pronounce itself on the photographs of the three skeletons from the altar space, and give detailed answers to specific questions that had given rise to acrimonious confrontations (ibid.: 385). The criminologists' statement was completed on March 30, and on April 7 Todorov signed his final report. This important document carefully summarized and weighed the two contending theses, and reached the conclusion "that in the church 'Sv. Petka Samardzhiiska' irregular burials have taken place after the construction of the church. Given the evidence which pointed to this church from before September 9, 1944, there is the great possibility that one of the skeletons might have belonged to Levski." At the same time, it indicated that "unfortunately, the bones have not been preserved, and the appropriate anthropological research, which could definitively determine whether or not, and which of the two burials could belong to Vasil Levski, cannot be made" (ibid.: 417).

The cover letter was worded even more carefully. It acknowledged that "in light of the newly found materials, the expertise, and the debates, certain conclusions were reached about later burials (after the construction of the church), which give serious reasons to begin a discussion, this time in the light of historical sources, about the possibility to place a memorial plaque at the church with an inscription stating that according to historical data, the Apostle of Freedom Vasil Levski had been reburied in the altar of the church by patriotic Bulgarians" (ibid.: 418). The wording was explicit that the archeological data were insufficient and did not preclude future discussion around historical sources. It suggested a compromise formula where the tentative scholarly formulation "according to historical data" would figure largely.[2] Finally, the letter reiterated the intention to publish all materials amounting to 810 manuscript pages.

---

[2] The distinction made between archeological and historical data is one between material and textual (written or oral) ones. That historical data (in this definition) can be contested is a permanent problem confronting historians.

3. No Redress, or Where are Levski's Bones?

When all was said and done, there were two lingering problems that at times were posed directly, at others present obliquely. One was the archeologists' question why all the noise when nothing could be proven categorically. Once it was clear that a definitive conclusion could not be accepted or imposed about the remains of Skeleton No. 95, this made the whole discussion a waste of time. After all, science deals only with proven theses. In a charitable version, this question can explain part of the implicit passivity of some archeologists. In a less charitable one, the passivity was just the outer syndrome of intellectual laziness and professional smugness as well as the iron *ésprit de corps*, which motivated the archeological team.

The other question that interested Khaitov and popular public opinion, was why, after all, confine the debate to the analysis of the archeological data. Why was it impossible to make the appropriate conclusions even without definitive proofs? Already the fact that the later reburial thesis could be launched as plausible provided, according to them, sufficient grounds for unequivocally accepting the possibility of Levski's burial. Also, Khaitov's team felt that the discussion had not been exhaustive and had missed one of the central issues: the whereabouts of the bones. After all, given the possibilities of contemporary science, there could be a very simple check, which would have made the waste of the whole mental and emotional energy completely redundant. Such a solution had been suggested already by Iordan Iotov at the 1981 *Rabotnichesko delo* roundtable. This was a simple DNA test. But where were the bones?

Let us address both questions by starting from the second and taking the suspense out from the outset: there are no bones. To this day my friend Diana says the bones will be found, just like many of the artifacts that were discovered in the storage places of the Museum of Sofia. Mikhailov intimated this in his 1980 publication in the journal *Sofia*: "Skeleton No. 95 was the best preserved and its bones are at our disposal" (Khaitov 2002: 232). Both he and Dzhingov maintained that the bones, together with the rest of the artifacts, had been carefully sorted out and packaged. However, in the documentary film "The Levski Legend," shown on the Bulgarian TV on July 16, 1980, Mikhailov said that "as far as I know, this skeleton had been sent to the City Museum" (Khaitov 2002: 233). When directly asked by Khaitov in 1985 where exactly the bones were, he exclaimed that he didn't remember what he had eaten yesterday, but that they must be either in the Archeological Museum or in the Museum of the City of Sofia (ibid.: 167). Dzhingov until his death seems to have believed that the bones were preserved. In the provincial newspaper *Iuzhno utro* of March 7–14, 1994, published in Stara Zagora, where he had arrived for a lecture, a local journalist asked him why the bones had disappeared. He answered: "The bones are in a secure place." When the amazed journalist required why they were not analyzed now, Dzhingov allegedly said: "And what if they belong to Levski? You know what will happen? Khaitov will become an academician and do you know what would happen to us?" (ibid.: 224–5). Khaitov did indeed become an academician, but nothing ever happened to the other side. Some archeologists continue to believe that the bones are simply misplaced. The more circumspect ones quietly muse that they must have been thrown away. In one of the protocols of the Kosev Commission from July 18, 1983, Ovcharov says: "I will tell you where the bones are. After Stamen Mikhailov became convinced that these were Roman bones [from the Roman period], they have buried them somewhere. This is what we archeologists do. They have not been preserved but they have also not been thrown away" (*BAN volume*: 167). But he carefully avoided further pronouncements, and his opinion was not included in the final report of the commission.

There is considerable and plausible evidence that the bones were actually taken out of the site soon after their discovery and embarked on a virtual odyssey. Consensus exists that during the excavations the bones of Skeleton No. 95 were placed in a sack. In the 1980 documentary film Dimitîr Rizov said he took the sack and brought it to the Theological Academy (ibid.: 119). Mikhailov never contested this, and Khaitov justifiably insists that the bones could not have been taken out of the site without his explicit permission. The two professors at the Theological Academy, Ivan Goshev and Giaurov, did not keep the bones but sent the servant of the archdiocese to hand the sack to the AI. The servant did so, but was told that the director Prof. Krtîstiu Miatev had ordered that nothing excavated on the territory of Sofia should be accepted but should go directly to the Museum of the City of Sofia. From here on, the versions differ. Buchinski, in his statement at the TV show in 1980, said that the servant then took the bones back to the excavation site and left them on a big box in the church (*BAN volume*: 119). However, this was not a witness account, since Buchinski had been away from Sofia between May 31 and June 13, 1956, and when he came back, the bones were already gone. Bobchev, on the other hand, had been struck by the unusual position of the skeleton and had asked Mikhailov to immediately launch a special investigation, but as a subordinate did not press further. When a few days later Giaurov appeared with the exclamation that they had discovered Levski's grave, "at that time, the bones had already disappeared." Bobchev, employed also at another archeological site, had no specific theory about where and how the bones had gone (ibid.: 124).

When Buchinski returned on June 13, the workers told him there had been quarrels on the site: some were saying the skeleton was ancient, Roman, others that it belonged to Levski. Apparently, some of the workers must have told him that the bones had been taken to the Museum of the City of Sofia, care of Stancheva, because he and Bobchev immediately decided to follow up on this but when they "went to Stancheva to ask about the bones, she said she would tell when she was ordered from above" (ibid.: 122). At the BAN debates, Stancheva was asked to comment on Buchinski's statement: "How can I say such a thing. This is a ridiculous response"(ibid.: 358). As far as her response goes, one might give credence to her objection, but one may be skeptical about her denial that the bones had been delivered to her Museum.

In fact, when the Kosev Commission deliberated in 1983, the directors of all three possible institutions, where the bones could have been delivered—the AI, the Museum of the City of Sofia, and the Central Historical-Archeological Museum of the St. Synod—wrote official letters, stating that the bones of Skeleton No. 95 were not only not preserved in their depots but had never been brought to them (*BAN volume*: 139). This, apparently, infuriated Mikhailov, because in 1989 he gave the following written answer to the representative of the

Committee for State and People's Control about the whereabouts of the bones: "All materials from the excavations have to be in the pitiful storage rooms of the Archeological Museum, and all bones have to be in the Museum of the City of Sofia, despite the fact that some of its employees deny it" (Khaitov 2002: 233). During the 1983 debates Kosev had asked Stancheva whether Levski's bones could be recovered, and she answered: "All bones discovered during excavations we send in packages to Boev's institute. When I later asked what happened to them, Boev's laboratory assistant told me that mice had eaten the packaging, the bones got mixed up and are not suited for work" (*BAN volume*: 171). She later insisted she was speaking in general terms, not about Levski's bones, which, judging from the turn of phrase is correct, but a disingenuous riposte, since she was responding to Kosev's specific question about Levski's bones. Stancheva, without knowing for sure, logically assumed that this is what had happened also to Levski's bones. It is also clear that in 1983, she implicitly accepted that the bones of Skeleton No. 95 had been delivered together with other bones from the site as had been ruled by Miatev in his directive that any skeletal remains be handed over to the Museum of the City of Sofia (Khaitov 2002: 9).

This is one of two possible versions of what had really happened. Either, as Ovcharov thought, the bones, after having been delivered back to the site, were discarded, buried back into the ground as Roman, or, they were sent to the Museum of the City of Sofia and from there to Boev's laboratory, where they were dispersed after mice had eaten out the packaging (*BAN volume*: 126–7). In any case, as the Kosev Commission nonchalantly concluded in 1983: "Later, the bones found in the altar space, including the ones which Giaurov thought of as Levski's, disappear." Just like that, into thin air. It is an amazing conclusion, not even followed by a surmise or question where and how the bones might have disappeared, given that this expertise was conducted by the leading Bulgarian historian of the day—Academician Kosev—and signed by a host of the most important specialists from history and archeology (ibid.: 138–9). No wonder Khaitov could not resist from spinning an elaborate conspiracy theory around this. He started with the inconsistencies in the archeologists' and Stancheva's statements, and concluded that the bones disappeared or were destroyed in the cellars of the Museum of the City of Sofia, with

Stancheva's full connivance. He makes a big issue of the fact that in the late 1990s, despite his numerous efforts to meet and interview her again, Stancheva studiously avoided any contact with him (Khaitov 2002: 234, 238). In the end, he holds five people responsible for the mishandling of Levski's remains: Dhingov, Mikhailov and Stancheva as archeologists directly involved, and two individuals representing the leadership of BAN, the director of the AI Miatev and above all, the president of BAN at the time, the philosopher Todor Pavlov.

Khaitov's publications before 1989 imply, but never fully develop his belief that there was a political conspiracy to prevent the "discovery" of Levski's grave. The farthest he went was to hurl a general accusation to the specialists for having gone "beyond themselves to prove that the Madara horseman was not Bulgarian; some of them denied that the Slavic settlement at Novi Pazar was Slavic; they questioned the inscription of the Chîrgubil Mostich; they questioned Kaloian's ring, and (the peak of self-denial), they trumpeted not only at home but also abroad, that Pliska, the capital of our first kingdom, was not Bulgarian but a whole intact Byzantine town found by the Bulgarians" (*BAN volume*: 214). After 1989, Khaitov who had been a privileged writer and personally close to many individuals in the party and administrative elite, but was not a party member and was a fervent nationalist, wrote up openly his suspicions which before he shared only orally and privately (Khaitov 2003: 258–9, 342–52). In June, 1990 a retrospective check-up at the AI by inspectors from the Commission for State Control triggered by Khaitov, discovered a report by Mikhailov, addressed to the then director of the institute Miatev. The report, dated June 1, 1956, written a day after the discovery of Skeleton No. 95 and after Giaurov had excitedly visited the excavations, informed that several burials had been discovered in the apsis space and that rumors were going around that these might be Levski's bones. Mikhailov further appealed to Miatev "to set up a commission, which would investigate *in situ* the position of the individuals buried in the altar space and the possibility that one of them is Levski" (Khaitov 2002: 5). On receiving the report, Miatev marked it with the word SERDICA, the medieval name of Sofia, and the report was filed by the secretary among materials from the excavations of the Serdica Fortress, which had been ongoing since 1952, and where the report was found in 1990. He never followed up on Mikhailov's suggestion to set up a commission.

Khaitov makes much of the erroneous filing of the report, insinuating that Miatev had hidden it. This is presumptuous: if he had wanted to get rid of the report, Miatev could have simply destroyed it. There is no doubt that Miatev was aware of the rumors. He had taken part in the 1937 military commission charged with finding the grave. He knew of the publication in *Trud* on May 17, 1956. Finally, he had been warned by his colleague Prof. Giaurov with whom he taught at the Theological Academy. At the same time, he never inspected the excavations even once, and never entered anything about them in his personal diary, regularly held between 1953 and 1958 (Khaitov 2002: 6–7). Khaitov never for a moment doubts that pressure must have been exerted upon Miatev not to follow up on Mikhailov's report. Remarkably, Mikhailov himself never ever mentioned this report during the BAN debates or the numerous interviews, although this would have undoubtedly alleviated some of the responsibility and he would have shouldered it with the already deceased Miatev. According to Khaitov, Miatev wanted to wash his hands, Pilate-like, and he ordered that all skeletal remains be handed over to the Museum of the City of Sofia, and then endorsed Mikhailov's thesis about the early burial. Khaitov never entertained the possibility that Miatev, like Mikhailov, may have sincerely doubted that these could have been Levski's bones and moreover, as a classical archeologist, he was not too interested in medieval sites, especially in the case of the saving operations around "Sv. Petka."

Instead, in an amazing flight of imagination, he introduces the figure of Todor Pavlov, at that time a powerful presence in Bulgarian academe and cultural life. A rather dogmatic Marxist philosopher, Pavlov had served as one of Bulgaria's postwar regents, and for many years was the powerful head of BAN. Khaitov's reasoning why Miatev did not form a commission is that he was aware of the negative attitude of Pavlov, that the latter had perhaps communicated over the phone. One can facetiously say that had Pavlov not existed, he would have been invented by Khaitov, because, like in physics, he was the hypothetical missing element needed to prove the theory. Khaitov devotes a whole brief chapter to "The role of Todor Pavlov as an organizer of the Marxist-Leninist revision of Bulgarian scholarship after 1946 and in deciding the fate of Levski's grave." For intrepid readers, there is the phrase that: "most likely, whether Skeleton No. 95 was destroyed on the personal order of Todor Pavlov will remain a secret forever" (Khaitov 2002: 11) but the whole ensuing chapter is built on this unproven premise. Khaitov represents Pavlov as the main party ideologue and trusted political stooge of the Soviets. His "Marxist-Leninist revision" of Bulgarian cultural life was profound and overbearing. In archeology it played itself out in the onslaught against the traditions of Bogdan Filov and Géza Fehér. In Khaitov's reading, Filov, "this great Bulgarian scholar executed by the People's Court" together with his Hungarian colleague Fehér, had made significant scholarly contributions about the proto-Bulgarian essence of the First Bulgarian state and its higher cultural status compared to that of the Slavs. The destruction of this tradition, designated as "Filovshtina" ("Filovdom") "meant in practice, the denunciation of the glory of the medieval Bulgarian state and its rulers, which until 1944 was feeding the national consciousness of the younger generations."

This is Khaitov's credo. An unabashed nationalist, he could never accept or understand the internationalism of the communists, let alone the quasi-internationalism after 1944, which served Soviet or Russian hegemonic rule. While Filov had indeed been a leading archeologist, this was not the reason for his trial and execution, but the fact that as prime minister in 1940 and regent in 1943, with his ardent pro-German, fascist and nationalist policies, he was instrumental in bringing Bulgaria into the war on the side of Germany. Fehér, a diplomat and head of the Hungarian cultural institute in Sofia, was an amateur art historian and archeologist as well as a charismatic figure, instrumental in promoting the political rapprochement between Hungary, Bulgaria and Turkey on cultural and ethnic grounds, downplaying Bulgaria's Slavic connections. While it is true that Slavic archeology in the aftermath of 1944 received unprecedented and unjustified precedence and the proto-Bulgarian component was downplayed, this was simply mirroring the extremes of the interwar period. Amazingly Khaitov, who questioned Mikhailov and Stancheva's expertise on the basis that they were not trained as archeologists but as classicists, would point to Fehér, whose forays into Bulgarian archeology, while feted greatly at the time, can be only described as wildly dilettantish.

The "ideologization" of Bulgarian archeology, according to Khaitov, began with the attempt to counter what was unfairly described as "wild Bulgarian chauvinism" but was, instead, the non-ideological, purely scholarly achievement of a whole generation of bourgeois scholars. The ideologization of the academic sphere, "was part of the grand-scale Stalinist program to denationalize the southeast European states, which had been handed over to the Soviet sphere of influence" (Khaitov 2002: 12). He offers a list of cultural "crimes," most of them were figments of his imagination. These included the order for the complete destruction of war monuments in 1946 that, in the course of a month, had been turned into gravel and inflicted the first blow on Bulgaria's national pride. That this is an unserious allegation is obvious from the scores of standing monuments dedicated to different wars before 1944. No monument for the Russo–Turkish war (1877–78), the Serb–Bulgarian war (1885) or the Balkan wars had been destroyed, and most monuments for the fallen in the First World War were preserved. Where he is right was that after 1944, textbooks were rewritten, and in the spirit of the new republic, royal titles were left out. Instead of Tsar Boris, Khan Asparukh, Tsar Simeon, students studied them only by their personal names. Equally, the irredentist calls were purged from history textbooks, as were nationalist poems and songs from literature ones. But it is completely false to assert that schools threw away the portraits of the national heroes and writers—Levski, Botev, Rakovski, Karavelov, Vazov, Elin Pelin—and substituted them for Bulgarian and Soviet Politburo members. Khaitov addresses Levski's treatment, linking it to the onslaught against the church, which introduced a skewed interpretation of him as atheist, with a predominant attention to Botev and Karavelov. He saw the same happening after 1989, only this time the face of de-nationalization was no longer Sovietization but Eurointegration, or "Euro-assimilation" (ibid.: 13). All of these charges Khaitov did not spell out at first. His verdict oscillated between accusations of unprofessional negligence to suspicions of conscious mishandling and planned destruction. Only after 1989 did he give free reign to his rather loose geopolitical imagination.

But where does Todor Pavlov come in? Khaitov's real grudge against him is over the Macedonian question, especially the handing over of Gotse Delchev's bones in 1948 to the newly created Macedonian state within the Yugoslav federation. Delchev (1872–1903) was a leading revolutionary of the Internal Macedonian Revolutionary Organization that led the struggle for an independent Macedonia. This region, part of Bulgaria according to the San Stefano

Treaty (March, 1878), was given back to the Ottoman Empire by the provisions of the Berlin Treaty (July, 1878). Delchev was a revolutionary in the style of Levski and Botev by whom he was inspired and, although clearly seeing himself as part of the Bulgarian revolutionary tradition, he opted for Macedonian autonomy, instead of annexation to Bulgaria. Killed during the abortive Ilinden Uprising in 1903, Gotse was buried in the Rila Monastery in Bulgaria, and immediately entered the heroic pantheon of Bulgarian national heroes. In the interwar period, after the demise of Bulgaria's ambitions, Macedonia was divided between Greece and Serbia with a small portion annexed to Bulgaria. The Greeks adopted strict anti-Bulgarian and Hellenizing policies toward their new Slavic citizens, while the Serbs treated the newly acquired territories and their population as Southern Serbs. There was also a parallel tradition alongside the Serbianizing attempts: the promotion of a separate Macedonian identity. This strategy, developed in the 19th century by the Serbian propaganda machine, proved to be a more successful anti-Bulgarian weapon. During the Second World War, Bulgaria occupied Macedonia as the accomplishment of its national unification, but its policies alienated considerable numbers of people attracted by Tito's partisans and the promise of a future independent Macedonia.

In the meantime, in the 1920s, the Comintern adopted the vision of a future Balkan communist federation, with Macedonia as an indelible part. It presupposed the dissolution of Yugoslavia within the federation and was not favored by the Yugoslav communists, who preferred a solution of the national question within existing frontiers. The mid 1930s saw a radical reversal of Comintern policies, adopting the principle of the united front. For the Balkan region it meant abandoning the demand for the dissolution of Yugoslavia. Instead, in 1934, the suppression of the Macedonian language was criticized and the demand for a separate Macedonian nation appeared. *The Great Soviet Encyclopedia* of 1938 for the first time had distinct entries on a separate Macedonian language and nation. During the war, attempts were made to devise a special Macedonian alphabet and promote Macedonian literature. Remarkably, the theoretical framework of Macedonian nationalism was developed mostly by Bulgarian communists, with the active participation of Pavlov. The compliance of Bulgarian communists with the policies of the Comintern in the highly charged atmosphere of the interwar period, when the Macedonian irredenta dominated Bulgaria's internal and foreign policies, and was the reason for the country's involvement in the war, made the communists easy targets as national traitors. After the war, with a Macedonian republic as part of Tito's Yugoslav Socialist Federation, there were negotiations about extending the federation to include Bulgaria. During the 1948 elections, inhabitants of Bulgarian Macedonia, although feeling Bulgarian, were forced to define themselves as Macedonian. This trend was reversed immediately after the Tito–Stalin split in 1948, and throughout the whole ensuing period until 1989 relations between Yugoslavia and Bulgaria were fluctuating and tense, but it left the bitter memory and perception of communists trying to de-nationalize authentic Bulgarians and be subservient to "socialist internationalism."

At the same time, the postwar period saw the building of national institutions in Macedonia and the writing of a new national history. Understandable as the defensiveness of this new nationalism and its nation-state was, particularly vis-à-vis Bulgaria, the appropriation of a number of already established Bulgarian national figures or events proved catastrophic for the relations between the two countries. After all, nationalism is by definition exclusionary, and the idea of sharing the same national heroes contradicted the very nature of nationalism. Gotse Delchev became one of the figures venerated in Bulgaria and Macedonia, but his undisputed stature in both national pantheons was seen as an oxymoron by nationalists on both sides: they could not imagine a pre-national condition, let alone a shared relic. It was in the brief period of warm relations before the 1948 split, and before Stalin had reprimanded the Balkan communist leaders for their initiatives toward a Balkan federation that the Bulgarian Communist Party, in a gesture of goodwill, decided to hand Delchev's remains to the new federal state of Macedonia and thus symbolically provide its need for heroes with some materiality. Todor Pavlov was the figure behind this action and, as Khaitov put it, "he personally extradited Gotse Delchev's bones from Bulgaria" (Khaitov 2002: 6). Pavlov also pronounced a speech on the occasion where he reiterated his views about the existence of a separate Macedonian nation and language.

It is this fact which is unpardonable for Khaitov's. By analogy, he attributes practically all the items on his "criminal" list to the deleterious effects of Pavlov's treacherous ideology and politics. He then jumps to the Levski affair and concludes: "Is it possible to expect from this party person, from this fanatical ideologue of socialist internationalism, that he would spare Levski's grave discovered on May 30–31, 1956? That he would allow to turn a church into a national holy place in the center of Sofia, especially in the immediate vicinity of the monument of Lenin that was planned to be erected only 80 meters away from this church?" (Khaitov 2002: 12). Even as he allows for some doubt, he adds: "Even if it hadn't been Pavlov, there were enough party fanatics both in the Central Committee and in the Medieval Section of the AI who would see to it that the emblem of Bulgarian patriotism would not receive his grave" (ibid.: 13).

That this is complete baloney can be seen from the report of Vŭlko Chervenkov, then minister of culture and Pavlov, sent to Todor Zhivkov, then chairman of the Council of Ministers. The report addresses the decision of the Council of May 8, 1956 to destroy the part of the church that protrudes above the street level, and leave only the structure below to be accessed through a special entrance. Instead, based on the archeological and historical studies of the "past several months," Chervenkov and Pavlov proposed that the church be elevated to a historical and artistic monument of national significance and preserved in its entirety: "The preservation of the church next to the Roman buildings in the yard of the Ministry of Electrification, to the mosque in front of the central baths and to the building of the National Museum, alongside other ancient cultural monuments, highlighted in the new municipal architectural ensembles, illustrate the great cultural legacy, created in Sofia throughout the centuries and enrich our capital." The report adds: "At present, research is being also undertaken linked to the statement that the body of the Apostle of Freedom Vasil Levski had been transferred and reburied in the church 'Sv. Petka Samardzhiiska.' This research is not yet completed but there are data substantiating this statement" (Khaitov 2002: 154). The most ironic circumstance about this report is, of course, that by the time it was written, the bones of Skeleton No. 95 might have already disappeared.

In the end, there is tacit agreement that the bones are gone. One could say that the conflict was not over "bones of contention" but over "non-existing bones of contention." Whether one believes that the remains were misplaced, thrown away or deliberately destroyed, as Khaitov, until his death believed they were, the fact is that at present the factual evidence is missing, and even if some day some bones would appear that can be traced to Levski's DNA, I soundly doubt these would be the bones of Skeleton No. 95. So, then, the response to the question posed by Khaitov and voiced by the public, namely why confine the debate to the analysis of the archeological data and not proclaim the church a temple even without definitive proof, goes to the motivations of Khaitov and team.

4. A Socialist Public Sphere?

At first glance, Khaitov's geopolitical confabulations might serve to delegitimize his general credibility. But one shouldn't apportion too much guilt by association. Khaitov's general motivations and his onslaught on the archeologists should be taken apart. His worldview, his *de facto* religion and deepest personal attachments were centered on nationalism, and he had devoted himself to rectifying what he thought of as the assimilationist and de-nationalizing tendencies of communism, and after 1989, globalization. The discussion with the archeologists was not his invention. He picked up an existing debate and turned it into a public event. That he succeeded in doing this, is attributable both to his polemical talent and popularity as a writer, as well as to the opportune conjuncture: the rise of Zhivkova and the general move to more openly articulated nationalism, especially in the decade preceding the 1,300[th] anniversary of the Bulgarian state. However, the scholarly issue with the archeologists was not his primary passion. He simply gave a powerful imprimatur of credibility to an alternative thesis which served his motives. This thesis not only had been voiced before and was suppressed or neglected, but received strong support from respected and serious specialists. In this sense, Khaitov became the *porte parole* of a significant faction of alternative opinion. In fact, at first Khaitov was not necessarily out to get the archeologists and put a blemish on their institution, let alone on their discipline. What he wanted was the public acceptance of the reburial version because this would clean the damaged reputation of Bulgarians who had not saved their greatest hero from an ignoble death and subsequent dishonorable burial. As Bobchev had put it earlier, it is important to know Levski's grave, because "Bulgarians have not left him unburied" (*BAN volume*: 126).

Had the archeologists agreed to such a solution, Khaitov might have left them in peace. But it came with a price, the cheapest being tacit admittance of unprofessionalism. This was not worth paying, and they reckoned they had enough power and influence to win the contest. The important point to make here is that there was a diversity of motives both between and within the debating teams, which turned out to be incompatible. The other question raised by the archeologists—about the redundancy of the discussions, given that the bones were lost,—goes back to the rationale for convening the debates. While the archeologists like to present themselves as victims of a party cabal, the truth is much more prosaic. Both sides had their supporters among the higher party echelons but with the highly charged renaming process at the center of political attention and with the growing economic difficulties, the issue of Levski's grave seemed too esoteric to command the highest attention, let alone direct involvement. Not worthy of high party intervention, the issue was, accordingly, handed to BAN to resolve.

In this respect and to add to the complexity of motives and framework, while the debates were not the initiative of Todorov, and his arbitrating role was imposed on him, once involved in the proceedings, he felt that the discussion had served an important function. This complicates even further the social drama by introducing yet another set of motives. Todorov's can be summarized briefly as follows. First was his belief, genuinely shared by some, but not challenged publicly even by the ones who didn't like it, that open and unrestricted discussion was the natural medium of scholarship. For Todorov it was also the natural medium for the democratic exchange of ideas. Thus treated the debates as a pedagogical laboratory where people were forced to enter into a civilized exchange, learn how to listen and debate in a refined way. No wonder that during his opening remarks on February 10, 1986, he explicitly referred to the practice of UNESCO, the international organization for cultural cooperation, where he had served, and put in place a procedure that would allow the calm exposition of standpoints and prevent the parties from interrupting one another. He believed that scholarship was not hermetic and immune against challenges coming from outside a scholarly discipline. Himself with a medical education before graduating in history, he was open to what we today call interdisciplinarity. Naturally broad-minded, disciplinarian parochialism did not agree with his vision. As a Marxist social historian, and even though Marxism was the dogma of the day, he was aware that to a huge number of historians of his and the older generation, the majority of whom was practicing a conventional type of political and less frequently intellectual history, social history was not really considered history but sociology. He was thus attuned to and opposed to the objections of "purists" and looked favorably to imaginative challenges to the status quo. Detesting the disciplinarian isolationism of "insiders," and deeply suspicious of what he considered a false opposition between professionals and dilettantes, he welcomed any thesis, as long as it was based on and defended with the conventional tools of scholarship.

Improbable as it may sound to the archeologists who have persisted in a partisan way to defend Mikhailov's thesis, one of Todorov's primary motives was to create a forum in which to cleanse once and for all the AI from accusations of deliberate destruction and lack of patriotism. He did not believe that this was the case, and expected the archeologists to muster all existing documentation and resoundingly refute the accusations. Khaitov saw very early through this motivation and was unhappy with it. Orally, he accused him numerous times of sheltering the archeologists, particularly Stancheva, for whom Todorov had great respect. Khaitov wrote that when the archeologists during the debates were exposed first for not giving all the photographs and then with "selecting" only some and offering merely copies, and his team asked for an official criminal investigation, "Academician Todorov did not agree so as not to throw bad light on one of the oldest units of the Bulgarian Academy of Sciences" (Khaitov 2002: 16, 78).

Todorov was ready to defend the AI from unsubstantiated accusations, but what incensed him particularly during the debates was the passive and cavalier attitude of the archeologists, who released the material sparingly or even went looking for it only after repeated admonitions, behaving as if they were above any kind of charge. Finally, he was thrown off balance when they introduced an explicitly ideological motive in their response to the final report. AI's memorandum of June 6, 1986, signed by Angelov and Gergova, was circulated widely to party and administrative authorities. It is of particular interest because for the first time it directly addressed some of the opponents' argumentation concerning architectural, medical or geodesical evidence. It reiterated the archeologists' position by characterizing their opponents' arguments as purely speculative. Specifically, it questioned the conclusions of the criminological expertise about the identity of the skeleton in the debated photographs. It also questioned the conclusion of the burials as irregular. The real issue of the archeologists was summarized in a lengthy litany against the manner of Khaitov and the negative repercussions of his campaign. Thus far the archeologists were staying within the realm of archeological proofs. But at this point, and for the first time in the discussion, they ended their memorandum on an ideological note as the final culmination and without any obvious link to the debate:

> A number of important questions linked to the revival process are about to receive scholarly support, as are also a number of other questions of a decisive political and ideological nature. The widely created general distrust towards the discipline fomented by Khaitov's book cannot be quietly overcome... The launching of the least plausible "church" thesis, unsupported scholarly or ideologically, continues, as well as accusations against the institute in nihilism and lack of patriotism. It is strange that in deciding the most important scientific questions the incompetents are becoming the most competent. Doesn't all this enfeeble the foundations of science, and its rights to play its ideological role, especially in deciding the national questions? (ibid.: 469)

The last sentence defended the rights of the AI "as an institute with ideological character" to state its opinion on the eve of the XIII Congress of the BCP, and declared that the question of the Apostle's grave did not have to be turned into a fetish. Todorov's response, written on June 26, 1986, is much angrier in tone than his final report. He points out that the leadership of the AI had been invited to produce a final statement and had agreed that all documentation be published in a collective volume. Despite this, it wrote yet another statement that it sent singlehandedly to a number of institutions, attempting to impose its own vision. This new attempt of the AI was "emotional, and not scholarly" and he squarely accused the archeologists of never seriously sticking to the main criterion during the debates, namely, to produce a methodologically sound interpretation of the facts. Instead, the leadership of the AI did not attempt even to find all the existing documentation, which was "discovered" thanks to his persistence and that of Khaitov's team. Todorov's real wrath, however, was reserved for the ideological:

> What is the goal of the authors of the memorandum when they stress that the AIM has an 'ideological character'? Which institute in the

humanities and social sciences does not, in a larger or smaller degree, have an ideological character?...How can public opinion be reassured, until we don't explain the exact fate of the bones, about which the participants in the excavations had been warned that they might belong to Levski? It is unbecoming for an institute like the AIM, one with an ideological character, to behave as if these questions do not exist. They have been raised not by Khaitov, but already in 1959 and nowadays they cannot be silently passed by or ignored.

I do not think that there is a general distrust against archeology, as the authors of the memorandum assert. However, the existing partial distrust, addressed against certain specialists, cannot be lifted by the bare denial of obvious facts and the repetition of old stereotypes without any argumentation, as in the memorandum, This can be achieved only in one way: through a complex, honest and objective laying out of the problems around the debates over the Apostle's grave. Looking for the truth around this grave is not "fetishizing the memory of Levski" as the leadership of the AI asserts, but the duty of our archeological and historical disciplines... This was the reason to organize the debates at BAN as the only correct means for a scholarly solution to the problems, followed by the decision to publish the whole documentation, together with the arguments of the two opposing versions in a collective volume. A scholarly debate should take place, and it should not be silenced through administrative pressure. In this particular case, the representatives of one of these theses have dominated over public opinion in the course of more than 30 years. Now we have a different situation, and the other thesis has achieved a relative predominance over public opinion. The publication of the BAN volume will allow the continuation of the debates on a scholarly basis (ibid.: 478).

It is symptomatic that the fate of this publication, supposed to be a culminating and natural result, the symbolic document of the redress phase and its resolution, became itself an apple of contention and might be said to have served as the documented open recognition of the schism. It is analyzed in detail below. Finally, when taking account of all sides in the debates, one should not underestimate the role of popular pressure. Numerous citizens' letters had reached the presidium of the academy, asking about the official position of BAN. Most archeologists were quick to dismiss these letters as organized pressure by the Khaitov propaganda machine, but they deserve a closer look. One of the most striking items in this collection of petitions is a thick student's notebook consisting of a cover letter and collected signatures.[1] The letter is addressed to the president of BAN with a copy to the newspaper "Literaturen Front." Dated February 18, 1986, it summarized the interest that Khaitov's book had generated among the reading public. It was the object of passionate conversations in every home and work place, because it dealt with Levski, "who is not only our national hero but our national saint, with whose name we all have received our first patriotic Holy Communion." It then states that since Levski is in the hearts of every Bulgarian, "it is imperative that we have a temple, a sacred place, our Bulgarian Jerusalem, where we can bow and feel the materialized presence of this great Bulgarian in Bulgaria's past, present and future." It ends with the request that BAN give Khaitov the opportunity to defend his thesis in front of historians, writers, journalists, and politicians at a level usually reserved for a dissertation defense. "If he manages to defend it as brilliantly as he did in his book, let the church "Sv. Petka" be officially pronounced to be the grave of Vasil Levski." It also asks that the ones responsible for the squandering of the bones be taken to task. The signatures are 589 individual entries, all from Varna, and a separate collective one stating that at their meeting on February 10, 1986, several hundred railway workers at the locomotive station "Nikola Karev" supported the letter. The signatures indicate name, profession and address of the signatories. They are captains and sailors, workers, doctors, dentists, school teachers, painters, engineers, students, retirees, drivers, construction workers, economists, actors, pilots, housewives, musicians, singers, a ballerina, economists, officers, athletes, accountants, seamstresses, mechanics, librarians, lawyers, journalists, cooks, people of all walks of life, and different levels of the social or professional hierarchy.

Of course, this petition could have been the result of Khaitov's lobbying. Most likely, however, it was initiated and seen through by the efforts of a local journalist, Dora Nikolova. She had brought the

---

[1] Archives of BAN, Personal archive of Academician Nikolai Todorov. This petition, as well as the other letters analyzed below, are in a file titled "Others."

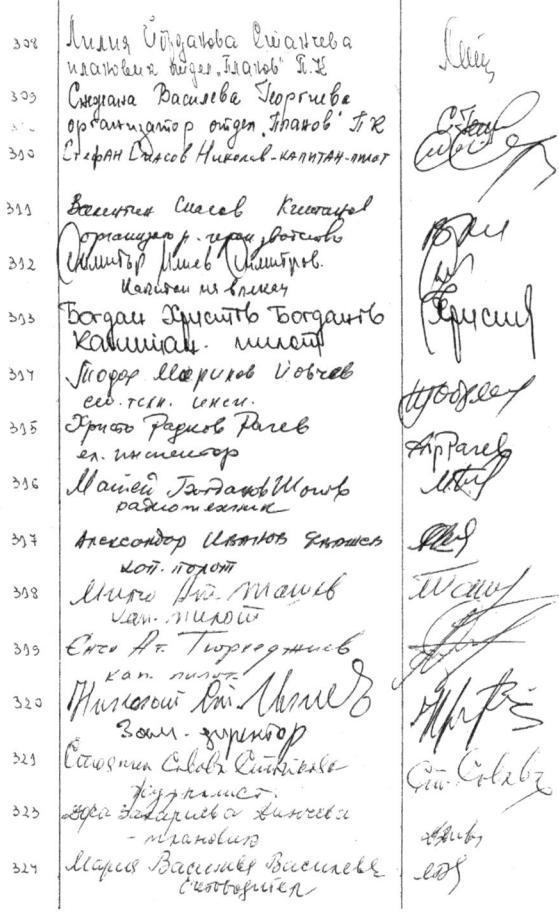

Figure 9. Page from the letter-petition signed by 589 citizens of Varna on 18 February 1986 and sent to the Bulgarian Academy of Sciences. Source: Archives of BAN, Personal files of Nikolai Todorov.

notebook with the signatures to the writer Evtim Evtimov and asked Khaitov to see it. The latter scolded her and asked her to take it back, because the "academicians would think that this was a campaign organized by Khaitov himself." Even if this was the case, however, how does it defy the character of a popular address? After all, these people were not forced to sign the petition. It did not come through any kind of existing official channels. Nikolova herself was obviously a local enthusiast. In another letter to Balevski, she commented on the public lecture of Dimitîr Ovcharov against Khaitov's thesis. Nikolova was unimpressed and concluded: "Where are the bones? Is this simple negligence or a conscious deed? The Bulgarian people want Levski to have a grave and this is why it celebrates the church and will celebrate it to the end of days, no matter what the scholars think. But still, let our scholars remember that they are eating the bread offered them by our people. And nobody is bigger than the bread." Nikolova also appended a poem she had written on the topic of the Apostle's remains, dedicated to Khaitov. Even weak poems testify to strong feelings... Nor was this the only poetic epistle. Another poem in impeccable rhyme was authored by Kamen Rilski, an obvious pseudonym, who appealed to the leaders of the academy:

> A pantheon we do not need,
> In our hearts is Levski.
> Our children through his grave will seek
> To bend their heads in silence.
> And now the honor falls on you
> It's in your power to admit.
> Today I'm sending this to you,
> This plea for your connivance.

A retired teacher also sent a letter. It was triggered by a radio show on Levski's birthday. She was deeply moved by the lofty assessment of Levski whom she considered "the only Bulgarian political saint," but was also worried by "the scholarly drama" which wanted to negate that Levski had been reburied in the church. For her, Khaitov's argumentation was impeccable, while Mikhailov was moved solely by professional pride and ambition. She addressed the academicians whose "moral duty and lofty task it is to tear the dark curtain of deceit" and proposed to place the Levski's hair in a large box in the church. On top, Levski's portrait should be hanged, flanked on both sides with small electric bulbs in white, green and red, the colors of the national flag, so that "eternal light should stream over the holy relic: Levski's hair."

Yet another powerful letter was sent to the editorial office of the historical journal *Vekove* with a copy to Balevski. *Vekove* had published a negative article of Khaitov's book by Stanislav Stanilov, and this provoked the letter of priest Todor Vodenicharov from the village of Karan

Vîrbovka, Ruse District, dated February 18, 1986. What is most interesting about this long, three-page single-spaced letter is its language. The priest's addressee is not "Comrade" but "Mister," the accepted address before 1944 and after 1989. The language is extremely vivid and colorful, poetic and at the same time colloquial, using folkloric and regional terms and phrases. It is peppered with Turkisms, of which Bulgarian nationalism was careful to cleanse the written language, but which was thankfully, although sparingly, preserved in oral speech. The priest writes about the effect Khaitov's book had on him, and of his dismay at the lack of official support for the reburial thesis. He then makes his point about the need for holy places. Even if the unconvincing thesis of Mikhailov was true, this should not prevent us from marking the church as a possible sacred place. After all, Botev's obelisk in the Balkan mountains was not erected at the exact place of his death that was contested. The important thing is to mark and remember not the something but the somebody, "to see from afar and to know that Botev had existed, no matter whether the bullet had pierced him at the very place of the obelisk." He gives the example of the 1950 Vatican congregation that revisited the list of saints, in the course of which it turned out that data about some saints were missing and they had to be taken off the list. One of the affected was St. Cecilia, the patron saint of church musicians, whose name the Musical Academy in Rome is bearing. "And so, you see what happens, everything was left as is, because what has been assembled in history should not be wasted but built upon."

Especially interesting are the priest's thoughts about the production of history. He is incensed that the debates are confined behind closed doors within the strictly "scholarly sphere" and is ironic about the selective use of "professionals' and "dilettantes" in Stanilov's article. "Scientific objectivity" is simply an euphemism for *esprit de corps*. Most striking is his comment on Stanilov's stated disregard for memoirs that he calls the litter of history. To Vodenicharov this is simply a strategy to classify uncomfortable facts or sources into a rubric that carries less clout. In a clear reference to the great discoveries of ancient archeology, he writes: "Isn't it clear to these professors that what somebody wrote or said at some point of time rests in the popular memory and in time under the name of history? And archeology as a scholarly discipline has in fact attached itself to this history reduced to 'litter' and has been only following its traces. Tell me, then, what here should be denoted with the word 'litter'?"

There is also the letter of the Metropolitan of Nevrokop, Pimen. Given his later ascendancy to the post of patriarch of the alternative Synod in 1996 and his role in the future canonization of Levski, this letter is of particular interest. Dated June 19, 1986 and addressed to Todorov, it states its approval of the concluding report of the BAN debates. Pimen finds Khaitov position more convincing. His careful phrasing can serve as a model:

> It is not in my competence to judge but it seems to me that during the excavations there have been deviations from the scholarly precision of the work that necessitated a more serious handling and preservation of the artifacts, so much so as informed individuals had affirmed that Levski had been reburied in this church. The timely signals of Professor Giaurov were also ignored. I know him personally and he is widely respected for his serious and critical mind. It was therefore a missed opportunity not to preserve the archeological material for detailed study at an opportune moment.

All of this deserves some, if only preliminary and tentative, theorizing attempts. My central question is: What is the proper category to describe the initiative of the Varna journalist and the petition of nearly 600 people? Or numerous private letters by people from all walks of life? Or poems written for the occasion, even if they are bad poems? As far as the Levski debate goes, there was, even within the perceived constrains, a remarkable openness for discussion: in the press, in the institutions and, most unexpected and surprising, a popular initiative to express opinions and pressure for their acceptance. Is all this not covered by the category 'civil society'? There are different strategies to pursue here. One is to explain off these and similar facts as being outside the realm of 'civil society' as it has been applied in Eastern Europe in the 1980s or, at very best, as modest sprouts of an embryonic one. Another is to abandon the strict definition and its normative overtones, and enrich and complicate it by the concrete historical ontology. Yet another is to discard the notion altogether. My inclinations are in the direction of the second option, and while my immediate interest is not so much in reaching a new theoretical explanation and in system building, the concrete goal is to contravene the intellectual straitjacket which the strict application of political science categories impose on the historical record.

There are varying and often contradictory definitions of civil society: from Hegel's designation of it as a sphere of needs distinct from family and state, and mediating between them, or Tocqueville's idea of a realm of secondary associations to present classifications including non-profit organizations only, or only self-organizing communities of common interest, or all forms of nongovernmental cooperation including big business, and finally, all forms of non-institutionalized human activity. Equally, the critique of civil society, whether coming from a normative (Hanna Arendt, Jürgen Habermas), historicist (Carl Schmitt, Reinhart Koselleck, Habermas), genealogical (Michel Foucault), systems-theoretical (Niklas Luhmann), or feminist critique (Seyla Benhabib, Nancy Fraser, Iris Marion Young) implies a different understanding of the categories state and society and their relationship, with both Foucault and Luhman squarely considering their posited stark opposition a false dichotomy (Cohen and Arato 1992; Falk 2003: 313–27; Holmes 1997: 267–303). Karl Marx adopted Hegel's term *bürgerliche Gesellschaft* but, in his attempt to demystify it, he interpreted it literally, as a synonym of bourgeois society and devalued the distinction between state and civil society (Falk 2003: 321; Mitchell 1991: 77–96). While for Marx civil society was first and foremost embedded in the market of which he was highly critical, for Antonio Gramsci its principal realm was public opinion and culture (Holmes 1997: 268). There is little doubt that if we apply a strictly normative definition of civil society, under communism it was largely curtailed, controlled and for all practical purposes marginalized. But it is equally imperative to revisit the famous paradigm of a lack of civil society bar the church (in its Catholic variety in Poland or its evangelical one in East Germany), and dissident or semi-dissident groups like "Solidarity" in Poland, "Memorial" in Russia, and the mushrooming ecological groups of the last decades under communism.

If we look at the historical genealogy of the concept, after its early use in the late 18th and early 19th centuries, it was largely abandoned, to re-emerge powerfully only in the 1970s, within the context of the crisis of the socialist regimes. Precisely the specificity of the East European context effected an interpretation of civil society such that the very notion as applied to Eastern Europe in the 1980s was premised on a complete opposition between society and the state, and the rhetorical claims of "antipolitics" were taken seriously (Konrád 1984). The turn to political society after 1989 made a joke of these claims. Pace Cohen and Arato's (1992: 67–68) noble hopes that East Europeans "would be able to resist the 'oligarchic' tendencies of modern political parties" and would avoid the dangerous example of Latin America where the turn to political society implied demobilization of civil society, this is exactly what happened. I am not questioning the lack or weakness of the principal norms of civil society under late socialism—the absence of guarantees for individual rights, privacy, voluntary association, formal legality, plurality, publicity, free enterprise—but these have been institutionalized heterogeneously and in a contradictory manner also in western societies. Nor am I preaching a pedantic ban of the category because of the multifariousness of its meanings. It is important, however, to emphasize its historical and contingent appearance and reappearance at particular junctures of the historical process, and to contextualize the concrete purposes for which it was mobilized.

In Eastern Europe in the 1970s and 1980s (much like for Enlightenment absolutist Europe), civil society was starkly posited as an emancipatory counterweight to the state, validated only by its potential oppositional qualities (Seligman 2002: 13–33). Yet, concrete research has shown not only the great variability between the separate East European societies, but has questioned the dichotomy itself. In particular, Chris Hann has suggested a useful distinction between political society in the narrow and in the broad sense. In the first case, he accepts it as an element of the dualist scheme that contrasts the state and its people, and where the political is encompassed entirely by the state institutions. In the broad sense, however, which is the main sense employed by anthropologists, it would correspond to a looser notion of civil society that does not presuppose an absolute opposition between state and society, or the political and the social. This is so, among others, because "in the communist context, virtually all social behavior had political implications" (Hann 1996: 13, 23–24).

To be fair to the historiographical record, the dogmatic opposition between state and society under communism had been questioned before, but so strong was the authority of the "antipoliticians" immediately before and especially in the wake of 1989 that seemed to have vindicated their claims, that these early interpretations remained isolated. Moshe Lewin had suggested already in the early 1970s that Khrushchev's and later Kosygin's economic reforms triggered the emerging phenomenon of a "civil society recovering." He explored state-society relations, and concluded that the introduction of "societal factors in our reasoning allows us to see Soviet history and state institutions as much more flexible and responsive to social realities than is generally perceived" (Lewin 1988: viii). As he nicely summed up "The world is, unfortunately, not immune to despotism and to oppressive states but, fortunately, no state has ever figured out how to master the complexity of human society" (ibid.: 29). Lewin warned that the analysis of civil society must not be predicated on definitions, but he offered one himself, stressing the possibility of serious dissidence in social complexes that do not necessarily oppose the state (ibid.: 80). He identified cultural life as the first arena for spontaneous actions but also the academic world and other groups of specialists that affected individuals, groups, institutions, and the state: "Civil society is talking, gossiping, demanding, sulking, expressing its interests in many ways and thereby creating moods, ideologies, and public opinion" (ibid.: 72–9, 146).

The notion of public sphere and lack thereof under communism poses similar problems. No doubt as a Weberian ideal type Habermas's public sphere is difficult, if not impossible to locate under state socialism, even in its last decades. Nancy Fraser (1996: 70) has pointed out the failure of the dominant socialist and Marxist tradition to distinguish between state apparatus and the citizens' public arena. If one were to stick to its theoretical elaboration as a space distinct from both the state and the official economy, one could posit the existence of an embryonic public sphere where people outside the immediate experts engaged in public debate. On the other hand, one can go a little further than simply apply the normative category that dooms the analysis of historical contexts outside the western "original" to narrative tropes depicting "lack," "lag," or "backwardness." To evoke Shalini Randeria's appraisal of the category for India:

> Rather than see civil society with Hall and Gellner as a unique Western achievement, and using its successful realization elsewhere as a yardstick to measure the difference or backwardness of non-Western societies, it may be important to see that the substance of the idea is

inherently elusive both in the West and outside it. This is in part due to the complex intellectual history and uneven political realization of the ideal of civil society over several centuries in the West as well as to the checkered history of its translation and conflictual domestication within the framework of colonial rule in most of the non-Western world (Randeria 2002: 290).

But even in the Western world, as revisionist historiography has demonstrated, there are "other, non-liberal, non-bourgeois, competing public spheres," and it is the failure of Habermas to examine these alternative spaces which may have led him to idealize the bourgeois public sphere"(Fraser 1996: 74). There is legitimate discussion, for example, about a black public sphere under the regime of Jim Crow. If anything, citizens in East European socialist countries after Stalinism fared incomparably better than blacks in segregationist America. Extending his work on multiple modernities and critiquing the assumptions of the liberal conception of civil society, Shmuel Eisenstadt (2006: 45–7) introduces the notion of a non-liberal civil society.

More importantly, instead of denying the existence of a public sphere under state socialism, one can speak of specific characteristic deformations of civil society and the public sphere under different regimes. The limitations under communism are self-evident and have been emphatically pointed out in numerous deliberations: party constraints, censorship, administrative and extra-administrative pressure. Western liberal democracies have suffered from an alternative set of limitations: corporate, legal, or media-related. There are a number that paradoxically seem to be common to both of these different social regimes and that cry out for comparative work, most blatantly the amount and character of self-censorship. Paraphrasing Mark Beissinger's (2006: 303) apt adaptation of Wittgensteinian philosophy to the application of the notion of empire in the Soviet context, one could say that civil society is not a clearly bounded transhistorical model but a "family resemblance" with significant variability over space and time.

The purpose of this excursus is not to attack the (uses of the) categories, but simply to appeal for their careful contextualization. The significant point to make is that, constrained as they were, these illustrations of an embryonic or different type of public sphere or civil society had to be taken and were taken into account, not necessarily for demagogic reasons. The Levski grave affair was not of such political importance that the party or state authorities would want to capitalize on it by either responding to or neglecting public pressure. A dense reading of the events and their consecutive recreation shows that the authorities were indeed responding to grassroots pressure. In a way, this is what one would expect to happen in a "normal" democratic society. And this is the reading that I am proposing. As long as they were not *seen* as directly challenging the existing political superstructure (either ideologically or personally), some kind of civil society and public debate were tolerated and even encouraged from the late 1960s on. What was not normal was that this "normality" was not expected and not seen as normal. After all, the memory of the late 1940s and 1950s, when party meddling was ubiquitous in culture, was too close to be forgotten, and had created a knee-jerk cautiousness among the generation which had lived through these decades. In addition, my emphasis on *seen* adds the element of arbitrariness and always expected "surprise" that was so typical for late socialism. One could never be sure whether what was logically totally innocuous, might not be *seen* by some apparatchik as dangerous in a most unexpected manner. And reverse, often serious and often calculatedly serious challenges were not noticed, that is *seen* by someone who was supposed to watch. I would add that the noticing or "seeing" procedure was not unconscious, a matter of oversight or stupidity but most often deliberate. As Miklós Haraszti (1987: 145) has perceptively observed in his notes on the "velvet prison," communication between the lines was the dominant feature of socialist culture in the post-Stalinist decades and "the opinions expressed there are not alien to the state but perhaps simply premature." It is this arbitrariness of the regime, rather than the easy totalitarianism-informed explanations of its behavior, that proved to be intellectually and emotionally exhausting. And then, again, one might choose not to overdramatize this.

5. "Professionals" and "Dilettantes"

When speaking of the BAN debates as Turner's redressive phase, what is peculiar about the Bulgarian case was that the whole framework upon which the redressive mechanism was based was itself in a legitimacy crisis from the mid-1980s on. By the 1990s it had completely collapsed and this is the most salient explanation why the redressive machinery did not "fix" the problem. What the BAN debates did demonstrate is that "it is in the redressive phase that both pragmatic techniques and symbolic action reach their fullest expression" (Turner 1974: 41). Their value and to some extent their revolutionary character, lay in the fact that for the first time the two opposing factions were forced to enter a mode of discussion. Until that moment the rival thesis was only spelled out in the public realm, even gained some notoriety, but did not have the imprimatur of expertise. Throughout the whole period, when it attracted the attention of the mass media and the broad public, the archeologists retreated in a pose of offended professionalism, refusing to take it seriously and *a priori* dismissing it. Once they were compelled to enter the debate, they retreated into another pose, of having been forced into an unnecessary, time-wasting exchange by the party *cum* government *cum* academy authorities, who allegedly were backing the hugely popular Khaitov and rewarding his lobbying talents. In fact, the authorities were largely responding to grassroots pressure. It is the general arbitrariness of the regime, the lack of any transparency that makes this simple explanation difficult to believe at first sight. As a rule, one was always skeptical of stated motives and the ground was fertile for conspiracy theories. To a large extent these rules of the game or, rather, the lack of strict rules, were recognized by all sides in the debates. Intellectual passivity was thus a logical cautionary behavior, implicitly cultivated and enjoyed by part of the ruling party bureaucracy. At the same time, prudence became an easy excuse for intellectual laziness. In the archeologists' case, I don't believe risk calculations were at play. Had there been even the slightest danger of genuine pressure, the invectives would have been toned down and measured. Another balance of power was at play.

Scholarship had always enjoyed a lofty, if not necessarily always secure or well-funded (with the exception of strategically important hard sciences), position under communism. Aside from the Stalinist follies that had had some early but limited repercussions in the newly set up postwar communist regimes in Eastern Europe, the sciences were seen as a semi-independent sphere, where real experts could find a tolerable space. This was true also for the humanities, with the exception of the most ideological "scholarly" concoctions, like scientific communism or sensitive research areas like contemporary history or the history of the Communist Party. The AI was seen and was self-perceived as the abode of specialists who were doing "real" science, far removed from the ideological and political conjunctures of the day. If archeology could be used for patriotic purposes, so much the better: it brought support and recognition, and did it really matter how it was used when what it discovered was "the truth"? This was the broad mindset reigning among archeologists (and historians), a mindset that during communism had changed little from the (usually German-inspired) positivist methodology, claiming a truth-discovering aura for their particular discipline. It is difficult to judge how much of this was methodological naiveté, wishful thinking, or technical narrow-mindedness. After all, archeology as a discipline in Europe and in the world has only "recently accepted the fact that its occupation is (perceived as) functional to political or nationalist agendas" and that, together with history, it has been instrumental in constructing the official "nation state monumental past" (Odermatt 1996: 115). This has been the case, as shown by recent scholarship, despite the fact of the universal and "almost unavoidable or natural relationship between archeology and nationalism" (Kohl and Fawcett 1995, 3–4). The peculiarly elevated status of Bulgarian archeologists and their respective inflated self-perception was the result of several factors. One was the role of the their discipline as a nation-state builder from the 19th century on. This is true also about historiography but the Bulgarian peculiarity lies in the fact that, unlike its Greek counterpart, political history could not by itself establish a direct link to antiquity. It was medieval history that supplied the elevated ties to statehood, which explains its equally lofty status, whereas archeology secured the connection to classical antiquity. It has to be understood also that in the lands of classical antiquity in general, there is an even stronger premium on rooting one's national project in antiquity, because of its high "social capital" among the developed world as the "cradle of civilization."

It is not only this functional explanation that allows us to understand the hypervalue attached to archeology. There was the strong influence of the elevated status of classical studies in Europe, where most Bulgarian interwar archeologists had been entirely or partly educated. Thus, when Khaitov made his allegation that "we care more about our Roman and Byzantine roads and mosaics than for our medieval ruins" he was on the spot despite protestations (*BAN volume:* 171). Bulgarian archeology even today has hardly moved from the paradigm of "a descriptive and a culture historical approach" and has been untouched even by the processualist traditions that have characterized western archeology from the late 1950s, let alone by the post-processualist or cognitive archeology after the 1970s (Bailey 1998: 97). Finally, there was the general suspicion against modern history (weakening but still persisting) and the belief in the greater "objectivity" of ancient or medieval studies. This suspicion was generated from two sources: the general development of European historiography, where the prejudices against *Zeitgeschichte* have been gradually overcome only after war; and the direct meddling of political authorities into scholarship with the ensuing (very often justified) perception that one was better hidden from ideological encroachments the farther away in time one specialized.

There was thus a heightened self-consciousness of professionalism that was not challenged by anyone and, in the mind of the practitioners, could not be challenged. There was also little tolerance for critique, none whatsoever for critique from outside the field, and little patience with even modest attempts at self-critical or self-reflective approaches that were dismissed as cowardly or relativistic. It was this self-consciousness that was challenged and wounded by the spirited although, granted, also aggressive intervention of Khaitov. His accusations had many overtones, but the archeologists rightly heard the strongest motive: the accusation of lack of professionalism. The simple scholarly controversy need not have necessarily blown into a real scandal around mutually incompatible positions. But what brought it about was the real stake the archeologists had not only in defending their professional competence in principle but because the scandal threatened their budget.

The preceding sections concentrated on the clash of divergent interpretations but there was little comment on the extra-scholarly rhetorical devices and actual actions taken by the participants. The emphasis was on the fact that this time the attack on the dominant version came from outside the scholarly field. It would be disingenuous to overemphasize this circumstance. Khaitov's spirited support for the counter-version, which succeeded in tipping the scales, had been tacitly "supported" from within. This fact has been conveniently overlooked, because the way the war trenches were defined, there seemed to be an exclusive opposition between professionals and dilettantes. When the first edition of Khaitov's book came out, it had received the imprimatur of two internal scholarly reviews, one from the highly respected classicist Velizar Velkov, at the time deputy director of the AI,. In his review, Velkov points out that:

> The work of Khaitov is very timely because for the first time it introduces a new, very serious argument in the discussion about Levski's grave, namely the diary of the excavations. The author has truthfully and consistently represented all opinions and has convincingly demonstrated that there had been serious possibilities for a genuinely scientific research on the bones, but these chances were squandered. I believe he has well assessed the archeological literature and has accurately shown its contradictions. The proposed work is without any doubt a contribution to the problematic of Levski's grave and has serious argumentation in favor of the opinion that Levski may have been reburied in the church "Sv. Petka Samardzhiiska." I recommend the publication of this work (Khaitov 2002: 164–5).

Upon the appearance of Khaitov's book, the Medieval Section of the AI held an internal debate. Velkov was urged to explain his review, and he stated that while he disapproved of Khaitov's tone, he still gave the book "a positive assessment because the facts known before the discussion in the section for medieval archeology allowed to come up with such a thesis." He emphasizes that the excavations had been compromised. All finds and objects had disappeared; so had the graphic documentation and the photographs. Even the diary of the excavations had appeared with additional entries only a quarter of a century later. "It was strange," Velkov remarked, "that, when years ago the same question had been discussed by the Medieval Section, neither Prof. Mikhailov, nor senior research fellow Dzhingov had been notified about [the existence of] this diary and, instead, discussed the issue without this documentation. Obviously, a scholarly publication on these excavations is needed." During the meeting, Velkov backed away from his review, saying that, in the light of Boiadzhiev's sketches, "the hypothesis forwarded by Khaitov can no longer be supported " (*BAN volume*: 188). Velkov was obviously under pressure. He was present at the BAN discussions in February, 1986 but his voice was never heard. Instead, he preferred to keep an extremely low profile, and fell back into the posture of a colleague who was not going to break the line, yet, at the same time, would not involve himself actively in defense of a weak cause against his own better judgment. I asked him about the affair when we happened to fly together on a plane to Vienna in early 1987. His reluctant but smiling response was: "defense of the profession." My recollection may be dismissed as partial, yet the few statements of Velkov, and the very fact they were so few, speak for themselves. Mikhailov himself did not fail to register his disappointment with Velkov's review:

> This work does not reflect well on the reviewers either, especially on one of them, the deputy director of the Archeological Institute and a specialist in classical philology, who lately also deals with ancient archeology, but is far removed from the problems of medieval archeology (*BAN volume*: 269).

This was obviously a blow under the belt. After all, Mikhailov himself, as Khaitov never tired to repeat, was not an accomplished archeologist, but a specialist in art history, when he started the excavations. More importantly, this reflects on something typical of Bulgarian scholarship at the time and still today: its incredibly compartmentalized specialization. In the field of history, one didn't dare pronounce oneself on anything even a couple of decades outside one's own designated period, let alone give legitimate opinions on neighboring disciplines. Interdisciplinarity was, and still is, a foreign category to scholarly praxis.

The discussion at the Medieval section of the AI, which took place on September 14, 1985, is a particularly apt site to investigate the nature of the exchange because, unlike the debates at BAN a few months later where the two sides were explicitly (although at times unsuccessfully) ushered to refrain from emotive attacks, emotions here ran high and were expressed accordingly. It is even incorrect to call this discussion an exchange because Khaitov was not invited by the archeologists to take part. His presence was a last-minute arrangement due to the intervention of Acad. Blagovest Sendov, a vice president of BAN. Khaitov had not been given the 76-page refutation of Mikhailov that the latter presented, and even at the meeting itself was refused access to the statement. This is why he taped the whole discussion and his response was submitted only in writing (*BAN volume*, 139–196). This is a detail that needs to be known in light of the misleading remark of Stanilov (1985: 77–9), who published a report of the discussion, that "at the meeting Khaitov confined himself to mere ripostes against the speakers in the style of his book." Khaitov was simply not given the floor for a thorough statement.

The discussion itself lasted two hours and heard the opinions of fifteen participants: nine archeologists, two historians, an architect, an anthropologist, a conservationist and a literary scholar. It opened with Mikhailov's statement, who argued for the harmfulness of Khaitov's book, and in an amazing tirade, called on censorship by scholars: "It would not be exaggerated to say that such low quality books, which increase scholarly mediocrity, have to be carefully and timely screened by specialists and not allowed to be published. And if [such books] do manage to appear because of negligence, they should be discarded just like this happens in industry, and the authors should be forced to give back their honoraria" (*BAN volume*: 143). Most of the speakers addressed not the factual aspects of the controversy, but stressed Khaitov's disrespect and the harm he had inflicted. This was the most frequent motive and it reappeared again and again both at this, as well as later meetings, and has been the dominant complaint against Khaitov, despite his equally frequent protestations.

In his response, Khaitov directly addressed the issue of professional competence and the juxtaposition of historians and archeologists to writers: "Why should the dilettantes (the writers) be opposed to the historians and archeologists when it is clear that historical science can ultimately fulfill its social goals only with the help of the writers, when history becomes epos, and historical knowledge becomes an ennobling emotion" (*BAN volume*: 194). He summarized the debates as "more of an exorcism rather than an authentic scientific debate" and felt confirmed in his belief in the existence of a professional cabal. Khaitov's polemic brilliance and his opponents' pitiful behavior should not leave the impression of a black-and-white duel between unprincipled knaves with vested interests and a quixotic hero. There was a genuinely held perception among the archeologists that Khaitov had a blessing from above and this affected their behavior. Conspiracy theories were not the figment only of Khaitov's imagination; they were a general explanatory device in the less than transparent atmosphere of late socialism.

Recently, the posthumous memoirs of one of the leading Bulgarian Byzantinologists, Dimitîr Angelov—at the time director of the AI—were published. There is a fragment dedicated exclusively to Khaitov and the BAN debates (2004: 168–172). While not dated, it was clearly written in the 1990s. Angelov repeatedly pictures Khaitov as a privileged stooge of the regime and the archeologists as its innocent victims. His arrogance is to be understood only because "he was leaning on the party-totalitarian machine," while today, after 1989, he attempts to present himself as an innocent victim of "this awful totalitarian machine." He was creating the legend that "the First" (Zhivkov) was supporting him in his endeavor to prove the reburial thesis. Angelov's fragment is not new or interesting for its argumentation: it is a faithful reiteration of the general arguments of the archeologists that they were unjustly accosted by a well-connected dilettante who had assembled around himself a group of quasi-experts and was playing on the nationalist feelings of the party and administrative bureaucracy; and that pressure had been exerted upon them and their defense was barred from the mass media. What is remarkable about the piece is simply the fact that it conveys the deep and sincere conviction of Angelov about this rendition of the events. No moment of hesitation, no second thought.

Angelov mentions that he writes his memoirs "not as a simple enumeration of facts but, rather, in the form of 'impressions,' 'visions' and 'evaluations.'" Indeed, because had he mentioned facts, he would have remembered that he had authored and signed the infamous memo of June 6, 1986, in which the scholarly debate was made hostage to ideological contingencies with the direct mention of the renaming process against the Turks. He also would have remembered that he himself was the co-signatory of a letter to "the First," in which the argument against placing a plaque at the church was made, among a host of other defensive arguments, on the basis of the fact that "by linking Levski to the church, are we not going to pay a high price that would denigrate our efforts at atheist education?" While posturing as a non-nationalist and accusing Khaitov of the sin, Angelov had no compunction in signing a letter threatening Zhivkov that if he were to endorse the discrediting of the historical discipline, "this can only please our ill-wishers in Ankara, Skopje, Belgrade and elsewhere." It is ridiculous to read the complaints of a host of party members (among them Angelov himself alongside three members or candidate members of the Central Committee) about Khaitov's omnipotence in the higher party echelons. Most importantly, the letter to Zhivkov worked, and the placement of the plaque was frozen. All of this, however, are facts, and since *de mortiis, aut bene, aut nihil,* let us assume that at a certain age facts are simply displaced by 'impressions,' 'visions' and 'evaluations.'

But Khaitov himself harbored the same complaints. He deposited two memos enumerating the publications in the press of the two sides of the debate in 1987 and 1988. There were altogether 20 articles and one TV show, written by archeologists and historians, who espoused the official line against the reburial. Against this, Khaitov listed 13 articles, which he had sent to different publication offices, and of which only two were published. Of the remaining eleven, six were rejected, and five never received an answer. As a whole, the archeologists repeated their argumentation avoiding to address the objections of Khaitov's team. However, all in all, the exchange between the two sides after the BAN debates, skewed as it may somewhat have been numerically in favor of the archeologists, was articulated in a scholarly tone and with a genuine desire to advance the factual knowledge and reach some well supported conclusions.

To doubt that both sides sincerely believed they were operated from above is to forget and deny the pervasive amount of manipulability under socialism. Journalists, in particular, were extremely sensitive to perceived trends in the upper echelons and the extent of self-censorship is staggering. But precisely because of this, one can suspect—judging from the amount of publications emanating from Khaitov in 1985–86, and then the reverse trend in 1987–88—that this may have been the result either of direct or perceived hints to the mass media.

In any case, it hardly had anything to do with strategic questions like the renaming process (as insinuated in Gergova's recollections) which were the unchanging political framework of the whole period until 1989. It is symptomatic that Khaitov in none of his numerous memoranda mentioned anything about the renaming process, while the archeologists distastefully and sycophantically alluded to "the revival process" in the Angelov-Gergova memorandum of June 6, 1986.

To recognize Khaitov's polemical gifts does not mean that his manner of debate and argumentation was above criticism. Sometimes his assertions would be forced and there are a number of instances that shed doubt on Khaitov's meticulousness and even credibility. In his latest publication he appropriately reproduced the whole text of the article in *Trud* from May 17, 1956, which summarized the general belief about Levski's reburial. In his analysis, however, Khaitov never mentions that the "prediction" suggested two possible sites in the church: either in the western part near the narthex or in the eastern part in the sanctuary. For someone who trusts him, and would not double-check the newspaper article, the reigning impression is that there is only one version. As Khaitov summarized it: "Thirteen days after [the newspaper article], on May 30, 1956 at 9 a.m., the diggers stumbled upon a 172 cm long male skeleton [...] at the exact same place suggested by *Mir* on March 6, 1937" (Khaitov 2002: 4). This is simply incorrect. The 1937 *Mir* recollection of Maria Poppavlova did specify the altar, but not the "exact same place" to the left of the altar stone, which was suggested only by her daughter Anastasia Bokova in June, 1956, after the discovery of the skeleton. And were we to believe Khaitov's logical conjecture that the author of the *Trud* article was Giaurov, then it is clear that before the discovery of May 30–31, 1956, he accepted as viable both versions: the narthex and the altar. There are other instances where Khaitov avoids the mention and analysis of inconvenient information, although he never falsifies it. At times he is unnecessarily pedantic when he overinterprets the phrase in Dzhingov's diary that the bones were "partly" under the church wall. He reasons that since they were partly under, this would mean that they were also partly over. This is sheer linguistic pettiness: it could be read simply as meaning that part of the skeleton was excavated, that it was in the open, and another part was under the wall, in other words, hidden. Khaitov's interpretation of one of the published 19th-century marginalia about construction works at the church in 1802—in the sense that the church had been thoroughly demolished and built anew at the beginning of the 19th century—is also forced (Khaitov 2002: 5, 34–5). He rightly complains about the elitist claims of the archeologists to be professionals, but he makes the same "under the belt" insinuations about Mikahilov and Stancheva that they were not real archeologists but trained as classicists, and therefore not professionals. Finally, there is his overall tendency to look for conspiracies. After 1989 in particular, they went rather wild.

All in all, and quite apart from his rhetorical abilities, Khaitov succeeded in putting forward quite a few convincing scholarly reassessments, not to speak of recovering needed material and exposing inconsistencies. The name Khaitov stands here often for the whole team which included a number of *bona fide* specialists. It is exclusively to the credit of the Khaitov team and his personal dogged stubbornness that the photographs, as well as additional material from the archive of the AI, were "discovered." It was also his team that exposed the mishandling of the photographs by Boiadzhiev (*BAN volume*, 346–347). Khaitov's personal achievement was to expose the diary of Dzhingov as a later copy. The archeologists were adamant that Dzhingov's diary be considered the only authentic document reflecting the excavations of 1956. Already at the debates Khaitov pointed to inconsistencies in the entries that most likely indicated that the notes were taken down not *in situ* but written up later. He went so far as to speak of a "manipulated copy of an unknown original" (Khaitov 1987: 85–7). Dzhingov categorically denied this and wrote an indignant letter (dated February 18, 1987) to the Central Committee of the Communist Party protesting Khaitov's allegations and calling for a criminal expertise of the diary. He ended with a call to "fight for the moral purity of socialist society" and "the importance to show the Bulgarian people the truth about Levski's grave, so as not to turn a random grave dating from many centuries ago into a national holy place" (Khaitov 2002: 200–201).

Then, in a surprising interview in a provincial paper on June 26, 1987 Dzhingov mentioned that the original diary was part of his personal archive. Always on the watch, Khaitov involved the Committee for State and People's Control. Dzhingov refused to let go of the original but deposited copies to the committee and to the archive of the institute. There are discrepancies between the original notes and the ones handed in as originals at the debates, and they appear indeed only after May 30, the day of the discovery of Skeleton No. 95 (Khaitov 2002: 80–82, 134–138). Dzhingov tried to explain them away, but at least in one particular case the difference is flagrant. The original notes contained the coordinates in centimeters of the skeleton vis-à-vis the adjacent walls and the altar stone, and these undoubtedly attested that the skull was in closest proximity to the altar stone and "touched" its masonry. That it could not survive intact had it been in place before the building of the church is obvious. These coordinates were missing from the sketches included in the copy of the diary! While Khaitov's conclusions based on these discrepancies are too categorical and cannot prove his contention that these are Levski's bones, there is no doubt that the diary was finessed in line with Mikahilov's version. Dzingov's diary was deposited by Mikhailov at the archive of the AI only in 1981, two years after Bobchev came in the open with his version of Levski's reburial, and the year in which the first roundtable at *Rabotnichesko delo* was held. Khaitov's meticulousness in exposing the inconsistencies in the archeologists' and historians' positions were characterized by them throughout as petty, arrogant, and the efforts of an amateurish sleuth (one of the archeologists even called him a bulldog) but they are a good example of professionalism that real scholars not only should aspire to but must possess if they have even the slightest claims to be professionals.

What is most exasperating is that the archeologists avoided addressing directly Khaitov's concrete facts but either repeated their own version or retreated in a general pose of offended professionalisms. Here is one of the few times that Mikhailov attempts to explain how No.95 could have remained intact: "This is a question we cannot answer, because we do not know where exactly, for what reason and at what depth the digging [of the foundations] took place. The important thing is not some such unknown details but the global fact that during the construction this area had been dug up, at which time some of the skeletons were damaged" (*BAN volume*: 259). This totally chaotic and illogical circular mental flow does not reflect too favorably on the scholarly pedigree of its author. Mikhailov presents the global fact that skeletons must have been damaged but he refuses, and is impotent, to explain the "unknown detail" about the intactness of No. 95 (*BAN volume*: 122).

One of the important arguments of Mikhailov's theory for the existence of an ancient necropolis under the church hinged on the claim that there had been a burial under the altar stone. The only mention of this burial comes from Dzhingov's diary, convincingly demonstrated by Khaitov to be a later edited exposition. The entry came on June 9, at the time when the debate was at its hottest and when the discovery of such a burial was incredibly welcome to Mikhailov. There is not a single photograph to corroborate the find, and Bobchev flatly denied that the altar stone had been lifted at all. All these counterarguments are simply waved off as unprofessional. The real apotheosis of Mikhailov's professional hubris comes in his conclusion: "One is amazed at the courage of a writer, a specialist in forestry, to oppose a whole scholarly institute, to question its competence, to teach the archeologists lessons, and instruct them in dating and digging... Following his method, I should teach him, say, about the vegetation of the Vitosha Mountain... No, I am not allowed to do this, just as Khaitov is not allowed to pronounce himself on my archeological excavations, because each discipline has its fine points which are not always accessible to the non-specialist." (*BAN volume*: 268). Nor was this the only dismissal of Khaitov on "professional" grounds. It is thus hugely uncomfortable on account of both historians and archeologists to read Khaitov's justified admonitions on scholarly ethics. A propos Kosev's curt dismissal of the reburial proofs as "unconvincing," he wrote: "In a scholarly debate it is easy to say something; it is difficult to prove it. But it is the duty of both small and great scholars to prove what they are saying" (Khaitov 1997: 43).

It has to be admitted, that once the debates went off on a bitter acrimonious track, they had a momentum of their own, and a psychological incompatibility built up from which there could be no retreat. In the end, however, the real bitterness of the debate is explicable not in terms of this psychological incompatibility. It is remarkable that behind the scenes some of the archeologists involved in the debate developed if not friendly, at least "gentlemanly relations" with Khaitov. Developing his understanding of the political, Carl Schmitt posited that "the specific political distinction to which political actions and motives can be reduced is that between friend and enemy." He warned, that "the enemy is not merely any competitor or just any partner of a conflict in general. He is also not the private adversary whom one hates. An enemy exists only when, at least potentially, one fighting collectivity of people confronts a similar collectivity" (Schmitt 1976: 26, 28).

Khaitov may have been hated by some for his personal arrogance, but the "political hatred" that he engendered stemmed mostly from the totally novel claim, revolutionary and unacceptable for the archeologists, that the production of history is not the prerogative only of institutionalized scholarship. This is not something that haunts only the Bulgarian scene:

> Debates about the Alamo, the Holocaust, or the significance of U.S. slavery involve not only professional historians but ethnic and religious leaders, political appointees, journalists, and various associations within civil society as well as independent citizens, not all of whom are activists. This variety of narrators is one of many indications that theories of history have a rather limited view of the field of historical production. They grossly underestimate the size, the relevance, and the complexity of the overlapping sites where history is produced, notably outside academia (Trouillot 1995: 19).

It takes, however, a historian of great talent and humility like Trouillot to acknowledge graciously that "the thematic awareness of history is not activated only by recognized academics. We are all amateur historians with various degrees of awareness about our production. We also learn history from similar amateurs. Universities and university presses are not the only loci of production of the historical narrative" (ibid.: 19–20). He pointed out that most people learn their first history lessons through media, celebrations, site and museum visits, movies, national holidays, and primary school books. The views they pick up from there are often challenged and subsequently modified by scholars: "as history continues to solidify professionally, as historians become increasingly quick at modifying their targets and refining their tools for investigation, the impact of academic history increases, even if indirectly. But let us not forget how fragile, how limited, and how recent that apparent hegemony may be" (ibid.: 20). Because of the conventions of historical articulation and "by virtue of its professional claims, the guild cannot express political opinions as such—quite contrary, of course, to activists and lobbyists." This often leads to the ironic situation that "the more important an issue for specific segments of civil society, the more subdued the interpretations of the facts offered by most professional historians" (ibid.: 21). This explains why many who genuinely care about history often look for historical interpretations on the fringes or altogether outside of academia.

This is the charitable look of an insider in the profession and, of course, many of us have been exasperated by the onslaught of historical journalism, let alone popularizing charlatans who have little patience with the rules of evidence and analysis. There is no doubt that Mikhailov and other archeologists sincerely believed they were caught in this no-win situation with the public. This feeling is particularly poignant in Mikhailov's concluding statement where his tone reminds us of the frustrations of a not very good but licensed doctor practicing conventional medicine, and what he feels are encroachers from alternative medicine, essentially quacks, but with charisma and success. After all, "by becoming a professional, a person set himself apart from the crowd and gained the ability, within his specialized field, to look beneath the surface appearances to the fundamental order of things." There was an additional pleasant thought that "his expertise was an unselfish, even democratic, service to the community" (Haskell 1998: 67).

Unfortunately, real life complicates even these simple and, on the whole, believable oppositions. In 1979, when the breach in the social drama occurred, the popular daily *Pogled* (N. 53, December 31, 1979) published a lengthy article by a mathematician—Borislav Dimitrov. Titled "With simple numbers toward immortality," the piece argued that simple numbers were ubiquitous in the Apostles life: the date and year of his birth and death, the years in which dramatic changes in his life occurred. The mathematician extracted and ordered these numbers in elaborate diagrams which produced a score of symbolic dates from Bulgaria's history. Numerology is an ancient human pastime and it is no surprise that the popular paper in its New Year's Eve edition was catering to an audience looking for historical interpretations on the fringes of academia when not altogether outside it. We can never be sure about the exact reception of the article by non-specialists but we are certain about its reception by specialists. In the same issue of *Pogled*, the editors printed a column "What the historians think" by three professors, two of whom were the widely accepted premier specialists on Levski: Undzhiev and Genchev. The article was sent to them in order to receive their imprimatur for publication. While cautiously worded, Undhiev, who died a few days later, gave an utterly positive review:

> I read this research article with genuine interest. It is the first mathematical work on dates and events from the life of the Apostle. The author, with great love for Levski's figure, identifies curious coincidences of simple numbers in important vital dates both in Levski's life and in our history. The article does not solve problems, nor does it explain important issues. It simply emphasizes and synthesizes the unity of the numbers. This is its contribution, the result of observation and thought. It deserves attention, it evokes interest and should be published.

Undzhiev's much younger colleague Genchev wrote a much more energetic endorsement:

> This work evoked in me an uncommon interest. I had not expected that the life of the Apostle can be approached through the "lens" of numbers. The arithmetic regularities are amazing and inexplicable. Maybe mathematical models in historiography have not yet been really introduced, which explains why we, the "classical" historians, are surprised by the results of Borislav Dimitrov. I think that this research will be broadly utilized in lectures, schools, illustrations of monuments. I therefore warmly recommend its publication and popularization.

The third opinion also lionized the piece as a contribution to the historical and mathematical disciplines, and made the pedagogical point that if teachers of history embellish their lessons with the numerical data of this research, the students will be able to remember and understand better and easier the glorious and heroic past." Numerology had been an *aide-de-mémoire* in medieval times and there was nothing wrong to step on such illustrious tradition but there was a certain world-upside-down quality to this page of *Pogled*, where three academics were endorsing an arcane arithmetic exercise and next to their column a fiction writer was publishing a short story under the title "Einsteinian celebrations." Already the graphic design of the page posed the question of where and to whom science belonged. A few days later, the hugely popular satirical weekly *Stîrshel* (N..1770,

January 11, 1980) published a parody by the well-known satirist Petîr Neznakomov titled "With simple numbers toward absurdity." He offered the funniest spoof of Dimitrov's article, playing with dates of his own life and ending on an appeal: "But enough! Let us give the word, as in the case of the article of Borislav Dimitrov, to the scholars." Who are the scholars, who are the quacks?

6. Recognizing the Schism, or What is Worse: Bad Professionals or Good Nationalists?

At the end of the BAN debates it was clear that a compromise, let alone a consensus, could not be reached. While Khaitov's imagination may have taken him too far—both in the deployment of political conspiracies and in his patriotic claim that the church had served as a burial pantheon for freedom fighters—his concrete analytical assault on the opposing version was devastating. It irrefutably demonstrated that the "professionals" had been anything but professional. The archeologists, although privately acknowledging mistakes, decided that even a partial concession would open a Pandora's box and publicly closed ranks behind the offended posture of professionalism. A reintegration à la Turner was impossible. The schism was recognized by the debating parties but they worked hard to deny the other side a niche of existence, and concentrated their efforts on securing exclusive recognition by the political authorities.

The archeologists were particularly active. Their first move was to suppress the publication of the debates. This was all the more flagrant, as all throughout they had appealed for a free press for all opinions. Angelov, in particular, had welcomed the prospective publication in flowery terms at the concluding meeting. In December, 1986, however, he sent a letter to Todorov stating that the materials should not be published before they were inspected, edited and approved by the Scientific Council of the AI because they handled mostly archeological issues. Todorov's response was that this was a documentary volume simply publishing the texts of the debates, and therefore did not need such approval. The archeologists then resorted to higher pressure. First, an official report was sent simultaneously to the secretary of the Central Committee Stoian Mikhailov and to BAN's president, signed by the then director of the United Center for History, Mito Isusov. Isusov's first objection was that the volume had been prepared for print by someone with no historical education. Most of his letter was a litany against the onslaught of "dilettantes who attack science with dishonorable means" and not "honestly and objectively." Finally, Isusov accused Todorov of attempting to publish the volume "in complete breach of the publishing norms and traditions of BAN." He suggested that the volume be discussed by the most competent scholars at the United Center for History. A little handwritten note appended to Isusov's report and addressed to Todorov's secretary Rumiana Radeva states: "Comrade Balevski ordered that the volume on Levski be held back." On June 16, while Todorov was in Paris for a meeting of UNESCO, the manuscript was taken from the publishing house and sent to Doino Doinov, the director of the State Archives.

After Isusov's intervention and the "confiscation" of the manuscript, Todorov addressed a written response to Iordan Iotov, the Politburo member who had been involved in greenlighting the above activities. He pointed out that the decision to publish all existing materials had been the result of a unanimous decision. Moreover, it had been sanctioned by the Presidium of BAN on the grounds that materials of a documentary or administrative nature that were not the result of individual or collective scholarly research did not need the approval of a competent body of scholars. This was a documentary collection, without corrections, additions or commentaries. Todorov ended his letter: "At this point I am again confronted with the efforts of some scholars to involve the Central Committee of the BCP with a decision on this publicly debated issue. It is an issue that should be analyzed exclusively within the academy. I am stunned at the attempts to suppress the publication of the volume. Why this fear before the truth?" (Khaitov 2002: 203–04).

Todorov also made the rounds to check on the fate of the volume. He first visited Iotov to protest the stopping of the book. Iotov told him that Kosev and Isusov had talked to him and strongly insisted that the publication be suppressed. In Iotov's words the book had not been stopped but only "held back" and Todorov should wait with the publication at least until the celebrations of the 150th anniversary of Levski's birth had passed. Doino Doinov at the State Archives, whom Todorov visited in order to get back the manuscript, told him that the accusations against him were ridiculous but the fact that none of the archeologists supported Khaitov's thesis made him uneasy. Stoian Mikhailov at first conceded that a decision had been taken to stop the volume altogether but after Todorov's written protest, they decided to only hold it back until after the anniversary. Finally, Balevski's official response to Isusov with a copy to Mikhailov followed at the end of July. It explained that the publishing norms of BAN effectively supported Todorov. In September, 1987, Todorov finally received the green light. He had decided to publish the volume in a circulation of 2,000 but there were already 7,000 demands, and he finally settled on 5,000. The volume appeared in the spring of 1988 to great acclaim. In July, *Pogled* announced that the volume was the most sought after book of the month. A literary critic explained the great public interest not only with the figure of Levski, the popularity of Khaitov and the public discussions around the grave, but explicitly linked it to the liberating and democratizing influence of the *Glasnost* process in the Soviet Union (*Pogled*, 28, July 11, 1988). Todorov received numerous personal letters of ordinary citizens who felt particularly grateful that the reader was allowed to form his own opinion.

The suppression of the volume was not the only attempt to silence further. The placing of a commemorative plaque followed a similar course. Already in 1979 Zhivkova harbored the idea to place such a plaque were the reburial thesis to prove sufficiently plausible. After the roundtable discussion in 1981, an editorial in the newspaper *Puls* of June 3, 1981 insisted that the bones be found and subjected to careful anthropological analysis. In the meantime, a plaque should be placed with the following text: "Here, according to the people's memory, was buried the Apostle of Freedom Vasil Levski." Of course, "people's memory" is a tricky thing but to any careful reader, its trickiness was explicitly suggested in its very inclusion. If anything, this was not simply a compromise proposal, it was scholarly enough precisely by including an imprecise category like "people's memory" in its careful wording. It never suggested that one was dealing with an indubitable fact. Indubitable facts are never introduced with "according to."

The final report of the 1986 debates recommended the possibility of placing a memorial plaque at the church with a similar conditional inscription stating that according to historical data, the Apostle of Freedom Vasil Levski had been reburied in the altar of the church by patriotic Bulgarians. In accordance with this recommendation, an inscription was prepared by the sculptor Mikhail Benchev. It was mounted not, however, with a decision by the government or municipality, but with the decision of the church council of "Sv. Petka." The plaque stayed in place exactly three days: it was placed on February 18, 1987, the day of Levski's hanging, and three days later was removed at night by unknown hands (Khaitov 2002: 198).

The archeologists fiercely opposed the recommendation and its implementation. So did a number of leading historians who signed a letter to Zhivkov on May 4, 1987 (*TsDA, ChP 130, File 21*). It started with the complaint that the specialists were being consciously eliminated from participating in the discussions around Levski's grave and that if hasty decisions were implemented, this would "have unfavorable ideological and political consequences." It alleged that Khaitov, in order to spread his unscholarly opinion, played with his popularity with influential individuals and the public at large. The "only deterrent against the enforcement of his opinion is the counter argumentation of the historians-specialists, who form their opinions on the basis of objective facts." Without at all touching on the argumentation of the Khaitov team, the letter simply stated that Khaitov and Co. used the negligence of some archeologists thirty years ago to compromise a whole discipline and to stir the public. In a shrewdly phrased sentence, the letter warned "that such public insults of the historical discipline aim at discrediting it, and this can only please our ill-wishers in Ankara, Skopje, Belgrade and elsewhere." The historians approved of the decision of the Central Committee to stop the public dispute over Levski's grave because of the existing danger of diverting public attention from the main issues of his legacy in the very year of his anniversary. The historians were surprised at the appearance of a second edition of Khaitov's book in an enormous circulation and were especially troubled by his insistence to place a commemorative plaque:

> The hasty placement of a plaque may bring about new complications. Quite apart from neglecting the historical facts, we accept the risk to split the people's devotion. The traditional pilgrimages to the Apostle's only monument in Sofia, which is the unquestionable and widely known place of his execution, would be diverted to a questionable object, such as the church "Sv. Petka Samardzhiiska." And who, by the way, would want such a diversion toward the church? By linking Levski to the church, are we not going to pay a high price that would denigrate our efforts at atheist education? Let us remind, in this regard, that this particular version about Levski's grave had been launched at the time

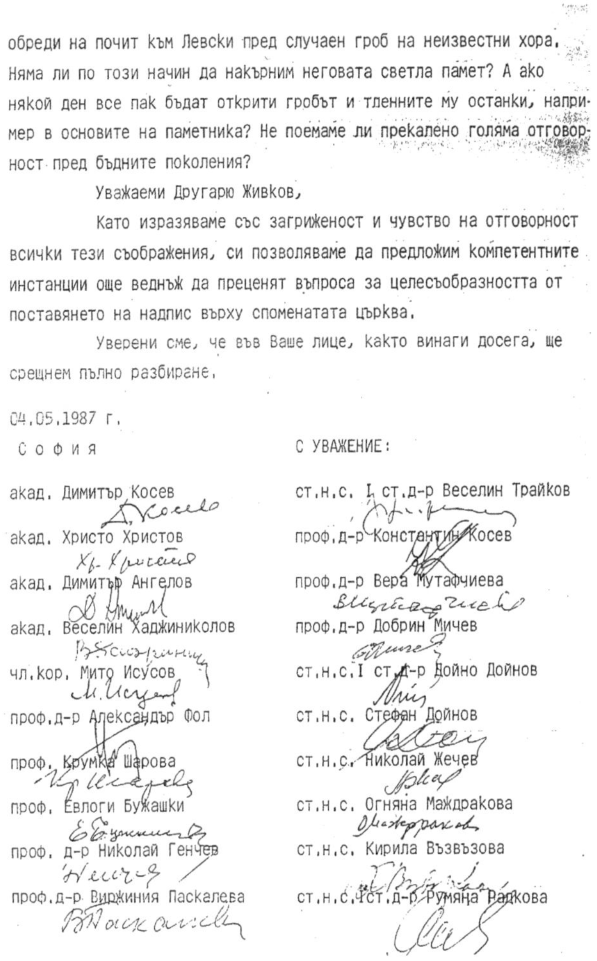

обреди на почит към Левски пред случаен гроб на неизвестни хора. Няма ли по този начин да накърним неговата светла памет? А ако някой ден все пак бъдат открити гробът и тленните му останки, например в основите на паметника? Не поемаме ли прекалено голяма отговорност пред бъдните поколения?

Уважаеми Другарю Живков,

Като изразяваме със загриженост и чувство на отговорност всички тези съображения, си позволяваме да предложим компетентните инстанции още веднъж да преценят въпроса за целесъобразността от поставянето на надпис върху споменатата църква.

Уверени сме, че във Ваше лице, както винаги досега, ще срещнем пълно разбиране.

04.05.1987 г.
София

С УВАЖЕНИЕ:

акад. Димитър Косев
акад. Христо Христов
акад. Димитър Ангелов
акад. Веселин Хаджиниколов
чл.кор. Мито Исусов
проф.д-р Александър Фол
проф. Крумка Шарова
проф. Евлоги Бужашки
проф. д-р Николай Генчев
проф.д-р Виржиния Паскалева

ст.н.с. I ст.д-р Веселин Трайков
проф.д-р Константин Косев
проф.д-р Вера Мутафчиева
проф.д-р Добрин Мичев
ст.н.с.I ст.д-р Дойно Дойнов
ст.н.с. Стефан Дойнов
ст.н.с. Николай Жечев
ст.н.с. Огняна Маждракова
ст.н.с. Кирила Възвъзова
ст.н.с.I ст.д-р Румяна Радкова

Figure 10. The page with the signatures of the 4 May 1987 letter sent to Todor Zhivkov.
Source: *Tsentralen Dîrzhaven Arkhiv, ChP 130, papka 21.*

precisely by members of the church with a definite goal, which now seems close to realization with the help of new supporters.

The letter was signed by leading historians, directors of institutes, editors of important historical journals. At least four of them had also important positions in the party hierarchy. The letter to Zhivkov worked, and the placement of the plaque was frozen.

There had been also a counter campaign. One petition to place a plaque was signed in April, 1988 by 150 writers. Another, signed in the spring of 1989 by 50 writers, professors and leading intellectuals was sent to Zhivkov but produced no result. Things at first seemed to have somehow subsided in the aftermath of November 10, 1989. To be sure, there were periodic polemic outbursts in the press but they were short-lived and inconsequential. One such exchange came in 1990. In January 1990 Khaitov gave an interview insisting on the placement of a memorial plaque. On February 16, 1990 Todorov published an article in *Otechestven Front*, summarizing the conclusion of the 1986 debates. He referred to the new democratic spirit in the country, in which the truth about Levski's grave could be handled differently and urged the placement of a plaque with the words "According to a number of data, the Apostle of Freedom Vasil Levski was reburied here in 1873." This article triggered a strong response by Stanilov, who after 1989 headed of the Medieval Section of the AI. It is remarkable for introducing a completely new tone in the debates, typical of the situation immediately after November 10, 1989. It was an unabashed *ad hominem* attack on "the two friends who wish to acquire the unfading fame of discoverers of a holy relic," and on Todorov who was not an archeologist and had not "the slightest idea of the specifics of this science" (*Rabotnichesko delo*, March 4, 1990). This was only Stanilov's modest debut. In a second article he attacked Khaitov as "the plague of Bulgarian cultural life," Todorov as "a family friend of the Pravets dynasty," both Khaitov and Todorov as "the two toadeaters on the table of Todor Zhivkov," among a score of other insults (*Vek 21*, 37, December 12, 1990). Finally, in a third article Stanilov caustically attacked Khaitov as a pathetic dilettante and a political opportunist hungry for fame and money. He also reiterated the old allegations about the illegality of the BAN volume and the decision of BAN taken "under the totalitarian pressure of academician Todorov" (*Svoboden narod*, March 27, 1991).

Stanilov's arguments and style should not be generalized about the archeologists as a whole. Others did not resort to his methods, nor were they taken up by the opponents, but they were indicative of the highly politicized atmosphere after 1989. One would have expected that with the passing away of what was officially pronounced as a politicized public space, debates would be held without flashing the political card but, quite to the contrary, this became ubiquitous.

Ironically, while in the latter decades of state socialism using a political argument to augment a point was as the peak of bad manners, hurling political qualifications and abuse became the standard manner of discussion in the first decade after 1989. This is quite natural. After the 1960s, socialism entered a phase of stability and, more or less, accepted rules that extended even over the period of growing illegitimacy of the regime, whereas a chaotic, anarchic and often hooligan atmosphere set in during the early period of transition. In the particular debate over Levski's remains, it played itself out in a visible shift of the main rhetorical trope from "professionalism" to "totalitarianism." Most significant about the post-1989 period, as it relates to the further development of the final phase of the social drama, is that with the exception of one participant, the issue had lost is existential urgency. For the archeologists, it was most often the power of inertia or the concern over personal reputations that triggered public statements. In the spring of 2001, however, a new polemic was set off that spilled out into the administrative and political arena. The immediate cause was the placing of a new commemorative plaque on the outside wall of the church. It was consecrated in the winter of 2001 by the Sofia Metropolitan Inokentii, head of the Holy Synod of the alternative Bulgarian Orthodox Church, to whose diocese "Sv. Petka Samardzhiiska" belonged. According to the priest of "Sv. Petka," Father Mikhail Milushev, the placing was initiated in late October, 2000 by a group of anonymous private donors. The inscription, unlike the careful wording in 1987, was unambiguous: "Patriotic Bulgarians reburied in this temple the Apostle of Freedom Vasil Levski in 1873." In addition, the image of Levski had a nimbus emphasizing his essence of a saint. When I asked Father Milushev why they had not followed the careful wording of the previous plaque, he laughed: "My dear, the conditional mood is for science. This is a church. People want positive knowledge."

The architect Andrei Mikhailov, son of the deceased archeologist Stamen Mikhailov, turned to the AI in April, 2001, and asked for its competent opinion on the question of the reburial. The Section for Medieval Archeology, headed by Stanilov, came up with a statement endorsed by the Scientific Council. Armed with it, Andrei Mikhalilov deposited a petition at the Commission for Education and Culture of the Sofia Municipal Council. He reiterated that the placement of the plaque was illegal and pleaded that it be dismantled. In the daily *Stolichen 24 chasa* of June 27, 2001 he disclosed his motives: "It is my highest moral and filial duty, in the name of and on behalf of my deceased father, to continue the struggle for scholarly truth, a struggle he waged until his last breath: against hypocrisy, falsehood and demagogy." At the same time, he qualified his authority as a fighter for scholarly truth by referring to the authority of the specialist: "As an architect, I have neither the scholarly nor the moral power to pass scholarly judgments and statements on the question. This right belongs exclusively to the competent specialists in this field. I would be happy if this basic truth gets recognized not only by me."

The socially accepted as well as self-designated "specialists in the field" produced the brief statement, serving as the fundamental scholarly argumentation of Andrei Mikhailov's petition. Entitled "Opinion of the scholars from the Section Medieval Archeology at the AI of BAN on the question of the identification of Vasil Levski's grave in the altar of the church 'Sv. Petka Samardzhiiska,'" it was approved "in an open vote at a regular session of the scholarly department with an existing quorum of habilitated persons," and signed by the section's head. The weighty title with the appropriate legal and scholarly accessories—"open vote," "regular session," existing quorum," "habilitated persons," "scholarly opinion," "authoritative institution"—is an apt illustration of rhetorical shift after 1989.

Comparing the tone of this late reaction to Stanilov's earlier writings, the absence of bitter acrimony is striking. It is a posthumous tribute to the memory of a colleague and a gesture to the hurt feelings of a son, rather than the anxious struggle of a faction in a debate. Indeed, the faction had no more stake in the debate. The whole infrastructure of how archeology was financed had practically disappeared. It is no longer a matter of striking a professional or patriotic pose. "Marketing" is the latest game and as a journalist hastened to conclude, "the so-called academic archeology is lately in fashion and becomes ever more worldly: archeologists appear in the media, people go to the museums." In the words of one of the most entrepreneurial archeologists, Nikolai Ovcharov, "Ten–fifteen years ago I firmly believed in the elitist science and, to tell you the truth, I looked upon tourists as a nuisance. During the last seven years, however, I became convinced that there was no advantage in scholastic science and the tourist aspect has become especially important for me. The steady flow of tourists is the only way our objects can be financed for research, restoration, conservation and upkeep" (*Kapital*, 44, Nov. 6–12, 2004, 9–10). Where before the AI depended entirely on the state budget and the support of the local municipal councils, today in the words of a critic "the state keeps its monopoly on the legacy but in the past 15 years has abdicated from its custody and has thus handed a *carte blanche* to the treasure hunters" (ibid.: 9). The spectacular Thracian gold mask from the excavations during the summer of 2004 under the leadership of the archeologist Georgi Kitov, brought 20,000 visitors to the museum. In nine days the cheap entry tickets (3 levs or $2 per person) made 60,000 leva, more than the 50,000 Kitov received to continue the excavations.

Today, the central item of revenue for the AI comes from its near monopoly over issuing excavation permits. In 2003, according to the institute itself, 290 such permits were issued. The inspection of the National Center for Museums, Galleries and Art maintains that the number is 890, but even the smaller figure indicates more ongoing excavations than in all other European countries taken together (*Kapital*, 44, November 6–12, 2004, 12–13). 90% of these permits are issued for so called "salvation excavations" and the rest is mostly *ad hoc*, when there is danger from treasure hunters. This monopoly has not been left without its critics but the point to be made is that the Levski issue, unlike its weight in the preceding period, is completely immaterial to their ongoing work. Tellingly, after 2004, when the split in the Bulgarian Orthodox Church was resolved in favor of the mainstream organization, and the commemorative plaque was removed by the official authorities around Patriarch Maxim, the archeologists remained indifferent. Now the controversy is exclusively within the ranks of the clerical establishment.

As Turner theorizes about the political field in the fourth phase, one has to pay special attention to the structure of the whole field that may have changed, as well as the nature and intensity of the relations between parts:

> New power will have been channeled into old and new authority and former authority defenestrated. Closeness will have become distance and vice versa. Formerly integrated parts will have segmented; previously independent parts will have fused. Some parts will no longer be-

long to the field, others will have entered it. Institutionalized relationships will have become informal; social regularities will have become irregularities. New norms and rules may have been generated during attempts to redress conflict; old rules will have fallen into disrepute and have been abrogated. The basis of political support will have altered. Some components of the field will have less support, others more, still others will have fresh support, and some will have none. The distribution of the factors of legitimacy will have changed, as also the techniques used by the leaders to gain compliance (Turner 1974: 42).

The one exception mentioned above, for whom the issue over Levski's grave never lost its urgency, was Khaitov. He moved in a kind of determined diachronic ardor through all acts of this dramatic opera, never once changing the words or pitch of his aria. A self-appointed defender of Bulgaria's national honor, for him the confrontation was "not the result of an ordinary debate between dilettantes and archeologists about Levski's grave. It is a debate with the thieves of Bulgarian glory and the falsifiers of Bulgaria's past, who, after fifteen quiet years again are raising their heads" (Khaitov 2002: 13). He not only did not change his position; his emotional involvement, if anything, intensified. From the outset, Khaitov had outlined four main arguments in defense of his crusade. The first was his assertion that it was part of human nature, indeed a vital need, to attempt to express in a material fashion its loftiest feelings of veneration toward a given individual by constructing memorial buildings: graves, mausoleums, pantheons. He called on the millennial record of humanity to support his assertion. He effectively countered the widely shared belief that such a material expression of devotion is unnecessary and, at worst, sheer idolatry. Not so, according to Khaitov. Surely the ones, for whom graves, mausoleums, and pantheons have been erected, also have their place in our hearts. "'For the sake of the next generation' and for 'His glory': this is why Levski's bones and grave have been and continue to be sought. Not because this is needed for his immortal spirit, but because it is ours, the living, vital necessity, as well as the need of those who are coming after us. Quite independently of, and maybe because of the fact, that he is in our hearts" (Khaitov 1989: vol. 3, 20).

Khaitov argued that if looking for the graves of the worthy was idolatry, we should reconsider our whole practice preserve the remains of deserving individuals. More concretely, he suggested we should not have brought back Rakovski's bones from Romania, nor reburied Khadzhi Dimitîr's remains in his home place, or erected a pantheon to the Bulgarian revolutionaries in Ruse, nor built the mausoleum for Georgi Dimitrov, or preserved the bones of the fallen in the liberation wars: "If immortalizing the memory of our revolutionaries by means of common graves, tombs, shrines, and mausoleums diverts us from their immortal ideas, is it not high time to think of their destruction? And to stop the television campaign to restore the monuments to the ones who perished in the wars?" (Khaitov 1997: 204–205). It is a powerful argument, not confined to the era of nationalism. Whether it is human nature is difficult to judge, but the urge to mark the graves of predecessors and especially of the select ones among the group, and to venerate remains, is certainly as old as human history. Some have called it a "hunger for facticity" (Lipcheva-Prandzheva 2001: 124) Graves are "the enduring units of society and provide the material symbol of their continuity" (Bloch and Perry 1982: 33). One may even sympathize with the enlightened or modernizing or simply ascetic ethos of the ones who despise the practice, but they will not win the realism bet: the long and often bloody wars on "idolatry" throughout human history have always been lost in the end. Khaitov's argumentation was the expression of a general worldview based on a strong attachment to tradition.

Khaitov's second argument pertained to the Bulgarian nation proper, its self-perception and self-esteem. The final verdict on whether Levski's bones were reburied would clean it from the charge that it was totally frightened and passive: "If so, let us deservedly carry the shame and the pain, but if the truth is different, why should we and the following generations be burdened by a non-existing guilt?" (Khaitov 2002: 21) This is an argument of someone for whom the nation and national allegiance is of prime importance. Yet again, it is not something necessarily archaic or Balkan. It is very comparable to the similar and arguably justified demands that the time has come for the German postwar generations to stop bearing the blame and shame for deeds they themselves had not committed. These demands do not come only from the right-wing fringe but have become a mainstream trope in a society whose democratic credentials no one doubts today. The third argument was in the same line: targeted the heart of what can be designated as the syndrome of weak nationalism. It addresses the alleged lack of historical feeling among the Bulgarians that Undzhiev had lamented already in the 1940s. Khaitov actually agrees with this self-accusation but thinks that the activities to find the grave, and even the fact that it cannot be found, may in reality counter it, if, indeed, the reburial had taken place.

It is, however, the fourth argument that is of particular interest here. Since the dispute over Levski's grave will not fade away, and people will always look for the truth, no matter whether pleasant or not, the crucial question is who has the right to look for it. The writer addressed specifically a letter of the AI, in which the Medieval Section claimed it was the only competent body able to pronounce itself on the objectivity of the archeological conclusions, and that Khaitov was a representative of a broad circle of. Not only was this unacceptable, when it comes to such a major question as Levski's grave it is also unprofessional. After all, the real question in solving the problem was not so much archeological but needed special reference to other disciplines, like architecture, engineering, and geodesy. Therefore, "there cannot be limitations on the procedures, and no academic institution has the right to monopolize the truths which are somehow linked to it. The truth—as long as it is the truth—is welcome, no matter when, where and in whose head it is reached" (Khaitov 2002: 22–3).

Well over eighty, and just a year before his death, Khaitov was after his idea with the commitment and ardor of a young athlete. There was something admirable in this dedication and dogged perseverance, quite apart from its exact motives. And it was infectious. The entry in my diary for July 5, 2001, after I had spoken to him, reads: "Khaitov is actually attractive with his full-blooded vitality and sharp mind but he is, at the same time, a quarrelsome and resentful hound who is intoxicated by confrontations." He continued to be active in the mass media. In February, 2002, he was interviewed by Slavi Trifonov in what is, arguably, the most popular show on Bulgarian television. Trifonov, who started out as a semi-alternative, folksy, somewhat crude but appealing leader of a popular band, has turned into something of an unofficial arbiter investing aspiring politicians and intellectuals with legitimacy, an unexpected combination of Jay Leno, Opera Winfrey and Jim Lehrer. Giving Khaitov the opportunity to present yet again his theses on Levski, he made sure the issue was alive and reached the widest possible audience.

Levski figured foremost in Khaitov's thinking, so much so that his personal relations were qualified through the Levski prism. His negative attitude toward Zhelev is well known. Asked to explain his antipathy, Khaitov responded: "My clash with him dates back to 1987, when I stumbled upon one of his *samizdat* pieces on Levski, in which he characterized me as a 'besotted jingoist.' So, even before the breaking out of democracy, it was clear to me what kind of person he really was" (Khaitov 2001: 38, 54). The piece in question was Zhelev's "Levski as a historical personality," but it was not true he had singled out Khaitov. He wrote in general about the "false patriotism of the cunning and the besotted jingoism of the dumb" (1995: 93). It was Khaitov's enormous self-centeredness, in addition to his self-crowned hypostasis as Levski's champion that made him oversensitive. Not only the perceived personal offence infuriated him. He was piqued in particular by Zhelev's statement that "We are reluctant to acknowledge even today that Levski had not been betrayed by separate individuals but by the whole Bulgarian nation which was not yet worthy of its freedom. Are not Levski's bitter words, pronounced at the trial, an illustration of this: 'Our Bulgarians desire freedom, but they will accept it only if handed to them on a plate in their homes.' This actually happened with the Russian–Turkish war of 1877–78" (ibid.: 90). Khaitov was angry but, and herein lies the remarkable trait of his brand of nationalism, while his reaction was emotional, his argumentation always strived to be scholarly. He accused Zhelev of sloppy scholarship, because he had decontextualized Levski's words, so that they would look like a total accusation hurled in the face of a whole nation. Khaitov was entirely correct to specify that Levski had differentiated between separate groups within the nation, and in support quoted his testimony before the Ottoman court:

> The educated Bulgarians who expected progress through enlightenment, considered it dangerous and inappropriate to demand rights with arms... The peasants in their desperate situation, and in the hope they could be delivered, whenever we talked to them of revolution, came wherever we would pull them (Vasil Levski 1952: 204–05).

It was not only Khaitov's nationalism, and particularly his identification with the peasant, the rural small man, that was offended by Zhelev's melodramatic overgeneralizations. Also offended was the aesthetic of his thinking: precise, documented, indeed scientific. Khaitov had plenty of old and new scores to settle, and was never averse to peppered attacks. It is remarkable how Levski always comes up in any, even the most tangential dispute. Levski's figure genuinely inflected Khaitov's view of the world and of separate individuals. His relationship with Iordan Radichkov who, together with Khaitov vies for the position of the most original recent Bulgarian author but was, arguably, the greater literary figure of the two, was strained. Khaitov's negative attitude, however, did not spill out to denigrate Radichkov's literary *oeuvre* as he did with other colleagues. His chief complaint against him was the latter's involvement in the activities of the Open Society Institute, and the fact that he had allegedly said in a documentary film that the financial reports of Soros were cleaner than Levski's famous notebook (Khaitov 2001: 30, 84).

After 1989, Khaitov openly deliberated on what he really thought about the "plot to destroy Levski's grave." The framework was the "political zombinization" of Bulgaria by Stalin. There is no room in Khaitov's explanatory word for chance, mistakes, or simply indifference. His ordered, sleuth-like mind needs to arrange everything in easily accessible and clearly marked boxes, linked in a transparent arrangement called causality. Bulgaria's history in the last half century in his worldview is boxed into several easily explicable sub-periods: *a) 1944–1956*, characterized by anti-nationalist campaigns, and attempts to obliterate the nation by curbing the existing prewar patriotism; *b) 1956–1989*. Todor Zhivkov's rule and the return to the national paradigm has great appeal for Khaitov; there is also the solidarity with the village boy who had made it to the top. Although Khaitov admits that in 1986 Zhivkov caved in to the demands to postpone the placing of a commemorative plaque, he nevertheless gives him a high rating as a national ruler. He is unequivocal about the positive role of Liudmila Zhivkova; *c) post-1989*, has seen a return to the anti-nationalism of the immediate postwar period that had been internalized by the generation of "the most de-Bulgarianized" Komsomol leaders socialized in blind devotion to the Soviet Union. They made no attempt to save the country from entering the orbit of the new great power that blew up the USSR. A significant part of the young generation, brought up in the spirit of "socialist and later capitalist cosmopolitanism" despises its own country (ibid.: 47–9).

Khaitov's penchant for conspiracy theory finally got the better of him. It did not pertain solely to the Levski case. In 2001, Khaitov collected many of his scattered essays in a new book—*Whoever Has an Ear, Let Him Hear*. It is a curious and deeply disturbing mixture of realistic down-to-earth, poignant, at times even courageous, assessments of the current economic and political situation, with the most far-reaching, extravagant unraveling of alleged internal and foreign conspiratorial plots. The "traitor" Gorbachev had sold Bulgaria to George Bush at their December meeting in Malta; the World Bank was implementing a plan to ruin Bulgaria's educational system, so that by 2010 the number of literate Bulgarians would be half today's number; the radiation from the depleted U-bombs thrown over Yugoslavia at the time of the Kosovo war in 1999 had totally devastated Northwestern Bulgaria; a demographic collapse was waiting to occur with over 750,000 Bulgarians abroad, half of whom with university and high school degrees, and another 300,000 waiting to emigrate; this was accelerated by the lowest birthrate in the world and an ethnic ratio at birth in which only 8,000 ethnic Bulgarians are born to every 40,000 births; the transformation of Kosovo into an American military base in the Balkans had been a military strategy since the 1970s, and was part of NATO's steady movement toward the natural resources of the East; the Euroatlantic policy towards Bulgaria could be defined as a war with diminished intensity; and last but not least, there was always the ubiquitous Soros, whose "outward role is that of a philanthropist, benefactor and theoretician of the new civic 'Open Society,' but whose actual role was devoted to one final goal: the closing of nation-states in the name of a new world order headed by one sole world power and one sole global government." One is almost tempted to exclaim in despair with the writer Boian Biolchev: "How could a writer with such talent enter the Association of Bulgarian Writers with his *Wild Stories*, and leave it so boringly with wild talk!" (*Kultura*, 43, October 29, 1999).

And yet, is it only the morbid suspicious imagination of an aging tycoon which is at play? What makes Khaitov's word resonate with people? It may be the brisk, accessible prose, the genuine passion, the obvious pain at the state of the nation, the often penetrating insights. Khaitov's description of the "ranked structure" with the US at the helm, followed by the NATO states of the EU, then "protectorates" like Poland, Hungary and the Czech Republic, all comprising the "civilized world," rings a bell. The rest of the world, including Russia, China and the majority of the Asian states, fall under the category 'barbarian.' When, in the aftermath of September 11, the leaders of the "civilized world" arduously joined a chorus chanting the hypnotic refrain about the assault on the "civilized world," eyebrows were raised even in the best salons of this civilized world. The rest of the world did not raise eyebrows, not even sneer; it did not expect anything else. A standard Bulgarian in the streets has not much time to discern the hair-splitting distinctions proposed to define the notion of "terrorist" in the New York offices of the UN diplomats. But a standard Bulgarian is curious and reads about the world, and usually has pretty strong opinions. From his vantage point, the world in his immediate vicinity looked like this: In neighboring Turkey, tens of thousands of Kurds were killed in a civil war in which they fought for their rights, but the Turkish government pronounced them terrorists, and despite verbal criticism, there was no real pressure because of American support; on the contrary, the country was bailed out economically, and was a most important NATO ally. This was the case until a few years ago, when the drive toward European integration produced a significant shift in the treatment of the Kurds. In neighboring Serbia, with the same structural problem, the fortunes of the Serbs have been reverse: they were bombed, and the Albanians pronounced freedom fighters. Hardly over a year later, these same Albanians were judged to be terrorists in Macedonia. Yet, in Macedonia, the government was not allowed to deal with them and defend its own territory. But in Israel, for decades now, the government is dealing without impunity with "terrorists" in illegally occupied territories. Bulgaria is being praised for its "ethnic peace," but foreign emissaries, NGOs, and scholarly institutions are interested only in the "minorities." And while Bulgaria was forced to sign the convention on minorities, neither Greece nor Turkey did.

This is no mere speculation. Every Bulgarian knows at least one Kurd, Palestinian, Serb, Albanian, Macedonian, Greek or Turk. They have listened to opposing viewpoints, have seen refugees, have heard NATO bombers in the air, feel that their fate is of no interest to anyone in the "civilized community." I repeat: this is more or less what one can hear openly in the streets or in coffee shops of any Bulgarian city or village, if one cares to speak to people. It is not highest on their agenda, but it is there, and Khaitov articulated it with verve. What he writes and how he writes about Bulgaria's geopolitical predicament, resonates well with the average citizen. Khaitov's words are not rallying calls, let alone battle cries. They simply "professionally" affirm the diagnosis that the sick and self-healing Bulgarian patient has given himself, before looking for the saving medicine abroad: emigration.

I was reading this latest book of Khaitov while riding the bus from Sofia to Vienna in the summer of 2001. I had closed the book and had closed my eyes. Why is it never simple? Why are "bad professionals" not really that bad, and why can "good nationalists" actually be good in many respects? True, Khaitov's style was too dramatic for my taste, his worldview reeking too much of conspiracy theory, but questions of interpretation and style apart, he was pointing his finger unquenchingly at the serious issues. The voice of my neighbor on the seat woke me from my slumber. A trendy young woman, roughly my daughter's age, who was visiting a friend in Vienna, she had just finished her beer, and had put a fresh layer of lipstick: "I see you are reading Khaitov. May I borrow the book? I really think he is the best."

When Khaitov died at age 82 on June 30, 2002, his funeral attracted thousands of admirers. The newspapers did not conceal the polarized emotions he had been evoking, but they all agreed on his magnificent talent and his larger than life presence in the cultural life of Bulgaria. In one of his latest interviews Khaitov had tried to strike a balance: "Sins I have but no qualms." The one thing for which he would give half of his life was to make a film about Levski. He didn't have time for that: as one of the newspapers summed it up: "God took in Nikolai Khaitov" (*Standart*, July 2, 2002). But Khaitov had already announced that "Levski is the Bulgarians' God" (*Standart*, February 18, 2001).

PART II

THE APOSTLE OF FREEDOM, OR WHAT MAKES A HERO?

In the summer of 1998, I visited the artist Todor Tsonev, who had become famous after 1989 with his exhibition of cartoons of Todor Zhivkov that he had painted during communism, one of the very few cases where the expectation of a "closet full of masterpieces" that were cached away from the forbidding eyes of censorship actually was vindicated. For a brief period of time Tsonev became the hero of democracy, the notion which in the first years covered the genuine democratizing transformations in the Bulgarian polity, as well as a pet of the "democrats," the label given in jest to the anti-communist political leadership. He soon disappointed both the "democrats" as well as the so-called reform socialists, the so-called "blue" and "red" factions, and reverted to caricatures, in which he exposed the pains and evils of "really existing democracy."

When I entered his studio, I was struck by an almost life-size portrait of Levski in uniform, on which the artist was working. It was not a spectacular piece of art. Tsonev was an excellent cartoonist, whose genius lay in the combination of quick and sparse line with strong civic consciousness. He was also working in oil, woodcarving and minisculpture, but these were not his forte. Following my surprised gaze, Tsonev explained that he had been arrested for a brief period in the early months of 1989. His interrogator was a young man, and quite humane, according to Tsonev. After Tsonev's release, he visited him from time to time. Then he disappeared for a longer period, and when Tsonev met him again, he had started a successful business. He asked Tsonev to paint a huge portrait of the Apostle that he wanted hanged in his living room. Obviously the portrait was accorded the role of an indulgence, only one is not sure whether it was supposed to atone for the pangs of consciousness of the former interrogator or the present businessman. Tsonev had no qualms about producing this portrait, no doubt because this particular interrogator had been good-hearted, and because he was making a living out of it. He himself held Levski and Botev as his heroes and saints, and told me that he had made arrangements about his own death. He should be cremated and his friends were to take the urn with his ashes first to Karlovo and sprinkle a handful of his remains in front of Levski's home. Then they should head off to nearby Kalofer and do the same thing in front of Botev's house. The rest of his ashes should be strewn in the fields between the two towns.

Levski has become the ultimate legitimizing authority and his name is the final imprimatur on any political initiative and business enterprise. Analyzing his consecutive and simultaneous appropriations allows one to see how boundaries within the framework of the nation are negotiated around accepted national symbols. Levski's relatively sparse written legacy, while interesting and significant in its own historical context as a testament to the vision of the national revolution in the 1860s and 1870s, has been elevated to the status of Pythia-like pronouncements, and relatively simple utterances have become slogans for wide political movements or programs. Bulgarians have been weaned on the popular "If I win, I win for the whole nation, if I lose, I am losing only myself." In the 1980s another one became fashionable: "The time is in us and we are in the time."

On July 18, 1996, the 159th anniversary of Levski's birthday, a monument was dedicated to Levski in front of the Bulgarian Embassy in Washington, D.C. It carries an inscription in Bulgarian and English of one of these brief thoughts that have achieved mantra-like quality. This time it was one that had hardly been used before. The text rendered in English is "Freedom and to each his own." While not a mistranslation, it is a misleading translation. Everyone I have asked about their knee-jerk reaction to the phrase (Bulgarians and Americans alike) interpret it as an illustration of Levski's dedication to individual liberties. Some suggest it shows Levski's understanding of the significance of private property, in other words it is unanimously a classical liberal reading. Thus, the monument is meant to transmit to the US government and the World Bank an assurance of the deeply ingrained individualism and property-abiding propensities of Bulgarians and their growing privatization potential, to counter the unfavorable stereotype of an irredeemably socialist infected population behind the Iron Curtain of culturally unreceptive and unreformable Orthodoxy. There are other innumerable attempts to domesticate a typical revo-

ОЧИТЕ НА БЪЛГАРИЯ към тебе са отправени
и всеки търси да открие нещо в себе си от теб,
ние всички искаме да бъдем с теб във времето
тъй както времето е винаги във теб,
ОЧИТЕ НА БЪЛГАРИЯ за тебе винаги ще жалят
както само майка жали за първо чедо,
за първороден син
защото ти израсна до бесилото като най-големия
и най-неповторимия ни исполин.
СЪРЦЕТО НА БЪЛГАРИЯ за тебе винаги ще бие
и няма сила, която да го спре,
то в теб ще бъде влюбено
дори да минат векове.
ОЧИТЕ НА БЪЛГАРИЯ и нас ще оценяват
един ден с твоите очи,
един ден внучето ще ни запита:
Къде е Левски в тебе дядо, бабо?
Какво направи за България след твоите деди?!

*Когато животът ме гневно притисне
със своята сила и груба ръка,
несетно си спомням за дякона Левски
в стихията страшна на тежка борба.*

ФОНДАЦИЯ "Лейди Дайана - Принцесата на народа"

Figure 11. Flyer of the charitable foundation "Lady Diana."

lutionary (or "terrorist"—he was hanged as one) into the politically correct neo-liberal idiom of market capitalism. Recently, I came across the flier of a charitable foundation, featuring Levski's portrait and a talentless appeal in rhyme. It is a supplication to Levski who is the sole solace in difficult times and ends with a grandchild asking the grandparents: "Where is Levski in you, grandpa, grandma? What did you do for Bulgaria after your predecessors?" The foundation is named "Lady Diana: Princess of the people."

The inscription on Levski's bust is one of those instances that illuminates the ambiguity of "the words of history." The phrase is encountered *in toto* or in parts in several instances. It is used as a verbatim slogan in a newspaper article of Levski published in Liuben Karavelov's paper *Svoboda* on February 13, 1871. The original dispatch of Levski had been sent at the very end of 1870 or the beginning of 1871, and after some editing and rewriting, Karavelov printed it as the correspondence of "d.L." It is one of the most powerful pieces where Levski develops his ideas that Bulgarians should rely only upon their own strengths. "The knife should be speaking; the ink does not help anymore," he comments on the uselessness of appeals to the European governments. Not only were they indifferent to the plight of the Bulgarians, but they were actively helping the decrepit empire stand on its feet: "Slavs-Poles are Turkish gendarmes, the French are Turkish engineers, the English—Turkish diplomats, Cossacks-Nekrassovs are Turkish police, Germans—Turkish spies, Hungarians—Turkish brothers, Czechs—Turkish musicians." It is worthless to complain and expect help from the outside; from now on "we devote ourselves to God and rely on our own muscles." The task of the paper is for one last time to inform the world that "we are humans and we want to live in a humane manner," and then throw away the ink bottle, and take up arms. This is followed by the pertinent paragraph: "Today's public opinion is such that each single nation, even the Turks, have to be free and live among us as people and citizens. Our banner which will be raised on the Balkan Peninsula, will carry only three words: 'Freedom and to each his own.'"

It is clear that in the context of the letter, the slogan "Freedom and to each his own" refers, in fact, to collective rights, or to individual rights, but the individual rights of the nation as an individual writ large. The whole pathos is in line with the liberal and democratic nationalism of Mazzini, and there is actually an indirect reference to him in the appeal that "Young Bulgaria" should look to Italy for inspiration. It is an echo of the universalist character of European nationalism as it was preached in the first half of the 19th century, before it lost its innocence in 1848, and before it was domesticated and harnessed in the carriage of establishments and the extreme right. In other dispatches Levski again used the same phrase. Writing to Gancho Milev in May, 1871, he mentioned his ideal of "freedom and a pure republic." The future Bulgaria will not resemble today's empire but "all nations will live under pure and sacred laws… everything will be equal for the Turk, for the Jew etc. whoever they are…. We do not chase away the Turkish people, or their religion, but the king and his laws, in a word, the Turkish government, which rules barbarously not only over us, but over the Turks themselves." Bulgaria will not have a king but a "people's rule" and "to each his own." In another letter to a wealthy Bulgarian in October, 1871, he stated (in the vein of Mazzini) that "our century is the century of freedom and equality for all nations," and it is our task "to build the temple of genuine freedom and give everyone his own" (Undhiev, Kondarev 197: 31, 37).

There are numerous analogous examples which demonstrate that Levski has already been constructed as a ritualized hero, malleable enough to be attached to most any cause. He has been evoked as the ultimate authority and has been on everybody's banner: believer and atheist, republican and monarchist, conservative and radical, all want him as a symbol. Indeed, the saga of Levski's posthumous fate, spanning already close to a century and a half, not only parallels the evolution of modern Bulgaria, it is in many respects its embodiment. The tribulations of Levski the hero are an allegory of the evolution of Bulgarian nationalism. This is a relatively weak nationalism in global terms, and in European terms one of the weakest. Bulgarian nationalism has not produced a powerful pantheon: Levski, as already pointed out, is by far the only uncontested figure. Compared to neighboring nationalisms in the Balkans, present-day Bulgarian nationalism is undoubtedly the weakest but, paradoxically, Balkan nationalism itself is much weaker than most other manifestations of European nationalism: its bitter defensiveness and sometimes nervous savagery is a symptom of its deep insecurity, and in the final analysis, its weakness. The analysis of Levski's consecutive and simultaneous appropriations by different social platforms, political parties, secular and religious institutions, ideologies, professional groups, even individuals, offers a fascinating glimpse into the development of Bulgarian political life, as well as into elite struggles over who possesses history.

At another level, the Levski story engages organically in a variety of general theoretical questions. Most broadly, it offers insights into the general problem of history and memory, with all its concomitant aspects: the problem of "public" or "social" or "collective" or "people's" memory as treated by historians; the nature of national memory in comparison to other types of collective memory; the variability of memory over time and social space; alternative memories; memory's techniques like commemorations, that are the mechanisms of creating and transmitting memory; the changing nature of memory over time, on the one hand, and on the other, the changing salience of memory over time. It is intimately involved with the question of historical heroes and the nature of hero worship. Is there anything specific about national heroes, or heroes of the age of nationalism? How does the understanding of heroes change over time? What is the correlation between historical heroes and literary archetypes of heroes? Who or what creates heroes and why? Finally, it is closely linked to the historical discipline itself: the nature of producing historical knowledge, the genres of history writing, the place of historiography compared to other memory-producing projects.

1. What is a Hero and are Heroes Born?

It should be no coincidence that the great interest in heroes as well as the beginning of the study of heroic myth falls on the high age of nationalism. It was also the high age of revolutions, the advent of mass politics, of science, and the passionate struggle between a numbers of -isms: conservatism, liberalism, socialism, republicanism, romanticism, anarchism. No wonder the great debate in an era that saw the shaping of several social science disciplines was about the role of individuals in history, notably heroes, versus the blind operation of structural forces and social laws, and the cumulative role of social groups, notably classes. It is not insignificant that the six public lectures on heroes that Thomas Carlyle delivered in 1840, published in 1841 as the famous *On Heroes, Hero-Worship, and the Heroic in History,* had been preceded by six public lectures on the revolutions of Modern Europe. He objected strongly to and caricatured what he thought was a prevailing belief that the hero was the "creature of the Time," that "Time called him forth, that Time did everything, he nothing," that "the individual is supposed capable of nothing," and that "there must be organization, classification, machinery ... as if the capital of national morality could be increased by making a joint stock of it" (Carlyle 1993: xxxv). For all his enthusiasm and polemics against what he considered the dominant spirit of the day, Carlyle was no gadfly. To the contrary: his obsession with heroes was a common and widespread preoccupation, and he represented a high point in mainstream Victorian thought. There were few dissenters and critics of Carlyle, among them T. H. Huxley, Thomas Macaulay, and especially Herbert Spencer who ascribed the popularity of the Great Man approach to the satisfaction of "an instinct not very remotely allied to that of the village gossip" and to the preference of explanations "easy to comprehend," summarizing his opinion in the famous phrase, "Before [the great man] can remake his society, his society must remake him" (Segal 2000: 3). These critical voices, however lucid and powerful, were totally lost in the storm of admiration and emulation.

For Carlyle, heroes were the creative drive in history. True, he never advocated complete voluntarism. His heroes did not impose their will arrogantly on history. Instead, their heroism intuited the direction of history set by God, deciphered the course of society and acted accordingly. As far as the etiology of heroes was concerned, Carlyle was convinced that the heroic is something immanent to the hero: "A Hero is a Hero at all points; in the soul and thoughts of him first of all" (Carlyle 1993: 25). It is the kind of belief that not only was coherent with the dominant spirit of the age but had a continued influence over generations of scholars and the reading public at large. It is shared by many, if not most people today, certainly shared by practically all writers, scholars and public figures dealing with the particular heroic cult of Levski, from the earliest (Zakhari Stoianov or Ivan Vazov) to the latest (Nikolai Genchev or Zheliu Zhelev). We are still, after all, within the *longue durée* of nationalism (even though past its peak) with its fixation on the romantic, the genuine, and the organic, and within the (everlasting) *longue durée* of human society with its need for the ideal, the inspiring, and the heroic.[1]

Carlyle expressed his belief in heroism and hero-worship as an immanent human characteristic: "Had all traditions, arrangements, creeds, societies that men ever instituted, sunk away, this would remain. The certainty of Heroes being sent us; our faculty, our necessity, to reverence Heroes when sent; it shines like a pole-star through smoke-clouds, dust-clouds, and all manner of down-rushing and conflagration. (Carlyle 1993: 174). He distinguished between six types or classes of heroes, and although the format in which he offered his spirited analysis was more essayistic than systematic, his work is nevertheless referred to as "Carlyle's theory of the hero." The six types were: the hero as divinity, exemplified by Odin and other Scandinavian gods; the hero as prophet, represented by Mohammed; the hero as poet, epitomized by Dante and Shakespeare; the hero as priest, represented by Luther and Knox; the hero as man of letters, exemplifies by

---

[1] Because I would like to depict here the sources of influence and mental world of the scholars and writers dealing with Levski, I confine this survey to Carlyle as the most prominent ideologue of the "great man in history" theory and hero-worship. For a systematic review of the scholarship on heroism, especially the constructivist trend, see Part III, Chapter 6.

Rousseau, Johnson and Burns; finally, the hero as king, embodied in the figures of Cromwell and Napoleon.

This last type—the hero as king—was the most important of Great Men and summarized all the various figures of heroism. Writing in the high age of monarchism and conservative triumphalism before the great conflagrations of 1848, Carlyle was at pains to discredit "all rebellions, French revolutions, social explosions in ancient and modern times" and preached that "there is no act more moral between men than that of rule and obedience" (ibid.: 170–1). Carlyle could not overlook or neglect "modern revolutionism" but he tried to domesticate it:

> May we not say, moreover, while so many of our late Heroes have worked rather as revolutionary men, that nevertheless every Great Man, every genuine man, is by the nature of him a son of Order, not of Disorder? It is a tragic position for a true man to work in revolutions. He seems an anarchist; and indeed a painful element of anarchy does encumber him at every step—him to whose whole soul anarchy is hostile, hateful. His mission is Order, every man's is. He is here to make what was disorderly, chaotic, into a thing ruled, regular. He is the missionary of Order (ibid.: 175).

"Modern revolutionism" began with Luther, and while the French revolution might have overthrown the divine right of kings and outwardly denied hero worship, the slogan for liberty and equality was, in fact, the repudiation of sham heroes. Napoleon was, at bottom, a man of order who hated anarchy but was one of the exemplars gone astray: his system, "this Napoleonism was *unjust*, a falsehood; and could not last" (ibid.: 220–1). In the end, the greatest hero "is called *Rex*, Regulator, *Roi*: our own name is still better; King, *Könning*, which means Can-ning, Able-man" (ibid.: 169).

Carlyle made the explicit distinction between the divine and the human, but allowed for mythic heroes to be considered as divine figures. Contrary to the academic convention to distinguish between mere heroes and gods, "heroism can blur the line between the human and the divine—not by demoting gods to humans but by elevating humans to gods" (Segal 2000: 6). This is achieved by hero myths. First in 1863 but systematically in 1871, Edward Tylor suggested that most hero myths follow a uniform plot. In his posthumous 1876 publication "The Aryan Expulsion and Return Formula" Johann Georg von Hahn described a sixteen-incident pattern defining a universal hero applicable to all human societies, and thus launched modern hero pattern research. This was followed by the studies of Adolf Bauer in the 1880s, Heinrich Lessmann in 1906, Emmanuel Cosquin in 1908. Otto Rank, applying Freudian insights, proposed a similar pattern, even as he avoided identifying incidents, in his most influential work *The Myth of the Birth of the Hero* (1909). Next came research by Karl Schmeing (1911), Paul Franklin Baum (1916), Eugene McCartney (1925), and Alexander Krappe (1933). Special mention should be made to the groundbreaking work of Vladimir Propp, *Morphology of the Folktales* (1928), about the place of heroes in fairy-tales. In the English-speaking world, most influential became the twenty-two-incident pattern of Lord Raglan in his book *The Hero* (1936), even as he was blissfully (or arrogantly) ignorant of previous work in the field. After the Second World War, the most significant contribution was Joseph Campbell's *The Hero with a Thousand Faces* (1956), as well as Alan Dundes's study on Jesus in the 1970s, although the steam of hero pattern studies has somewhat subsided since (*In Quest of the Hero* 1990). What characterized most theorists before 1945 is that, as a rule, they were little concerned with the historicity of heroes. They did not explicitly deny that heroes may have been based on real historical figures, but they posited that the concrete aspects of their heroism weren't. The attention was on the analysis of the structural components of myth and ritual, and the psychoanalysis of the myth-maker and the reader's ego. Lord Raglan, in particular, was adamant that heroes had no claims to historicity and that "the traditional narrative has no basis either in history or in philosophical speculation, but is derived from the myth; and that the myth is narrative connected with a rite" (ibid.: 109).

    Lord Raglan distributed his twenty two incidents characterizing the hero pattern in three groups around the three principal rites of passage: birth, initiation, and death. In a tongue-in-cheek survey of the Levski case and juxtaposing it to this model, it will be clear that he corresponds significantly to the pattern. The first seven incidents pertain to the hero's birth: the mother is a royal virgin, the father is king, often related to the mother, the circumstances of the conception are unusual, the hero is reputed to be the son of a god, there is an attempt (usually by the father) to kill the son, but the son is spirited away and saved. Clearly these incidents around the birth do not correspond with the Levski case (as they mostly do with Jesus, whom Lord Raglan did not take into account), but Raglan himself does not posit royal parentage as a condition *sine qua non*: it is only "whenever there are royalties available" (ibid.: 148). The same element in Rank's scheme is "child of distinguished parents" (ibid.: 188) and Levski's hard-working and honest parents were deemed "distinguished" in the moral universe of 19th and 20th century Bulgaria, where the most "noble" background is of poor, but alert and industrious people. In the other two rites of passage —initiation and death—the Levski case conforms splendidly with many incidents. For instance, we can find analogues of the next four items of Raglan—the hero is reared by foster parents in a far country (8), we are told nothing of his childhood (9), on reaching manhood he returns and goes to his future kingdom (10), he is victorious over a king or a giant, or dragon or wild beast (11)—in Levski's difficult religious apprenticeship with his maternal uncle, running away from him, and then joining the Belgrade legion of Rakovski, where he enters his future kingdom—the revolution and serving the liberation of his people, and achieves such distinction that he is nicknamed "the Lion" (Levski).

Raglan's next incidents are the marriage of the hero to the princess, his becoming king, his reigns and prescribing laws (items 12 to 15). The absence of marriage is an obvious difference, also a glaring absence in Jesus, and Alan Dundes makes much of this by providing an interpretation of Mediterranean family relations in Oedipal terms, claiming it was this male-oriented worldview that produced the lack of marriage as a significant element of the Christian ideal. The Freudian framework is not particularly evocative, nor is there anything particularly Mediterranean in askesis. Moreover, if one were to take askesis as a spiritual ideal more seriously, then one could also trace the presence of a metaphoric marriage (to the national revolution in the case of Levski, to the Christian ideal in the case of Jesus) and the subsequent service to the idea, in the realm of the ideal kingdom. Raglan's last batch of incidents focusing on the end of the hero (items 16–19: losing favor with the gods or the subjects, being driven from the throne, a mysterious death, often at the top of a hill), can find fairly straightforward analogues in Levski's life: his frustration with the revolutionary work toward the end of his life, his contested leadership, his trial and execution at the gallows that were immediately seen as a symbol of Golgotha. The last items (20–22: the hero's children, if any, do not succeed him, his body is not buried but he has one or more holy sepulchers) are again relevant. While Levski had no children, the disarray in the revolutionary movement following his death can be interpreted in the vein of the mythical pattern.

Levski is too historical and recent a hero to make it possible to trace the hero pattern and be able to disentangle folklore from biographical fact. However, there are elements of his historical life that "fit" the pattern so well that this, in turn, immediately reflects back and "heroicizes" the life accordingly. But if this is the case, then the legitimate question is: are heroes born? Is there something ontologically heroic, immanent to a certain human type, or else, is the heroic an attributive constructed characteristic? Better still, is it at all productive to separate the ontology of heroes from their construction? Let us summarize the bare facts of the historical life of our hero.

Levski was born in 1837 in Karlovo in a craftsman's family. Upon the death of his father in 1851, he helped his mother in procuring for the family. He became a novice to his maternal uncle—an abbot—and in 1858 was ordained as monk with the name Ignatii. In March, 1862 he abruptly left for Belgrade where he joined the Bulgarian legion organized by Rakovski whose aim was to train young Bulgarians for future military clashes with the Ottomans. There Vasil Ivanov Kunchev acquired the nickname Levski (from *lev, liv,* "lion"). With the disbanding of the legion—having become an embarrassment to the Serbian government in its attempt to reach an arrangement with the Porte—Levski left Belgrade in the fall of 1862 and returned to Karlovo where he served as deacon. In 1864, at Easter, he broke with his religious career, and in his own words took the vows to serve "the fatherland...to serve it until death." In the next two years he taught in a couple of villages, and in early 1867 emigrated to Romania in order to join the *cheta* (military band) of Panaiot Khitov. As the standard-bearer, Levski criss-crossed Bulgaria, later joined the second Bulgarian legion in Belgrade, and after its disbanding returned to Bucharest. By that time, he was deeply disappointed with the existing tactics of revolutionary struggle, and believed that only a solid and meticulous preparation within the country could be effective. He managed to convince one of the émigré organizations to send him on a tour of Bulgaria, and in 1868 and 1869 traveled through the country twice, creating a network of revolutionary committees. On his return to Bucharest, he became a co-founder of the Bulgarian Revolutionary Central Committee (BRCC), and in the course of a year tried hard if not very successfully to persuade his fellow émigrés that the center of the revolution should be moved to Bulgaria proper, and the movement should be emancipated from dependence on foreign powers (Serbia and Russia in particular). In May, 1870, Levski returned to Bulgaria, and in the next two years he was a veritable legend with his enormous energy and singular ability to evade arrest. He organized hundreds of revolutionary committees, and formed a second, internal center in Lovech. He also worked on the statutes of the organization, the best source for his political views. In April–May, 1872, he participated in the first general assembly of the BRCC that adopted an official program and statute. Some of his ideas were adopted, but in general the documents reflected the ideas of the revolutionary emigration headed by Karavelov. The organization would have only one center, in Bucharest. The newly elected six-member Central Committee was chaired by Karavelov; Levski was elected member. He returned to Bulgaria in July, 1872 and began feverish preparations for the national revolution. In the fall of 1872, an abortive operation by his estranged and undisciplined deputy, not authorized by Levski, led to the arrest of a number of revolutionaries. Their careless disclosures jeopardized the organization, and on his way to Bucharest to discuss the aggravated situation, Levski was captured by the Ottoman police (December, 1872). Tried by an emergency court, he was condemned to death and hanged in Sofia on February 18, 1873.[2]

This brief biography should not be seen as a travesty on a national hero on whom tomes have been written that could easily fill a library: there have been some 4,300 works (biographies, academic monographs, scholarly and newspaper articles, belles-lettres, poems) published on Levski until 1986 (*Vasil Levski. Bio-bibliografiia* 1987). Contemporaries knew much less than that, and one could argue that until at least after the First World War, there was no ritualized celebratory attitude toward an abstract, essentially generic, national hero. Between 1872, the year before Levski's death, and the beginning of

---

[2] This is the correct date of Levski's execution but the widely known and officially commemorated date is February 19.

Bulgarian independence in 1878,[3] there were only 28 literary pieces (newspaper entries, polemical letters, poems) that mentioned Levski or were dedicated to him. With the exception of his mention in Khitov's memoirs, all the rest were triggered by his execution in 1873. Thirteen (maybe fourteen) belonged to Karavelov and were printed in his Bucharest edited revolutionary paper "Independence," eight were written by Botev in his papers "Banner" and "Freedom," one was Khitov's memoir, two unsigned ones lamented his death. These materials were all published by the Bulgarian émigré press in Bucharest and authored by Levski's closest associates. Only three pieces came out in the loyalist Bulgarian press in the Ottoman empire: one a short news piece about the trial and execution in *Dunav* and two in *Turtsiia*, accusing Levski of misleading the Bulgarian people, calling him "a lowly person and a *haidut*," and maintaining that he, as well as Karavelov, did not enjoy public support. It is therefore impossible to endorse the view of one of Levski's early researchers who, in his analysis of Levski's first important 1883 biography wrote that while Zakhari Stoianov had to struggle in order to popularize Botev's greatness and oeuvre, "this was almost redundant for Levski, since Levski had become immortal and the favorite among a great part of the enslaved Bulgarian nation already during his life" (Karakostov 1943: 5). Levski was indeed a popular figure but he was not yet singled out and, according to the testimony of the same researcher, by 1881 Botev was the one who held the imagination of the Bulgarian youth (ibid.: 6).

One of the best-known specialists on Levski, Nikolai Genchev, has been at great pains to insist that although a minority, the major figures of the national struggle did recognize Levski's prominence and superiority. He based his evidence first and foremost on Karavelov and Botev,

---

[3] Bulgaria, after partitioning by the Congress of Berlin in June/July, 1878, comprised only the lands north of the Balkan mountains and the region of Sofia, and had autonomous status with an elected Christian prince under the suzerainty of the Sultan. Eastern Rumelia south of the Balkans, was given a measure of self-rule, but under the direct rule of the Porte. Macedonia was unconditionally returned to the Ottoman Empire. In 1885 the Principality of Bulgaria and Eastern Rumelia declared their unification, and the country acquired full independence in 1908. For all practical purposes 1878 is considered the birthdate of Bulgaria's independence. In history books and everyday speech, it is referred to as "the Liberation" (*Osvobozhdenieto*).

and on some additional, but very brief and scattered, pronouncements by other revolutionaries (Genchev 1987: 139–41). The relationship between Karavelov and Levski was not always smooth. There were basic differences on how they understood the strategic and tactical aspects of the revolution, especially the issue of the primacy of the internal organization over the one in emigration, and dependency on foreign support. Levski insisted on moving the center of the revolt to Bulgaria and was highly critical of the contemplative position of the émigrés and Karavelov in person. In February, 1871, Karavelov published a brief report of Levski, and added that it was written by "an honest, patriotic and active individual, ... whom we wholly trust." In the same issue of the paper, he addressed himself to Levski (a way of communication that was adopted by the revolutionaries), stating: "We wish you luck, but at the same time would advise you to speak little and work a lot. It is difficult to change from a horse to a donkey." These are the only two written mentions of Levski coming from under Karavelov's pen during the Apostle's lifetime. The patronizing tone of the latter is unmistakable, and it seems that doubts over Levski's ethos and behavior were shared at some, albeit brief, moments, by Karavelov (ibid.: 142–3). Genchev rather summarily asserts that in the minds of his contemporaries the living Levski was present as a synthetic image, "the premier Bulgarian and main figure of the national revolution" (ibid.: 144). This is a forced conclusion, and Genchev was closer to the truth when he wrote that "Levski had not been the commonly accepted leader of the liberation movement. His rights as the main leader were questioned by solid journalists, by scholars and poets, and by leaders of the *cheti*. In the eyes of the cabinet revolutionaries in Bucharest he passed for someone simple and uneducated. Some internal revolutionaries too, dared compare themselves to him, questioning his extraordinary powers" (ibid.: 139).

It was Levski's execution that dramatically changed Karavelov's attitude. As chairman of the organization, he felt responsible for the blow. Strangely, he kept silent for several months and only on August 11, 1873 published an obituary, describing the Apostle's last days. It is a dramatic and passionate piece but thoroughly unreliable. In a kind of testimonial prose, Karavelov describes how Levski was tortured in his cell, all his teeth pulled out, his flesh torn piece by piece with tongs, and his body pierced by the bare knives of the surrounding soldiers. It ends with his execution: "When the Turkish legislator saw that nothing would come out of the mouth of this Bulgarian saint, it ordered that he be hanged. Levski was hanged half-dead. May his memory live forever" (ibid.: 147). Even before that—in June, 1873—Karavelov wrote authoritatively that Levski had been betrayed by Pop Krîstiu, and a year later reiterated his accusation by calling him Judas, monster and ostracized by popular consciousness. That Levski's death became a crucial turning point for Karavelov has been well documented. By 1874 Karavelov had despaired over the revolutionary alternative and began preaching the evolutionary road, through the dissemination of science and education.

Botev, on the other hand, was even further radicalized after Levski's end, and perished, weapon in hand, during the abortive April Uprising of 1876. He had shared an abode with Levski and in an early letter wrote that his character was unparalleled, that he would be joyful and singing even during the greatest cold and starkest hunger. Botev lamented his loss in terms comparable to Karavelov's and was equally devastating of Pop Krîstiu's alleged betrayal. He extolled Levski's significance, writing that his and his collaborators' activities make them "rare apostles of the revolution not only for our nation but also for the more advanced ones" (ibid.: 150–1). Botev also published his famous wall calendar, in which Levski figures as a martyr. Additionally, he wrote his famous poem dedicated to Levski's death, in which the Christ-like image is unmistakable:

> O mother mine, deal land of my birth,
> Why do you cry so bitterly, dismally?
> You, dread raven, accursed bird,
> Over whose grave do you croak so grimly?
> .....
> Weep! For there by the city of Sofia
> Stands a black gallows-tree verily, verily,
> There you finest son, Bulgaria,
> Hangs from the gallows-tree heavily, heavily.
>
> Horribly, grimly the raven croaks.
> Wolves are out howling, the dogs run wild.
> Old folk hotly their God invoke
> To the sobbing of women, the screams of a child.

While Genchev was right to point out that Karavelov and Botev shaped the public discourse on Levski as it developed in subsequent decades (the earliest evaluation as martyr of freedom, his political canonization, as well as some factually debatable tropes, like the treason and its agent, the trial, the execution), it is impossible not to speculate about what would have happened had the revolutionary vision and verdict not become the Whig interpretation of history after 1878. This does not mean denying the heroism of a figure like Levski but only qualifying that it is possible merely within a specific intellectual framework: the teleology of the nation (and the nation-state). Just for illustration, one can briefly articulate an alternative (or counterfactual) version. That Bulgaria became an independent nation-state in the latter half of the 19th century was an intended but not predetermined outcome. With hindsight, taking into account the end of both the Ottoman and Habsburg Empires after the First World War, the British and other colonial empires after the Second World War, as well as the Soviet Union (increasingly interpreted as an empire) in the 1990s, one might seal the fate of empires in the age of nationalism, and speak of the law of imperial entropy. But I doubt that the emergence of independent nation states can be formulated as a law. As Ernest Gellner (1983: 43) has remarked, "the number of potential nationalisms which failed to bark is far, far larger than those which did, though *they* have captured all the attention." Greece became a nation-state; so did Serbia, Bulgaria, Romania, and Albania. But Kurdistan never did. And until 1992 nobody was thinking seriously of Bosnia as an independent state, while now we already have a substantial academic output arguing its historical roots and its glorious Hegelian march to self-achievement, understood as state-achievement. This is true, in some cases to a lesser degree, about Slovenia, Slovakia, Moldova and other of the newly emerged independent states on Europe's map.

Had Bulgarians had the fate of Kurds, for example, and given that they would also have an intelligentsia dedicated to the national cause, Levski probably would have made it as a hero in an alternative history, or would have received honorable mention in some outside account by an author interested in exotic identities. If mentioned at all in an imperial account dealing with botched secessionist movements, he most likely would have been depicted either as a terrorist or even less glorious, as a burglar, the way he was sentenced, and executed by the Ottomans in Sofia in 1873, and then buried in a mass grave in the cemetery for criminals. Even allowing that in the case of Bulgaria, given the general parameters of great power struggle and balance in Europe at the time, its emergence as an independent entity was inevitable, this is not the case with the timing. The country could have emerged after the First World War, with the final collapse of the Ottomans, like Albania or Macedonia, and judging from small power appetites and plans in the 1860s, there could have even been attempts at partitioning it among the earlier comers on the Balkan scene. If that was the case, Levski most certainly would have made it into the pantheon of heroes any nation-state worth mentioning bothers to create, but it is uncertain he would have presided over them.

Even dedicated nationalists of the variety called patriots (moderate nationalists, without the excesses of chauvinism) would make allowance for such an approach. What would be unthinkable to them, is the meddling with the ontology of the hero. "The clue for understanding Levski's personality and especially his constant presence in Bulgarian life after his death, is to be found first and foremost in the meaningful substance of his work, in the reality and lofty significance of the very struggle for national liberation, in the fact that the struggle of Levski and his associates was not a pursuit of utopian ideas, not running after empty chimeras" (Zhelev 1995: 83). It is the lack of historical distance, sometimes the lack of sensitivity or strong values that, in this reading, prevents the timely recognition of heroes, but the underlying assumption is that heroes exist objectively, completely independently from whether they are recognized or not, and it is the great merit of poets, historians, and the like, to discover them and shed the light of recognition onto them, much like objective nations were discovered and released from the realm of forgetfulness.

2. The "Making" of Vasil Levski

The first post-Liberation decade—the 1880s—saw the publication of the first biography of Levski by Zakhari Stoianov (1883) that immediately engaged contemporaries in a heated debate about the assessment of Levski's role. Now that the outcome of the Russo–Turkish war had vindicated the effort of the revolutionaries, there were no doubts about the general assessment of Levski, similar to the ones voiced in the pre-1878 period by individuals or groups suspicious of revolutionary radicalism. There was also no question about recognizing his important presence in the revolutionary movement; the debate was around his place relative to the contribution of the other revolutionaries, and also to the different social groups participating in the national movement, particularly pitching against each other the movements of the so-called "old" and "young" which, after 1878, had coalesced around the two opposing party formations of Conservatives and Liberals.

The image of Levski that Stoianov offered to the public elevated him to the peak of the revolutionary achievement and focused on the link between his human ordinariness and simplicity, and the extraordinary and sophisticated achievement of his activity: "the modest deacon, the psalm-singer, the teacher from Voiniagovo who had nothing but his upright character, determination and passionate patriotism, what a strong and famous hero he became" (Stoianov 1883: 59). Clear autobiographical overtones could be seen in this portrayal, especially the identification with Levski of someone without any formal education, who had made it from a humble shepherd to speaker of parliament. A strong critique of Stoianov's biography was voiced by S. S. Bobchev who objected that the subscribers had not paid him in order "to raise Levski on stilts and put him way above all other revolutionaries" (Genchev 1987: 163). He accused Stoianov of inaccuracies and partisanship, particularly misrepresenting the contribution of the circle around the brothers Georgievi. He maintained that committees had existed even before Levski, and that Stoianov was exaggerating his contribution. Technically, Bobchev was right to question Stoianov's factology, but in the end the clash was about the general assessment of the conservative and liberal wing in Bulgarian political life. Implicitly, the debate was about intellectual and political legitimacy, and about social control and cultural hegemony. Even after Levski emerged as the unchallenged revolutionary patriarch, these were still the basic disputed questions. Only the discourse had shifted from the evaluation of Levski's relative place to who had ownership over him in his absolute presiding position.

During this entire period, one can observe the gradual growth of a commemorative industry around Levski: the early and slow initiative to build a monument in Sofia (inaugurated in 1895), the first modest provincial celebrations, the 25th anniversary of his execution in 1898 and the publication of a small volume, the celebrations in his birth town of the 30th anniversary and the inauguration of a monument in Karlovo in 1905 (Plate 1). Beginning with the 50th anniversary of his death, and especially with the solemn and scrupulously organized 100th anniversary of his birth in 1937, an elaborate and systematic commemorative ritual came into place. It had its ebbs and flows, but was never suspended. Indeed, there was a geometrical progression in the size of the literary output on Levski: until the 100th anniversary of his birth, some 740 titles had come out; until the end of the Second World War, the number had doubled; the next 40 years had added another 3,000 titles. This does not take into account the avalanche of publications in the late 1980s and during the 1990s. So, when Zhelev sardonically asked whether any serious Bulgarian could ever harbor the thought that a mausoleum or a memorial for Levski or for Botev would add anything to their achievement or to the charisma of their personalities, he had forgotten that there had been an industry which had been doing precisely this for over a century. In fact, the president himself asked his question at a speech delivered at the monument of Levski in Sofia on the 120th anniversary of his execution.

Genchev outlines three layers in the memory literature dedicated to Levski. One comprises the memoirs of the first generation of contemporaries at the end of the 19th and the beginning of the 20th century, such as collaborators who knew him personally, revolutionaries who had no personal contact with him, and his relatives. The second is the material gathered by Dimitîr Strashimirov under the auspices of the "National Committee Vasil Levski" immediately after the end of the First World War. The third is material "completely legendary, assembled around 1937, when the 100th anniversary of Levski's birth was celebrated and the press was filled with all kinds of fables, which have no value as historical evidence" (Genchev 1987: 155). This periodization is persuasive, although the differentiation between the first and second period is artificial, the only criterion being intentionality: in the first case the memoirs were written and published without any outside impetus, in the second case, triggered on the urging of researchers. More problematic is Genchev's evaluation of the evidence emanating from the separate periods. One can actually posit that any material stemming from the period after 1878, and even after Levski's death in 1873, has about itself something of the legendary, insofar as it is marked by a retrospective glance.

Still, there is a certain virtue in separating the material before 1937, insofar as most of it can be defined as having been based on lived experience. I very pointedly don't privilege categories such as immediate or authentic knowledge or experience, although Walter Benjamin (1969: 100) actually implied the element of immediacy in his definition of storytelling where the bodily presence of the story-teller and the story-listener supply the parameters of the lived experience: "A man listening to a story is in the company of the story-teller." Every experience is mediated, except perhaps the narrow philosophical definition of experience as a sensuous empirical reflection of the external world, the "immediate sentient observation, which is generally prior to any reflection on its meaning" (Jay 1998: 44). Yet one should not be crucified over "the sterile choice between naïve experiential immediacy and the no less naïve discursive mediation of that experience" (ibid.: 78). I do not go here into the distinction between *Erlebnis* and *Erfahrung*, the two German notions for experience that denote, on the one hand, the immediate pre-reflexive response to external and internal stimuli and, on the other hand, the knowledge accumulated in the process of interaction between self and the world. More useful might be the distinction made by Edward Bruner (1986: 6) between life as lived or reality (reality being what is really out there), life as experienced or experience (how that reality presents itself to consciousness), and life as told or expressions (how individual experience is framed and articulated). Although it is difficult to define in any coherent quantitative or qualitative terms the distinction between experience resulting from how reality presents itself to consciousness, and experience resulting from the expression of someone else's experience of reality, I still would endow lived experience with some unique qualities, though this does not guarantee that the sources coming out of this experience are better or necessarily more reliable.

The first full-fledged literary portrait of Levski was created by Ivan Vazov, the unchallenged patriarch of modern Bulgarian literature. It was his way of articulating ideas and emotions about Levski that modeled the way subsequent generations have been thinking about this hero. In 1881 Vazov wrote his enormously popular epic poem "Levski," but Levski had been part of his poetic pantheon from 1876 and on to 1905. Without ever having met him in person, he introduced Levski's physical appearance in his 1883 novel, *Nemili nedragi* (*Outcasts*), and most Bulgarians know this opening by heart: "Levksi was of average height, thin and slender; eyes grey, almost blue; moustache reddish, hair blond, face white, round and haggard form incessant thought and vigil, but animated by a constant and natural mirth! Strange! This young man who was preaching the dangerous thought of freedom and death, who subjected himself daily to dangers, this son of the night, of the desert, of adventures, possessed a cheerful nature" (Vazov 1996: 82). It is an extremely effective as well as efficient introduction, following on Vazov's regret that Levski's only existing photograph could not convey the loftiness of his character: "Art had been unable to represent his striking face." By calling the photograph "art" and positing its weakness when faced with the power of reality, and by placing himself implicitly outside the realm of art, Vazov secured a claim for documentary authenticity to his own word. Indeed, the physical portrait of Levski follows the criteria with which, in the 19th century, Ottoman tax records would describe an individual—height, eyes, moustache and hair—a convention still very familiar to the first post-Ottoman generation that was reading him (Plates 2–5).

Vazov focused on Levski's character, particularly the two qualities that made him tower over all other revolutionaries: persistence and tenacity. Levski's spirit was "the manifestation of a force emerging from centuries of suffering, from an ocean of humiliation." He crisscrossed Bulgaria in the course of seven years, "visited about a hundred villages and towns, founded committees, taught, encouraged, threatened the wealthy ones, angered the Turks, steady to the point of impossibility, persistent to the point of madness." This is how Vazov recapitulated Levski's essence:

> Such was the individual known under the names of the Deacon, Vasil Levski, the Apostle, whom fate had sent to lead a host of preachers and martyrs of freedom, in order to move the masses, to generate events, to engender the future!... A small Hus, who could not become a giant, since he lacked the space in which to unfold, and who would have been crucified in Judea, and burnt at the stake in the Middle Ages, just as he was hanged in the nineteenth century...Three tortures, three symbols: the crucifixion, Torquemada's fire, the gallows—three deaths, invented throughout the centuries to punish the dishonorable and the immortal. (ibid.: 84–85).

Vazov established Levski in the genealogy of archetypal heroism and martyrdom, something achieved in almost the same turn of phrase, but in rhyme, in the poem "Levski." In fact, the characterizations that Vazov used, even the exact turn of phrase have been so deeply internalized that they were verbatim reproduced to me in oral interviews with Bulgarians whom I asked why they considered Levski their hero. One can approach *Nemili-nedragi* as the prose version of Vazov's powerful *Epic for the Forgotten*. The two works are contemporaries, and Vazov must have worked on them simultaneously, although technically the poem "Levski" preceded the novel. *Nemili-nedragi* was published in Plovdiv in 1883, and the twelve poems of the *Epic* Vazov wrote in two spurts, the first five poems in three days in 1881, the remaining seven in 1884. But these were not two identical works in accompanying genres. The *Epic* dealt with the great historical personalities, whose glory encompasses both their own heroic deed, as well as the unnamed deeds of their collaborators. The first, Vazov perceived as already perched on their monuments' pedestals, and depicted them accordingly in verse and an intonation replete with pathos. The latter, most of whose names have been lost, continue their historical life only through the medium of their unnamed achievement, and Vazov celebrated them in a good-humored, nostalgic and close to autobiographical prose. Levski was present briefly but emblematically in *Nemili-nedragi*, but his cameo appearance was a veritable montage, different in tone and execution from the rest of the text and identical to that of the poem.

Since 1880 Vazov had moved to Plovdiv, the capital of Eastern Rumelia, where he co-edited the newspaper "People's Voice." He incessantly satirized the new society whose ideal was the "practical man." His "forgotten" ought to be understood not literally: numerous monuments in their honor were being raised but the post-Liberation society was not moved by their lofty ideals of self-sacrifice and heroic deeds. It had turned entirely to a new idol: the golden calf. Vazov deplored the ignorance of Bulgarians of their history and geography. A Bulgarian would not visit Sliven, and will know better "the whereabouts of New Orleans in North America or of Algiers, than the unfortunate birthplace of Khadzhi Dimitîr...But what can one expect of a nation which is proverbially apathetic and ignoring itself" (Vazov 1950, vol. XXI: 68–69). This was an open challenge to the syndrome of underdeveloped nationalism, and Vazov took it upon himself to redress the aberration.

In creating what has been characterized since as the Bulgarian poetical iconostasis without peer, as the most powerful instrument of national education, Vazov had three immediate inspirations. Two of them challenge the paradigm of a hermetically sealed, organic national culture, but are an apt illustration of the powerful and creative absorptive and adaptive genius of this national culture in the making. In his conversations with Ivan Shishmanov, the Eckermann to Vazov's Goethe, and a leading intellectual figure, Vazov reminisced on the conception of his epic cycle. He had read in a Russian book about the Finno-Swedish poet Runeberg and his cycle of odes to Swedish patriots, and this constituted a powerful motivation. There is no indication that Vazov was familiar with Runeberg's poetry itself. He was however, intimately familiar with and deeply influenced by Hugo's *La légende des siècles*: "The pathos and form of *Epic of the Forgotten* I owe to Victor Hugo. I had just read his *La légende des siècles* and I was charmed by the élan, the broad range of the French poet" (Shishmanov 1976: 232–3). At the same time, Vazov's statement was misleading. He had received *La légende des siècles* as a gift from a friend after he had already written the first five poems of his cycle, including the one on Levski. Therefore the readings characterizing his own *Epic* as a reminiscent echo, textual dependence, or synthesis of a foreign genius with native talent, are forced and naïve. The phenomenon has to be approached through the concept of intertextual relations, and "the existence of an identical language that was 'caught' in the texts of

Hugo and Vazov by means of different redactions of its development." (Lipcheva-Prandzheva 2001: 20–1).

The most immediate impetus came, however, from an article by Zakhari Stoianov, the great memoirist of the revolutionary struggles, a revolutionary and active political figure in the new Bulgaria, and the first biographer of Levski. His article, published in April, 1881 in the newspaper *Rabotnik* in Eastern Rumelia, dealt with revolutionaries who had ended their life with suicide. It was a defiant celebration of the proud romantic suicide against conventional Christian attitudes. Stoianov wrongly included Benkovski in this list while himself describing his murder in his masterpiece "Notes on the Bulgarian insurrections" whose first volume came out in 1884. Likewise, the alleged attempt of Levski to kill himself in prison during the trial, has remained unproven, most likely the abode of legend. Vazov was stimulated simply by the list of names published by Stoianov; the motif of suicide was not at all the moving force. In the case of Levski, he completely disregarded it, maybe because the hanging of Levski had become the most powerful image already with Botev's, and because it allowed him to elaborate on his powerful metaphor of the gallows as the Cross.

> In splendor and shame, like the crucifix, hallowed!
> The sight of your victims has made our hearts ache,
> We've seen from your bar bodies swing and shake
> And southerly winds with the dead limbs playing,
> And jubilant tyrants their venom displaying.
> O glorious scaffold! You shine with the light
> Of heroes who died here! Most holy sight!
> A terrible token, a sign of that freedom
> For which in your shadow folk die and lie bleeding,
> The lion, the hero: all honor is due
> To those who to this day still die upon you.
> For in that dark age we refer to as "bondage"
> The rogue and the spy and the man with no honor
> Would peacefully die in their bed, their conscience—sold,
> But death on your bar, holy scaffold, was always
> No mark of disgrace—but on earth fresh glory,
> A summit from which a brave heart could survey
> Toward immortality the straightest way!

The absence of Botev from the gallery of the "Bulgarian poetical iconostasis" is glaring. True, Vazov had immortalized him (without mentioning his name) in the poem "Radetski," written in 1876, but the immense popularity of the poem was due mostly to its arrangement as a popular march, arguably the best-known melody and song among Bulgarians. The argument about a more limited gallery, based only on Stoianov's list is weak, because the suicide motif is present neither in Rakovski's, nor in Paisii's, nor Benkovski's lives. If anything, Botev's gesture could be and has been interpreted as suicidal and his popularity and stature as martyr was unequalled and comparable only to that of Levski. Most likely, given that Botev was also widely accepted as an unrivalled poetical genius, Vazov prudently kept silent on his one brilliant literary competitor, even though Botev's oeuvre produced in his short tumultuous 28-year-old life, was incomparably smaller. It is symptomatic that until 1891—twenty years after he had met Botev for the first time—Vazov never said a word about Botev's poetry, and the first time he pronounced himself on his dead rival was in a long critical essay that he published anonymously. Vazov allows for Botev's originality and poetic genius but at the same time finds that not a single one of his poems reaches beyond good quality and is always beneath perfection. The gist of his ire was in the elevated status Botev had reached in the first decade after 1878 that rivaled Vazov's aspirations to be the sole prince of poetry: "Botev has been allotted the honor of enjoying a kind of unconditional cult that is based more on a patriotically exalted emotion rather than on a sober and mature evaluation of his merits… In its extremes, this idolatry reaches comic overtones… This emotion, brought to its extreme, is turning into a national vice" (Dafinov 2006: 123). To counter this, Vazov concentrated on creating an "unconditional cult" around Levski who obviously was no threat to him in the realm of words.

While the *Epic of the Forgotten* became an instant classic, and Vazov enjoyed the patriarchal seat in Bulgarian literature already during his lifetime, his work did not remain unchallenged during his day. This was especially true by the turn of the century when the literary circle *Misîl* ("Thought") came forward with a program not only challenging but squarely denouncing and denying the social and aesthetic basis of the older generation presided by Vazov. Dr. Krîstev, a German-trained philosopher and editor of the journal *Misîl*, one of the first pro-

Figure 12. Ivan Vazov, 1950-1921.

fessional literary critics, accused Vazov of only superficially describing Levski, never reaching a profound psychological portrait, of overstated and empty rhetoric, of creating an inflated and pathetic image, far removed from the genuinely revolutionary, unique and original figure of Levski. Vazov readily admitted to the excess of pathos: "I emulate the solemn, elevated, philosophical tone of [Hugo's] odes," and about the poem "Levski": "It is entirely Hugoan—his majestic phraseology, the grave, exalted tone of his odes," particularly his "Evirandus," to which "Levski" bore literal resemblance (Shismanov 1976: 232–3).

There was more to the anti-Vazov hostility that burgeoned in the decade before the Great War, than mere rejection of style. A new generation of intellectuals had emerged overthrowing what it thought of as the localism, provincialism, traditionalism, national romanticism and unimaginative social realism of the old generation of whom Vazov was the most illustrious representative. It came with a new modernist philosophy and aesthetics, opposing a Nietzschean individualism to the strong collectivism of the old guard, preaching psychologism and pure, non-social art, that, in the Bulgarian case, never quite reached anti-social overtones. Thus, in the last two decades of his life (he died in 1921), Vazov's was not an undisputed voice. He was challenged by an influential group whose much shorter life-span coincided with his own (of the four major figures of *Misîl*, Pencho Slaveikov died in 1912, Peiu Iavorov in 1914, Petko Todorov in 1916, and Dr. Krîstev in 1919).

What is significant about the challenge to Vazov's rendering of Levski by the Bulgarian avant-garde literati is that it did not question his elevation of Levski to the peak of the Bulgarian pantheon. For Dr. Krîstev, Levski remained the most noble son of Bulgaria and he made a special effort to supply an alternative reading that would nevertheless confirm his stature. This reading was imbued by the fashionable psychologism of the times. Neither Stoianov's self-educated simplicity, nor Vazov's false phraseology and empty rhetoric could solve "the enigma" of Levski. Only an approach inspired by insights into the character and temperament of the individual could shed light on his essence. Levski was characterized by "a quiet temperament, a maidenly mildness, and humility," and this meekness of the heart was linked uniquely with an exemplary consistency, immense determination and even mercilessness. Therefore, Krîstev concluded, "great is not the one, on whom nature has abundantly heaped some quality, but the one, whom it has endowed with contradictory powers and disposition, and who exercises enormous will to bring them in harmony." The greatest clue to Levski's character lay in the deed of unfrocking and embracing the revolutionary path. All of this made "even the most revolutionary *words* of Botev pale before Levski's revolutionary deed" and in a self-critical but rather murky gesture Krîstev pronounced Levski as the sublimated practitioner whose "deed cannot preserve the transcendental purity which we, the literati, rave for."He went so far as to pronounce himself on Botev, who likewise had perished in the uprising, that "there is practically no merit in a deed, which is effectuated by some such passionate revolutionary temperament, an individual emancipated from any respect toward the sacred, such as Botev." When, however, the same deed results from "a modest, quiet nature, which lives in accord with the morality of trite mediocrity, from a personality which is stimulated neither by mighty passions, nor by an enlightened philosophical mind, we don't know how to name it but as an act of genius." (Krîstev 1898: 110–4). The only reason so much space is devoted to these arbitrary pronouncements, unsupported by the record and rather pompous and pretentious, if understandable in the framework of the intellectual *Zeitgeist* of the time, is that in the 1980s and especially after 1989, there was a temporary return to this kind of rhetoric and approach, if not in mainstream historiography, then certainly in popularizing essays and conversations. This was to be explained only partly by a reactive attachment to psychological explanations against the officially imposed, most often reductive, communist sociological analysis. Mostly, it was the unreflective and uncritical rehabilitation of anything produced before the Second World War, especially by the "ivory tower" intellectuals of the turn of the century, with whom intellectuals a century later liked to identify.

Vazov's authority was questioned not only on philosophical and stylistic grounds. The open anti-clerical and even anti-religious pathos of the poem "Levski" attracted its own critics. It seems that it was precisely Vazov's interpretation, and the subsequent emphasis on Levski's break with his holy orders that contributed to the complicated and ambiguous attitude of the church toward the hero. Vazov himself appears to have harbored profound religious doubts, if not an openly stated position as a non-believer, but projecting this onto Levski seems to have been forcing the evidence. Despite these challenges, there is no question that the poem "Levski," alongside "Paisii" and above all "Shipka" from the *Epic of the Forgotten* had become the most popular Bulgarian poems. They were recited at patriotic gatherings, commemorations, school meetings. The poem "Levski," as well as Vazov's short stories about the hero, figured as a central item in all commemorative volumes published on the occasion of Levski's anniversaries. Vazov's literary image of Levski became the essence of the historical portrait that was disseminated through the school system. In a sense, Vazov became the Pygmalion to the mythical Levski: his words brought the myth to life.

It took some time before Levski was turned into a legend. A look at the first history textbooks after the creation of the independent state can best illustrate the case. Textbooks have lately become a favorite subject and source for historians. They provide the documentary evidence not only for the content of national ideas inculcated in the population but are the best illustration of the mechanism employed to produce a relatively homogeneous population sharing a common body of knowledge and values. This essentially instrumentalist approach is not necessarily a great methodological insight of historians in the past decades. It was well understood and articulated by contemporaries in the 19th century. Practically all history textbooks would be prefaced with reflections on the need to know the history of the nation. This need was deemed natural because the nation was believed to be an organic whole, and while "we all, peasants or townsmen, artists or merchants, educated or ignorant, laymen or clergymen, are different in our way of life, we share the same fatherland, speak the same language and are one great family, called the Bulgarian nation" (Manchov 1880: i).

In the two decades before 1878, a remarkable network of modern schools was built up in Bulgaria: altogether, over 2,000 elementary and high schools were opened. The number of schools and students rose drastically after 1878, and with it the need for more and updated textbooks. This became especially urgent after 1876 with the publication of Konstantin Jireček's *Geschichte der Bulgaren*, considered the first comprehensive scholarly treatment of Bulgarian history. The first textbooks in the Bulgarian Principality were not regulated: there was no provision in the first law for public education from 1885. Writers and publishers had no limitations, and teachers were free to choose from the variety of textbooks offered. This went on until 1897, when a "Statute for Textbooks" was adopted by the Ministry for National Education. Until the late 1890s, therefore, textbooks were a most reliable barometer of the ideas and knowledge shared widely by the educated Bulgarian elite, and deemed appropriate for pedagogical and nation building purposes.

The most popular and widely used of the newly published history textbooks were authored by Dragan Manchov and Stefan Bobchev. Manchov was the most significant Bulgarian publisher alongside Khristo Danov, and the author of at least two history textbooks already in the early 1870s. His updated history textbooks passed through numerous editions after 1878. The third edition of his brief history, compiled for elementary schools, came out in 1880, and covered the events of the 19th century in barely three pages. There was no mention of Levski or of any revolutionary initiative, organization or individual. On the other hand, the full text for the public schools devoted half a page to Levski. He was described as the organizer of a network of secret committees comprising thousands of members. His activity was known to the Turks but he was difficult to capture because of his unusual agility. Finally, as a result of unintended negligence on the part of a friend, he was caught by the Turks, tortured, and hanged in Sofia. While Manchov's prose was controlled and sparse in praise (he mentioned simply that Levski struggled courageously before he was caught, and did not betray his friends), Levski's revolutionary activities were the only ones mentioned between a survey of the school system and the outbreak of the Eastern crisis in 1875.

Bobchev, the future influential legal historian, began publishing his history textbooks in the early 1880s. By the mid-1990s, his high school history had become the most prestigious text in the school system. The first edition of his *History of the Bulgarian People* (1881) had the subtitle *After Dr. K. Jireček,* explicitly indicated that this was a school adaptation. In this 300-page work, Bobchev devoted a 10-page chapter to political-revolutionary movements and literature. Having described the activities of Rakovski, Khitov, Khadzhi Dimitîr and Stefan Karadzha, and especially Karavelov as the central figure of revolutionary organization and propaganda, Bobchev devoted slightly under a page to Levski. He published also two brief versions of his history: one for elementary, another for high schools. In the latter, Levski was introduced as the most prominent of Karavelov's assistants. The text for the elementary schools stressed the tortures to which Levski had been subjected after his arrest and described him for the first time as martyr, but he still was not the exclusive figure that he had become a century later. Still the inclusion of the element of inhuman tortures and martyrdom was a first step in the direction of mythologizing the figure. In fact, as is well attested and historians would agree, Levski was handled respectfully by the Ottoman court, and was not subjected to any physical abuse. The legend of the tortures during the trial was spread by Karavelov, in a brief message in *Nezavisimost* (III, no. 47, 11 August 1873), which one can read also the first formulation of Levski as a "Bulgarian saint." This assessment of Levski continued also after the regulation of school textbooks in 1987. Thus, the 1899 edition of Bobchev's *History* put its emphasis again on Rakovski and especially Karavelov as his heir in the revolutionary struggle. Levski was praised as courageous, intelligent and resolute, the most important figure in the revolutionary circle of Karavelov.

Post-liberation textbooks offered patriotic accounts with a very clear idea of the educational effects of historical knowledge. The bulk of these surveys was devoted to the medieval period: the two Bulgarian empires from the 7th to the 14th centuries. The aim was to disseminate in a popular form the knowledge assembled by Jireček. His history itself emphasized the medieval period (over two thirds of the text), describing the Ottoman centuries as the Dark Ages. Jireček had conceived of the history in the early 1870s; his narrative spanned the period from antiquity to 1875 but the account ended with the results of the struggle for church autonomy in 1870. The history's last three chapters covered the beginnings of the new educational movement, the church struggle, and a brief survey of modern Bulgarian literature. It was Jireček's contribution to popularize the achievements of Bulgaria's cultural figures. There was no mention, however, of the existing political attempts at emancipation, and of any revolutionary leader, with the one-page exceptions on Rakovski's legion and the *chetas* of Panaiot Khitov and Philip Totiu. There was, consequently, nothing on Levski in the first edition. Although Jireček was intimately familiar with Levski's case and post-independence Bulgarian development (between 1879 and 1884 he resided in Bulgaria holding high administrative positions, among them minister of education), Levski did not make it to the main text of the later manuscript addenda, either. Characteristically, Jireček ended his penultimate chapter with the following statement: "The Bulgarians, a peaceful and industrious folk, maybe yield to the Serbs, Greeks, Albanians and Romanians in militancy and national pride; in industry and agriculture, however, they are far ahead of their neighbors… What these wonderful lands, lavishly endowed by nature and populated with an industrious people, need most, however, is a more humane and reasonable government… The outbreak of the Hercegovinian insurrection (1875) gave an impetus for a new state of affairs. The next year Bulgaria was befallen with the awful, well-known catastrophe, whose description falls out of the framework of this survey" (Jireček 1876: 561–2).

This left the authors of the post-Liberation textbooks to write up their own versions of the political and revolutionary struggle. In terms of format, the textbooks were almost wholly built around the biographical principle. Students were exposed to the biographies of Bulgarian khans and tsars as well as the great religious and cultural figures. This reflected not merely contemporary historiography but first and foremost the romantic endeavor to present the historical message around strong individuals, the builders of history. It is all the more symptomatic that while Levski definitely figured among the major revolutionary figures, he was described in a matter-of-fact fashion, devoid of the immoderate superlatives of a later period. Textbooks reflected the ideas circulating among the educated elites who were making a conscious effort to forge a nation out of a comparatively passive population. They were using all possible methods to instill pride in the heroic history of their fatherland, and the respectful rendering of Levski's activities

Figure 13. Official program for the inauguration of Levski's monument in Sofia, 22 October 1895.
Source: *Sofiiski Gradski Okrŭzhen Arkhiv*, Fond 1k, op. 3, a.e. 192.

without the elements of later glorification has to be taken to reflect the dominant views harbored about him in this period.

On October 22, 1895, Levski's monument in Sofia was inaugurated amidst criticism leveled at the ruling circles for their lack of involvement and interest in this figure. As far as the opening ceremony was concerned, the accusations were not entirely fair. The committee, one of whose members was Vazov, had prepared an elaborate program. On the eve of the inauguration, Vazov's drama *Khîshove* was staged in honor of Levski. At 9 a.m., a memorial service took place "for the soul of Deacon Ignatii Vasil Levski" at the metropolitan church. Half an hour later, a solemn procession took off for the monument. It was arranged according to a strict protocol, led by the orchestra, followed by Levski's collaborators and students, his relatives, ministers, members of parliament, municipal authorities, military officers, officials, professors and teachers, students, the home guard, and a number of different societies, closing with ordinary citizens. The monument was opened by the prince, after the consecration of the clergy, and there was an elaborate musical program, military parade and wreath laying. The evening ended with an official dinner for Levski's relatives and fireworks for the public (*SGODA*, Fond 1k, op.3, a.e. 192, 2–6).

Raising a monument dedicated to Levski had been initiated already in the first months of the post-Ottoman administration. In November, 1878, it had been decided to begin a fundraising campaign. In February, 1879, circulars were sent to all district centers, asking for support to commemorate the deed of the Deacon Ignatii Levski (*SGODA*, Fond 1k, op. 3, a.e.151, 1). The fundraising initiative was not very successful. There were positive responses from different places, but the total sum gathered was insufficient. In their letter, the representatives of the town council of Stara Zagora wrote: "As you would know, poverty is rampant in our town and we could barely gather 20 franks." The Vratsa council sent 102 franks and praised the "holy initiative." It also asked about the approximate price of the monument, because it wanted to raise a monument to Botev who had been killed nearby (ibid.: 3–36). The building of the monument was discontinued because of financial difficulties, and a new fundraising campaign began in 1884 (*SGODA*, Fond 1k, op. 3, a.e.166, 1–14). It is at this point that the construction of the monument resumed, and was completed in 1892.

In her otherwise pioneering article on the beginnings of Bulgarian commemorative culture, Claudia Weber makes the hasty assertion that the reluctance of the population to contribute donations to the projected monument illustrates that "the veteran Vasil Ignatii Levski was to a great extent unknown to the Bulgarian population and the motivation to give money for his monument did not gain strength for many years." Based on this observation, she concludes: "The Levski cultus in the last decades of the 19th century was in any case regional and his inclusion into the canon of national martyrs needed further 'work on the myth'" (Weber 1999: 160). The claim for Levski's "regional" status is wholly arbitrary, and conforms better to the latest theories on nationalism rather than with 19th-century Bulgarian realities. When Stoianov published his Levski biography in 1883, the 3,000 copies of the book disappeared from the bookstores in a few days, 2,000 of them alone in Plovdiv, not Sofia. Weber is right on target about the gradual maturing of the Levski myth. She is also right about the gradual process of making "peasants into Bulgarians." However, she is conflating two issues: the absence of a strong or universally developed national consciousness with the readiness to donate. Poor or impoverished people, especially with war on their minds (1877–1878, 1885) can hardly be expected to donate money for monuments with little to survive on. Passionate national movements in their beginning phases are least of all concerned with monuments, which mostly feed the retrospective glance of already established polities.

Equally problematic is Weber's claim that "the Bulgarian 'invention of tradition' was at the outset an extra-state undertaking," which "throws remarkable light on the weakness of the Bulgarian state as the bearer of the national commemorative culture" (ibid.: 159–60). According to her, there were two groups that took up the task of creating repositories of memory: the temporary Russian administration and the network of local veterans' committees. Indeed, the first monuments dedicated to the Russo–Turkish war were erected during the two-year term of the Russian administration and teams of Russian engineers and architects toured the country to find appropriate places for war memorials. Equally, it was the veterans' organization that initiated the building of a monument for the Tsar-Liberator Alexander II, and the state gave its decisive support only in 1899, opening the way for the successful completion of this magnificent monument in 1907. But Weber does not take into consideration both the decisive state financial support for Levski's monument, and the fact that the state had initiated another huge undertaking coinciding with this project. This was the decision, taken already in 1879 to build a "temple-monument for our fatherland's liberation," the future "Alexander Nevski" cathedral in the capital city. In 1882, the foundation stone

Figure 14. An early sketch of architect Kollar for Levski's monument. Source: *Sofiiski Gradski Okrîzhen Arkhiv*, Fond 1k, op. 3, a.e. 169.

Figure 15. Levski's monument in Sofia. Present view.

was set. It was hoped that the construction would be completed by 1885, but the war prevented this. The cathedral was completed and officially consecrated only in September, 1924, a good 45 years after it was planned. At the same time that the campaign to gather donations for Levski's monument was going on, a parallel campaign for the support of the temple was launched. If the state should be characterized in any way, it was not as a "weak bearer of the national commemorative culture" but, rather, as a selective one. Most of its efforts went behind the erection of the grandiose temple that had the enthusiastic support of the church; was a unifying symbol of independence, rather than only a monument of one strand in the liberation movement; and served as a gesture of gratitude to the liberator Russia. In this respect, the accusations leveled against the ruling elites of an ambivalent, if not quite indifferent, attitude toward Levski, are more to the point. Three years after the inauguration of Levski's monument, at the time of the commemoration of the 25th anniversary of Levski's death in 1898, the Ministry of War was criticized for keeping the army and the officers away from the commemorative initiatives. For several decades after independence there were debates around the proper evaluation of Levski, the general assessment of the revolutionary movement, and his exact place in the revolutionary pantheon. Once the highest place was accorded and became unchallenged, the debate shifted to which movement, party, ideology or institution best represented his ideas, in a word, to who owned Levski. The watershed came after the end of the First World War.

3. A Banner for All Causes: Appropriating the Hero

The voluminous body of scholarly work on Levski, among which some genuine and masterly contributions stand out, is focused entirely on the historical figure and its activities. The first and only analysis of Levski's posthumous fate is Genchev's chapter on "Vasil Levski in the Bulgarian historical memory," published in his 1987 book on Levski. Genchev attempts to explain the abrupt turn in the Levski discourse after the Balkan Wars and the First World War. He contends that history itself vindicated Levski's ideas. The reason for this was the critical reassessment of the political platforms, characterized by excessive dependence on great power patronage, that led to the two national catastrophes in the second decade of the 20th century. Looking back to the lessons of history, the new generations refuted these disastrous policies and opposed them with the national platform of Levski which maintained "that only an independent and unengaged development, only a society of guaranteed political and social liberties, only a complete spiritual upsurge can bring out the Bulgarians from the enslaved chaos of their history and psychology" (Genchev 1987: 176).

This murky explanation replete with romantically inflated 19th-century abstractions, is also patently untrue. For all the attraction of Levski's ideology and revolutionary practice, history did not vindicate him. *Realpolitik* in the 19th century meant balance-of-power, and straightforward great power patronage for the rest. Bulgarian liberation was achieved as a result of the Russo–Turkish war of 1877–78, sanctioned by great power consensus at Berlin. Nor was this the exception to the rule. The representation of the Serbian and Greek historical myth has managed to shift the attention to the internal effort, but neither the First Serbian Uprising can be envisaged without the Russo–Turkish war of 1806–12, nor is Serbia's subsequent autonomy and independence conceivable without the treaties at Adrianople (1829) and Berlin (1878). The same is true for Greek independence that came as the end-result of great power bargaining, in which the status of the newly formed state was raised from autonomy to independence in direct correlation to the cut in size. Despite the strong republican strain in the Greek and Bulgarian national movements (of which Levski was a powerful exponent), alternatives to monarchies were not even mentioned, let alone discussed or considered. Genchev, however, was entirely correct with the timing—the early postwar years—and the result: "All doubts in Levski stopped as if cut off by a knife. What followed was a crazy race to appropriate his historical immortality. Every political force, party or trend in Bulgarian life was in a hurry to put his fair image on its banners, to recommend itself as his followers" (ibid.: 176).

Thus, in the 1920s, the Levski myth was finally shaped, and the whole mechanism of transmission was in place: the sacred text, its dissemination through textbooks, the regularized educational system reaching each and every child through normative texts, the elaborate commemorative ritual. The standard explanation has it that the reason Levski began presiding over the heroic pantheon was the result of the vindication of his ideals. No doubt the humiliating defeats of Bulgaria as a result of the Balkan and First World Wars (known as the First and Second National Catastrophes), served as a sobering shock to the jingoistic irredentist nationalism. The crown, in the person of King Ferdinand, was completely compromised and accused of reckless adventurism. Not only did this cost Ferdinand the throne—he abdicated in favor of his son Boris—but it cost the medieval Bulgarian kings the throne of the heroic galaxy. They were demoted, and if before the greatest heroes were Tsar Simeon, Khan Asparukh, Tsar Ivan Asen II and other political and military leaders, only gradually and distantly followed by the constellation of 19th-century national revolutionaries, now the order was reversed. One could say that here was a vindication of their republican and democratic ideas, together with their internationalist nationalism (if this oxymoron is allowed). This, however, is not the sole satisfactory explanation of Levski's personal ascendancy.

It is my belief that two circumstances were decisive in this respect. The first concerns the fact that the generation of Levski collaborators or simply contemporaries was, as a whole, extinct by the 1920s. This meant that there were no alternatives to a unified, unchallenged and presiding heroic assessment of Levski. After 1878 there could be no dispute about the construction of Levski as hero. His elevation as the ultimate Bulgarian hero, however, could and did encounter fair resistance. After the 1920s, living memories could compete no longer. In the second circumstance, the generation of contemporaries of Vazov— the author of the standard text which became *the* body of basic knowledge and evaluation of Levski—was likewise gone, and so were the critics to Vazov's view or simply rivals to his style. Just as this passage of the contemporary generation was necessary for the literary "canonization" of the hero, so it was needed for the "canonization" of the text. That the two coincided in time was an outcome of the fact that Levski (1837–1871) and Vazov (1850–1921) themselves were contemporaries; it should not have any further methodological significance.

So, in a way, the old prejudice against what the Germans call *Zeitgeschichte*, or contemporary history, may be justified, after all: one needs the distance of time in order to begin a levelheaded and "objective" quest. Live contemporaries can be an impediment to this. It is all like the Swahilli maxim that contends that the deceased who remain alive in people's memory are called "living dead." Only when the last to have known them passes away are they pronounced completely dead (Lowenthal 1985: 195). Only, myth seems to need the services of this exact same time distance. Myth is not used here in its popular connotation of traditional story or in its pejorative meaning of false story. Rather, I employ Bruce Lincoln's classification of narratives from the point of view of the narrators' claims and their reception by the audience. There are, in this model, four types of narratives: fables, legends, histories and myths. Fables do not make truth-claims, but present themselves and are accepted as fictions. Legends claim truth-power but they enjoy neither credibility nor authority over their audience. Stories that offer accurate accounts of past events and have credibility are history. Myths are the small class of stories possessing both credibility and authority. Building upon both Malinowski, who describes myth as a social charter, and on Geertz's notion of "model of" and "model for" reality, Lincoln posits that "a narrative possessed of authority is one for which successful claims are made not only to the status of truth, but what is more, to the status of *paradigmatic* truth... Thus, myth is not just a coding device in which important information is conveyed, on the basis of which actors *can then* construct society. It is also a discursive act through which actors evoke the sentiments out of which society is actively constructed" (Lincoln 1989: 24–25). Levski is the literary hero of both these narratives.

It is symptomatic that serious historical research on Levski began precisely in this period. At its first meeting on April 24, 1923, the newly founded "Vasil Levski" People's Committee decided to launch "a strictly scholarly and critical" volume, which was to include Levski's biography, as well as memoirs of living revolutionary collaborators. The person charged with this task was Dimitîr Strashimirov, himself a permanent member of the committee and a well-known scholar who in 1907 had published the valuable "Archive of the Revival." One of the main tasks was to secure funds to finance Strashimirov's research trips around the country, assembling documentary material and interviewing people. By 1924, the committee had opened a "Levski" account at the Sofia Popular Bank, where, among others, moneys collected from school performances were flowing in. The committee's protocol book makes it clear how onerous a task the compilation of Levski's biography was. Five years after undertaking the job, Strashimirov reported that the first documentary volume was ready for print, and it came out in 1929. While work on the second had advanced, he was waiting to include the Ottoman documentation on the trial against Levski, on which a team of Turkologists was working. Overwhelmed by petty squabbling and suffering from bad health, in 1929 Strashimirov resigned from the committee but promised to deliver Levski's biography. This he never managed to complete before his death in 1939, at age 71. Already during his illness in 1938, Strashimirov's assistant Ivan Undzhiev was asked to take on the task of producing the scholarly biography. While Undzhiev stepped on the enormous research work of his predecessor, it is no doubt that the first scholarly biography of Levski was his own achievement.

The publication of Levski's scholarly biography was not the committee's sole activity. For years it deliberated to restore Levski's birth place, a task completed by laying the foundations of the future Museum of Levski in Karlovo. The peak of ambitions was to launch a proper national celebration of the 100th anniversary of the Apostle's birth in 1937. In 1936, when the committee first approached the government for permission and support, the prime minister refused to even grant an audience, and later the sum of 150,000 leva promised from the state budget was crossed out by the minister of finance. The committee continued its lobbying efforts. Some of the members were prepared to settle for a local celebration in Karlovo but others insisted that only a general national commemoration merited the great achievement of the Apostle. In the end, the celebrations were postponed and were confined to Karlovo. The government did not commit and no financial backing was received, but the Ministry of Education at least gave permission for morning meetings in Sofia and some other cities, organized by actors and literati. It also allowed journalists and writers to issue a commemorative paper on the day of the event, and for school lectures dedicated to Levski to be initiated by the committee through the Ministry of Education (*TsDA*, ChP 940).

That the government was weary of giving green light to a nationwide celebration had little to do with Levski and everything to do with the nation. After a couple of turbulent decades, since 1935 Bulgaria was under the royal dictatorship of Boris III, and the price for relative political stability was the complete curtailment of parliamentary freedoms. Boris relied on particularly uncharismatic politicians, and did not allow for a national election until 1938, when candidates ran individually in a strictly controlled campaign, since party lists were banned. In such a highly authoritarian climate it was little surprise that the government was cautious not to endorse public gatherings that might run out of hand, given Levski's democratic grassroots appeal. This knee-jerk reaction of the government is much reminiscent of Ioannis Metaxas' famous ban in neighboring Greece of studying Pericles' funeral speech at schools, not because it was anything but "truthfully grand of democratic ideas," but because it "may be misunderstood by the students as indirect criticism of the vigorous governmental policy and, in general, of the trend of the present state" (Stavrianos 2000: 673).

Levski and what he stood for had little, if anything, to do with the attitude of the authorities. In the circumstances of the 1930s, they could not be accused of neglecting a revolutionary figure as had been done at the end of the 19th century. After the 1920s, Levski's image had already become the object of a universal cult and a receptacle of most incommensurable views and visions. As the volume published by the Karlovo Society on the occasion of Levski's centenary put it: "Much had been said and written about Levski to date. Where only his image has not been hung! His name today is a legend." The volume itself was conceived in the accepted manner of similar editions: starting with Levski's autobiographical poem, followed by the mandatory pieces of Vazov and other poets, writers and scholars. This particular one had added also a contribution in harmony with the contemporary *Zeitgeist*: an "anthro-genetical-biological" essay by one Dr. Vasil Bakîrdzhiev, a student of Ernst Kretschmer. Applying Kretschmerian typology, Bakîrdzhiev defined Levski as a mixture between the athletic and the pyknic type, and as a typical cyclothemic personality, in full contrast to the schizothymic nature of Botev. Anthropologically, he was said to belong to the Thracian racial group and particularly to the blond anthropological type (blue eyes, blond hair, white skin). All of these features corresponded to a host of characteristics so marked in Levski: sociability, naturalness, responsibility, realism, thriftiness, decisiveness, adaptability. Little surprise, Bakîrdzhiev's analysis concluded with enumerating the main features of the "complete cyclothemic genius" such as Levski. These included first and foremost his qualities as leader. Even his insurrectionist, revolutionary activities were praised primarily for their leadership aspects. He was also defined as a "statesman with definitive and correct views on our near and distant neighbors," citing two brief and somewhat critical pronouncements on Serbia and Russia, completely taken out of context. And, of course, equally taken out of context, were quotes indicating his endorsement of the "Bulgaria-Thrace-Macedonia" ideal (*Vizpomenatelna kniga* 1937: 125–32).

In the mid-1930s Levski had already become everybody's acceptable hero but not quite yet as elevated above the rest as half a century later. One can see this in the 1935 statutes of a quasi-Masonic organization—the Fraternity of the Bulgarian Spirit—that circulated around the capital (*TsDA*, Fond 177, op. 2, a.e. 697, 64–66). This was a nationalist organization calling on preserving the Bulgarian spirit in "all lands populated with Bulgarians," the most popular interwar slogan with a focus on Macedonia. A central duty of the members was to preserve and remember the advice of Bulgarian leaders: "secular and spiritual, civilian and military, fighters and saints-martyrs." Levski was one of four 19th-century national revolutionaries chosen next to three revered kings as a fighter for liberty. The patron of the organization, however, was King Boris-Mikhail. His icon, next to the Sts. Cyril and Methodius was to be placed in the house of every brother.

A few years later, on October 1, 1940, the Mayor of Sofia announced the renaming of three central Sofia arteries that henceforth were to bear the names of Italy's King Victor Emanuel III, Benito Mussolini and Adolf Hitler. He proudly emphasized that one of these streets was starting "from the monument of our most sacred national hero Vasil Levski" (*SGODA*, F. 1k, op. 3, a.e. 880, 31). By that time, Levski had been already appropriated by the extreme right as well but again, not as the exclusive summit of heroic achievement. Much like the majority of East European regimes in the interwar period, Bulgaria was dominated by authoritarian and nationalist politics, nourished by the open wound of the Neuilly fiasco, and gravitating mostly around the anti-parliamentarianism of the crown. At the same time, its fascist organizations, although with much greater strength than the latest historiographical fashion would like to accord them, never quite reached the social prominence and mainstream influence that their analogues in neighboring Romania or Croatia did, let alone their ideological models in Italy and Germany. Of the great variety of organizations gravitating to the extreme nationalist right, several in the 1930s were openly espousing a pronounced fascist ideology, the most prominent being the Union of the Bulgarian National Legions (*legioneri*, Legionnaires), founded in 1931, and the Warriors for the advancement of Bulgarianness (*ratnistsi*), founded in 1936, both with ambivalent and often hostile relations with the crown. Without going into the ideological discussion of whether these were authentic fascist formations or only unduly labeled as such, there is little doubt that both consciously and openly fashioned themselves after and emulated Hitler and Mussolini, alongside all the usual repertoire of the extreme right: strict hierarchy with a Leader; military organization; anticommunism; antidemocratic, anti-liberal and anti-parliamentarian position; nationalism, racism and anti-Semitism; loyalty to the Third Reich; and in the case of the Legions, in particular, a mysticism consciously reminiscent of Corneliu Zelea Codreanu's Legion of Archangel Michael in Romania (Poppetrov 1991: 54–55).

What interests us here is to what extent and how exactly these organizations evoked and coopted the legacy of the 19th century revolutionary democrats, Levski included. An influential publication was the Plovdiv based monthly "Might: Journal of Fascist Thought which disseminated corporatist, anti-Semitic and racist ideas. What is striking is that the language of the contributions is completely universalist, Bulgarian history proper rarely mentioned, and neither Levski nor any of the 19th-century revolutionaries are evoked as predecessors. Much the same is true of "Turning Point," the journal around which the Legions' movement coalesced. Its subsidiary issued by the youth organization published numerous nationalist articles evoking the ideals of the "fighters of the pre-liberation period" as models for the young generation in a formulaic manner, but none of the figures were mentioned by name. The only exception was a casual mention of Botev, a fact quite ironic in itself, given that Botev was the only leader with pronounced socialist ideas.

The claim to continue the national liberation struggle was implicit in the very name of the Legions, harking back to the first Bulgarian legions created by Rakovski in Belgrade in the 1860s, whose participant Levski had been. The one explicit mention of names is in the Legionnaires' oath: "We, the Bulgarian Legionnaires call on you to wake up to fight for the ideas of Georgi Sava Rakovski, Levski and Botev. Let us unfurl our national flags on which the holy message of our history is written: Fatherland! Bread! Liberty! God and Bulgaria call on us to take an oath, and live and die for it!" (Simeonov 1999: 33). The same impression follows from reading the works of the Legions' leader Ivan Dochev (1906–2005). His first publication, where he popularized the platform of the Legions, gave mention of only one historical figure: Father Paisii. Dochev's other writings were exclusively and monotonously obsessed with his anti-communism. No doubt Levski was held in high esteem by the Legionnaires but he was not separated from the rest of the national revolutionaries, not did the latter figure prominently in their ideology.

The reason to go into some detail of how the 19th-century revolutionaries were evoked in the thought and practice of the extreme right-wing fascist organizations is to see to what extent the widely shared belief in the 1970s and 1980s, promoted by Genchev, that Levski was not the preferred figure by the communists, is based on reliable evidence. Genchev founded this allegation on a double argumentation: first, that since Levski had become the patron of the Legions and their hero, he was seriously delegitimized in the eyes of the communists who had named the external communist radio, communicating from Moscow during the war, after Khristo Botev; second, that because of Botev's explicit espousal of communist ideas, he had always been held on a higher pedestal than Levski, particularly after 1944. The first argument, as demonstrated above, is an obvious misreading of the evidence. Neither the fascists, nor the communists in the interwar period split Botev and Levski, or claimed them as exclusive ideological representatives. In fact, Botev figured laudably in the writings of the most prominent fascists. Genchev's second argument was equally gratuitous.

For all the plasticity Levski's (and Botev's) image had acquired, and for all its wide and various utilization, Levski continued to be an unquestioned hero of the left, and his ideas were subjected to much more detailed analysis and nuanced appreciation in their midst. He was one of the symbolic heroes of the socialist movement, and an analysis of his place within this ideology in the first half of the 20th century is not only appropriate, but also mandatory. The reasons for this are twofold. On the one hand, with the monopoly of the communist cause after the Second World War, the evaluation of Levski by the socialists was transformed from one among existing interpretations and appropriations to the dominant one. This, while the obvious, is the more conventional reason. After all, while the socialists certainly emphasized Levski's democratic ideas and his stature as a genuine representative of the people, the image in their writings did not differ significantly, if at all, from the one articulated by other political groups. A consensus had developed and, especially in the interwar period, it was a matter of appropriation and legitimation in his name, rather than one of reinterpretation. Levski had become a paradigmatic symbol and, as with any symbol, its different uses managed to mobilize disparate audiences who believed they shared a similar understanding. The other reason is much more interesting and has to do with the place Levski acquired in the 1970s and especially the 1980s, the last decade of state socialism. It is directly linked with the oeuvre and influence of Genchev, and the curious twist he introduced, that resulted in a relatively broadly shared perception of Levski as not appropriately valued by the communists, and therefore elevating him to a quasi-dissident symbol. While this is the subject of the last section, here I will give a close reading of how the socialists, especially Dimitŭr Blagoev, the founder of the Bulgarian Social-Democratic Party and Georgi Bakalov, one of his closest but independent-minded associates, dealt with Levski and his legacy, in an equally close juxtaposition to the interpretation offered by Genchev of this issue.

The first mention of Levski by Blagoev came as early as 1886 when he published a lengthy critical brochure in response to Zakhari Stoianov's memoirs on the revolutionary movement which had appeared in the previous years to great acclaim but also to critical scrutiny. According to Genchev, Blagoev in this piece lay emphasis on Botev, Karavelov, Angel Kînchev and Volov as the great revolutionaries, while Levski came out as someone with a 'talented nature,' but without a clear idea about the power relations within the revolution. Genchev accused Blagoev of attributing all the great ideas of the revolution to Karavelov and Botev because they were "espousing 'the great ideas of present day's humanity,' that is, the ideas of socialism." He therefore concluded that Blagoev "lay the foundations of a permanent banter vis-à-vis Levski, defining him as a simple-minded and uneducated fantast who, in contrast to Botev and Karavelov, even while being of a 'talented nature,' did not know what he was doing... The socialists gave all their preference to Botev at the expense of Levski, because they were sympathetic to the utopian ideas of the former" (Genchev 1987: 165).

This interpretation became very influential among Genchev's students and close circle, but it was a complete and deliberate misreading of Blagoev. It thus begs for a close re-reading. Blagoev in this strongly polemical brochure accused Stoianov of merely adopting or rather aping the revolutionary discourse while remaining completely alien to the quintessence of the great revolutionary ideals of the period. The main thrust of Blagoev's argument was directed against the irresponsible accusation of Stoianov that no learned or wealthy person had been risking anything for the nation's liberty. In this respect, Stoianov, himself undereducated, although of great literary talent and still greater political ambitions, was making a claim about the character of the authentic national revolutionary heroes. For this reason, he identified with Levski and Benkovski as social types, and elevated them high above the other revolutionaries. Blagoev was protesting against Stoianov's cheap populism and particularly against the latter's conflation of knowledge and education with wealth. He was essentially defending the intelligentsia's role as a revolutionary force. He was absolutely explicit about this: "Everyone knows that V. Levski and

Benkovski, whom, due to [Stoianov's] understandable affection for them, he specially emphasizes and repeats, had been apostles and organizers of the revolution according to the plan, prepared by the 'Central Revolutionary Committee' headed by L. Karavelov and Khr. Botev." The most one can conclude from this is that Blagoev may have underestimated Levski's personal ideological contribution. Yet, even after a century of research on the Bucharest Revolutionary Committee, nobody denies that Levski was a member of the Central Revolutionary Committee headed by Karavelov, and that the debates among them concerned mostly issues of strategy. In his polemic, Blagoev did not juxtapose Levski to Karavelov and Botev, but countered Stoianov's juxtaposition of the "true" revolutionaries Levski and Benkovski to the "intellectuals": "[Stoianov], while emulating Benkovski in his hatred against the 'grammarians,' goes so far as to forget that the present circumstances, in which our nation lives, are different. Now knowledge and 'learned heads' are necessary" (Blagoev 1957, I: 229–31).

It is in this context that Blagoev enumerated the names of Karavelov, Botev, Angel Kînchev, and Volov, known to have been well educated. Karavelov and Botev in particular had left considerable oeuvres, and were the two most important publishers and revolutionary ideologues. It was only natural that Blagoev would not mention Levski in the same line. First, Levski was exempt from Stoianov's cheap anti-intellectualism, and it was Blagoev's goal to polemically counter it. Secondly, anyone reading Levski's modest prose will come to the natural conclusion that we are dealing with the work of an intelligent and honorable person, but one who lacks a protracted formal education and does not have either the literary ease or years-long practice to articulate his thoughts in writing. There is nothing shameful or patronizing in this. After all, there exist enough educated but unintelligent individuals. Besides, the socialists were neither the first nor the only ones who "underestimated" Levski's lack of formal education. According to Vicho Ivanov, editor and publisher of the officially sponsored commemorative volume for Levski's centenary: "Vasil Levski did not have the acquired culture of his more learned brothers—Rakovski, Liuben Karavelov, Khristo Botev. But Levski was where the people were—with their suffering and hopes, with their sorrows and small joys. With his elemental nature, with foresight, with a healthy and original feeling for the historical mission of the people, he raised himself high up not only in the consciousness of his contemporaries but also among the following generations" (*Vizpomenatelna kniga* 1937: 99).

True, in this brochure Blagoev focused mostly on Botev and Karavelov, and referred to Levski only peripherally. He characterized Karavelov and Botev as "the main leaders of the revolutionary party" and their ideas as the ones "espoused by present day's humanity." But there is no reason to allege that he valued their ideas only because they were socialist, as the shrewd and unwarranted insertion by Genchev suggested, namely that his praise was because they "espoused 'the great ideas of present day's humanity,' the ideas of socialism" (Genchev 1987: 165). In fact, in all his comments Blagoev defined Karavelov and Botev first and foremost as republican democrats, specifying Karavelov as a political radical, and Botev as a radical and utopian socialist revolutionary or, in his preferred terminology, as a *communard*. Blagoev's attitude to Botev is of particular interest, given the cavalier way in which Genchev accuses him and the socialists in general of elevating Botev at the expense of Levski and pitting the two heroes against each other. During the first independence decades, and up to the Balkan Wars and the First World War. Botev, quite apart from any socialist propaganda which in this period was relatively marginal any way, was the most popular hero of the youth. Ivan Shishmanov, in 1905 minister of education and least of all a socialist sympathizer, pronounced himself to be "a fanatical admirer of the Bulgarian national genius and in this respect having the rare pleasure to share the idol of our youth—Botev" (Blagoev 1959, X: 281).

Blagoev was careful and adamant not to claim a direct link to Botev's utopian socialism. In his 1901 response to an article presenting Botev as a typical representative of Bulgarian socialism, he wrote that "the socialist ideas of Khristo Botev were rather utopian or a mixture of the petty-bourgeois ideas of Proudhon, the anarchic ideas of Bakunin and the utopian socialism of Chernishevskii, as were the socialist ideas of most socialists in the world in this period, and especially the Russian ones, with whom Botev had lived. This, of course, does not prevent us from appreciating Botev highly" (Blagoev 1958, VI: 598). Blagoev's other pronouncements, chiefly in critical reviews, never contrast Botev to Levski but are directed against the attempts to de-politicize and present him simply as an anodyne poetic genius. If there is any comparison at all, it is with the ideas of Karavelov, especially their different approaches to the idea of a Balkan federation. If Blagoev's oeuvre leaves the impression that there is somewhat more on Botev than on Levski, this is in part because Botev was often depicted as a precursor of Bulgarian socialism, and Blagoev took great pains to explain the differences between Botev's utopian and anarchic socialism and his own "scientific" variety. All in all, Levski, Botev and Karavelov are allotted the same space as the post-1878 politicians Petko Karavelov and Stefan Stambolov. As a whole, however, the national revolutionaries, for all of Blagoev's admiration toward them, were not his central referent points. Looking at the name register of his *Collected Works*, the most mentioned names are Karl Marx, Friedrich Engels, Eduard Bernstein, Karl Kautski, August Bebel, Ferdinand Lasal, Georgi Plekhanov, Wilhelm Liebknecht, Karl Liebknecht, Rosa Luxemburg (the last three are mentioned about the same amount as Levski and Botev), and of the Bulgarians social democrats of the period.

Speaking of the national revolutionaries as a whole, Blagoev normally referred to the triad—Karavelov, Levski, Botev (in changing order)—as the leaders of the revolution. His interpretation of Levski focused on his role as a practical revolutionary. Whenever he dealt with ideology, he spoke of Karavelov as a "radicalist," aiming at a democratic liberal republic of the Swiss and American type, and of the "communards" around Botev with their utopian socialism. In 1898 he dedicated a special article to Levski. Having laid out the stages of the revolutionary tactics, culminating with the idea of a broad internal revolution, Blagoev concluded: "The idea was prepared, the plan arranged. But to put it in practice, a man of strong spirit, iron will and heroic courage was needed. A practical genius was needed, a genius organizer, someone able to fire up the slaves, to stir them up for struggle. This practical genius was found in the person of the former deacon Vasilii, in the person of Vasil Levski" (Blagoev 1957, IV: 547). Blagoev singled out Levski for his personal charisma, a motive which has continued to be a most powerful aspect of the Levski cult: "Levski belongs to this rare species of social figures whose image is immune to human malice and slander. His image remains pure and radiant despite the desire of his enemies to find some kind of stain, the tiny feather of a wing that may throw even the faintest of shadows upon him. Levski is the epitome of the brightest national organizational spirit devoid of any self-interest; he personifies the pure and ideal aspirations of this spirit" (ibid.: 549). Levski's ideals—his democratic and republican ideology, and specifically the idea of a Balkan federative republic—remained unfulfilled. For Blagoev, it was the serendipitous meeting of two geniuses—the theoretical of Karavelov and the practical of Levski—that put the revolutionary idea in practice. Such an "underestimation" of Levski's ideological contribution was considered to be a crime by Genchev, and he attributed the same tendency, as well as the opposition to Botev, also to Georgi Bakalov, the most prolific and influential Marxist literary critic of the interwar period.

A look at Bakalov's work will demonstrate not only that an artificial opposition between Levski and Botev was not perpetuated but that any such attempt was being opposed. Bakalov's debut on the topic started in 1924 with his book *Our revolutionaries—Rakovski, Levski, Botev*, but most of his work on the great 19th-century figures fell on the decade of the 1930s. The opening to his one explicit essay on the relations between Botev and Levski could not be less ambivalent: "Equally sweet beat the hearts of these among their heirs who care about their deeds, when they think about the one or the other. In terms of appeal, admiration of their personalities and love, they don't have rivals in the memory of the following generations. In the Bulgarian pantheon of the immortals the first place is reserved for them" (Bakalov 1938: 27). He then follows the way in which the two men reached their revolutionary credo: Botev, more in a speculative, theoretical manner, shaped under the influence of Russian revolutionary democratic ideology; Levski, through the difficult road of personal experience, of self-taught practice. What brought them together in complete accord was their belief in the revolution as the only effective strategy and tactic for liberation. Bakalov presents Levski as a practitioner of genius, and he attributes to him "the purely Levskian idea" of preparing the revolution by means of a whole system of committees that covered the whole country. He insists that this "idea of genius" belongs to Levski, who not only applied it in practice but also conceived of it, and he specifically opposes the attribution of the idea to Karavelov who, according to Bakalov, only gave it its literary shape. It is in this context and as a defense, not as an accusation, that Bakalov writes: "Nobody considered Levski, whose education was rather wanting, as a theoretician. This, however, does not mean that he did not have his own, original ideas which enriched the treasury of the revolutionary ideology" (ibid.: 28–9). This irked Genchev immensely and, instead of giving it the proper contextual analysis it deserves, he introduced the quote with "he [Bakalov] does not fail to remind us that 'nobody considered Levski, whose education was rather wanting, as a theoretician'" (Genchev 1987: 180). We are back to the populist anti-intellectualism of Zakhari Stoianov.

If Bakalov can be considered somewhat unjust, it is in the direction of Karavelov, never towards Levski. Neither is Botev elevated in any way. The whole tenure of the essay was the parity between "the two greatest Bulgarians before the liberation." It bears mention that, similar to Blagoev, in his other works Bakalov also made it clear that according to him Botev should not be considered a forerunner of Bulgarian socialism, except in the most symbolic and conditional sense. He considered Botev a revolutionary democrat permeated with the ideas of utopian socialism very much in the line of Lenin's characterization of Chernyshevskii. At the end of the day, he defined Botev, as well as Levski, as leaders of the agrarian/bourgeois-democratic revolution in Bulgaria. This interpretation of Botev brought Bakalov the characterization of not being "correct and consistent," of being misguided by an erroneous political interpretation. Luckily, it came after the Second World War, when he was no longer alive. All of this is not meant to elevate Bakalov's analysis to the pedestal of a "correct" interpretation against the subsequent dogmatism. In fact, Bakalov himself was inspired by an unabashed presentism in his evaluation of the historical legacy of Botev and Levski. What he chose to stress was their dedication to the revolutionary program and tactics, their elevation of the avant-garde professional revolutionary organization as the natural leader of the movement.

Keeping in mind the period when Bakalov wrote his essays about Levski, with the Bulgarian communist party banned and open repression against left-wing ideas, his analysis of Levski presaged the famous periphrastic of the communist period. Bakalov described in detail the character of Levski's clandestine military struggle, the principles and tactics of an illegal and centralized revolutionary organization, and the qualities necessary for an effective professional revolutionary who "has to possess all the qualities enumerated by Levski: judiciousness, perseverance, courage and magnanimity, all in agreement. If only one of these qualities is missing, Levski foresees the disgrace of the revolutionary" (Bakalov 1934: 19). The interests of the organization are, according to Levski, above anything else, and this is what prompts him to use violence as well as advocate iron discipline and severe punishment, the capital inclusive, for any activities that might jeopardize its security. Levski's "secret police" is the terrorist organization of the party whose goal is to create "a sound conspiratorial organization as an avant-garde of the popular revolution." (ibid.: 41). Only Levski could be the legitimate garb for this unabashed revolutionary manual.

It is clear that in the interwar period there was an acute struggle to appropriate Levski as the authentic representative of a class, party, or movement. The same can be said for the figure of Botev, since both had achieved enormous legitimation power. These attempts, however, did not necessarily starkly falsify their ideas and activities, nor did they pitch them against each other, either by the political left or by the political right. It was a matter of highlighting or exclusively emphasizing the nationalist component of their legacy (by the right) against the same tendency of underscoring their revolutionary potential (by the left). It is actually very interesting that incompatible worldviews which often clashed in bloody armed struggle (in the 1920s, as well as the 1940s), never really adopted one figure to the exclusion of the other. While Botev's socialist ideas were stressed by the socialists, they were rarely used to discount his inspirational presence for the extreme right. When Levski's nationalism or his religiosity were underscored by the right, this never served as a pretext to distance themselves from him on the left. Both Levski and Botev had been explicitly accepted as common national figures: it was rather a matter of who was more loyal to their legacy.

It is therefore difficult to accept Genchev's contention that three different conceptions of Levski floated in the ideological space in turn-of-the-twentieth-century Bulgaria: one belonging to Stoianov "who elevated him on the pedestal of a great organizer of the national revolution;" another espoused by Bobchev and Zaimov who, while equally admiring Levski, sided with the ones "who were looking for more reasonable ways to achieve independence;" finally the socialists who allegedly "gave all their preference to Botev at the expense of Levski, because they were sympathetic to the utopian ideas of the former" (Genchev 1987: 165). Genchev never explained clearly what the difference between the three conceptions is. It seems that what he defined as "conceptions" were rather three different emotional attitudes and levels of appreciation. Equally, his contention that Blagoev, alongside Stoianov and Dr. Krîstev, initiated the tendency to set Botev and Levski against each other in an unhealthy comparison, is not supported by a careful scrutiny of these authors' oeuvre. It is a position that Genchev needed, however, in order to construct his own emancipation of Levski. In his attempt to raise Levski to the potential pedestal of the dissidents' banner or at least to an accepted quasi-oppositional icon to the communist regime in the 1980s, Genchev himself was forcing the evidence and pronouncing Levski as the central, exclusive and most prescient ideologue of the revolution, setting him far apart from all other 19th-century revolutionaries.

4. Contesting the Hero

In 1898 when Blagoev mentioned that Levski had his enemies, and was lamenting the insufficient attention to his person and ideas, he was not far off the mark. Despite the icon-like and, as we shall see in Part III, literal iconic status, as well as the correct impression of his universal acceptance, there were questions raised about his personality or his interpretation both by his contemporaries, as well as today. The story of the hero's contestation, while muted as a whole and without much real effect, deserves to be told, because it allows for a more complex glimpse into national debates and at social cleavages. The only open and thoroughly negative assessments came from among some of Levski's contemporaries. The story can appropriately begin with Khristo Georgiev, the wealthy Karlovo merchant, whose monumental seated figure together with his brother Evlogi, flanks the main entry to Sofia University. During his first tour of Bulgaria in 1868–1869, when he began to build his carefully organized network of committees, Levski tried to collect funds for his expeditions and for arms purchases from wealthy Bulgarians in Walachia. This came at the height of the tension between the groups of the "old" and the "young." While there had been differences of opinion about how to organize the national movement in emigration, the clash over tactics was exacerbated after the Crimean war and especially in the 1860s. The brothers Georgievi, especially the younger Khristo who was considered its leader, were the most influential members of the organizational nest of the "old" in Bucharest and were vehemently opposed to the clandestine preparations for a revolution, to the military actions, and to what they saw as the radical ideology of the "young."

In April, 1869, Khristo Georgiev responded to the message of Naiden Gerov, the Bulgarian man of letters serving as Russian consul in Plovdiv between 1857 and 1876, who had reported on his meeting with Levski. Georgiev informed Gerov at length about the activities of Theofan Rainov whom he characterized as a "chief Turkish spy," how he "spends well for himself" and supports Kasabov of the Secret Bulgarian Revolutionary Committee: "Every Bulgarian knows that Rainov is a Turkish spy, and he is approached only by the likes of Kasabov, for the lucre." On the last line of this letter, as a kind of postscript, Georgiev advised Gerov not to trust Levski: "Let me stop here, tell [people] not to believe in the tales of the Deacon." (Undzhiev 1947: 248). On May 30, 1869, Gerov wrote to Georgiev again, informing him of the proclamations Levski was distributing around the country. In his response on June 14, 1869, Georgiev wrote: "The proclamations that you have seen have been printed here by Rainov and Kasabov, and were given to the Deacon for distribution. The Deacon is the one who concocts the false letters for Rainov to recommend himself as a good spy. Whatever Rainov, Levski is the same; both would sell their father for money" (ibid.: 254).

There has been a persistent trope about Levski's intention to kill Khristo Georgiev who had refused to give financial aid to the revolutionary movement. It comes from another revolutionary figure, Khristo Ivanov, and was first mentioned by Zakhari Stoianov who had evidently consulted Ivanov's unpublished memoirs, but was bypassed by all other biographers. According to Ivanov, Levski did not go through with his plan, because he could not secure from Karavelov the key to a house where he would hide after the murder. Undzhiev considers this information unreliable and thinks that there was only a verbal threat behind this. He clearly wanted to cleanse the image of Levski from accusations of terrorism, and judging from today's reception of Levski, has largely succeeded. A former friend of mine with whom a few years ago we discussed the 19th-century revolutionary figures exclaimed that she liked Levski because he was "so mild, non-confrontational, unlike Botev, whose discourse is intolerant." When I pointed out to her the epistolary evidence of Levski himself, she offendedly pursed her lips but insisted Levski's blue eyes were not fanatic.

It is instructive to go to Levski's accusatory letters themselves. While the archives do not have evidence for a concrete threat on Georgiev's life, several letters dating from 1871 have been preserved. With a circular letter from the Bulgarian Revolutionary Central Committee dated March 10, 1871, Levski was given the right to apply the terrorist principle. The circular took the shape of a letter with a generic addressee "Mr...." It warned that whoever refused to give everything for the cause of liberty "will be damned and very soon will be sent... you figure where. The traitors, the rich, the tyrants and the Turkish toadies will hang on the same tree as our enemies." The letter further stated that the revolutionaries would provide a receipt for everything received but if "someone does not take part in our popular movement, he will be considered a traitor and enemy" and urged the receivers to quickly decide whether they were "with us or against us" (Vasil Levski 1941: 191–3). There are at least two preserved letters of the kind written in Levski's handwriting. While the terrorist tactic was applied very sparingly and from that point of view Undzhiev's assertion that this was mostly meant to intimidate may be true as a whole, there were instances where there was a genuine follow-up. In a letter to Karavelov from 1872, in which he complained of the behavior of Dimitîr Obshti, Levski mentioned in a postscript that "Velichko effendi will be exalted one of these days head down." Velichko Stoianov of Ruse managed to escape but the assassination plots against the Deacon Paissii of Lovech and many others did succeed (Sharova 1991, 6–9).

The aim of all this evidence is not to make the point that Georgiev's wrath against Levski was justified or to demote Levski to a terrorist, alongside all the other revolutionaries. It simply aims at historically contextualizing a genuine revolutionary of the type Europe knew in the second half of the 19th century, and to contravene today's stale politically correct tendency to denounce "illegal" violence as terrorist, while tacitly underwriting the "civilized" and "legal" violence of the powerful. It is also to remind that heroes are not uncontested and that there were fierce social and ideological cleavages in Bulgarian pre-independence society that have been smoothed out only by the Whig pen of later historians. Nevertheless, it is only fair to mention that neither the trope of assassinating the internal enemy or the assembling of money through raids for revolutionary purposes, much as they figure as genuine or at least tolerable revolutionary acts, became part of the national mythology. They were silenced without falsifying them, and Levski's popular biography was subconsciously cleansed of these deeds that gave way to other mythological structures.

The most uncompromising attacks on Levski's integrity came from the Istanbul-based Bulgarian elites as well as from the ones close or integrated in the Ottoman governing apparatus in the provinces. Nikola Genovich, editor of *Turtsiia*, the organ of the Turkophile Party in Istanbul, wrote in a comment about Levski's trial: "Can a whole nation be called a rebel, because Karavelov is a Serb agent and publishes a mutinous paper in order to cheat the corn-growing Serbs out of their gold, with which he buys lowly individuals and *haiduts* such as the recently hanged in Sofia Dimitîr Obshti and Vasil Levski" (*Turtsiia*, IX, 7, March 31, 1873). While Genchev asserts that this was the only written slander against Levski after his death, Sharova shows that both the provincial newspaper *Dunav*, as well as the capital based *Turtsiia*, published virulent attacks on Levski as "assassin," "scoundrel," and "haiduk" who fooled the naive Bulgarians (Sharova 1997: 26).

Nor was the critique of Levski confined to the circles that refuted any radical activity. His stature among the revolutionaries was not unambiguous. His frictions with his aid Obshti are common knowledge, and are reflected in every school account of the last year of his activities where it is the unilateral action of Obshti, his capture and subsequent immoderate boasting of the scope of the organization that allegedly dealt it an unrecoverable blow. Never is there mention of Obshti's motives, beyond psychological explanations of impatience and adventurism. These were, however, widely discussed within the revolutionary circles at the time and during the first years after independence. Sharova, one of the best researchers of this period, demonstrates convincingly the inevitable contradiction between the centralizing and decentralizing principles in the revolutionary movement. She insists in particular that the crisis in the organization preceded the Arabakonak adventure of Obshti, and was an inbuilt problem of its structure and tasks. The central question for the revolutionaries, after the initial creation of the network by Levski, was the collection of money for arms. The organization, created by penniless émigrés, and drawing its membership mostly among petty artisans, merchants, poor teachers, clergymen, and peasants, never disposed of the needed resources. Wealthy Bulgarians refused to contribute and this triggered the above-mentioned circular extortion letters, but these proved ineffective. By the spring and summer of 1872 the internal revolutionary organization had reached a critical state of affairs. Levski returned to Bulgaria on July 1, 1872 and decided to resort to attacks, and apply the principle of revolutionary terror. His motivation was to procure funds, as well as to forestall the dangers of betrayal.

What followed was a series of political assassinations: an attack on a reputedly corrupt and greedy potentate from Etropole; the already mentioned assassination of Deacon Paisii of Lovech who promised but did not give money, and threatened to speak; the assassination of a Liaskovets prominence; the unsuccessful attack on the house of Dencho Khalacha and the murder of his servant that is the mostly wide known instance of these terrorist activities (it was leveled as an accusation against Levski during his trial, and he bitterly regretted and was repentant about this incident). There were also plans, albeit unsuccessful ones, to murder high-standing Bulgarians, and a host of others to be observed and, if needed, liquidated. According to Sharova (1991), and contrary to Levski's conviction that the secret revolutionary police would easily and cheaply deal with the problems, this turn of events cost the organization very dearly. It alerted the authorities who followed up with arrests and surveillance, and it upset the organization's other plans, creating unease and fear among the committee members. All of this coincided with the growing activity of the Ottoman government against the Bulgarian movement after Midhat Pasha became Grand Vizier in the summer of 1872. He immediately closed down the democratic newspaper *Makedoniia* and arrested its editor-in-chief, Petko Slaveikov, accusing him of contacts with the Bucharest-based committee of Karavelov. He also sent directives to the police to be especially watchful against the Bulgarians.

This attack on the Ottoman treasury convoy at Arabakonak has been traditionally attributed to Obshti's single-handed decision and blamed for the subsequent demise of the organization. Sharova calls for a revision of this thesis, showing that Levski himself was considering this operation, only he wanted to better prepare it and leave Obshti out or at least not leave it entirely to him. The attack itself, quite contrary to today's received wisdom, was well prepared and carried out, and for a whole month the authorities had no lead. To this date it is unclear how and through whom the Ottoman police managed to get to the perpetrators but most likely this was by means of infiltration of spies into the revolutionary network. The conflict between Levski and Obshti may have also had personal psychological dimensions but at its heart it was the irresolvable conflict of opposing strategies: one, embodied by Levski, focusing on centralism as a *conditio sine a qua non* of any kind of clandestine revolutionary work and insisting on his extraordinary powers as leader of the internal organization; the other, represented by Obshti, calling on the majority vote as the highest principle of the organization and insisting on a broad distribution of revolutionary tasks among the leaders. The clash had apparently gone out of hand by the summer of 1872 and when in September Levski asked the committee in Bucharest to remove Obshti, he added that the latter "has in many respects deserved a death sentence but will be pardoned for now" (Sharova 1991: 15).

That it was a matter of colliding viewpoints about strategy and not simply the clash between two individuals is evidenced by the series of opposition to Levski, by both individual members and whole committees who were alienated by some of Levski's activities. For example, in July, 1872 Levski decided to convene a general assembly within Bulgaria. The Etropole and Teteven committees were against; so was the one in Tîrnovo, headed by a very close and trusted friend of Levski. The reason for this opposition was that people were cautious about the activities of the Ottoman police and fearful to invite recrimination by the authorities. In their refusal however, they were careful to act according to the Statute of the Revolutionary Committee, quoting the principle of majority vote. Levski was furious with the cautious response and sent letters to Karavelov complaining of the committees cowardice. Another factor contributing to the crisis was the structure of the internal organization itself. It had grown in size, the local committees had an increased appreciation of their own abilities, and the organization could no longer be managed by a sole person. Levski resorted to two strategies, without dismissing the centralizing principle that he strongly believed in. One was the creation of regional centers with whom he would have contact, and they would further communicate the decisions to the smaller local committees. The other was delegating powers to assistants. The criteria for his choices apart from personal trust were unclear.

Finally, there is the case of the priest and member of the Lovech Revolutionary Committee, Pop Krîstiu, who was accused of having disclosed Levski's whereabouts and bore the brunt of national archtraitor. The historiographical controversy about his alleged betrayal is explored in the next part, but worth mention here is his opinion of Levski. In 1879, Pop Krîstiu sent a letter to the Plovdiv newspaper *Maritsa*. It was never published and became known only when it was found in 1882 after his death in his prayerbook. In this letter, he speaks with disgust about the punitive tactics of the revolutionaries, Levski in particular: "These people, who were honest and wise and knew how to proceed with their work in a reasonable way, why did they resort to such nonsense and barbarisms, in order to bring the whole cause to this end? Who killed the Deacon Paisii and why was he killed when he was an innocent man who, even when he was dying, did not betray his assassins, although he knew them. Who killed the innocent young man in Lovech (in Dencho's house) and why? And why did he go there? To raise a nation or to rob homes and kill people?" (Strashimirov 1929: 680).

It is only natural that the open dismissal of Levski would come from among his contemporaries and, almost exclusively, during the pre-1878 period. As already Georgi Bakalov perceptively noted: "This aspect—the obverse side of attitudes toward Levski—today can hardly be researched. The result from Levski's activities, albeit not direct— the liberation—was so positive that all dark spots were forgotten. Who would dare criticize and judge the historically vindicated Levski and boast one's disagreements and debates with him as a special merit?" (1938: 4). Hereafter, the story of attitudes toward Levski is based not on immediate experience but exclusively on the competition about the appropriation of a central national symbol. The distinction should not be overdone, however, because in both cases the opinions are inflected by the horizon of desired expectations for the future of the polity. While this was the topic of the previous section, it is worth highlighting the tropes and places where the contestation of Levski took and still takes place.

For the early Bulgarian socialists and future communists in the interwar period, Levski, alongside the whole radical revolutionary movement, was an endorsement of the legitimacy of political struggle through revolution. Bakalov's 1938 book *Revolt against Levski* opened with the rhetorical question whether it was even possible that someone would dare attack or renounce the great Apostle. It had not yet come to that, but the direction taken by many historians was leading surreptitiously to it, and this tendency was the "renunciation of political struggle (and in the circumstances of complete injustice this struggle could be nothing but revolutionary)." Accordingly, Bakalov dealt with the conflict between Levski and Obshti in light of the developments within the socialist movement at the time. It had been split between the factions of the "narrow" and the "broad," reflecting different approaches to the strategy of the organization. When Bakalov exclaims that "the revolt against Levski was the fruit of a hazardous deviation and factional blindness, a damaging display of political and moral decay," one can clearly hear the overtones of the later political debate within the socialist movement. When he endorses Levski's "iron discipline, which would not stop even before applying the highest punitive measures" against the adventurousness of Obshti, one can again see his support for the "narrows" cause (ibid.: 3, 14, 17).

Throughout the postwar period and until 1989 this became the dominant historiographical interpretation and, by far, the only official one. The first gentle hint at reassessment began with Krumka Sharova, a respected historian of the Revival Period and specialist on Karavelov who, in the early decades of communist rule, did much to uphold Karavelov's stature as a significant leader of the revolutionary organization against the dogmatic tendency to brush him off as a mere educator and oppose him to Levski as the organizer and practitioner, a tendency that had its roots already in the prewar period. She called for an end to repeating the simplistic scheme whereby it was Obshti's single-handed adventurism and lack of discipline that led the organization into a cul-de-sac and pointed out that the crisis was brought about with the application of revolutionary terror. She introduced the explicit notion of revolutionary terror in the practice of Levski for the first time, substituting for the hitherto euphemistic definitions: "The actions aimed at forceful seizure of money and capital punishment for real or potential traitors are forms of revolutionary terror, known also among other clandestine revolutionary organizations" (Sharova 1993: 15).

Still, this was a mild form of criticism: "the heroic romanticism of the era took the upper hand over Levski's sober realism. Romanticism, by the way, is typical for any revolutionary movement, especially an underground one" (Sharova 1991: 14). The criticism was slightly more explicit in a 1999 lecture course on the Bulgarian Revival which summarized the existing dogma as resting on "two untruths": the fictitious opposition between Karavelov and Levski and, more importantly, the postulate that "the authorization of Levski as chief apostle in the country is something natural and determined, something positive, without which the cause of the national revolution would have suffered." This effectively "imposed on the revolutionary organization the principles of conspiracy, the secret mail system, the secret police and revolutionary terror" and was the chief reason for the symptoms of crisis. "It contradicted the principle of majority vote—the Bulgarian Central Revolutionary Committee's basic principle" (Mitev 1999: 116–7). Again, as in the case of Bakalov and as is normal with every consecutive historiographical reassessment, one can hardly avoid hearing the overtones of today's *Zeitgeist* with its professed credo in democracy and majority rule. At the same time, this is the farthest that a tentative criticism of Levski would go. After all, we are still living in the regime of sovereign national states, despite the new understanding of sovereignty, and Levski is without any doubt one of the major figures of the national pantheon. Contrary to Genchev who thought that Levski was not valued enough during the communist period, it is today that in the historiography he is being carefully "demoted" from the exclusive peak of the national pantheon (or, rather, the exclusive peak is being populated with a number of other figures).

It is difficult, if not impossible, to decide whether there had been critical notes toward Levski among the broader population. There is an interesting passage in the writer Khristo Radevski's memoirs, published only in 2000. The entry of his diary for September 17, 1972 recalls overhearing the conversation of two six–seven-year-old girls during his stroll through the park: "Do you know what kind of butcher he was?" "Who, Levski?" "He, of course. If someone didn't obey, he would come and cut his head off." Radevski was distressed but ends this brief report with something reminiscent of a written sigh: "This is a conversation overheard by an adult." (Radevski 2000: 114). While certainly not widely held, it is a view that had been obviously held and discussed in family circles in the capital city. There is another, equally if not more interesting, passage coming from under the pen of one of the most talented and idiosyncratic Bulgarian writers, Chudomir (1890–1967). In the interwar period he was a frequent contributor to the left-wing press, and after the Second World War until his death chaired the "Iskra" education club and was director of the Historical-Ethnographic Museum of Kazanlîk. His diary spanned the period 1947–1967 and was first published in 1994. On February 26, 1951, Chudomir noted that one of the first socialists in Bulgaria, Kosta Bozveliev, had died bequeathing his library and archive to the "Iskra" club. Chudomir was delighted and had been going through and arranging his papers. The entry ends with a comment: "A nice person, wonderful soul, human, honest and ... vain. All Bulgarians are like that. Levski and Botev too, all photographs, all posing, all skulls and knives... Same thing with bai Kosta: everything is separated, arranged, signed, waiting only for the biographer or the historian to come and begin. I don't reproach him. This seems to be a human quality. I only note" (Chudomir 1994: 125).

This is not criticism directed specially to Levski. It is not even criticism but a good-hearted chuckling observation. Still, it is an important glimpse into what I would maintain is a dominant attitudinal trait in a majority of Bulgarians. The genius of Chudomir and his immense popularity as with most Bulgarian writers lies in his unrivaled ability to capture and represent this mixture of self-irony, sometimes cruel mockery, practical idealism, and skepticism against everything which smacks of inflated loftiness. Virtually every Bulgarian, I think, would agree with Chudomir as a whole, but virtually every Bulgarian would exempt Levski from his list, maintaining that Levski's simplicity, ordinary speech, and modesty set him apart. One may even say Levski's man-of-the-people posture is his most appealing trait that has won him the popularity among the nation. Having written this sentence, I realize that it would evoke a storm of protest: that it is not *posture* but precisely Levski's authenticity as a man of the people. This, of course, invites us to deconstruct notions such as authenticity as well as rigidly held ideas of what it means to be "of the people." Yet, for our purposes here this is not necessary. What is significant is that, quite apart from Levski's ontology that may indeed have contributed to his being singled out, there is a public readiness and desire to construct one's authentic hero as a counterpoint to the standard version and image of a heroic figure.

This section will end with a counterpoint, making room for probably the only expressly negative evaluations of Levski in recent years. They are in no way typical either in terms of Levski's reception or in terms of any kind of social representativeness but it is precisely their exceptional character than can shed additional contrasting light onto the image of the hero. One is written by a young historian who offered a view in his book "Christianity and History" (1998) that harked back to the church's early 20th century repudiation of the national revolutionary movement but without exempting Levski. In a bombastic prose that matches the extreme laudations of Levski, he introduces this "dubious figure, imposed on the Bulgarians as their national hero and propped up at any price, even sacrificing the whole Bulgarian nation." Inspired by his own royalist and Christian Orthodox values, the author's portrait of Levski is a litany of unmeasured invectives: "a semi-literate former legionnaire from Belgrade," "a rebel intoxicated by his own greatness," a mere athlete without intellectual qualities, "a criminal killer of a fourteen-year-old boy," whose philosophy "merely substituted the pagan idols of the pre-Christian period" and led directly to atheism, and whose republicanism is a virtual treason of the Bulgarian historical tradition. At the same time, it is an account that correctly locates the beginnings of the Levski cult in Vazov and while not original in any of its allegations, is nonetheless surprising in refusing to succumb to the mythology.

The other denunciation comes from Dimitîr Bochev who had studied philosophy in the 1960s and defected to Germany in 1972. He worked for the East European radio programs of *Deutsche Welle* and *Free Europe* and, after 1989, published several literary works in Bulgaria. In an interview he gave for the widely read *168 chasa*(July 10–16, 1998) he was asked about Levski:

> "The Apostle for me is above all a child-assassin. It is well known that he strangled a youth in order to avoid the risk of betrayal. But Dostoevski writes that if at the entrance of the gates to Heaven there is a single child's tear, the one who provoked it, should not be admitted. The heroic deed is not worth the child's tear. There exists no heroism that is not ready to sacrifice human life for an idea. According to me, man should live imperceptibly, causing as little evil as possible."

"You mean heroes are criminals?"

> "Heroism is a crime, and heroes are demons of evil. Sometimes I wonder what kind of scoundrels live in the memory of this nation, from Khan Krum to Todor Zhivkov. Khan Krum drank wine from the scull of his military adversary Nikiphor, who had fought honestly and valiantly. We, his descendants, are proud with this fact, instead of being ashamed of the kind of barbarians our gene has started."

The rest of the interview is prone to similar overarching outbursts: for example that Darwin had become religious at the end of his life and this definitively overthrew his theory of the origins of species; or that history was just an accumulation of facts whereas literature is a spiritual act. Some of these outbursts are garnished with Nietzschean overtones, namely that the only important thing in life is ecstasy, which Bochev had allegedly achieved in a commune in Germany with narcotics; or that the writer has no responsibilities, but writes only for himself. On the other hand, there are also a number of accurate if banal instinctual verdicts and insights about the barbarization of the world and the lack of human progress punctuated with the excesses of the Middle Ages and Dachau, as well as about Bulgaria's provincialism, nationalism, and present criminality. In the end, as a potential indictment of Levski, this piece is especially impotent given the contrast between the professed philosophy of imperceptible life and the typical bombastic absurdities of a self-described gadfly.

This survey of attempts to contest Levski's eminence as the sublime Bulgarian hero can reach the only conclusion that the challenges have been rare and rather indecisive. The only serious ones came during his lifetime when he was not yet a candidate for heroic status; after that they have been, to say the least, half-hearted. A widely accepted ethical taboo to question his lofty position exists. Before going into the final twist of Levski's posthumous fate—his elevation even higher than his heroic peak, into a position of dissident hero, which during the communist era would confer upon him an absolute sacredness—let us briefly survey the different genres in which he has appeared.

5. The Literary and Visual Hypostases of the Hero

For a long time the "novelization" of Levski was resisted. Vazov's oeuvre introduced the fictional genre in the treatment of Levski (both in his poetic ode as well as the short stories), but the latter somehow acquired the status of documentary evidence in public perception, although Vazov had never (and did not pretend) to have met and known Levski. Levski's biographer Stoianov also had never met Levski and suffered profoundly from this "deficiency." His first attempt at biography (moving away from the memoirist genre) was Levski, and he was adamant that it was true to facticity and resisted the temptations of any literary modeling. Yet, the choice and arrangement of facts and, especially, the silencing of others, already was bespeaking the imagination of a literary creator.

Levski has not had the luck to interest writers of the caliber of Thomas and Heinrich Mann, Lion Feuchtwanger or Ivo Andrić. Most of the prominent Bulgarian writers who produced historical fiction after Vazov—Stoian Zagorchinov, Fani Popova-Mutafova, Dimitîr Talev, Emiliian Stanev, Anton Donchev, Gencho Stoev—avoided the topic. The one significant exception is the work of Stefan Dichev. Stefan Dichev (1920–1996) is, without any doubt, the writer whose work symbolizes Levski's fictionalization. The author of numerous historical novels, Dichev fictionalized themes from antiquity to the 19th century, and did not confine himself to Bulgarian history. In 1956 he published a huge novel "For Liberty," consisting of two parts: one, dedicated to and entitled "Rakovski," the other one on Levski. In 1959, the novel was awarded the prestigious Dimitrov Prize for 1954–1958, and underwent numerous editions. It is a work that is amazingly well researched. In a way, Dichev can be defined as Undzhiev plus some literary talent, and a larger palette. He has learned his history in all details, and has delivered some captivating scenes and images, especially the complex character of Midhat Pasha, the Danube vilayet governor and future Grand Vizier, in his relationship to the Bulgarian question. He has painted a full-blooded portrait of Levski against the international diplomacy and ideologies of the 19th century, as well as against the intricacies of the Bulgarian revolutionary movement. Still, the book is more of a literary illustration of a historical narrative, rather than a novel using a historical theme or, to formulate it differently, an arrangement for direct speech of a well-known composition in indirect speech. It is a book that is also broadly "correct," according to the exigencies of the day. Dichev has not allowed himself any arbitrary deviation from Levski's dominant interpretation. Pop Krîstiu is the traitor, there are the depictions of class conflict among the Bulgarians, there is the odd but moving scene of "class solidarity" with the Turks, there are the differences of ideology and tactics with the other revolutionaries. For all this, it offers an emotional and dynamic narrative that has remained largely unsurpassed.

The book begging comparison with Dichev's is the equally voluminous novel *Levski* by Iana Iazova. Written as part of the trilogy *Balkani* in a first draft between 1952 and 1955, it was published in full only in 1987. Iazova (1912–1974) was a poetess and celebrity figure in the 1930s but did not publish after the war. She shared her manuscript with friends who encouraged her to offer it to the publishing house "Narodna kultura." She sent a copy to the press in November, 1960, and received a positive review but with editorial suggestions in July, 1961. There were problems with the size of the manuscript (2,579 pages) but she insisted the book should be published in full. In 1972–73 she copied and corrected the manuscript again, but this copy was lost. Iazova died in 1974 without descendents, and her papers went to the Central State Historical Archives. Petîr Velichkov found the first 1960 manuscript in the archives, and published large excerpts in the periodic press in 1984. The whole manuscript of the trilogy was prepared for publication by Velichkov, and came out as three separate volumes in 1987, 1988 and 1989: *Levski*, *Benkovski (The April Uprising)*, and *Shipka*.

The Levski volume (1075 manuscript pages, 830 printed pages) produced a hype in the literary circles. Part of it had to do with the *femme fatale* stature of Iazova in the interwar period, and the ongoing idealization of this period, especially in the literary sphere among intellectuals in the 1980s. The literary critic Iordan Vasilev (husband of the poetess and future Vice President Blaga Dimitrova, and himself a relentless anti-communist) wrote a review of the book in 1988 (*Plamîk*,

32, February 2, 1988, 163–169). I was familiar with the review before I got hold of the book only in the late 1990s when I was already working on this project. It was an incredible laudatio: Iazova was compared to Zakhari Stoianov, Simeon Radev, Ivan Khadzhiiski, Geo Milev and Nikola Vaptsarov, all authors who were recognized sometimes decades later, often posthumously. Her book was said to be equal to the ancient Greek mythology, to an ancient tragedy whose hero was the whole people. I was mostly intrigued by Vasilev's comparison of Iazova to Eco: "If we overcome the snobbish fascination with the sensational, until recently, novel of Umberto Eco 'The Name of the Rose,' we shall surely acknowledge that our compatriot has produced, decades before him, something similar in appearance but with far greater spiritual value." Now, this was some verdict and since I continue to be snobbishly dazzled by Eco, my curiosity was heightened.

It has to be said that, similarly to Dichev, Iazova had done massive preparatory work and from that point of view only, her work is a phenomenon in the history of Bulgarian literature. In terms of both ideology and style, this was the antipode of Dichev's. Where he was building a typical realistic novel, replete (although tactfully) with the ideological pathos of the postwar years, she was still in the realm of the nationalism and her typically romantic, even melodramatic style of the interwar years. Where he was sending an internationalist message, trying to highlight the co-existence and cooperation between ordinary Bulgarians and Turks, she set out with stark dichotomies already in the prologue to her trilogy. This brief essay introduced the Balkans as a stormy crossroads and offered a romanticized version of Bulgarian history from antiquity to the 14th century. Bulgarians had accepted Christ as a sign of goodwill and desire to live in peaceful co-existence with the Christian peoples of the peninsula. Their internal bickering, however, brought the Ottoman hordes to the "crossroads of nations," and the Bulgarians "defended themselves alone, holding a sword in one hand, and lifting the cross in the other." When their sword fell, they kept to the cross "as a sign, by which they could be distinguished from the Turks... For five hundred years the Turks called themselves *Aghas*—masters, and the Bulgarians *reaya*—slaves." The return to the simple nationalistic pathos of the prewar years held a definite appeal and was supported both by the then communist authorities (discreetly) and today's government (openly).

Iazova's Levski was described in all the disguises the historical record had documented: a Turk with a turban; a European banker in a suit; a simple peasant; a rural bumpkin; a shepherd; a wandering Gypsy, a silver-haired monk, a teacher; a dervish; a one-eyed beggar, etc. But when she turned to her own description of his real physical image, Levski was coming directly out of her maiden dreams in the 1920s. This was "a luminous young man with golden blond hair and a sunny merry look in his eyes with the color of the clear skies." He was dressed in "European clothes from the finest material in the latest fashion, as if this man was used to wear only well tailored clothes." It is the Great Gatsby directly out of F. Scott Fitzgerald (played by Robert Redford). One has to agree with Vasilev about one thing though. Trying to maximize Iazova's achievement in the postwar years, he compared it to her two novels of the interwar period. They were liked and brought her prizes and prestige but, in his words, "were of the type of the average literature for the middling bourgeoisie." This is where she stayed and this, in principle, should support Vasilev's prediction that her Levski novel would be "devoured by the people," but I doubt it.

Propelled by the same elevated and slightly pompous romantic nationalism, but immeasurably more talented in terms of literature, is the over 200-page-long dramatic epic poem, penned by the poet and classicist Radko Radkov. This was not the first poetic rendering of Levski after Vazov. Unlike historical fiction, poetry renders itself easier to a brief emotional outburst, and the majority of poets have written at least one poem dedicated to Levski in their lifetime. In 1987, a comprehensive anthology of poetry on Levski was published, collecting the century-long production on the topic. A number of other writers preferred the safer middle ground between literature, historiography and journalism. The best is surely Vera Mutafchieva's *The Trial 1873* (1972) because, unlike most of her other colleagues who have nothing more to add except illustrate the Levski theme, she used it for a fine reflection on the relationship between historiography and literature, objectivity and imagination, written and oral testimony, the value of the archive and of silences. Whatever one would think of the quality of a number of other works that have come out in the last few years, they seem to be at least driven by a genuine desire to share one's thoughts and feelings about Levski.

Dichev's novel became the basis for the sole, but quite successful and popular, feature film about Levski until 1989. Dichev himself wrote the script for the ten-series TV film *The Demon of the Empire*, released in 1971. The film was directed by Vili Tsankov, and its consultant was Undzhiev. It featured a cast of the most prominent actors of the time. Its popularity stemmed exclusively from the fact that it was staged as an adventure film, a kind of national Western, with a focus on Levski's agility, and was fondly referred to as the "Dzhingibi" film (*cin gibi*, Turkish for "demon-like," the epithet for which Levski was known among his persecutors whom he successfully eluded). In a recent interview in *Standart*, XIV, 5216, July 18, 2007, Tsankov shared that there was pressure to drop the film, mostly due to protests from Turkey, alleging that it made fun of the Turkish army. Zhivkov himself defended the film, jokingly leaving it to his foreign minister to settle the problem. Asked why today no one dares make a film about Levski, Tsankov replied: "When we were shooting *The Demon of the Empire*, the times were romantic. The Apostle was our hero. Now completely different things are on the agenda. Even the outward similarity would be irrelevant. Our theater and cinema relinquished the chance to experience and emphasize the spiritual. Only the show is valued."

Physically, Levksi's image today is ubiquitous. In all its guises—portraits, sculptures, monuments, paintings, drawings, illustrations, medallions, coins, stamps, cartoons—it keeps close to the realism of the photographs. The version that—purely graphically—is the most interesting, insofar as it deviates from the canonical realistic image of the photograph, was Levski's canonical image as an icon. Even there, of the three known iconic versions, two stuck pedantically to the portrait. Apart from the seven known photographs, the first artful rendering of Levski's image is a naïve drawing from 1879–1880 of Levski's execution. In the 1880s and 1890s, the artist and national revolutionary Georgi Danchov, who knew Levski personally, produced a series of portraits (oil canvases and lythographs) that became widely circulated and immensely popular (Plate 6).The great painter Ivan Mîrkvichka also added illustrations to Vazov's stories in the 1890s. One of the most recognizable images of Levski, also from this period, is the fine bronze medallion (in high relief) on Levski's monument in Sofia, crafted by the Viennese sculptor Rudolf Weir (Plate 7).Painters and sculptors seem to have been far less coy with the Levski theme than writers.

184   The Apostle of Freedom, Or What Makes a Hero?

Figure 16a. Banknote with the image of Levski.

Figure 16b. Stamp with Levski image from 1929 by Khristo Lozev.
Source: Zhechko Popov, *Vasil Levski v bîlgarskoto izobrazitelno izkustvo*, Sofia: Bîlgarski khudozhnik, 1976, Reproduction 95.

All in all, several dozen portraits or sculptures were produced until the Second World War, and hundreds after the war. Practically all most significant artists touched upon one aspect or other of the Levski topic (Popov 1976: 5–46).

For all of Levski's ubiquity, remarkably there has never emerged a lucrative commemorative industry around his image. True, a few postcards exist (usually reproductions of artists' work, and on sale usually at Levski's museum in Karlovo). A few times stamps with his image were issued: one in 1929, two in 1953, one each in 1957, 1963, and 2007. He is used very sparingly on money signs. Twice in the history of the modern Bulgarian state, commemorative silver coins were cast with his image: once, in 1973, for the 100th anniversary of his execution, and then again, in 1987, for the 150th anniversary of his birth (Plate 8). Levski was even taken out of the banknote images during the last change. Until the end of 1999, his image circulated on the 1,000 levs banknote, next to other prominent historical figures of the Bulgarian Revival period. The money signs after 1999 utilized new images spanning the course of Bulgarian history.

There does not seem to be any particular criterion for the choice of images aside from the desire to circulate more nationally significant names among the population. However, when talking to people in the streets about this, they would not ponder on the symbolism of the images but approve of taking Levski off the banknote: it does not behoove his purity to be soiled with money.

Levski can rarely be seen on t-shirts, and the only tiny pin with his image is on sale at his Karlovo museum, next to two small magnets, one with his portrait. Still, it is difficult to resist the commercialization of about everything, and even the official keepers of the Levski flame—the Bulgarian Committee "Vasil Levski"—are making use of it but in a solemn fashion. Preparing for the festivities dedicated to the 170th anniversary of Levski's birth (July, 2007), they have issued 170 medals with his image that will be distributed to worthy Bulgarians. The medal is accompanied by a DVD of the group "Episode," performing patriotic rocks pieces, of which the hit "Levski" based on Vazov's lyrics. Finally, there is a recent fashion of tatoos with Levski's image, carried proudly by its bearers as something sacred (Plate 8A).

His name is used more often but, as a rule, for serious purposes, like naming streets, schools, and libraries (Plate 9). Levski has also become a toponym. Scholars from the Bulgarian Antarctic base on Livingston Island have named after him a mountain peak, rising to approximately 1,430 meters in the western extremity of Levski Ridge, Tangra Mountains, Livingston Island in the South Shetlands Archipelago. Even such a central and sacred national hero as the Albanian Georgi Kastrioti Skanderbeg, whose ultimate position in the Albanian pantheon is reminiscent of Levski, has a famous three-star brandy named after him, and another cheaper version coming from the "George Kastrioti Distillery." Levski thus far has escaped the appetite of gourmands. But both Skanderbeg and Levski have lent their names to the most popular soccer teams of their countries, in Skanderbeg's case in a charming case of split personality, with "Skanderbeg" (Korca) playing against "Kastrioti" (Kruja). Still, while soccer fans passionately roar *Samo Levski* (Only Levski) in the stadiums and in the streets, and the respective graffiti decorate walls and fences, in their minds this "Levski" is completely dissociated from the Real Levski. Remarkably, the team itself does not capitalize on the name as can be seen from a perusal of its organ—the popular newspaper "Levski."

186   The Apostle of Freedom, Or What Makes a Hero?

Figure 17. School photograph, 1987. "Levski, with pioneers, a teacher, two marginals and a portrait of the dissident as a young man."

This section on Levski's image ends with a photograph from the late 1980s, depicting a classroom of third-graders. They have been recently admitted to the membership of the pioneer organization which gives them the right (and obligation) to wear red scarves. The photograph shows the ubiquitous Levski portrait and one could entitle it blandly *Levski in the schoolroom,* were it not for the fact that such a typical title borders on the boring. Instead, I have called it *Levski, with pioneers, a teacher, two marginals and a portrait of the dissident as a young man.* The two marginals are the two melancholy figures to the right, white shirts but without their red scarves. The entire class has been asked to wear their uniform for the day of the photograph. The two have apparently not yet been admitted into the ranks of the select, since they have not forgotten to put on the white shirts. Could one read resignation, if not alienation, in their faces? The boy to the right of the teacher, well within her clutch, does not even wear a white shirt, let alone the red scarf. I have tentatively called him the dissident. I am not sure whether he (purposely) forgot to wear what he was supposed to or whether his mother "was away on business." In any case, it makes a nice figure of speech. The dissident's name is Alex. He is my son.

6. From Hero for All to Dissident and Back

The review of Levski's reception and appropriation in the interwar period, especially in comparison to the respective reception of Botev, shows that both figures, despite certain idiosyncratic trends in their legacy highlighted by different political groups, had been explicitly accepted as common national figures. Both were truly heroes for all. The assertion that Botev and Levski were pitched against each other already in this period, and that after 1944 the communists had elevated Botev as their exclusive symbol at the expense of Levski who was allegedly largely forgotten, was a later hyperbolic interpolation, dating from the 1970s and 1980s, and serving a particular political idea. This does not mean that Botev had not become the slightly preferred figure in the first couple of decades after the war. With his explicit endorsement of the communist ideal, he had been raised as the banner of the communist movement. The whole tenure of communist historiography at the time was such as to posit a teleological and ideological evolution that had to be crowned with an embrace of the socialist idea. At the same time, Levski as the patron of the fascist Legion movement, in no way diminished his status as a major figure in the heroic pantheon. On the contrary, September 9, 1944 was posited to be the materialization of Levski's dream of a "pure and holy republic." The best way to define the official attitude until the 1960s is to say that there was no fascination with Levski comparable to the one that began in the 1970s and continuing until today.

Even as Botev might have been slightly privileged, there was no obsession with him. A look at Politburo protocols dealing with anniversaries in the 1940s and 1950s, shows the emphasis on celebrations of communist events and figures: September 9 (1944) and the Bolshevik Revolution, as well as commemorations of Georgi Dimitrov. Nor did they entirely monopolized the public space. In 1946, the main events and individuals to be commemorated (outside of the official national holidays) were: the 70th anniversary of 1876 uprising; the 2nd anniversary of the heroic death of 138 partisans from a partisan brigade; the 70th anniversary of Panaiot Volov, a national revolutionary; the 64th anniversary of Dimitrov; the anniversary of Iane Sandanski's death (in 1915); the 330th anniversary of Shakespeare's death; the 10th anniversary of Maxim Gorkii's death; and the millennial anniversary of St. John of Rila, the venerated medieval saint-patron of Bulgaria. There were celebrations scheduled to commemorate Botev's 100th anniversary in 1948 but the budget was comparatively modest. The 80th anniversary of Levski's death was commemorated in 1952 and the 80th anniversary of Botev's death in 1956. In the deliberations, there is nothing to indicate any ideological preference. If Botev's name is mentioned somewhat more often, it is because the day of his death—June 2—had become the national day commemorating the roll of honor from the struggles for national liberation against the Ottoman Empire, as well as against capitalism and fascism. By the 1960s there seems to be complete parity: Levski's and Botev's 90th anniversaries were commemorated in 1963 and 1966 respectively and the centenary of Levski's death in 1973 received special attention (*TsDA,* fond 1, op.6, a.e.531, 568, 2829, 5032; op.8, a.e.187, 3092; op.35, a.e.3147).

The scholarly output largely continued the trends set up in the interwar period, although there was, of course, the growing allegiance to the new Marxist jargon, especially in class analysis. Undzhiev's seminal biography, started in the 1930s and continuing Strashimirov's work from the 1920s, was completed in 1945 and published in 1947. The 1940s and 1950s saw the publication of other specialized works by hisorians, whose research had started in the interwar period. The veritable boom in Levski studies occurred, however, from the 1960s on, at the time of his two anniversary celebrations: the 100th anniversary of his death in 1873 and the 150th anniversary of his birth in 1987.

At the time of the 1973 centenary commemoration a trend was set that elevated Levski in the subsequent decade to the role of dissident icon. This process can be traced directly to the work of Nikolai Genchev (1931–2000), a much celebrated and popular historian. In 1973 he published a booklet of 150 pages: "Levski, the Revolution and the Future World." Because this book and its author achieved a mythic status, it is mandatory to look at it in some detail. Years later, in his memoirs written in the mid-1980s but published posthumously in 2005, Genchev wrote that this book "slipped through the authorities' fingers, and they were really mad against its author, this time with good reason" (2005: 254). There is the question about the "authorities." Genchev lets slip in the next pages that even though the press committee sent a telegram to bookstores to stop selling the book till further notice, two thousand copies had already been sold, and he adds that the remaining eight thousand were released soon (ibid.: 256). Who in a small country like Bulgaria could publish 10,000 copies of an academic book without the "authorities"? Obviously someone with direct access to them. The complexity stems from the simple fact that the anonymous "authorities" were a many-headed hydra, and Genchev was friends with only an assortment of these heads.

His memoirs allow us to extrapolate a brief biography in this respect. Born in a poor and uneducated peasant family in 1931, Nikolai Genchev was only 13 at the end of the Second World War, and his vitality, alert mind and charismatic presence made him a natural leader: by 1949 he was already head of his high school's communist youth organization in Tîrnovo where he had moved for his studies. Although he could enter the university in 1949, he preferred to join the District Party Committee. In 1951 he decided to pursue higher education and during his student years, he again headed the communist youth organization of the history and philosophy department, already as a party member. Upon completing his education in 1956, he had offers to join the Institute of the History of the Bulgarian Communist Party, to become director of the Tîrnovo Historical Museum, or a professional party functionary in Sofia. After he arrived in Tîrnovo to assume the directorial post, he was offered to join the city committee of the BCP instead. Genchev refused and through a variety of close friends and colleagues, whose names were later well known in the upper echelons of the party nomenclatura, managed to receive a position as head of the university youth organization of the Engineering College in Sofia. In 1957 he was in charge of the propaganda department of the Lenin District in Sofia, and by 1958 had joined the Central Committee of the Komsomol. Already disappointed in party politics since the time of the Hungarian Revolution, his fervor tamed, by 1959 he became assistant professor at the Department of History of Sofia University. His first book, co-authored with Ilcho Dimitrov, was on the history of the communist youth organization in 1944–1947.

The year 1963 was a turning point. For one, he fended off yet another offer to join the party nomenclatura and "forever bid farewell to a political career, in the sense of a party functionary" (ibid.: 112). Secondly, he got involved in a "happening" that set in motion his subsequent lifelong engagement with Levski as well as his reputation as an unpredictable and courageous maverick. The event took place on December 8, the traditional university students' day that had not been celebrated since the war. In 1958 there were voices to reinstate it, and Genchev takes credit for being among the ones initiating the campaign. The celebration among the historians took place on the first floor of the department with a lot of food, drinks and music. There was temperamental dancing on the tables amidst glasses and plates, and around 3:00 a.m. Genchev called on the group "to go to the monument of Levski to pay our respects according to tradition." Everyone headed to the monument that was a 5 minutes' walk away, singing a popular patriotic 19th-century song with the refrain: "Enough slavery and tyranny." It is worth hearing the professor's voice:

> Drunk and decisive, I climbed the pedestal and ordered in a loud voice: "Get to your knees in front of the spirit of the greatest Bulgarian!" After this I held the following speech to the silent and kneeling assembly: "Dear colleagues, we have knelt here in reverential respect before the Apostle. But why did we forget his three precepts: Levski taught us to love our people, and respect democracy, while we run after every despot. Levski showed how to die for Bulgaria, while we give pledges to foreign states and foreign interests." The moment I pronounced "It is a shame, my students and colleagues," I saw that the silent kneeling assembly is surrounded on all sides by jeeps and militia. At this moment Ilcho Dimitrov pushed me from the pedestal and started explaining something to the students. I must have thought that, if the militia had heard my words, it would start dispersing the meeting, so I climbed back on the pedestal and shouted: "Let us not forget the nice traditions of this holiday! Whoever is ready, follow me to break at least some shop windows on Ruski Boulevard" (ibid.: 113).

His friends tried to dissuade the students from listening to him, and finally they all went back to the university to go on with their drinks, continuing to sing patriotic songs. The militia dispersed without any incidents. It needs to be specified that among Genchev's friends at the event, he names two: Ilcho Dimitrov, his close friend and co-author, future Rector of the University and minister of education in the 1980s, and Georgi Atanasov, likewise friend and colleague, at the time secretary of the Central Committee of the Komsomol and future prime minister under Zhivkov in the 1980s. Next morning, Genchev woke up with the feeling that he had done something irreparable. "It was clear to me that if the authorities learn about the events at the monument, however veiled the meaning of my speech, I won't get away with it." One can only note that some of the "authorities" were next to him at the happening. For several days Genchev was expecting to be summoned for an explanation. Finally, at the end of December, Ivan Abadzhiev, another Komsomol leader who missed the happening at the monument simply because he retreated earlier with a female student to the cloakroom, asked him to visit him at the Central Committee of the youth organization. Without ever mentioning the incident, he offered him the post of councilor on youth affairs to the Algerian government. He added that this would offer Genchev the opportunity to see an interesting part of the world and, "most importantly, would allow me to make some money, improve my lot and buy myself a car" Genchev thought the offer over for a day and concluded that his friends were trying to get him out of the Bulgarian atmosphere, although he did not specify what dangers lay ahead had he stayed. In any case, he defended his dissertation in February, 1964, and on March 1, 1964 was already in Algeria where he spent a year, underutilized by the Algerian government but accumulating materials for a book on the Algerian Revolution that he published in 1967 (ibid.: 114–22).

When he returned in 1965 and resumed his position at the university, Genchev became closely involved with the journal "Youth," whose editorial board he joined. He was instrumental in publishing an article by the philosopher Nikolai Iribadzhakov attacking the long-time Politburo member and godfather of academic life Todor Pavlov (incidentally also the founder of the journal in the 1920s) who had become, in the apt phrase of Genchev, "the father of Bulgarian communist conservatism." While Genchev unconvincingly pleads innocent ignorance and claims that at the journal they were not informed about the political configurations in the highest echelons of the party, the critical article against Pavlov earned them Zhivkov's benevolence. The editors of

Mladezh were invited to an official dinner at the former royal residence Vrana. Zhivkov entertained the group with crude jokes, loud laughter and drinks and told them, inter alia:

> I am a modern person like all of you but my position obliges me to conform to Marxism. Don't think, however, that I am a fool. I even know that this nineteenth-century teaching cannot explain the phenomena of our electronic era. But the people and, especially the youth, need to believe; without belief nothing can be achieved with the young generation (ibid.: 128).

Encouraged by this highest benevolence (Genchev with his usual wittiness stressed as a typical Bulgarian characteristic that even the greatest liberals and the most extreme heretics loved to receive a pat on the shoulder by the Sultan), he submitted an article to the journal that was published in August, 1966. This article, entitled "Magistra vitae, but when?" became, for Genchev, "the most dramatic moment in my life, the source of all my subsequent tribulations and misfortunes." Its gist was an attack on the national nihilism of the Bulgarians who had settled for a crudely falsified version of their past. Kievian Rus was only a pale copy of medieval Bulgaria but today it had acquired the radiance of a world cultural and political center while Bulgaria was known only to the specialists. What was the reason for the Bulgarians' slow progress, asked Genchev, was it something genetic, was it "because we had not enough real men like Levski"? The article, as he summarizes it, "was a spontaneous journalistic outburst of the outrage that was boiling in me, and not only in me, against the continuous and conscious falsification of Bulgarian history after September 9 [1944], deliberately pursued by the Bulgarian communists in the interests of the USSR" (ibid.: 125–31).

Bulgaria's official subservient and sycophantic attitude vis-à-vis the Russians was widely deplored and widely (though privately) discussed but, while nationalism had received the green light in the 1960s, anti-Russian articulations were taboo. Genchev thus spelled out what was on the minds and hearts of many intellectuals. The journal issue with his article (*Mladezh*, 1966, No. 8) virtually disappeared from the kiosks, and it became the buzz of the city. More important than its contents was the style, out-and-out Genchev: epigrammatic, conversational, making big and splashing generalizations, quick, witty, often risky, often populist, often plebeian, very virile, with frequent sexual innuendo. It was the accepted style of the semi-intellectual café culture but one that few, if any, dared bring openly into the institutional corridors of academia or power. Genchev was performing it with gusto, not only at his lectures, but now also in writing. There should be no doubt that he was endowed with considerable charm: this was the common consensus of both admirers and detractors. Of course, charm is not a commodity that is easily quantifiable, let alone comparable or generalizable. It does not have a gold standard or unit of measurement. Nonetheless, it would be safe to say that Genchev had a particular charm that had (and has) a particular valence in Bulgaria.

The French *Le Monde* and the foreign press in general, picked up on Genchev's article and, since *Mladezh* was the official publication of the Komsomol, came to the conclusion that "Bulgaria was returning to nationalism and attempting to differentiate itself from the Soviets" (ibid.: 137). This was true but this was not how it was scripted above, and Genchev's escapade had some, although not fatal, repercussions. He was reprimanded at the Central Committee of the BCP for being irresponsible, but his fate was to be decided by the Komsomol organization. The then Rector of the university, Academician Kosev, called him and told him the Komsomol wanted him fired. Kosev was prepared to fend off the danger for another week but advised Genchev to get directly to Zhivkov. And this is what Genchev did, using the channels of his university male support group, in this case Alexander Fol who was close to Zhivkov's daughter Liudmila. A couple of days later, the Central Committee of the Komsomol received a phone call from Zhivkov who told them not to touch either the editorial board of *Mladezh* or the author of the article (ibid.: 142–150). Crisp and efficient. It is also the pattern of Genchev's relationship with the authorities. What is more amazing is how this tolerated *enfent terrible* of the regime managed to acquire the reputation of an authentic dissident.

The next few years following this incident Genchev describes as "tough years," punctuated by a series of drunken raucous affairs (mostly whiskey and cognac) taking place exclusively in the company of very highly positioned party gentlefolk. Genchev describes them in painstaking detail, the culmination being his row with Fol at the apartment of Zhivkova in 1969, and their subsequent physical fight at the time of the World Congress of Historians in Moscow in 1970. Interestingly, Zhivkova warned Genchev to be more careful because "our regime is multi-layered, the different layers acting independently of each other so that, while one layer can tolerate you, another can crush and suffocate you" (ibid.: 218). He also found room for scholarship. After having published his first two books in 1964 and 1967, Genchev began work on a study of Bulgaria's foreign policy in the period 1938–1941. He tried to reconstruct a more complex and nuanced picture of Bulgaria's entry into the war by showing the attempts of the monarchy to maneuver in the complicated situation after the Ribbentrop–Molotov Pact, and downplayed the role of the communists. The work was completed at the end of 1967, deposited at the *Nauka i Izkustvo* publishing house and, having finally been reviewed positively, awaited its publication. Apparently 5,000 copies were printed but after the 1968 events and the invasion of Czechoslovakia, as well as the incident with a pro-1968 student group among the historians, the book was destroyed. In fact, Genchev managed to publish its several chapters in different academic publications in 1968, 1969, 1970 and 1972, but it came out as a separate book only in 1998. It was this event, however, that finalized his decision to work henceforth only on the 19th-century Bulgarian Revival period, "still naively thinking that this was neutral terrain where the communists were not directly affected, and I could stay true to myself" (ibid.: 138–50).

Genchev's dedication to the Bulgarian Revival lasted for the next couple of decades and is decisive in turning Levski into a symbolic dissident. He had regularly written journalistic pieces dedicated to Levski even before but they were rather anodyne. In 1973, his aforementioned book came out, written according to him in a fortnightly spurt of inspiration. In his memoirs, Genchev explains that his inspiration and ease stemmed from the greatness of Levski, from the fact that he knew all the documentation practically by heart, and "third, because Levski with his undying ideas and deeds majestically rose against all ugliness of our contemporary life. Shown in his full stature, he would expose the contemporary rulers as miserable usurpers, tyrants and nonentities" (ibid.: 255). The book itself consists of an introduction and four parts, dedicated accordingly to Levski's theoretical and practical contributions to the national movement, his ideas for the future, and his personality. The introduction explains that Bulgaria "does not need to substitute the clear tones of the original sound of the genius with the surrogate voices of interpretation," and then goes on to offer 150 pages of interpretation meant to "enrich his image with a novel view," "defend him from the dilettantes who tailor him according to their taste and desire," and bring us back to the "genuine Levski" (Genchev 1973: 6, 9, 19). Inspiration often doesn't follow the sounds of logic but rhetorically we are prepared that this writer has a direct line to Levski's soul.

The book is indeed an inspired apology of Levski, and rereading it today (as well as reading it back in the 1970s), I was amazed that it produced such an uproar. Already at the time (and today again), I felt uneasy with the cheap jibes at the Ottoman Empire (always called Turkey or the Turkish Empire) as "a "barbarous Asiatic machine," "a laughable sack of rubbish," "an Asiatic barbarous system," "a doomed decayed empire, unable to integrate itself in modern society, where any attempt at progress would lead only to the birth of "oriental Asiatic monstrosities." This wouldn't have triggered a backlash from the authorities; if anything, it was in line with the general assertion of nationalism. True, "Asiatic Turkey" may have been meant to be read also (but not only) as a metaphor of Russia and the Soviet Union, a safe way to direct the invectives, and this interpretation was widespread among his students, not a little cultivated by Genchev himself. Levski was described as the emanation of all the glories and achievements of Bulgaria, and pronounced to be the embodiment of all of Bulgaria's heroes' individual qualities, "inspired and ennobled by the humanism of the Renaissance, the light of the Enlightenment, and the liberal free-thinking of the 19th century" (ibid.: 148). If anything, this pompous turn of phrase would enhance Bulgaria's grandeur and Europeanness. Nor was it objectionable at the time (but uncomfortable to read today) to lambaste the theological literature for trying to depict Levski as a religious person: "In his personality and deeds he is a complete negation of God and his terrestrial and subterranean worlds; he is a complete negation of the false and hypocritical Christian morality" (ibid.: 10).

There were only a couple of passages, well buried in the text, that could have produced an adverse reaction. One was eulogizing Levski's patriotism, his vision for a free united nation "there, where the Bulgarian lives, in Bulgaria, Thrace and Macedonia." These were Levski's words but they were accompanied by a commentary that this radically distinguished him from later politicians who are ready "to trade like grocers the historical rights of the Bulgarian people" (ibid.: 109). Given that Thrace and Macedonia were shed from the foreign policy program of Bulgaria after the Second World War, it was a transparent criticism of the communist regime. The other extolled Levski's political perspicacity, in interpreting his vision for the future government as a division between judicial and executive powers: "in this our remarkable democrat saw guarantees against the totalitarian regime, against tyranny and despotism" (ibid.: 112). This was a par excellence instance of East European periphrastic. "Totalitarian regime" was the keyword and synonym for communist power, and this was a direct shot, although one that was well calculated and well camouflaged. Genchev himself mentions "several transparent hints" that infuriated the authorities. First was his assertion that Levski was the greatest Bulgarian figure, and "communists cannot calmly accept such a historical verdict when not addressed to one of their own theoreticians or leaders." This, in view of all the preceding analysis, is rather lame. The second and third "hints" are the ones highlighted above: that Levski had been appropriated by everyone, including totalitarian regimes, and "it was clear to everyone, that here the communists were meant;" and that Levski espoused democratic ideas contrary to the ideas and practices of the communist regime (Genchev 2005: 257–8). In all other respects, and despite the fact that Genchev described his effort as thoroughly revisionist, the book developed ideas that were not politically objectionable.

Writing, as he does in his memoirs, that this book "slipped through the authorities' fingers" is a huge exaggeration. He sent his manuscript to the editor in early July, 1972, and she immediately edited it. Fine points like peer reviews and formal board decisions were apparently not necessary for him. The only thing needed was the signature of the editor-in-chief Mantov but he was about to leave on vacation. Genchev "called Mantov on the phone and chided him for making me stay in Sofia during the summer in order to finish the manuscript, while he dodges and will ruin the publication." So, Mantov promised he would sign the same evening as he was leaving next morning. Which he did, without having read the manuscript (ibid.: 255–6). A month between the delivery of a manuscript and its going to press is a record that can make many a writer in any political regime envious. It was only in February of the following year, after two thousand (of the 10,000 printed) copies were sold, that the book was stopped. What followed was a meeting in the office of the then head of the "Propaganda" division at the Central Committee, Dimitrov. After the meeting, at which he was livid and ordered sanctions against the editor, Dimitrov left in his car and had a bad accident. Sofia was filled with the rumor: "This bacho Kolio (the popular name under which Genchev was fondly known) is a holy man; whoever pesters him will suffer." Immediately following this sentence, without further explanation, the memoirs report that a few days later, the remaining 8,000 copies were released and sold out practically in a morning. Genchev had to find additional copies from provincial cities. (ibid.: 257). This is the saga of a book that had the reputation of a banned and dissident work but whose 10,000 copies were printed at breakneck speed, and effectively sold.

It was not so much what was written in the book that created the reaction against it but, rather, Genchev's self-advertisement of what he meant to say with it. He had always been (in a tradition typical for and cultivated especially among Bulgarian university historians) better in oral than in written articulation. The same goes true for the politicians. Rather than waste their time reading, they heard what others were saying. And what was being said was that "bacho Kolio" had put the proper dots on all the "i"s: read Turkey, understand Russia and their local stooges. Moreover, looking at the exact sequence of events, it seems it was not "the authorities" in general but one particular person—an apparatchik who apparently had been alerted—who reacted to a signal, and after his ominous accident, there was no follow up, except Genchev's enhanced reputation of a courageous gadfly. All of this does not deny that several times in his life Genchev did suffer some kind of sanction. His 1973 book was eventually distributed but the introduction he had written to the documentary collection of Levski was taken off. His monograph on Russian–Bulgarian cultural relations was virtually destroyed immediately after it was printed. His endorsement of Zhelev's "Fascism" (as internal reviewer) cost him his position as chair of the history department. But it shows the erratic and essentially arbitrary way the regime was reacting to challenges. "Exposing" Genchev's successful self-mythology also does not mean that much of his critique did not build on real aberrations, even as they assumed hyperbolic dimensions. Moreover, the positive reception of his actions and works, and his immense popularity were apparently triggered by a profound unease and displeasure with the official and stale ideologese. By the 1960s it had lost its initial fresh appeal, and the new generations, the ones already born and brought up under socialism, rarely fell under its spell as had Genchev and his generation. As aptly summarized, Lenin had given way to Lennon.

What actually comes as a surprise is how long pedagogical efforts and textbooks lagged behind this disenchantment so obvious in the public sphere, how little they adapted to the new constellations. On the other hand, they offer a glimpse into how hero worship was formed from the youngest age. A textbook for teachers at the kindergarten level from 1976 enumerates the different elements constituting the natural and social environment that children should be gradually exposed to. Six elements are defined as comprising the social environment: labor; cultural institutions; national heroes and political leaders; social, political and private celebrations; space (town, village, neighborhood); an idea of the Soviet Union and other socialist countries. As for detailing national heroes, this consisted in acquainting children with the figures of Vasil Levski, Khristo Botev, Georgi Dimitrov and the heroes of the antifascist struggle. This was, more or less, replicated in the more elaborate 1979 textbook that also gave a concrete breakdown of themes introduced at the different kindergarten levels. Three Bulgarian heroes—Levski, Botev and Dimitrov—exemplified the theme "Motherland." Of course, these were not themes that monopolized the curriculum, and they were a relatively small part among topics on the family, nature, plants, birds, animals, cooking, cleaning, travel, medicine, but the sequence in the particular sub-field of heroes is a telling one.

These books are distinguished from the ones published after 1989 in that they are much more general, deal at greater length with child psychology, and do not offer regimented thematic programs. Yet, the older textbooks are still utilized. In 1998, I visited a kindergarten in one of the central districts of Sofia and spoke with the director and a schoolteacher. I was interested in how children were introduced to historical themes, especially national heroes. Both teachers emphasized they were trying to do this discreetly and juxtaposed their present freedom to experiment with methods to the previous bureaucratic approach and strict discipline when they were careful to conform to the rules. I asked how abstract notions like heroes are explained to the children. "This is easy: a hero is one who does things for the rest." When I asked the director —a well educated pedagogue who quotes Piaget and a host of new luminaries I haven't heard about—how exactly the children are introduced to national heroes, she was critical: "For example, Levski is always introduced beginning with the gallows. This creates tension, negative emotions among the children, just like with the 'Turkish yoke' and the violence. It produces people without optimism and self-respect, but instead with complexes and feelings of victimization." I asked why she unconsciously gives the example of Levski, when I posed my question about heroes in the most abstract, and whether he was for her the greatest national hero. "Who else? How otherwise?" When I persisted, she became impatient: "I have read enough and it is not a matter of manipulating me; I am able to contextualize." I told her that textbooks at the end of the 19th century had not yet elevated Levski to the peak of the pantheon. "Fine," she retorted, "it is possible that in different periods political considerations predominated but in the end the real character shines through." She likes to speak of the *truth*, of *real values*, and that *the people* instinctively know and are the final *objective* arbiter. But it is too much to expect deconstruction from children's pedagogues when historians shy away from it.

Genchev's own work is a good illustration of this. Between 1973 and 1989, he published no less than 23 popular journalistic pieces specifically on Levski. He passionately broadcasted his ideas in an accessible prose (especially his interviews that retained his inimitable oral talent). Finally, his major opus on Levski came out in 1987. It included his 1973 work with an important excursus on the reception of the hero. Yet, he never transcended the deeply ingrained understandings of authentic truth, genuineness, real values, objective criteria that characterized and continue to characterize the, as a whole, empiricist physiognomy of Bulgarian historiography. Genchev was no methodological revisionist or innovator. He also was less of a political revisionist than he liked to believe but he did, indeed, achieve no small feat. While insisting on Levski's universal human message and appeal (against explicit attempts at appropriation), he, in fact, appropriated him as a dissident banner. That, in the process, he erected himself as Levski's bard and avatar, goes without saying.

It was this dissident ethos of Levski, as popularized by Genchev, that was embraced by his friend Zhelev, the leader of the anti-communist opposition after 1989. Ironically, it was Zhelev, one of the few authentic Bulgarian dissidents, who put an effective end to Levski's dissident status, once Levski's portrait founds its place on the wall behind the desk of the newly elected President Zhelev. Ever since, Levski decorates every incoming president's office, and is again evoked as the official imprimatur on any political philosophy or action. He is again a hero for all. Again, he is utilized for a myriad "jobs." It was announced that with his prescient ideas, Levski had laid the basis for the future Eurointegration. Twice each year, on July 18, his birthdate and, especially, on February 19, the day of his execution, Bulgaria's top managers—president, prime minister, speaker of parliament, city's mayor—dutifully appear before his monument in the center of Sofia in an elaborate ceremony, replete with military honors, wreath laying, and actors' performances. The same, on a lesser scale, goes on in other towns, particularly Karlovo. In the meantime, the ecclesiastical authorities organize memorial services in all major churches of the country, and the number of citizens who participate is growing by the day. It is becoming truly an addition, if not a challenge to Bulgaria's national day, March 3. Levski is the patron of temperance societies, and the inspiration of prisoners. People run in races, swim across the river Danube and climb Mount Everest in his honor.

The scholarship on Levski after 1989 continues unabated. Most of it is in the serious factographical tradition of the previous decades, and much comes from historians with an already earned reputation in the field but there is also a lot in the popularizing and commemorative genre. An interesting addition are the contributions of non-professional historians, especially on the issue of Levski's capture and betrayal, a phenomenon that became possible with the decentralization and liberalization of the publishing business. A continuing and obviously successful venture, given the constant laments about the shrinking book market, is the publication of new and revised editions of Levski's documentation, as well as the reprinting of some of the better known works on Levski. While the style of writing has not changed, there are two subtle modifications: one is the addition of new topics, some of them quite arcane (Levski as pedagogue, Freemason or linguist); the other is the general suffusion of the works in a new discursive field where the principle vegetation is of the genus of "democratization," "constitutionalism," "communication," "tolerance," "anti-terrorism."

All these illustrations are at the level of the *production* of individual and group, social and political, moral and historical identities. It is more difficult to find evidence for the analysis of the receiving end of the phenomenon, the level of *reception*, that would show how this production—historiographical, journalistic, fictional—is being internalized. In 1998, I launched questionnaires at different school levels, in the hope that this would allow to have a glimpse at the reception end of the process, and its articulation. The cluster of material comes from two locales: Sofia and Plovdiv. The Sofia responses are from one school and comprise 115 answers. The Plovdiv responses—a total of 139—come from three different schools. The clusters are of different quality: the Sofia school is one of the top educational institutions with a focus on the Italian language, whereas the three Plovdiv schools are not ranked among the top. Accordingly, they are treated separately.

Two questions, offered independently of each other, so the answer would not be implicitly suggested by the question, were posed to the Sofia students. Three classes were asked to write on "Who is the greatest Bulgarian hero?" Of the 87 respondents, 62 chose Levski, and in another 9 cases Levski figured in a cluster with other heroes, paired with Botev, Khan Asparukh, Tsar Simeon and Stefan Stambolov. The answers are, in their majority, quite unemotional. An opening statement asserts Levski as the greatest hero, followed, almost without exception, by a factual (often lengthy and pretty correct) recitation of his biography and main achievements. It is the clichéd history-textbook version, as it is memorized and internalized by good and ambitious students in one of the leading high schools in the capital, but some of the answers also contain elements of Levski's adventures as they must have been remembered from previous exposure in their childhood or early school years to the stories of Vazov. Even though Levski is chosen as the greatest hero, this seems to follow some kind of received wisdom, as he is not juxtaposed to the other Bulgarian heroes and nothing specific is singled out, beyond his sacrifice for liberty and the fatherland.

The answers to the second question "What do you know about Vasil Levski?" produced the same biographies, as if they had been asked the same question but without the option for choice. This unemotional, factual approach is true also of the ones who dissent from the standard choice of Levski. The only conclusion that can be drawn from these responses is that issues about national heroes or national pride do not evoke strong feelings, let alone passions. The young people have internalized the textbooks and produce the answers expected of them, but are doing it in a matter-of-fact way, devoid of affect. It has to be added that these questionnaires were prepared at the end of the 1990s, when the "emigration virus" among young people was particularly active. This particular cohort of the Sofia high school subsequently had one of the largest proportion of students studying and attempting to stay abroad. One could interpret their reception of the Levski theme as the accumulation of useful knowledge, needed to get over the hurdle of the final high school exams and preparing for the university entry exams, rather than identity-building information.

The Plovdiv students' responses don't differ from the Sofia ones in terms of affect but strike one as more spontaneous even if much shorter. More interesting is the comparison of the Plovdiv high school cohort to the Sofia one. The 54 tenth to twelfth-grade students from Plovdiv responded, as already mentioned above, in a very informal way, producing brief, often hurried answers on tiny pieces of paper. One response to the question "What is your opinion about Vasil Levski?" by an unnamed student from the tenth grade of the "Konstantin Preslavski" school stands out:

> According to me, the present generation rejects and renounces Vasil Levski. These questions are old-fashioned and passé. Only during the literature periods, because it is mandatory and because students aspire to get a better grade, they praise him and say what the teacher wants to hear. The new twentieth-century generation has other, completely different, idols. Levski valued and defended his homeland, and nowadays every Bulgarian is trying to run away abroad. Many change their beliefs easily and everything is radically different.

This is not shared by all. A two-sentence response says: "Levski for me is the ideal individual." An even briefer one offers a curt: "Levski is not a national hero, he is something much greater." Yet another student, writes that Levski is "Bulgaria's idol. I think, that today such individuals do not exist. Maybe I am proud to be a Bulgarian and have such a hero." This is the most poignant "maybe" that I have ever encountered!

Bulgarian school kids are no different from school children in other European locales. Despite the assertion that the phenomenon of globalization makes Madonna more popular than Joan of Arc or Garibaldi, popularity is not tantamount to notions of heroism, and the concrete data corroborates our skepticism. Thus, French students in the 1990s spontaneously connected "the hero" to notions of sacrifice, justice and courage, all of which are closer to Joan of Arc and Garibaldi than to Madonna. "Political figures were most often associated with heroism, followed by anonymous and fictional figures. The 'heroes' of show business were allotted a mere 13%, and only scholars and artists, as well as athletes were assigned even less (5% and 3% respectively), a soothing reassurance for academics who are always ready to trail after athletes" (Centlivres 1998: 980100).

If this evidence for the reception of Levski's cult was generated with an external stimulus, other manifestations are, if not completely spontaneous, at least propelled by some internal urge. Several Levski websites are regularly visited and passionately commented on. Levski came again in the focus of public attention when, on the eve of Bulgaria's accession to the European Union in January, 2007, the National Television organized a contest about "Great Bulgarians." In December, 2006, Bulgarians were invited to vote through their cell phones for the foremost historical personalities. On February 17, 2007, the results of the contest were announced. Levski won the first place with 60,000 entries. Much to everyone's surprise, Petîr Dînov emerged second with 20,000 votes. While this was no scientifically conducted opinion poll, it reflected the public's aversion to the present political scene, and elevated a relatively marginal though charismatic spiritual figure to the second position. Levski may have been a politician but he had the luck to have never been in power, and in the past years his proverbial honesty, modesty, frugality and scrupulous book-keeping have been constantly contrasted with the wholesale corruption of the political and economic elites.

Another way to gauge people's reception is to look at a relatively untapped source: visitors' books to museums. One reason they have been distrusted as evidence is that a disconcerting number of entries follows a bureaucratic pattern, or are full of uninspired but expected platitudes. Surprisingly, the so-called "books for impressions" at the Levski Museum in Karlovo yield more than commonplace remarks.

There is a display of real emotion and one of the books—for 1976—bears the highly unconventional title of "notebook for emotions." There is a regularly kept series of these "impression books" beginning in the 1970s. True, a greater number of entries before 1989 are predictably more rigid than the ones written later, but there are enough that give the impression of authentic spontaneity, even as the articulation may seem trite. A majority of entries comes from groups, most often school groups. Many oscillate between cliché and pathos, but some are surprising. An entry from June 21, 1981, signed by "a group from Tolbukhin and Varna," reads: "'I would sacrifice my life for love; for liberty, I would sacrifice even love'—these are the words fitting the Great Levski." Quite a few elevate Levski on the highest pedestal. He is "the greatest and unrivalled among all Bulgarians," "there is no Bulgarian greater than this Bulgarian," "Vasil Levski is the only honest Bulgarian," and there are appeals: "Let us bow to the only one!" and "Let us honor the memory of the greatest Bulgarian." There is an unmistakably political entry of April 18, 1993: "We came to honor the only Bulgarian who is a democrat. What a pity he could not find followers among the builders of contemporary Bulgaria." A group of socialists, returning from the celebrations of the 100th anniversary of the foundation of the socialist movement in Bulgaria address Levski: "You, Deacon, are in our hearts with your immortal ideals for a pure and holy republic" (August 4, 1991).

If one were to draw the geography of visitors to Levski's museum, the whole of Bulgaria would be on the map. There are entries in different languages: Polish, Czech, Hungarian, Russian, French, German, Italian, Spanish, Dutch, English (from Canada, Australia and the US), Arabic, Greek, Croatian, Hebrew, even a Laotian poem. Some of these group entries are ideological and, at first glance, predictably in line with what is expected, but neither sycophantic nor, upon reflection, opportunistic, given the obscurity of a museum book entry. As usual, most interesting are the individual and personal entries. A few visitors have come, who are the offspring of grandparents that have known Levski or have been active in the 19th-century national revolution. Others are moved by some kind of local patriotism. Donka Karastoianova adds at the end of her thoughtful comment: "Blessed and happy is Karlovo for having given Levski to Bulgaria!" (October 6, 1992). An angry note from June, 1982 by "a pure Bulgarian" chal-

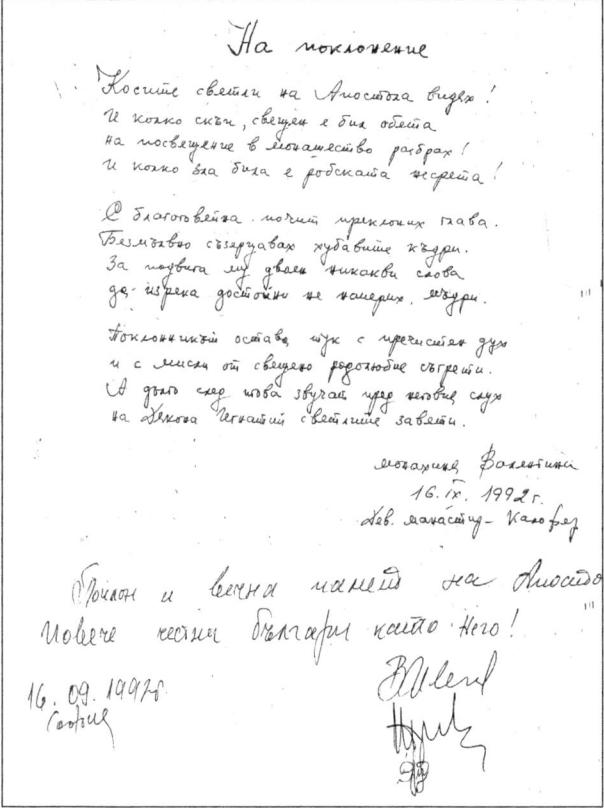

Figure 18. Poem dedicated to Levski by the nun Valentina from the Kalofer cloister, 16 September 1992.
Source: Visitor's books to the Karlovo museum.

lenges the inhabitants of Karlovo to rectify the part of the exposition that unduly emphasizes the contribution of the Lovech Revolutionary Committee. Disregarding the well-established historical fact that Lovech was indeed the center of Levski's revolutionary network, and playing on the shared belief of Pop Krîstiu's betrayal, the "pure Bulgarian" writes: "Isn't it high time that Karlovo's inhabitants stop the bragging of these insolent traitors... The way things are moving, they will soon say Levski was born in Lovech."

A self-critical note alludes to the fact that Bulgarians had participated in the trial against the Apostle and agreed to the death sentence, and had left his remains and his grave in oblivion (September 14,

1979). Another (from May 29, 1981) deplores the fact that the ideals that inspired Levski, and which are the only ones that could make the country great, do not exist any longer. This is as far as it gets in criticizing communist reality in the visitors' books. The post-1989 entries are more explicit, and a lapidary one, added on the Apostles birthday on July 18, 1992, reads: "Bulgaria! How much grief, impudence, shame, desolation. Oh, Deacon, bring them to their senses!" A number of post-1989 entries are written by believers, who unequivocally refer to Levski's faith and image as saint and martyr. There is the beautiful melodic poem of a nun who has come on a pilgrimage from her monastery in neighboring Kalofer. A prayer by a citizen of Omurtag on September 14, 2003 pleads: "Lord Jesus Christ, discover the second Levski, so Bulgaria can be saved." One entry is signed by a young couple—Aglika and Angel—on June 8, 1996. They are inspired by the faith of the Apostle, by his ideals, and his life and death. According to them, today Bulgaria needs the Apostle's spirit in order to overcome the terrible sin which weighs upon her and suffocates her. Only then will the country be free and Jesus Christ will reign as its holy Lord. Angel adds that "together with Agi, who is my fiancée, we believe we shall meet him in heaven."

Some Christian entries display a more biblical wrath. Milhail Penushliev from Sofia writes on March 9, 1990, very soon after the fall of the regime: "Now we need Levski's light and fire in order to overcome the legacy of the slave-totalitarian regime. We know that the totalitarian censorship had encroached even on Levski's correspondence, but this has come to an end. Place candles in the home of the Deacon. He has not been an atheist." But the atheists would not disagree. As the couple Vildanka and Dodio from Gabrovo expressed it already in April, 1987: "We are proud of and grieve for Levski. Why do we need God, when we have Levski!" There are the odd and unexpected figures of speech, some moving, others funny. A young woman from Iambol shares her long-standing view that "death in the name of an idea is a very unreasonable act. But, having come here, I think I may change my mind" (she is putting the date the American way: 07.27.98). A group of eight illegible signatories have visited the museum on June 8, 1996. "Especially today," they write, "when we are so desperate with everything that happens around us in our country, it is nice that there are such individuals who can raise one's national self-esteem. Today, in particular, when we expect the victory of our national soccer team, we are going to think of Levski." Someone has added the popular *Samo Levski*, that usually reverberates in the soccer stadium.

For me personally, the most moving among this rich parade of entries are two brief ones from 1993. One (June 30 is signed by Zekiye, Ali and Hasan and says: "I, a Turkish woman, deeply admire your courage, your intelligence, and your great deed. Let us bow before your purity and holy memory, Apostle!" The other one, entered on Levski's birthday, July 18, reads: "My ethnic consciousness is Turkish, but the Bulgarian I respect is Levski, because he is the most noble Bulgarian figure!" In April, 2004, one Gülay has added "Thank you for everything you have done for us." There is also the standard school entry signed by twelve-year olds from the fifth grade of a school in Khaskovo on December 11, 2004. The class is mixed, half the names are Turkish, half Bulgarian. One rebellious child has added a brief note (with orthographic mistakes): "Bulgaria is the dullest state." These are not isolated cases. During her 1992 field work in Razgrad (a mixed Bulgarian-Turkish region in northeast Bulgaria), the ethnographer Ekaterina Anastasova came across the legend of a female Levski among the Turkish population. It was rumored, at the time of the renaming of the Turks and their subsequent exodus, that a woman from the village of Kaolinovo, Ruse district had organized protest actions. "We have an organization and we have our Levski," the Turks would say. "Only, he is not a man but a woman, so you cannot catch him!" Some denied the existence of a leader, others said the woman was a secret police provocateur, and Anastasova could not establish more reliable facts (1993: 159). The reality is besides the point. Levski, by all measures the quintessence of a fierce and passionate national struggle, has acquired a supranational appeal. His figure, the gender change notwithstanding, has become the ethnically syncretic symbol of resistance.

Levski also has a worshipper—the self-described psychoanalyst, Doctor Dimitîr Sirakov—who regularly visits Karlovo on July 18, the Apostle's birthday. The doctor signs as the chairman of the branch of the World Health Organization called BIOMAG-92-BALKANIA, and lives in Thessaloniki, Greece (he has even entered his address and telephone number). Interestingly, he announced the canonization of Levski as having occurred in 1992, and greeted Levski in his address of July 18, 1992 for the 155th anniversary of his birth and the first anniversary of his sainthood. One can only assume that it was Sirakov himself who officiated at this canonization. Sirakov is the discoverer of the "leptonic arms for the twenty-first century" and on the day of the Holy Apostle's 160th birthday, he declared a "leptonic cosmo-planetary war on global imperialism, the cancer of the epoch we inhabit." Yet, while Levski's canonization did not occur in 1992, except in the fiery imagination of Sirakov, his prescience cannot be denied. The canonization did take place, although a few years later, and this is the subject of the following part.

PART III

THE NATIONAL HERO AS SECULAR SAINT: THE CANONIZATION OF LEVSKI

On July 14, 2000 in the tiny and, as yet, empty interior of the newly-built chapel "All Bulgarian Saints," part of the Vasil Levski Museum ensemble in Karlovo, a couple of men were leveling a marble and glass container. This was the only other object in the chapel aside from the iconostasis. It is a pretty *objet d'art* made of a green marble base, carrying a glass case flanked at the corners with four gilded lion heads, and crowned with a gilded cross. The glass case was supposed to house Levski's hair. "This is a reliquary," I exclaimed. Only instead of presenting what St. Hieronimus called *ossa veneranda* (venerated bones), or rather because of their absence, it displays *capilla veneranda* (venerated hair). "Far from it," I was told, "it is simply an air-conditioned museum display box." It didn't matter that even the word employed—*khranitelnitsa*—is that for reliquary. What was happening? Has the religious sanctuary acquired a primary function as a museum in our secular age? Or the reverse? Or are we in the presence of an intelligent ploy to impose the formal canonization of Levski on the Church's agenda? The latter, in fact, had already partly happened (Plates 10–12).

On July 1–4, 1996, a Church National Council was convened by what some consider the "secessionist church" or "schismatics," and the conveners called the only legitimate Bulgarian Orthodox Church. The council made two profound personnel changes that cemented its difference from the existing church administration of Patriarch Maxim, referred to as the "comrades of the red church." It elevated former Metropolitan Pimen the status of Patriarch. It also elevated Bulgaria's most popular national hero to the status of saint. Pimen's election was widely reported in the press, and received due attention by observers of the ecclesiastical split. The canonization of Levski, by contrast, remained unnoticed although it was the more momentous choice. Pimen, after all, is mortal, and died in the meantime, while Levski was propelled from one immortal hypostasis (national hero) to another (saint), a kind of immortality insurance policy that behooves this age of ephemeral values and abrupt changes in fortunes. The news of Levski's canonization came out only on his birth date on July 18, when a service was held at "St. Paraskeva," the headquarters of the Pimen-led church. It was rebuffed by Patriarch Maxim as an act of populism, in contradiction to the Orthodox tradition and canon. Still, it was considered so unworthy of attention at the time that when, in the summer of 1998, I spoke with members of the Church Historical and Archival Institute of the Bulgarian Patriarchate (CHAI), they were under the impression it had taken place in February, 1997. Even priests of the Pimen-led church hierarchy believed the year to have been 1997.

Contrary to its early underestimation, the event had a crucial significance for the future of the church, as well as the character of national symbols. It became the central differentiating sign of Pimen's church that gave it cultural legitimation, apart from the exclusively political power rhetoric used up to this moment. At the same time, it triggered subdued debates within the official church, as well as a grassroots process that, despite strong protestations and firm official opposition, is moving in the direction of Levski's canonization in the future. By looking in detail into the intricacies of the church split and the political implications of Levski's canonization, I hope to indicate my interest and stake in a project aptly described as "enchanting" politics with a richer sense of what it might consist of or, as Clifford Geertz defined it, "to elaborate a poetics of power, not a mechanics" (1980: 123).

To be sure, the interest and study of the links between symbolism and politics had its forerunners in several branches of scholarship. This came as a corrective to the neglect of politics or reductionism in interpretations of the political in the traditions that dominated historiography after the Second World War: the *Annales* paradigm, social science history, influenced by functionalist sociology, orthodox Marxism. The decisive influence came from contemporary cultural anthropologists—Mary Douglas, Clifford Geertz and Marshall Sahlins—who gave historians

> ways of seeing politics as a form of cultural interaction, a relationship tied to broader moral and social systems. Political symbols and acts of persuasion carry with them complex networks of social customs, aspirations, and fears... By reading these 'metaphorical' acts, sym-

bols, and pronouncements, much as an anthropologist reads everyday events and rituals, the historians hope to fuse our understanding of power, cultural expression, and political consciousness" (Wilentz 1985: 3-4).

It is the interest in the "poetics of power" that informs the analysis of Levski's recent canonization. Looking into the mystique of politics shows its logic most clearly because, "a world wholly demystified is a world wholly depoliticized" (Geertz 1980: 30). This analysis should be applied not only to the present post-socialist period. It would be equally deficient to foreground it only against the socialist baseline. Instead, it should be analyzed in the *longue durée* of ecclesiastical and national history. For a decade the church had a Janus-like Levski: one face already with a *nimbus*, the other a saint in the making. But Levski had already been conferred a non-canonical holy status as martyr and saint of the nation. Methodologically, the events of recent years pose additional problems: the correlation between hero worship and sainthood in the era of nationalism; the different genres that effectuate this interplay; finally, the symbolic repertoire of nationalism in the era of post-communism.

There is an additional methodological issue. How exactly can we write a poetics of power? Poetry, even at its most abstract, is most powerful in its metaphoric use of detail. This attention to detail and the veritable elevation of the concrete, flourishes first and foremost through narrative. It might seem superfluous that narrative should need special justification here, in a work written by a historian, after the decades-long debates about overcoming the narrative, returning to the narrative, and the basic philosophical consensus that our understanding of the world is narrative, and that history is a narrative project. This is not a return to the outdated division between descriptive and nomothetic scholarship. Historians, whether they admit it or not, or are conscious of it or not, provide narrative interpretations of often several orders of previous interpretations. This interpretive character of the historian's project necessitates what Gilbert Ryle introduced as a category, and Geertz made famous—"thick description"—arguing that how cogent our explications are, should be measured "not against a body of uninterpreted data, radically thinned descriptions...but against the power of the scientific imagination to bring us in touch with the lives of strangers" (Geertz 1973: 6, 16). This imperative speaks directly and dearly to the heart of the historical profession, with the only distinction that there is an additional chronological distance about the historian's strangers: they are not only of another place but also of another time. It shows as well how close the disciplines of history and anthropology have come together in their philosophy and methods.

It is within such approach that I situate several narratives of what happened, and construct a reading of them. The first is about the recent church split, and the political background within which the canonization has to be contextualized. Taking a close look at the succession of events, it is based largely on the contemporary press and, more often than not, approaches the journalistic genre. The second narrative is partly interpretive in that it provides a sociological explanation of the main protagonists' position, but its main purpose is to show dominant discourse in which the canonization was argued by both adherents and opponents. Insofar as it approximates in style an old-fashioned historiographical narrative, it will have succeeded in conveying the manner of argument advanced by all sides in the controversy. The third narrative explains the equivocal position of Levski in the church. It is written in the genre of classical critical historiography, and offers a critical narrative of other narrative genres in which Levski's case has been emplotted: memoiristic, biographical or historiographical. The fourth narrative—about the spontaneous but also often orchestrated grassroot *cultus* of Levski—is closest to the ethnographic approach with all implications about the genre of writing. The point is to provide a set of rich and detailed narratives, so as to be able in the end: "to draw large conclusions from small, but very densely textured facts; to support broad assertions about the role of culture in the construction of collective life by engaging them exactly with complex specifics" (Geertz 1973: 28). The last two chapters bring these four narratives together by subjecting them to an interpretive reading. To be sure, creating and situating narratives is itself a construction, and the subsequent "reading" is simply a consecutive self-conscious construction of a further order. If, however, the first four narratives implicitly suggest a number of theoretical interpretations, the last two chapters provide an explicit theoretical framework. The fifth chapter engages with issues of ritual and commemoration, nationalism and religion, and links them directly to the socio-economic and cultural processes of post-communism. The sixth chapter probes into how the hero-creating process depends on the historical context, and whether there exist typological differences between the place of heroes in the theocratic state, the ancient city-state, imperial formations, the nation-state, or global communications settings, and specifically the link between sainthood and heroism. It finally locates Levski within the international "family" of national heroes or the genus of human heroes at large.

1. The Split, or How a Bicephalous Organism Functions

The birthday of the split was May 25, 1992 when the director of the Office of Religious Affairs (ORA), an agency directly under the cabinet of ministers, issued decree No. 92 declaring Patriarch Maxim and his Holy Synod illegitimate, and appointing in its place a new Holy Synod under Metropolitan Pimen as its *pro tempore* president. This act legitimized the internal secession of five metropolitans a week earlier, who had announced the formation of a new Synod headed by Pimen. The decision rested on the argument that Maxim's election in 1971, during a totalitarian and atheist regime, was a violation of the Holy Canon and the Law of Confessions. It contended that Maxim and the central leadership had not been registered properly, and rendered their election illegal.

This birthday had been preceded by a two-year long gestation period. Immediately following the fall of Zhivkov on November 10, 1989, different institutions looked for ways of reforming themselves by changes of personnel, a kind of spontaneous lustration. In the church, this happened by an unwieldy alliance of individuals propelled by very different motives. The intellectual force was the professor of the Theological Academy Radko Poptodorov, by all accounts a well-educated and cultivated scholar but embittered by feelings of underappreciation, who, in an article in *Otechestvo* in January, 1990 articulated the basic charges against the ecclesiastical leadership. The driving political force was Father Khristofor Sîbev, a lapsed nuclear physicist turned monk in the 1980s, whose only permanent quality in a flamboyant and unpredictable career was his erratic character. Known to the public as "Fori the glow-worm" for the candle-light night vigils he organized in the early days of democracy, this mercurial individual offered the single most non-religious and realpolitiker's motivation for the split in an interview for *Demokratsiia* (September 22, 1992) the official organ of the Union of Democratic Forces, the anti-communist coalition: "You have to understand, with the coming elections the MRF has its religion and temples, and the UDF also needs its own church. It needs religious support. This is not mixing politics with religion. Just tell me who will Maxim's lot vote for in the new elections? They will vote for the BSP, they are in a symbiosis with it, let our people have no illusions." The MRF is the Movement for Rights and Freedoms, unofficially known as the Turkish party, and BSP the Bulgarian Socialist Party, the renamed former communists. As MP since 1991, and Chairman of the Assembly's Committee for Religious Affairs, Sîbev secured the directorship of ORA for an ally. In March, 1992, ORA sent a letter to the Holy Synod explaining the illegitimacy of the 1971 election, and ordering a new one. Then came the famous decree of May 25, 1992, poignantly flanked by the meteoric rise of Sîbev, who had his eyes on the patriarchal post. The newly established Synod, however, encountered serious difficulties as a number of early supporters backed off. Of the ones who stayed, the most active was the Metropolitan Pimen, implicated no less than Maxim in the intricate relationship between church and state in the years of communist rule.

The next few months witnessed a display of rocky relations punctuated by the accompanying turbulence of the political scene that culminated in the fall of the UDF cabinet in 1992. First was the thwarted attempt to take possession of the Synodal headquarters (May, 1992), and the Patriarchal Cathedral "Alexander Nevski" (June, 1992) where on Ascension Day (June 4, 1992) both Pimen and Maxim tried to hold the divine liturgy, against the musical background of the magnificent church choir, and the less harmonious but equally audible shouts of the lay audience. Then came the dramatic occupation of the Theological Seminary on August 31, 1992 by Pimen's people, and the promulgation of Poptodorov as Rector. This was followed by the counter-storming of the premises on September 13 by seminarians, and the eviction of the occupiers. The final attempt was the attack on the Diocesan Headquarters on Sunday, October 1, 1992. It failed after a four-hour-long fight with students from the Theological Academy and the Seminary. All throughout, the church bells of Sofia were tolling a funeral knell that prompted the following exchange. Emil Kapudaliev, member of the National Assembly from the governing UDF party complained to the clerics of the nearby "Alexander Nevski" cathedral: "Stop the bell, we simply cannot think," whereupon a clergyman allegedly murmured back: "Your mind is stunted anyway." In addition to the Sofia events, there were attempts, with varying success, to seize monasteries and the dioceses in Lovech, Tîrnovo, Varna, and Plovdiv.

While the UDF government gave Pimen's church legal and moral backing, it did not provide it with physical support. Upon the issuing of ORA's decree, Patriarch Maxim appealed to President Zhelev who referred the appeal to the Constitutional Court. The latter ruled on June 11, 1992 that ORA had acted in violation of the Constitution but left it to the Supreme Court to decide on the Maxim's legitimacy. On July 2, 1992, the Supreme Court refused to consider his appeal on the grounds that it had been submitted 24 hours beyond the stipulated seven days period. In addition, it ruled that since Maxim's church had not been registered with the Directorate of Religious Affairs, it was illegitimate, and thus not entitled to petition the Court (Raikin 1993: 21–22). This Catch-22 decision encouraged the representatives of Pimen's church to ask for armed support in acquiring the offices of the Sofia Diocese but this was not given either by the Attorney General, nor by the Mayor of Sofia who had otherwise obligingly registered the new Diocesan Council of the secessionist church. By October, 1992, Sîbev bitterly complained that "the police sides with Maxim, and has interfered against us for the fourth time" (*Demokratsiia*, October 2, 1992).

The same month saw the culmination of the political conflict between President Zhelev and the cabinet of Philip Dimitrov. Zhelev had accused the prime minister, among others, of having declared war on the church. On October 28, 1992, the Dimitrov's government fell, and in January, 1993 Liuben Berov formed a new cabinet. In March, 1993, the director of ORA was dismissed, his position passing to a history professor at the University of Sofia. He promptly invalidated decree No. 92, and the Attorney General's Office advised Maxim to make the appropriate steps to legalize his position. Maxim did not follow up, never having considered his position illegitimate. By 1995, the next cabinet under the BSP leader Zhan Videnov, took further steps to consolidate the Orthodox church under Maxim. In a letter of November 13, 1995, following the orders of the socialist Vice Prime Minister, ORA formally restored to Maxim the official juridical leadership of the Orthodox church. In a further step, when in June, 1996, the hierarchs around Pimen announced they were convening a Church National Council, and approached the socialist government with requests for financial aid, the vice premier flatly responded that as far as the government was concerned, the Holy Synod of *pro tempore* president Pimen did not exist, that it supported the leadership of Patriarch Maxim, and that the convening of a council would amount to creating a second Orthodox church.

The UDF in opposition actively supported Pimen. The dismissed director of ORA published an accusatory article about the Orthodox church as "a strategic link for Moscow's politics," on May 9, the Red Army's victory day in the Second World War (*Demokratsiia*, May 9, 1994).The Church National Council was officially opened in the "Sv. Paraskeva" church in Sofia on July 1, 1996, in the presence of key UDF leaders. When it ended on July 4, it had a newly elected patriarch, and a newly canonized saint. Despite the socialist government's unambiguous pledge that it would not recognize the new Synod and its patriarch, the cabinet itself had problems in being recognized as a credible and legitimate leadership. On the church conflict, there was the obvious split between the BSP cabinet and the UDF controlled Supreme Court. In an atmosphere of heightened economic tensions, and wildly running inflation, the UDF won the presidential elections in October with Peter Stoianov elected as president. Under increased pressure Videnov resigned, but only six days earlier, on December 13, 1996, in a last-minute attempt to strengthen Maxim's position, the socialist government registered his Holy Synod, despite previous claims that this was unwarranted. When an interim government was appointed, Pimen challenged Maxim's registration. At its hearings on March 5, 1997, it was canceled by the the Supreme Court, the Attorney General stated that Pimen was the only legitimate patriarch, and that his legal proclamation would follow soon. The stakes seemed favorable since, at his inauguration, President Stoianov had invited Pimen to administer the oath despite previous assurances that he would act as a non-partisan president, and would work toward the reconciliation of the church. He did not, however, openly condone the Supreme Court's moves, and in the next years behind-the-scenes pressure was exerted on Maxim to step down and open the road to reconciliation, but to no avail. The limbo situation was summarized by the Vice Premier that neither patriarch was legitimate.

And so the situation persisted. The Bulgarian Orthodox Church (Pimen), basing its claims on the May 25, 1992 decree, and the March 5, 1997 decision of the Supreme Court, maintained it represented the only legal leadership. It was baffled that the UDF executive, while giving it lip-service support, did not carry out these decisions. The Bulgarian Orthodox Church (Maxim), on the other hand, while feeling pressured, was confident of its canonical status, and had time and tradition on its side. People, while cognizant of the church's ambivalent status during communism, and often critical of Maxim, did not single him out as a sinister collaborator, anymore implicated than any of his contemporary prelates. The common sense attitude of the majority of the congregation was that, with the passing of this generation of church leadership, a reconciliation would inevitably take place. Preserving the institutional unity was far more important than what was perceived as a simple power struggle within the higher echelons. Of the circa 1,500 priests and monks, 1,267 priests and 80 monks sided with Maxim, and only 117 priests and 15 monks with Pimen. A 1997 poll of 1,389 individuals gave Maxim 55% support, Pimen 6%, and 39% disinterested respondents. In addition, Maxim's church scored several important international and domestic victories. The National Movement for Unification of the Church, founded in 1992, decided to back Maxim in 1997. Pope John Paul II, invited by President Stoianov to visit the country in 1997, declined on account of the church split, something widely interpreted as an indirect endorsement of Maxim. When the Pope finally visited Bulgaria in May, 2002, he had an official meeting with Maxim and the members of the Holy Synod.

The most spectacular endorsement came from the heads of the other Orthodox churches on September 30, 1998. It was, as a journalist put it, a pan-Orthodox meeting that took place in Sofia 1,655 years after the Council of Serdica (Sofia's ancient name) convened in 343 A.D. The meeting was called by the ecumenical Patriarch Bartholomew to discuss the Bulgarian schism. Present were the heads of twelve Orthodox churches: the patriarchs—Bartholomew I, Antioch's Ignatius IV, Alexandria's Peter VII, Russia's Aleksii II, Romania's Theoctist, Serbia's Pavle, Albania's Anastasios, Bulgaria's Maxim; and the archbishops—Cyprus' Chrisostomos, Athens' Christodoulos, Poland's Sava, and the Czechs' Simeon. It was a spectacular gathering. The former head of ORA, who had denounced the council the previous day as a new Warsaw Pact, found it diplomatic to meet the ecumenical patriarch at the airport. The council's message was unambiguous: reconciliation had to occur, otherwise Bulgaria risked excommunication because the sin of a schism cannot be absolved even with martyrs' blood. Pimen's prelates could return to the church only by following the canon, that is penance and renunciation of their posts. Maxim's Synod would demonstrate magnanimity, and would re-ordain them within the month. There were speculations that a solution had been reached, the church conflict was over, Pimen's people had repented and Maxim would retire to a monastery.

It never came to a resolution. By the summer of 2000, the situation was identical to 1997. The public was waiting for biology or God to have their say. Pimen did oblige in 1999, people jested it was Maxim's turn. There were anemic attempts to keep the public's interest alive with a war of words. In April, 2001, the alternative Synod headed by Metropolitan Inokentii convened a supreme ecclesiastical court to give a final verdict on the legality of Maxim's 1971 election. The chief prosecutor, Professor Poptodorov, supported the claim that the election was rigged. Unsurprisingly, the ecclesiastical court gave a verdict, which effectively "retired" Maxim from his post. Maxim's Synod gave a brief dismissing answer that the event deserved comment only after Inokentii's Synod was recognized. Schism fatigue had set in, however. More importantly, the church question was no longer a political trump card; it had become an embarrassment. The ideological polarization of the early 1990s no longer commanded the political discourse. A new political class had emerged, still circumscribed within the inert structures of inherited party affiliations, but with a vested interest in preserving power, and a tacit professional solidarity across party lines. The elections of June 17, 2001 provided an additional twist. The new prime minister (and former king) Simeon Sakskoburggotski firmly supported Maxim, and the patriarch was at the opening ceremony of the parliament. For three years Simeon did not articulate any special policy toward the church conflict, although he strongly encouraged reconciliation, and did not shy away from taking sides. Then, the summer of 2004 brought the unexpected closure. July and August—the "dead" hot vacation months—are preferred for taking dramatic decisions aimed at undramatic reactions. According to the newly adopted Law of Confessions, Patriarch Maxim was appointed the sole legitimate leader of the Bulgarian Orthodox Church. On July 21, 2004, following a prosecutor's decision and backed by the police, Maxim's Synod received back more than 250 items of church property (churches, restaurants, shops and other realty), which had been appropriated by the alternative Synod. Of these, some 28 are in Sofia. Despite the lame protests of some politicians, and without much fanfare, Bulgaria had again a unified church.

2. The Canonization and Its Implications

This is the background against which the elevation of Levski to a sanctified status has to be understood. To reverse the popular definition of historical background as the limbo inhabited by people who do not really interest us, it is precisely the inhabitants of this limbo who capture the attention in this story. For the clergy of the alternative Synod, the canonization was a move that propelled their activities out of the heretofore exclusively political field, into the field of culture. Was this a deliberately calculated and carefully staged act intended to exploit a powerful national symbol in order to deliver a much coveted national popularity? In hindsight, it seems to display an inordinate and unsuspected sense of acumen in acquiring some powerful symbolic capital. However, the way in which the activists at the Pimen Church National Council spontaneously and initially crudely went into the act of canonization belies such a belief. The act can be better explained by resorting to Pierre Bourdieu's notion of *habitus*. It provides both a unifying category that subsumes the protagonists of the canonization as well as their opponents in an explanatory matrix, and emphasizes the intuitive over the premeditated aspects of their behavior. For Bourdieu, *habitus* is the result of a long process of inculcation, beginning in early childhood, which in the end becomes second nature. It represents a set of structured and determined attitudes or dispositions, which generate structuring and determining practices and perceptions. Bourdieu specifically emphasizes the durability of these structures, because they act over a lifetime, as well as their characteristic of being "structured structures" insofar as they are the product of objective social relations and conditions. He also stresses their dynamic and organizing power which, in turn, makes them "structuring structures," which accounts for the similarity in the *habitus* of agents from the same social class (Bourdieu 1990: 53).

This explains why the most challenged addressees of the canonization act—the prelates of the Maxim-led church—despite formal resistance to the "structuring structures" and the resulting practices, respond to the challenge in much the same way: they are passionately debating in private the pros and cons of canonization, some carefully preparing the ground for a future canonization despite official protestations. Their "feel for the game," their *sens pratique* inclines them to act and react in a manner that is not always calculated and is often unconscious. On the other hand, this theoretical framework helps appreciate the complexity of the agents' (here Pimen's adherents') actions: they are both deeply rooted in and, at the same time, actively challenge the existing structures in which they are inculcated (and implicated). Bourdieu's definition lays stress on the questionable mastery needed in order to attain the aims, which is another way of emphasizing the intuitiveness of the activity. This resonates much with the clumsy way in which the actual canonization took place, and was undervalued by its own advocates. There were no fanfares about Levski's canonization back in 1996. It was not publicly and widely advertised. None of the theological argumentation about his canonization was published in the press. A year later, one could not even buy a copy of his icon, although another one was on display in the church "Sv. Petka Samardzhiiska." The representatives of the Pimen-led hierarchs at that time did not deem it important to discuss Levski's case with lay visitors. Ironically, at first the cultural capital of the canonization proponents did not allow them to fully appreciate the symbolic capital of their act. This occurred only very gradually, and only amongst some of the church leaders who recognized that "through ritual... those claiming power demonstrate how their interests are in the natural, real or fruitful order of things" (Bell 1997: 129).

Things had changed considerably by 2000. In July, I made four visits to the Synod of Pimen's church, two of which were close to two-hour conversations. The most interesting and informative exchange was with Father Anatolii Balachev, at that time the secretary of the St. Synod. An intelligent and cultivated interlocutor, he reminisced that in the 1960s, as bookkeeper to the Holy Synod of Patriarch Kiril, he helped in preparing the canonizations of Father Paisii of Khilendar and of Sofronii Vrachanski. At that time he approached Bishop Partenii with the idea that the church should not stop with Paisii but that it needed also other saints. "Maybe you'd like Levski," the Bishop countered, "but he is the assassin of an innocent youth." Balachev's argument that the already canonized Tsar Boris-Mikhail had also resorted to violence, as had all military saints, did not seem to impress the bishop. Memory is a slippery and unverifiable notion but the least that can be said about this piece of reminiscence is that it indicates that there is (or there is an attempt at) continuity and perseverance in the efforts to elevate Levski to the status of saint at least from the 1960s on.

In the 1990s a special commission was formed to establish the grounds for Levski's canonization. These were then submitted to the Synod which ordered the compilation of a brief *vita* and a service for the saint. The *vita*, Balachev assured me, was written but the service was not yet completed. The act of canonization had been prepared by Radko Poptodorov, in consultation with Apostol Mikhailov, both professors at the Theological Academy. The grounds for sainthood, comprised the following four criteria: healing powers of the holy remains; holy life; service for the fatherland; martyrdom. Levski fulfilled all conditions, except the first (his remains being unknown), and was accordingly canonized as a *sveshtenomŭchenik* (holy martyr). Of course, Balachev added, Levski had already become a saint in people's souls and hearts, and the church was simply following in the wake of something that had already been attained. Why was Maxim opposed to the canonization? "Comrade Maxim and Co. are against because they cannot stand someone higher, someone with qualities superior to theirs." Could I see the written act of canonization as well as the brief *vita*? By all means, only I had to come another day. And so I did, on several days during the following weeks but the documents never materialized. This in itself requires a comment.

There can be no doubt that Levski was canonized by the Church National Council convened by Pimen, July 1–4, 1996. This was, however briefly, documented in the press at the time. The fact, though, that no documentation could be produced of such a crucial decision, leaves one skeptical of its existence.Father Balachev was eager to place it at my disposal, and was extremely apologetic that he could not produce it. His assistant went even so far as to muse what might have happened to the document: "In those days everything was so tense, who knows where the document might have landed! And these, the reds, they used to steal!" The latter already sounds like an alibi. Most likely, what happened in July, 1996 was a spontaneous oral act without a meticulous preparation, and no formalized procedure. This was quite enough for the years 1996 and 1997 when the priorities were high on institution building, and there was an acute political conflict at hand. By 2000, on the other hand, there was the need for cultural clout and a legitimate written record. This may actually appear, only it most probably will have been produced *post factum*.

A visit to "Sv. Petka Samardzhiiska" corroborated this indirectly. This small church, the place of Levski's alleged reburial, was the first and for a period of time the only one with an icon of Levski on permanent display. Painted and signed by Nikola Orozov in 1996, this depiction of a haloed Levski carries the inscription St. Holy Martyr, Hierodeacon Ignatii. Father Mikhail Milushev, an energetic, well-educated and humorous man, a priest of the Pimen affiliated hierarchy, and staunch believer that Levski had been buried in his church and ought to be canonized, opined about the canonization: "It was done in a slapdash fashion without preparation. Such an act should unite, not divide the congregation. They started where they should have ended." Indeed, a canonization needs a careful preparatory period, and this was what Balachev was trying to convince me had taken place before the act of 1996 (Plates 13, 14, 15 and 15A). Preparation or not, the Maxim-led hierarchy, without officially giving their formal reasons, had refuted Levski's canonization. In 1998 and 2000, I had a number of interviews with members of CHAI, priests, professors and students at the Theological Academy, all part of the mainstream church. All described Levski as the greatest Bulgarian national hero but a secular figure at the pinnacle of the secular pantheon, not in the church. The reasoning was different but noone resorted to a political argument. It was based on differing interpretations of the canon or Levski's relationship to the church. Some pointed out that Levski had unfrocked himself, and thus broken his vows. Others objected that although he had left the church, he had remained deeply religious; they insisted, however, that in the absence of miracles, his canonization was illegal. Still others maintained that Levski was guilty of the murder of an innocent young man, and therefore could not be pronounced a saint. The counterargument that many a Christian saint has committed more than one murder works with some but not with others. Only privately, and after some pushing, some would concur that Levski actually has all the credentials to become a saint, but that Pimen and company's precipitous act is now the major obstacle to a legal and consensual canonization.

What emerges from this exchange is that people differ, often incompatibly, not only over the specific arguments on Levski but, in general, over who can become a saint. More significantly, the argumentation pro and con is deeply grounded in historical reasoning. In a society in which political discourse in the past two centuries has often taken the form of disputes over archeological discoveries and historical rights, as is the case in practically all European societies, there still is an enormous premium on the persuasive power of an erudite and abstruse academic argument. In the case of prelates or church scholars, the argumentation attempts to acquire the guise of a legal argument, referring to the canon. Inevitably, the discussion of the canonization's legal aspects has a political dimension and far reaching practical implications, and the parties concerned are aware of this. What is remarkable is the complete domination of the traditional style of objectivist and positivist academic rhetoric. The detailed survey of the history of Orthodox canonization in the next pages, is not an end in itself, but attempts to give an immediate taste of the nature and density, but also style, of the actual discourse that takes place among the parties involved.

The reason that different, often clashing, views are displayed is not due to ignorance of the canon but to the fact that no strict canon exists in the Orthodox church that regulates sainthood. The ancient church had not developed a formal process of canonization. For Christians in the first centuries, sanctity was something obvious, and the problem of proof, so significant in Christianity of a later period, was irrelevant. In both the western and eastern medieval worlds, popular veneration preceded and induced official recognition of the church. As summarized by Alice-Mary Talbot, "usually a cult developed first at the local level (e.g., at a parish church or monastery): pilgrims would flock to the saint's tomb in hope of receiving healing from his or her relics; there would be a special annual commemoration, usually on the anniversary of the saint's death, which became the saint's feastday; a *vita* might be written and an icon painted; eventually the saint might be recognized by the local church hierarchy and his or her name inscribed in a register of feastdays" (1996: vii). When Balachev says that Levski had already been sanctified in people's souls and hearts, and the church was simply following in the footsteps of tradition, he is actually expressing the ancient practice.

Canonization became formalized much later and only gradually. It began with decisions issued by the Patriarch or the Pope in the 9th and 10th centuries but, while in the Eastern Church saints could be added at the discretion of the local prelate without a formal patriarchal endorsement, by the 12th century the Roman Church forbade the worship of saints without papal sanction. The first historically attested papal canonization by Pope John XV was that of Bishop Ulrich of Augsburg in 993, twenty years after his death. This became a strictly regulated procedure for the Western Church in 1234 during the papacy of Gregory IX (1227–1241). No earlier than fifty years after his death, a threefold investigation in the life and miracles of the candidate for saint, initiated by the local clergy and bishop, was effectuated by a congregation of rites (*congregatio ritus*). Following this, the congregation voted to promulgate the dead to the status of blessed, beginning the process of beatification. Local veneration was then allowed for the beatified. If additional miracles happened, one could proceed with canonization. Some of the conditions for canonization included: belonging to the church; a proper age to distinguish good from evil; the state of being deceased; a holy life; a miracle; an already existing church tradition of veneration; petition for canonization; the existence of a *vita*. It was during the pontificate of Pope Urban VIII (1623–1644) that the two-level beatification-canonization procedure found its final formulation, and a radical reform in the canonization process took place. The most elaborate theory of canonization was the work of Cardinal Proper Lambertini, the future Pope Benedict XIV (1740–1758) who published a treatise in 1734 and a papal decree in 1741 (*New Catholic Encyclopedia* 1967: 55–61). Intricate as these rules are, the Western Church does not always strictly stand by its own rules, especially when it comes to the "waiting period," as attested by the recent spree of beatifications and canonizations under Pope John Paul II. In addition, while in principle following the rules for accepting a saint, the Catholic Church did not develop a canonical model for sainthood that was to be followed by all communities. Instead it relied on the saints themselves, and their followers and admirers to develop their own interpretation of holiness.

The Orthodox church has not elaborated a formalized canon, even the term *canonisatio* was unknown in the Eastern Church until the 17th century when it was first mentioned by the Patriarch of Jerusalem

Nectarius (Nektarios). In the early centuries sanctity was recognized by the consent and acclamation of a local community. From the 4th century A.D., the veneration of saints in the Byzantine church was more widespread and stronger than in the West. At the same time, this veneration was highly regionalized and there was only a limited number of common cults. The late 13th and 14th centuries during the Palaiologan period saw a change in the recognition of sanctity toward a more formal procedure. There are several canonizations by decree during this period, and in the opinion of Ruth Macrides, this was brought about by contact with the Latin Church during the 13th century. With the fall of Byzantium under the Ottomans, however, this trend came to an end (Hackel 1981: 83–7).

Still, if one were to scrutinize the practice of the Eastern Church, it actually follows, in its main lines, the same rules that are accepted in the Western Church (Zhivov 1994: 35–8). At the same time, while the conditions for canonization are more or less the same, they are treated in the Eastern Church less legalistically, emphasizing their sufficient rather than obligatory character. The differences between the Western and the Eastern churches are actually less ones of substance but rather ones of procedure. While canonization in the West is more formalized and exclusively effectuated from the center through Papal authority, the one in the East seems to be stressing more the grassroots process, following tradition, that is the public opinion of the congregation. It still has an administrative character, insofar as the process of adding to the rank of local saints is effectuated at the local level by the diocesan prelate or the metropolitan, and in the case of a more generalized *cultus*, by the archbishop or the patriarch. Evelyne Patlagean, in particular, stresses that the public recognition of sanctity is effectuated by its entry into the liturgy (Hackel 1981: 103). In practice, this happens by appointing an annual celebration in memory of the saint, usually the anniversary of his/her death or another significant date as, for example, the finding or transfer of relics. It is punctuated by adding the name of the saint to the menology (the monthly calendar) in the church. Often, the composition of a short *vita* of the saint for liturgical needs indicates the act of canonization (Bakalova 1991: 175). Balachev, well aware of this, went to great lengths at insisting how well prepared the canonization was, and how the Synod, in anticipation of the canonization act, had ordered the writing of a short *vita*, and the composition of a liturgy. The *vita*, he said, had been prepared; there had been not enough time for the liturgy, and at this point there existed only an antiphon (*tropar*) for the saint. As with the document for the canonization, neither the brief *vita* nor the *tropar* could be produced.

While all of this makes the procedures in the Eastern Church seem less cumbersome and informal, the absence of a body of broadly accepted formalized prescribed rules that can be strictly imposed opens the ground for different readings and opposing opinions. A rare case, where an official opinion about canonizations in the Greek Orthodox Church has been articulated, comes from the 1930s. In November, 1930, the Romanian Patriarch Myron requested the opinion of the Ecumenical Patriarch on the issue of recognizing saints. A special synodal committee on canonical questions was convened in Constantinople in February, 1931 that drew a relevant report, which was transmitted to the Romanian Patriarchate together with a letter from the Patriarch Photios. The committee's report was styled like a sermon, and it drew on several precedents. One was the statement of Nektarios of Jerusalem (1602–1676) who, in a refutation of the Friars of Jerusalem, articulated the essential elements of holiness: "There are three things which testify to true holiness in men; first blameless orthodoxy, second attainment of all virtues, amongst which is resistance on behalf of the faith unto death, and finally the manifestation on God's part of supernatural signs and miracles." The proclamation of saints was done by the church, either as a whole or by any particular local church. The ecclesiastical authority sanctioning the canonization depended on the characteristics of the saint: "Each province, each city celebrates with special zeal its particular martyrs and saints, but the whole Church regarding those who are most distinguished amongst them as her own property, has honored and revered them as Catholic saints." In the end, it was "the common consciousness of the shepherds and the flock [that] discerns and affirms those who are really saints." One of the precedents cited was the opinion of Patriarch Philotheos, the great Hesychast scholar who was patriarch twice: 1353–1354 and 1363–1376. He wrote a Panegyric of Gregory of Palama who had been canonized by the Synod. Philotheos points out that "we have proclaimed him a Saint, not waiting for the summoning of very great Synods and (the giving of common) votes, which are often intercepted by time and sluggishness and tardiness and many other human things, but being satisfied with the decree and proclamation from above and the sight of things which are manifest and cannot be called in question" (Canonization 1931: 86). The final validation was clearly common custom. The canonization of Gerasimos the Younger (1579–1599) occurred in 1662, when a great synod of metropolitans, archbishops, bishops and clergy, with the participation of the patriarchs of Antioch and Jerusalem, and under the presidency of the Ecumenical Patriarch Cyril Lucaris, proclaimed him saint: "The pious assembly taking into consideration the good results of honoring those who lived according to the will of God, used to expose their deeds and achievements in pictures and sermons... following therefore the common custom of the Church we decree and define ... that the aforesaid Gerasimos should be honored by annual sacred festivals and ceremonies" (ibid.: 87).

The accompanying letter of Patriarch Photios of Constantinople to Patriarch Myron of Romania was organized around a prescriptive structure, but it also left room for interpretation and adaptation to local custom. It bears citing *in toto* since it is a rare case where rules are spelled out:

> In accordance with our tradition the following general principles are followed in the recognition and placing amongst the Choir of Saints of the church, of persons glorified by God.
>
> 1. The verification of the elements of holiness must be made by a Synod, composed of all the Metropolitans, Archbishops, Bishops, and official clergy of the particular church.
>
> 2. This verification is superfluous in the case of those holy persons whom the general consciousness of the Church—of both shepherds and flock—has for long ages recognized and celebrated as such. Of such holy persons who have been tacitly recognized up till now as sanctified and glorified by God, a merely formal recognition is given by the Church in accordance as we have said above.
>
> 3. At the proclamation there is a proper ecclesiastical procedure of which the enclosed copy of the Procedure in the consecration of St. Gerasimos the Younger—which took place under the blessed Patriarch Cyril Lucaris at the beginning of the seventeenth century[1]— may serve as an example.

---

[1] Clearly an error. The canonization took place in 1662.

4. The Deed of Proclamation is solemnly signed in the church, the proper ecclesiastical ceremony being as follows: The whole Synod having come down into the Church and the Book of the Gospels being placed in the center, the following troparia are sung— "Blessed art thou, O Christ our God," "When He (the Holy Spirit) descended," then the Deed of proclamation is signed by all members of the General Synod who are present and immediately after are sung the troparia "Holy martyrs who fought well," "The tortures of the saints which they suffered for Thee," "The blood of Thy martyrs throughout the world."

5. At a convenient time a special and suitable Office, within the framework of the hymnology and ceremonial of the Orthodox Churches, is naturally composed for the most noteworthy of the canonized saints, for use in the churches.

6. Of equal necessity is the translation of the relics, if such are preserved, and their anointing with Holy Chrism. At the translation of the relics it is customary to have vigil services and solemn liturgies. (ibid.: 88–9).

This is as close to an official set of rules as one can come across in the practice of the Eastern Church, and it demonstrates the leeway of maneuverability within a generally accepted framework. At the same time, it displays a growing desire and even tendency to formalize the canonization process. One can speculate that a contributing factor for the persistence of informal canonozation in the Orthodox church in the course of so many centuries was its delicate position in the Ottoman Empire. Martyrs are an especially beloved object of devotion, and the new martyrs (the term is used for martyrs after the iconoclastic period, to distinguish them from the ancient martyrs)—chiefly the martyrs of the faith who had perished during the Ottoman period—have their special place in the Greek Orthodox Hagiologion. In addition, saints whose *cultus* revolves around their relics have a special value because their number is comparatively small. While the church tacitly approved of the veneration of new martyrs, it is not difficult to see that even if there had been an elaborate system of canonization in place, it would have been impossible to sustain. The new martyrs of the Ottoman period were usually victims of official or tolerated acts on the part of the Ottoman authorities, and their authorized canonization would have been considered an open breach of loyalty, and an endorsement of disruptive and rebellious activities. The example of George of Neapolis, a priest in Asia Minor, is a case in point. Compromised as a Russian supporter in the 1770 Orlov expedition during the Russo–Turkish war of 1768–74, he was imprisoned and later beheaded. Buried in Malakope, his body is said not to have decomposed. At the time of the population exchange in 1924, his relics were translated to Neapolis of Perissos, Nea Ionia. Today, the whole body reposes in the Church of St. Eusthatios, Neapolis, Nea Ionia, Athens, and is commemorated on November 3. An earlier case is Apostolus from Hagias Laurentios who had accompanied his fellow villagers in 1864 to Constantinople, to petition for their rights. Arrested, he suffered martyrdom, and is commemorated today on August 16. Parts of his body are in the Zographou Monastery on Mount Athos, and others in the St. Agathon Monastery in Ipati, Lamia. A famous case is that of Patriarch Gregory V who at the time of the Greek Revolution was hanged over the gateway of the patriarchate on Easter Day 1821. His body was then thrown into the Bosphorus but found by a Greek captain six days later. His relics were transferred in 1871 to Athens and today repose in the Cathedral Evangelismos, Metropolis, Athens. There are dozens of similar cases (Meinardus 1970: 132–3, 145, 184–5, 187).

While all these men were venerated as martyrs, it is easy to understand why there was no official act of canonization. The church could afford to only quietly acquiesce and support the popular veneration. It treated the holy persons "as sanctified and glorified by God" because "the general consciousness of the Church—both shepherds and flock—has for long ages recognized and celebrated" them as such. It adapted creatively to the problem by utilizing an "Anonymous service to any new martyr." Composed by Nicephoras of Chios, is explicitly circumvented the difficulty of an official proclamation during the centuries of Ottoman rule. The relevant passage reads: "As the majority of the new martyrs do not have a service—one to honor his fellow countryman, another to honor someone known to him personally, yet another to someone who has helped him in some need, I have therefore composed an anonymous general service for any new martyr. May he that so desires, sing such a service to that martyr whom he venerates" (Challis 1980: 241).

The Russian Orthodox Church, which did not face similar constraints, developed over time a highly formalized ritual, stopping short of writing down and imposing a strict procedure. In the 17th century, a central part of the church reform was to standardize the rituals of the Greek and Russian Orthodox churches in view of the future unification of orthodoxy under the Russian crown. Originally, the ecclesiastical authorities simply approved popular cults and introduced them into the formal liturgy. With the trend towards centralized control in the 17th century during the rule of Tsar Alexei Mikhailovich and Patriarch Nikon, canonizations were carried out exclusively by the Holy Synod. By the 18th and 19th centuries, they had turned into virtual state canonizations, although very few saints were canonized. Today, there is an unmistakable tendency throughout the whole orthodox world to go through the formal process, one that began in the past century with the orthodox churches of the independent nation states that seceded from the Ottoman Empire. Two examples from the list of relics of Greek Orthodox saints aptly illustrate this trend. Saras of Kalymnos was a monk in the Skete of St. Anne on Mount Athos. After years in monasteries in Palestine, Aegina, and Patmos, he finally retired to Kalymnos where he died in 1948. Officially canonized in 1958, his whole body reposes in the monastery of Hagioi Pantes on Kalymnos. Another popularly venerated but not yet officially canonized saint is Magdalene from Kalymnos. Born in 1847, she became a nun in 1867, and spent her long life in the monastery Evangelistria in Argos, which was built by her wealthy father. She died at age 105 in 1952, and her body reposes and is venerated in the monastery (Meinardus 1970: 210, 245). The phrasing of the entry for this nun is significant, because it clearly indicates where the tendency and the expectations point to: "Magdalene has not been canonized *yet*" (italics mine).

The case of the Bulgarian church is identical to the Greek, although on a smaller scale. During the Ottoman period, it was an integral part of the Constantinople patriarchate—the centralized Orthodox church institution under the Ottomans—until 1860, when it symbolically and unilaterally seceded, and 1870, when the secession was recognized by the Sultan. Its inception effectively coincided with the formation of the independent nation state. The first attempt to compile a list of Bulgarian saints belongs to Paisii, celebrated as the precursor of modern Bulgarian historiography. The last chapter of his 1762 "Slavobulgarian history" contains a list of 29 saints, 23 from the pre-Ottoman period, and only 6 after the beginning of the 15th century.

Paissii had compiled his list according to written—printed or manuscript—sources. Bulgarian Orthodox calendars from the 1850s to the 1870s—at the height of the church conflict with the Constantinople Patriarchate—published lists of saints where, alongside a majority of commonly venerated Orthodox saints, they highlighted specifically Bulgarian ones, beginning with Sts. Cyril and Methodius. These calendars were compiled by writers, journalists or publishers, without explicit ecclesiastical sanction. Khristo Kîrpachev's calendar of 1868 identified over 100 Bulgarian saints, 40 from the Ottoman period. Dragan Manchev's calendar of 1875 listed 26 saints from the "Turkish period." Its 1877 edition added "5,000 martyrs from Batak" in commemoration of the victims of the 1876 April Uprising that precipitated the Russo–Turkish war, and eventually underwrote Bulgaria's independence (Stoianov 1982: 166–7). The Russian Archbishop of Cherinigov Filaret in his description of the lives of the saints of the South Slavs, published in 1865, included the vitae of 51 Bulgarian saints, 30 Serbian ones, 15 early Christian saints from the South Slav territories of the Roman Empire, 7 general Slavic saints (Cyril and Methodius and their disciples), 5 unspecified ones, and one Czech saint (Sviatye 1865). The orthodox calendars from 1875 and 1876 published by Khristo Botev, that add revolutionary figures to the pantheon of martyrs for the faith and are analyzed further in the text, belong to the same genre. In the majority of cases, especially as far as the neo-martyrs from the Ottoman period are concerned, their entry into the calendars was based not on written sources but upon memory and oral tradition.

This was in line with the attitude of the Orthodox church to respect popular veneration, and acknowledge that some saints were more local, while others were widely or generally recognized. There are numerous examples: the last Bulgarian Tsar Ivan Shishman, venerated in folk songs, whose memory was commemorated on September 11, appeared as a saint and defender of the Bulgarian state and of Christian faith in the calendars of Kîrpachev, Manchev, and Slaveikov. He is not, however, present in the modern-day Bulgarian Synaxarion—*Zhitiia na svetiite* (1974). Neither is he entered in the ecclesiastical calendars for 2000 and 2001. Alexander from Thessaloniki (Aleksandîr Solunski), killed by the Turks in 1794 in Smirna (Izmir) appeared in all three 19th-century calendars, but was dropped from the 20th-century ones and from the above-mentioned *Zhitiia*. Angel Bitolski from Florina was said to have been killed by the Turks because he refused to convert in 1750, and was mentioned as a saint by both Father Paisii and in the Zograf Bulgarian history. He has entirely disappeared from the 20th-century saints' lists. Some martyrs are more obscure, and have not even been recognized by the publishers of the 19th-century calendars. Instead, they appear in marginalia to clerical texts or in other manuscripts. The martyrdom of the Samokov Metropolitan Simeon, who was believed to have been tortured and murdered by the Turks in Sofia on August 21, 1737, was reported solely in a marginal note to a 16th-century panegyric preserved in the National Library in Sofia. The same holds for the Okhrid Archbishop Varlaam beheaded by the Turks on May 28, 1598, whose record comes from a marginal note to a 14th-century prologue preserved in the Library of the Bulgarian Academy of Sciences (Stoianov 1982: 171). We do not know how long or how widely held their veneration was at the time: did it last only a generation, was it confined to a specific locale? Of the 55 entries for saints and martyrs from the Ottoman period that Maniu Stoianov (1982) published on the basis of different nineteenth and early 20th-century calendars, manuscripts, and marginalia, only 30, slightly more than one half, appear in the 2000 and 2001 official Orthodox calendars.

The absence of strictly prescribed rules and approved lists occasions the episodic lack of correlation between different sources that are otherwise contemporaneous. Georgi Sofiiski Stari who was martyred on March 26, 1437 by being burnt on the stake for offending Islam, appears in the 2000 and 2001 calendars but is not allotted an entry in the *Zhitiia*. Conversely, Anastasii Strumishki, martyred by the Turks in 1794, has a brief *vita* in *Zhitiia* but is absent from the calendars altogether. But this is a feature typical of orthodoxy in general. Eve Levin (1989: 25), commenting on the compilations of saints' lives in the medieval Slavic world, notes that far from aiming at comprehensiveness, the editors of different calendars chose materials that fitted central themes, and accorded some saints special honor by including their *vitae* and prayers in praise of them, while only briefly mentioning or altogether dropping others.

After its resurrection as a Patriarchate in 1954, the Bulgarian Orthodox Church embarked on a road of formal canonizations as its Greek sister church. The 1960s saw two major canonizations, although there was no follow up in the subsequent decades. The first was that of

Father Paisii of Khilendar (b. 1722) on June 26, 1962. The brief *vita* in *Zhitiia* defines him first and foremost as a national writer and educator: "When the Bulgarian nation was in its worse predicament under the double five-centuries-old Greek–Turkish yoke, God elevated the Reverend Paisii of Khilendar who wrote his remarkable *Slavobulgarian history*, and through it breathed national consciousness and resilience into the Bulgarian people, extracted it from its despair and set forth the Bulgarian revival." The whole *vita* differs little from the hagiographic biographies in secular textbooks. At the end, there are a couple of meager attempts to fulfill the standard conditions for sainthood. It is emphasized that Paisii was characterized by a typical monastic humility and that he himself indicated his asceticism by drawing the reader's attention to his stomach pains and headaches (to the compiler of the *vita* these were proofs of his excessive fasting and sleeplessness). His manner and time of death are unknown, let alone his body's whereabouts, but the author of the *vita* makes the conjecture that he "may have died in martyrdom: if not from a hostile hand, then broken by overexertion." (*Zhitiia* 1974: 299–300).

The second canonization followed some three years later: on December 31, 1965, the bishop of Vratsa Sofronii (1739–1813) was elevated to the status of saint. As in the case of Paisii, he was a widely respected figure in the pantheon of national men of letters. He is traditionally honored as the co-founder (alongside Paisii) of the Bulgarian Revival. An early copyist of Paisii's history, his name was immortalized by the publication of the first printed text in modern Bulgaria in 1806, the authorship of an autobiography hailed as a masterpiece of South Slavic literature, and his political activities evaluated by some historians as the first political program of the Bulgarian emigration to solve the Bulgarian question. These are clearly sufficient grounds to reserve him a prominent place in every history textbook and in that body of internalized historical knowledge that passes under the name of historical memory. Even less than in the case of Paisii, there are no indications of the traditional criteria for sainthood: miracles, or possible martyrdom. Sofronii was even left out of the 1974 collection of *Zhitiia*, and this has not been corrected in the subsequent 1991 edition: a mere oversight maybe, but a telling one. Neither in Paisii's nor in Sofronii's case, do we have any evidence of local religious veneration. Both canonizations can thus be interpreted as political acts on the part of the church which was looking for ways to bolster its image and, at the same time, elevate figures were acceptable to the secular authorities, especially during the communist period. From a legal point of view, these precedents seem to have cleared the way for the subsequent possible canonization of Vasil Levski, a towering national symbol and a figure intimately linked to the church.

Even though in Bulgaria as in Greece, a tendency toward growing formalization of the canonization process is discernible, still a rigid set of rules for all of orthodoxy is missing and there is considerable tolerance for local practice. There exists broad consensus among Bulgarian specialists about a few obvious criteria: the saint has to have been a Christian; s/he has to be deceased; there have to be legends about miracles; and there should be some tradition of veneration, like chants. If miracles at the grave are a *conditio sine qua non*, Levski clearly does not meet the criteria. But if others are met, and they comprise sufficient reasons, then the road to sanctification is open. In fact, the Bulgarian pantheon of saints has numerous precedents: the remains of Boian-Enravota, Tsar Boris-Mikhail, Tsar Peter, Patriarch Evtimii, Georgii Sofiiski Nai-Novi, Zlata Mîglenska, Paisii Khilendarski and others are unknown, and there have been little or no legends of miracles, and in some cases no *vitae* or liturgies, connected to their early *cultus*. Bulgarian hagiography, while in general following Byzantine patristic models, has some unique characteristics, the absence of miracles standing out as one of the most remarkable already in the medieval period (Bozhilov 1995: 312). While relics are the focus of the *cultus* of saints in the Western Church, the veneration of icons replaced to a great extent the centrality of relics in the Eastern Church (Wilson 1983: 5).

Is it the case, then, that the difference in the stated attitudes of adherents of Pimen and of Maxim (even within the bodies of their churches) calling on the canonical tradition for support, is an attempt to obfuscate a simple power struggle behind arguments seeking canonical legitimation? This, to a great extent, seems to be true and a tacit movement is going on among supporters of the Maxim-led church, preparing the ground for the subsequent canonization of Levski, despite the firm official opposition. The precipitous canonization act by Pimen may have postponed what would have been a natural process; on the other hand, it may have stimulated it. But, if indeed either option is the case, why wasn't Levski canonized sometime over the previous century?

3. Levski and the Bulgarian Church: Memory and Narration

A few comments about Levski's standing in the church while he was alive are in order. While there exists consensus between most biographers on the main stages of his career, there are differences in interpretation, and nuances of articulation that are important for the overall assessment of his relationship to the church. Vasil Kunchev entered in the service of the church at age 15, in 1852, as a novice of his uncle, a hieromonk of the Khilendar Monastery of Mt. Athos. This was an arrangement between his recently widowed mother and her brother, the monk Khadzhi Vasilii, who employed the young Vasil as his assistant in collecting alms and, in return, promised he would secure his nephew's education and preparation for the priesthood. While residing in Karlovo, for the first three years, Vasil took lessons in church singing, and his angelic voice was highly appreciated in the services of the "Holy Virgin" church. In 1855, the couple moved to Stara Zagora where Vasil was enrolled in the local school. Again, he stood out with his voice in the church choir. In his third year at the school, a year's course was organized to prepare candidates for the priesthood of whom the country was in great need. Vasil completed the course as the best student in his class, and his uncle promised to send him for further education to Russia. However, he postponed his promise, preferring to utilize the free services of the young man who had already turned 21. Returning to Karlovo in 1858, he persuaded Vasil to enter the monastic order before pursuing further education. On December 7, 1858, Vasil assumed the name Ignatii. He continued to serve his uncle for free, and to sing in the church.

In the absence of an extended autobiography or correspondence from Levski to explain his motives, it is only natural that his biographers were seduced to supply their own reading. The first, Zakhari Stoianov, himself a revolutionary, produced a biography from which Levski emerged as a person of fiery temperament, a born revolutionary whom only circumstances and poor fortune had temporarily put in the church's captivity, before his revolutionary vocation won in "the struggle between the black cassock and the passionate soul." In his words: "If Levski had not been 18, and his taking the vows had been postponed to the period 1862–1866 when the brighter and more progressive ideas of 19th-century skepticism had taken roots among the Bulgarians, we would not have had to describe the Bulgarian hero in a black cassock and long hair" (Stoianov 1990: 26). Levski was not 18 but 21 at the time, and Stoianov is notoriously untrustworthy as a historian but he is equally powerful and influential as a writer, and his views shaped public perceptions very early and influentially.

Levski's most authoritative biographer Undzhiev remarks about this episode that while he had little choice, the thought of becoming a monk was not alien to Levski. He makes a special point to emphasize the sincerity of Levski's religious feelings: "We are going to discover the religious spirit in all of the Apostle's subsequent activities that for him have always been a form of public worship. His faultless moral purity, the mysticism of his self-denial, as well as the puritanic earnestness of his life have to a great extent a religious base" (1947: 88). Undzhiev was actually making the point that nationalism is religion, a theoretical interpretation that reached its most elaborate articulation in the work of Carlton Hayes. He had insisted on an imminent human need to believe in transcendent reality, and that with the weakening of Christianity in the age of Enlightenment rationalism, the nation became a supplement to religion. Nationalism not only appropriated religious traditions and symbols; the nation became a substitute for God:

> On his own national god the modern religious nationalist is conscious of dependence. Of His powerful help he feels the need. In Him he recognizes the source of his own perfection and happiness. To Him, in a strictly religious sense, he subjects himself. Moreover, the religious nationalist not only is disposed subjectively to acknowledge his dependence on the national god, but also he is ready to acknowledge such dependence objectively through acts of homage and adoration (Hayes 1966: 104–05).

This can be easily demonstrated in the case of Levski. The uniqueness of his story is precisely the point that he had already dedicated himself once to the Christian God. Is it then the case that there was a complete shift of religious feeling and fervent commitment from the God of traditional Christianity to the God of modernity, that is the nation? This is a matter of interpretation in the existing literature. Undzhiev unequivocally insists that for Levski this was not substitution but complementarity: "One should not think, however, that Levski had feeble religious feelings, that he was wearing the monk's cassock with insufficient sincerity, that he was alien to a deeper religious thought." In making this point, Undzhiev entered an already ongoing debate about Levski's equivocal position in the church that had been going on for several decades. It comes as no surprise that after the Second World War, the dominant preference was to downplay Levski's religiosity, and stress his revolutionary final break from the church. Mercia MacDermott who, in her almost fictional biography, relies most heavily on Undzhiev, prefers in this instance to picture Levski as "not enthusiastic about the idea" but having no choice (MacDermott 1967: 39).

One year after he took his vows, in 1859, monk Ignatii was ordained as deacon, and among the many names under which he was known, *Deacon Ignatii* or simply *The Deacon* became the most popular alongside *The Apostle* and Levski. Disappointed with his uncle's unwillingness to fulfil his promise and send him to continue his education, in 1862 he secretly left Karlovo, and joined the military legion of Rakovski in Belgrade. He had cherished the idea for some time because in a later letter of 1872, Levski indicates 1861 as the year when he made his crucial decision: "I have dedicated myself to the fatherland already in 61 to serve it unto death and to work according to the will of the people" (Undzhiev 1947: 90). It was during his stay in the legion, either at some of the training sessions or at one of the fights with the Ottoman garrison, that Vasil also received his nickname Levski (the Lion), most likely from Rakovski himself (ibid.: 110–2). In many works, 1862 is given as the year when Levski symbolically "threw away the cassock." Literally, of course, in Belgrade he had cut his hair, and had been dressed in a military uniform, but after the disbanding of the legion, and his return to Karlovo in 1863, he again put on a cassock, and resumed his functions as deacon.

On Easter 1964, Levski carried through the symbolic act that attracted wide attention, and was interpreted by some as his final break with the church. He cut his long hair, entrusting it to his mother, and became a teacher. The episode of Levski's second defrocking has been interpreted differently by his biographers. Stoianov insists that the choice of Easter was a deliberately powerful blow against religion and the church, a symbolic act intended to shock public opinion out of its slumber. Undzhiev agrees with the latter but refuses to see in it a final break with the traditional faith (ibid.: 136–8). This difference of opinion is no small matter because on it depends the evaluation of Levski's subsequent career: whether that of a layman and non-believer, or that of a devout individual and servant of the church who had simply prioritized his devotion to the fatherland during his temporal existence.

The third and decisive episode of Levski's biography that underlay his uneasy relationship with the church, are the circumstances of his capture, alleged betrayal, and execution. Following the robbery of the Ottoman mail in the Arabakonak Pass in the fall of 1872, and the subsequent arrest of the attackers, the revolutionary network was in jeopardy. The attack was organized by Dimitîr Obshti, his deputy, who was in conflict with Levski over organizational issues, and had not received his approval for the particular timing. Obshti made encompassing revelations about the revolutionary organization in the hope of attracting foreign attention to the maturity of the movement and, at the same time, of deflating severe punishments as the government, faced with a broad conspiracy, would not risk international disapproval. Numerous arrests followed, Levski's physical description was circulated to police stations all over the country. On his way to Romania to discuss the situation with Central Committee in Bucharest, Levski tried to salvage the archive of the Lovech Committee, and was caught by the Ottoman police in December, 1872 at a nearby inn (at Kîkrina, which has assumed the symbolic weight of Golgotha). Bulgarian historiography is almost unanimous in attributing Levski's capture to treason. For over a century it has also been almost unanimous in pointing to a local priest from Lovech—Pop Krîstiu—as the traitor. Rumors about the priest's betrayal circulated already before 1878, and a few years later he died leaving behind a letter denying all accusations. There is to date a significant literature on the problem of whether there was treason at all, and whether Levski was caught as a result of an accident, even his identity being established only after his arrest. There is a no less numerous literature around Pop Krîstiu, ranging from confident accusations to no less positive acquittals. Quite apart from the factual interest, the significance of this obsession should be understood in the framework Bulgarian na-

Figure 19. Leaders of the Bulgarian community in Lovech. The priest in the front row is Pop Krîstiu Totev Nikiforov (1836–1881).
Source: Khristo Ionkov and Stoianka Ionkova, *Vasil Levski i bîlgarskata natsionalna revoliutsiia*, Sofia: Izdatelstvo na BAN, 1987, 77, n. 144.

tionalism, especially discussions over Bulgarian national character and/or collective identity. This, however, is the object of a separate analysis.

Here, I am trying to trace how the betrayal thesis shaped the attitude of the church toward Levski. "Two individuals," Balachev told me, "are to be blamed for Levski's alienation from the church. One is Zakhari Stoianov, for he was an atheist; the other one is Vazov who was hostile to the church because the Holy Synod publicly criticized him for his debauchery." Stoianov was indeed a non-believer, though not a pronounced or active atheist, and he painted a devastating Judas-like portrait of Pop Krîstiu in his 1883 biography. He did not, however, make the additional step to generalize the priest's personal behavior on the whole clergy. Vazov, on the other hand, made this step, most probably for poetic rather than ideological reasons. In his 1881 poem *Levski*, part of Vazov's poetic cycle *Epic of the Forgotten*, Pop Krîstiu is not mentioned by name, but there is the laconic verse that all subsequent generations of Bulgarian students have recited and know by heart:

> But he was betrayed, and betrayed by a priest!
> This groveling worm, this despicable beast,
> This outrage to God, on the Church this foul blemish,
> Through whose vicious treason the deacon would perish!

Nor was Vazov at the time at odds with the Holy Synod over his *joie de vivre*. His proverbial debauchery manifested itself, and triggered the reaction of the clergy, much later, at a more advanced age. Nonetheless, the openly anti-clerical and even anti-religious pathos of the poem (quite apart from the verdict against Pop Krîstiu) attracted its own critics. Vazov himself appears to have harbored profound religious doubts, if not an openly stated position as non-believer. In his conversations with Shishmanov, Vazov explains: "As a child I was very religious. But when I started living with the revolutionary exiles, my faith began to waiver significantly. These people were mostly non-believers . My skepticism was reinforced because of the undeserved sufferings of my people. How often I have asked myself: 'Where, where is the divine justice?'"(Shishmanov 1976: 141).

This (rather than his debauchery), given Vazov's exalted status on the literary scene, was a challenge the church could not afford. That the general alienation of the intelligentsia from the church and, often, from religion altogether, was considered a real and important problem by the church is evidenced by its painful attempts to prove the non-existence of the problem. Thus, a 1942 article asked the question "Are the Bulgarian poets and writers repudiators of religion?" Its predictable answer, based on an analysis of Botev, Vazov, Nikolai Rainov, Ivan Grozev, Konstantin Velichkov and others was that there was "no data for an affirmative answer" to the question. Only Botev, according to the author, could be described as renouncing Christianity but even in his case this was ascribed to isolated moments of skepticism and despair, and his textual mentions of the word "God" were brought in as proof of a much more accommodating attitude, a clear attempt to domesticate Botev as well as other socialist and communist poets and writers (Arkhimandrit Evtimii, 1942: 4).

Since Vazov, with his direct accusation against Pop Krîstiu, and graphic descriptions of a corrupt and cynical clergy, was considered responsible for arousing a negative attitude toward the church, he was allotted some length in this article. It takes a real leap of imagination to accommodate Vazov in the fold of traditional religiosity and Christianity, but his canonical status in literature was apparently a challenge, and the way the author (himself a high-ranking prelate of the church, an arkhimandrit, one step below bishop) handled it, was by providing, without comment, a number of quotes with the mention of God, faith, and Christ. What emerges from them is at best a deist. Vazov's God is "not the God of Moses, of Zoroaster, and of Buddha, but the God of pure Reason, of the great Truth, the God of progress"; it is in nature that he looks for providence and God; he even describes himself as "a bit of a pantheist" (Arkhimandrit Evtimii, 1942: 5–7). Nor did Vazov harbor any doubts as to the views of Levski himself. In his story "*Chistiiat pît*," Vazov glorified Levski as the quintessence of moral purity, an example of Christian morality and yet, in Vazov's terms, "a skeptic." Here is the whole excerpt, as it is often quoted in parts so as to prove one of the opposing theses:

> [Levski] is not only valorous, he is also virtuous: a victorious rebuttal of the theory that honesty is an element incompatible with revolutionary activity. Vasil Levski reminds one of the early Christians, the people called him 'The Apostle.' Never has a name been given more truly. As an apostle in his message and his fanatic faith in his God—Bulgaria's liberty—he reminds us of Christ's pupils, both in his life style, his abstinence, his moral purity, as well as his unimpeachable purely Christian morality, despite the fact that he was a skeptic. Levski did not drink, did not smoke, never stole, like Charles XII, did not know a woman; a timeless wanderer, vagabond, pauper, he managed to become the incarnation of ideal honesty."

Apart from the fact that Vazov's interpretation of Levski's "skepticism" can and has been challenged, there is little doubt that it was his poetic vision, and its subsequent broad public reception, of the betrayal as well as the emphasis on Levski's break with his holy orders, that made for the complicated and ambivalent attitude of the church toward the hero.

The reasons to go into such detail about seemingly unimportant biographical instances are twofold. One is to show that the difference in interpretation about Levski's link to the church long predated the communist period. There is a tendency nowadays to ascribe the attempts to disassociate Levski from religion and church to the atheistic and anti-church propaganda of the communist state that attempted to push Levski "into the swamp of atheism." This propaganda existed, but it simply reinforced an interpretive trope that had appeared a century earlier, at the very beginning of the attempts to make sense of Levski's legacy. This trope had its philosophical roots in the general crisis of traditional religion during the 19th century, and the different outcomes triggered by secularization and skepticism: deism, agnosticism, and atheism. It was complicated at the turn of the century by the reception of a variety of general European philosophical currents that came to define Bulgarian modernism, and was reinforced during the interwar period with the radicalization of the political and ideological scene. Within this interpretation, it was tacitly assumed that Levski had outgrown his religious commitments as well as consciousness, and that the rupture with the church was final. Almost immediately, a parallel interpretive trope insisted that Levski never did break with the church. For obvious reasons today, after decades of official atheism, this interpretive trope is vocal but it is neither new, nor any more intense than when it first appeared more than a hundred years ago.

This polarized interpretation has another, more concrete provenance. The heroicization of the national revolutionary movement and its main figures—Rakovski, Karavelov, Levski, Botev—has become so much the Whig interpretation of Bulgarian history, that one tends to forget that it needed several decades after 1878 to become dominant. It most easily and quickly entered the schoolbooks after the radical political outcome of the Eastern Crisis 1875–78, when the rise of yesterday's revolutionaries to the political helm of the country vindicated their revolutionary vision. But it was neither an easily conceded nor unanimously accepted outcome. An editorial of 1898 published in the series "Religious stories" entitled "Hierodeacon Ignatii or Vasil Levski, Was he an Atheist?" argued strongly against the appropriation of Levski for anti-church propaganda. The article reacted to the manifesto of the commission entrusted to organize the 25th anniversary of Levski's death, where he was said to have "thrown away the monk's cassock and the begging in the name of the church, and stopped to raise his voice to a God who was deaf to the prayers of the slave." (Ierodiakon 1898: 52).

The reaction, however, was not directed solely at proving Levski's religiosity. There was a vicious polemic against the whole revolutionary movement. There had been, the article maintained, two strategies of national struggle. One belonged to the church and the schools, and had produced a restrained and enlightened literature; the other one, produced by and producing the revolutionary community, was overwhelming and immoderate, and "atheism and unbelief was the most popular idea of the revolutionary literature." These rebels "had elevated unbelief, atheism, hateful crimes like murder, theft, bank robberies and others to the level of virtue, if these crimes were seen as a means to the accomplishment of the idea: the liberation of the Bulgarian fatherland." As a result, "thanks to this language, this style, and these thoughts, a whole generation has been raised amongst us which, among its other virtues, cherishes unbelief and atheism as the greatest virtue" (ibid.: 55). The rest was dedicated to proving the moral heights of Levski in stark contrast to the norms and activities of the other revolutionaries. Levski emerges as a true son of the church who never broke his vows (with special emphasis on his virginity), his last words being: "I am dying for faith and fatherland!" So powerful was the polarization at the end of the 19th century that the article concluded in no uncertain terms: "If such an anniversary takes place, if there are proclamations, pamphlets and speeches offensive to faith and church, the church should be closed for this celebration, the clergy should not participate in such a celebration" (ibid.: 71). Nor was this attitude confined to written polemics. When in the 1880s, Zakhari Stoianov had collected materials for a biography of Botev and applied for a publication subsidy to the Ministry of Education, the response of the then minister Georgi Zhivkov was that he would not give money for the poetry of a "ne'er-do-well." Stoianov allegedly stormed out of the minister's office pledging to make Botev the idol of the Bulgarian people.

Two aspects have to be emphasized. One is that Levski had not yet become the uncontested figure of the Bulgarian heroic pantheon who, while constantly appropriated by different groups and platforms, was yet by common consent the property of the whole nation. At the end of the 19th century we witness a fierce and uncompromising contest over who he belongs to. The other is that the church's ambivalence vis-à-vis Levski stems not merely from the different possible interpretations of his own relationship to it but from a broader difficulty to accommodate the revolutionary period and its actors during the national struggle. The mutual hostility was great, the accusations on both sides devastating, and their roots deep in the two decades of the 1860s and 1870s. The accommodation happened only gradually, mostly after the first generation of contemporaries had passed from the scene. The present historiographical consensus of complementarity rather than conflict between the movements for church and political independence was achieved slowly and painfully over a whole century. By 1937, the 100th anniversary of Levski's birth, the sharply conflictual verdicts had been tempered, and the language adopted by the church did not differ from the tenor typical for the general national discourse. Nothing but the author (episkop Antim) or place of publication (*Tsŭrkoven vestik*, XXXVIII, 9, February 27, 1937) reveals the following opening as the position of the church: "Great historical events which create epochs in the history of nations, have to be remembered not only by their contemporaries; they have to serve as an example to the next generations. A nation which knows how to esteem the individuals with special merits to the Motherland, to point to them as an example for the youth, such a nation deserves to live and enjoy the admiration of the community of nations." Most writings in this period, stemming from the church, stressed Levski's religiosity but without a hint at the earlier enmity toward the revolutionary movement. On the contrary, the Whig interpretation had become so organic that the stress was on how much Levski relied on the clergy, and the latter's participation in the revolutionary struggle. Of course, there were exceptions, and in 1939 Stefan Tsankov, a *protopresviter* and author of a history of the Orthodox church after 1878, still lamented that "one of the most unfavorable internal conditions for the activity of the Bulgarian Church in our age was the antireligious and antichurch spirit of our intelligentsia" (Tsankov 1939: 7).

 It is only natural that in the first decade after the communist takeover, writings about Levski in the ecclesiastical press followed closely the dominant formulae, but they were not significantly different in style and tone from the ones during the interwar period. The focus was on Levski's devotion to "a pure and holy republic," to his ideas about the brotherhood of nations, even on his revolutionary democracy. There was no emphasis on his religious ideas and standing in the church, but absent at the same time was the insistence on any alleged atheism. By the late 1950s the reconciliation had taken place. In the atmosphere of an ideological thaw, and the elevation of the Bulgarian

Church to the Patriarchate in 1954, the compromise discourse was shared by all sides: on the one hand, the greatest figures of the national liberation struggle were posited to be the revolutionary democrats; on the other hand, the Bulgarian Orthodox Church was accepted as the single most important institution which had preserved the nation throughout the 500 years of the yoke.

A perfect illustration is a lengthy study about the Orthodox religion and church published in the Yearbook of the Theological Academy in 1970 by Radko Poptodorov, the future ideologue of the split and of the canonization. With the exception of the couple of pages that replicate Undzhiev's arguments on Levski's attitude toward the church, every other word or phrase could have been authored by any researcher from the Institute of History, the University of Sofia, or any other secular institution at the time. The symbiosis between formerly struggling evaluations reached its culmination in the conclusion about the April Uprising of 1876: "In it, the people's Bulgarian Church not only took part, but often in the person of its clergy and the monastic order, it even became the motor and leader of the people's revolutionary masses. In general, [the church] played a great role in the preparation and realization of the anti-feudal bourgeois-democratic and, at the same time, national-liberation revolution, and the revival of the Bulgarian state. This revival was finally completed in 1878 with the selfless help of the brotherly Russian people" (ibid.: 256). If Poptodorov would claim today that he was under pressure to write this pro-Russian statement, he surely cannot claim that somebody forced him (or prevented him from) writing the following florid patriotic paragraph that had become the consensual position of the Church and the secular communist authorities alike: "The Orthodox-Christian faith has been in the course of the five-century long Turkish yoke a spiritual armor made of steel over the body of the Bulgarian people which saved it from Turkish assimilation... During the dreadful five-centuries long hardships of slavery, the Orthodox-Christian faith and the Bulgarian people's church were the pulse of the people's life, thanks to which our people survived, hardened, and will last forever" (ibid.: 257).

Within this new consensual climate of reconciliation, when the revolutionaries were domesticated, it was perfectly natural to read that "the church never regretted the defrocking of Levski..., because it knows that to fight and sacrifice oneself for the good of one's fellowmen is a great and blessed deed"(*Tsîrkoven vestnik*, LXXIV, 5, February 12, 1973: 10). To a great extent, the reasons for the church's ambivalent assessment of the hero were shaped by the way in which Levski was emplotted in the two influential master-texts of the period immediately following independence: one, Zakhari Stoianov's biography, but first and foremost, Vazov's oeuvre. But Levski was emplotted in many more narratives and, while they are not mutually exclusive, they allow us to illustrate different ways of assembling and handling evidence, as well as different approaches to biography.

The nature of the biographical genre as a type of history writing poses general methodological problems about the nature of evidence, the problem of memoirs as historical sources, and the fibers of memory. Most of Levski's biography was based on written and oral memoirs or, as we would say today, it was to a great extent a project in oral history. It was conceived by the National Committee "Vasil Levski" (1923–1950), established exactly half a century after Levski's death. Its first task was the publication of a "strictly scientific and critical" commemorative volume that would contain a biography, documents and memoirs of live contemporaries. The person in charge of this initiative was Dimitîr Strashimirov, at the time chief librarian of the National Library. He was entrusted with funds to tour the country, buy existing manuscripts, copy documents. He also was appointed to produce the official biography of Levski, a task on which he worked incessantly over the next 15 years until his death in 1939. Much of the deliberations of the committee concern financing and the constantly postponed completion of this project. The first volume of Strashimirov's great collection of materials on Levski was published in 1929. The publication of the next volume was delayed because he was waiting for the translation of newly arrived Ottoman documents, and he resisted producing a hasty dilettantish biography. In the late 1920s he brought in his young assistant Ivan Undzhiev who, with Strashimirov's terminal disease, was commissioned to complete the work. This he did by the end of 1943 but, with the bombings over Sofia by the allied forces, the printing started in 1945, with the book coming out in 1947. In the spring of 1943, while reporting to the committee about the completion of the biography, Undzhiev emphasized the difficulties he and Strashimirov had encountered. One was the absence of a Bulgarian biographical prototype to emulate; another was the lack of scholarly monographs on separate aspects of Levski's and the revolutionary movement's activities. The most serious one, however, was the "enormous burden of legends, arbitrary statements, and impossible hypothesis, dubious memoirs and unfounded communications" (*TsDA*, ChP 940, Protocol 64 (March 12, 1943). Yet, in the absence of a reliable documentary information, Undzhiev was forced to work primarily with memoirs. Even Levski's birthday was reconstructed on the basis of personal reminiscences, and not baptismal registers or other documents. There had been no serious debate about the year of birth. The day, however, was disputed. Stoianov in 1884 stated that Levski had been born around St. Peter's Day in 1837. Stoian Zaimov in 1895 defined the day as July 6/18, basing his reconstruction on gathered recollections. The decisive reminiscences came from a cousin who in the 1890s was an active member of the Levski family council. He remembered one particular wedding, at which Levski's father was present but his pregnant mother could not attend. Following an elaborate logical scheme taking into account the customs around St. Peter's Day, and the wedding traditions in this period, Zaimov concluded after numerous consultations with Levski's relatives that July 6/18 was the most probable date, accepted since as Levski's authentic birthday. Clearly, the date is probable, possible, even very likely, but not unquestionable. The point here is not to question the date. After all, what does it matter whether Levski was born on July 6, or 5 or 7? The issue at stake is how we communicate information stemming from memoirs, and how we interpret them.

Had Undzhiev been pedantically true to his requirements of a "strictly scientific and critical" work, he would have used much more often the conditional form. Instead, Chapter 2 begins with a simple affirmative sentence: "Vasil Ivanov Levski, the apostle of freedom, saw the native skies on July 6, 1837." True, this sentence is referenced by a lengthy note narrating the whole story of the dating but this note appears some 691 pages later, and few readers are steadfast note consumers. Moreover, the biographical genre itself relegates methodological explanations to notes. The body of the text is supposed to present a smooth (and instructive) narrative of the real life. It is like the reconstruction of an ancient vessel where the missing parts are filled out with modern substitutes but, on top of it, the vessel is given a fresh varnish to cover the patches. Again, this dating is a simple example without any momentous interpretive repercussions but because of its simplicity, it neatly fleshes out the tension between genre conventions and scholarly ethos.

There are more complicated examples that pose more difficult questions. The dramatic act of Levski's second defrocking on Easter Day 1864, the cutting of his hair, was vividly preserved in the minds of the contemporaries, writes Undzhiev. It involved the visual memory of an act that had all the underpinnings of a carefully staged theatrical scene. Levski could have cut his hair as he had done in 1862 without any witness. Instead, he called his friends Georgi Pop Khristov and Khristo Vasil Pulev, took them to the locality Altînchair, and asked them to cut his hair. Terrified, both refused, so in the end he did it himself. He then folded his hair carefully, and gave it to his mother to preserve. After that, already in civilian clothes, he reappeared at his usual place in the church, and produced the turmoil and "vividly preserved" memory. This is the brief version of the event in the biography. The accompanying note specifies that the only source for this event was the story of one of the witnesses, Pop Khristov. The story itself was recorded only in 1903. Other recollections of contemporaries, both ones considered valuable by Undzhiev as well as others dismissed as untrustworthy, are, in the final analysis, based on this initial story. How is all of this to be interpreted? How do we juxtapose the two following statements of Undzhiev: one, in the main text of his narrative, that "the act of the defrocking was vividly preserved in the minds of the contemporaries"; the other, in the accompanying note, that "the act of the second defrocking of the Apostle was made known to the generations by the witness to the event—khadzhi Georgi Pop Khristov. Many Karlovo inhabitants had heard from him the story about the episode at Altînchair" (Undzhiev 1947: 133–5, 783).

What do people remember decades after the event? The event itself or the story as it was delivered to them by the witness? What had become of Pop Khristov's initial story once it was shared with the rest of the community? Did it/how did it differ from the version that was noted and published 40 years after the event? How reliable was it in the first place? Why was there no similar story by Pulev? What makes Undzhiev believe parts of the story, and consider others "not very convincing"? Was Levski a singularly intuitive and effective public relations manager who knew the value of a dramatically staged public event?

Did he intentionally bring his two friends so as to assure the circulation of eyewitness accounts? Or is the "staging" of the story to be attributed to the witness himself, for a number of different and plausible motives? How conscious was Undzhiev of all these questions? Did he avoid them on purpose or did the conventions of the biographical genre dictate the rules of the narrative, making him oblivious to the conventions of the dominant historiographical style? Should we hear in his lament about the absence of a Bulgarian biographical prototype the tension of this methodological quandary? Finally, is there really a methodological quandary?

One last example that goes back to the problem of the relationship of Levski with/within the church. The person who in 1873 communicated Levski's death to his mother was Archimandrite Konstantin, later Bishop of Vratsa. His recollections, published in 1903, describe how the devastated mother shared with him the episode of Levski's defrocking, and the handing of his hair. The Archimandrite gave a verbatim rendition of Levski's words as they were communicated by his mother: "Mother, the people's voice has called on me to run to the assistance of my enslaved fatherland; therefore, I can no longer fulfill my ecclesiastical duty, and I resign from it. Take my hair and hide it in your wooden chest, for I am leaving you, and when you hear that I have perished, take it out so that a funeral service can be performed over it and that it can be buried, because I may have neither funeral service, nor a grave" (Undzhiev 1947: 135–6). A few years later, Konstantin, already a Metropolitan, gave a speech where he again referred to the mother's recollection. Published in 1933, the speech had little in common with the first quote. This is how it sounded in the second version: "Mother, I take off the cassock but I will never and under no circumstance renounce the vows to serve God and his holy church. I am putting on civilian clothes only to be able to preach freely and unhindered among my compatriots. When I perish for the fatherland, hand my hair to the clergy which should perform over it the funeral service as it befits the deacon's rank" (ibid.: 783–4).

Undzhiev was understandably suspicious of the second version, and published it only in his footnotes, while giving the first version the scholarly imprimatur of authenticity. Also understandably, it is the second version from the footnotes that is nowadays put forward as the authentic soliloquy of Levski. What is surprising was that Undzhiev never voiced any questions about the first version. He took it at face value, and reproduced it as he would do a document or a letter. There can be no question about Undzhiev's meticulousness and his methodological sophistication within the framework of historiograpical positivism. Had he written a scholarly monograph or article, he probably would have reached the same analytical conclusions about Levski's sincere religiosity, and that the act of defrocking was not an act of refuting his faith. But he would have, no doubt, provided all the conditional interpretive paraphernalia to this recollection in the main body of the text, and would have most likely rephrased it, and refrained from rendering it in direct speech. That he chose to do otherwise was due, it seems, to the clear consciousness that he was working in another genre, about whose conventions he was not entirely certain but that he assumed to be much more flexible and able to accommodate a piece of fictional (though plausible) memory. As has been half-jokingly remarked, the *biographie romancée*, where facts are a little hazy and dialogues and private thoughts are freely invented, is usually shelved in libraries under "Biography." In contrast, more serious and scholarly biographies are placed under "History." But is the distinction so obvious?

Biography's genesis can be traced back to the tradition of exemplary lives, gospels and hagiography that sought to contribute to the public good. The "critical and scholarly" biography of the 19th and 20th centuries was not trying to do away with this stated function but it prioritized values such as objectivity and verifiability over the predominantly prescriptive and moralizing tenure of earlier writings. This it shared with the national historiographies and the realistic novel, which had the same vision of their functions and legitimation—the public good—as well as the same methodological predilections. All three genres were informed by the belief still dominant today among practicing historians that the past is "another country" that can be reconstructed from traces left behind. There is another view, making its way slowly and unevenly into the mainstream of the historical profession: "The past is myself, my own history, the seed of my present thoughts, the mold of my present disposition" (L. S. Stevenson, cited in Tonkin 1992: 1). In this view, both biography and history can be essentially reduced to a kind of intellectual autobiography. Fundamentally opposed as these two understandings of historiography are, in both frameworks there is no intrinsic cognitive contradiction between the biographic and historiographic genres except *qua* genres. What Jerome Bruner has to say about autobiography applies equally to biography and history:

> "[a]utobiography is life construction through 'text' construction. To look at a life as if it were independent of the autobiographical text that constructs it is as futile a quest for reality as the physicist's search for a Nature that is independent of the theories that lead him to measure one rather than another phenomenon... The principle instruments by which the culture [creates the paradigms that guide our construction] are its narrative forms, its genres, its modes of 'packaging' forms of life" (Bruner 1993: 55).

Undzhiev functioned comfortably within the first discourse, and his uneasiness was not methodological: after all, the scholarly biography has been collapsed into the larger historiographical field. His anxiety stemmed from the trepidations of a pioneer of scholarly biography within the younger and smaller tradition of Bulgarian historiography where he could not hide behind a widely accepted model. Still, the biographical genre seems to have afforded broader presumed license on both the manner of articulation as well as the treatment of sources. It was also a genre that gave Undzhiev an easier and maybe more effective venue to fulfill his self-described mission both as biographer and historiographer: "The Apostle Levski as a historical figure reveals himself in new and unsuspected depths, and emerges as the most majestic figure of our past. Now, when [future] generations will already know his life thoroughly and correctly, he will rise in everybody's mind as the most perfect expression of the Bulgarian genius" (*TsDA*, ChP 940, Protocol 64, March 12, 1943).

Symptomatically, 20 years later, in a completely different political context, and deeply involved in the project of Marxist historiography, the English historian Mercia MacDermott replicated the exact same strategy, drawn to and unconsciously guided by the conventions of the genre. She also had a mission, and it was even more grandiose than Undzhiev's, in that it was appropriately international compared to Undzhiev's national claim: "Had Levski lived and worked in a larger, less unknown country, or had he written in a more widely understood language, he might already have had an honorable place in the international pantheon of revolutionaries and liberators" (MacDermott

1967: 86). Writing for an English-reading audience, MacDermott made the appropriate analogy between Levski and the legends of Sir Galahad and Robin Hood. The documentary evidence, according to her, did not destroy this romantic figure; what it added, though, was incorporating him as the primogenitor in another romance, that of revolutionary Marxism. For MacDermott, Levski anticipated if he did not strictly speaking inaugurate the revolutionary practice of the 20th century: "To an astonishing degree, the principles upon which Levski built his revolutionary organization foreshadowed those of Lenin and the Bolsheviks, but the familiarity of many of Levski's principles must not mislead us into overlooking the fact that when Levski formulated them in the late 1860's and early 1870's, they were original and had no parallel in other European movements" (ibid.: 16).

The obvious distinctions between Undzhiev and MacDermott, especially their ideological underpinnings, can be better understood in the framework of the dialogical principle rather than within stark explanations of political and ideological exigencies. Elizabeth Tonkin has argued that one cannot detach the oral representation of pastness from the relationship of teller and audience in which it was occasioned (1992: 2). This is also valid for written representations. The relationship between teller and audience need not be unmediated. As Lotman has shown, not only communication but thinking itself is dialogical by nature. In the 1930s–1940s, Undzhiev was in an internal dialogue with a projected audience within a sphere in which religion was a contested but dominant signifier. In the 1960s, MacDermott practiced this internal dialogue within a sphere where religion had been relegated to the periphery but also, in the particular Bulgarian circumstances, did not represent a viable challenge and strong threat to the dominant Marxist discourse. She, therefore, easily conceded that "Vasil's rejection of the cloister was not intended as a conscious rejection of the Church" and that he "felt neither the compulsion nor the desire to cut the umbilical cord which bound him to the Church." Her projected audience was supposed to have a different hierarchy of priorities, one that corresponded to her reading of the world and, consequently "Levski had felt an urge to lay his life upon an altar, to live morally and meaningfully, but it was in the revolutionary movement, not the Church, that he found complete spiritual satisfaction" (MacDermott 1967: 86–7). For all the posited contrasts between the pre- and postwar periods and historiographies, they functioned within the same semiosphere: nationalism. What in Undzhiev was carefully depicted as the transposition of religious ardor from the transcendental to the secular sphere, in MacDermott's brush turned into the somewhat pompous portrait of a harmoniously developed Renaissance man: "He was full of an almost pagan *joie-de-vivre*, and his delight in physical existence was closer to the spirit of Ancient Greece than that of Byzantium... Vasil was essentially an earthly person, and his asceticism was that of the athlete rather than the saint" (ibid.: 87). Levski's hypostasis as an athlete, as well as an athletes' "patron-saint," is well known, but MacDermott may have been too hasty in dismissing his hypostasis as a saint.

4. The Orchestration of a Grassroots Cultus

The "Holy Virgin" church in Karlovo cuts a handsome profile with its blue and white bell tower. The bell tower is relatively new, from 1897, but the church building, as the inscription above the western entrance tells us, dates from 1851. Before they began constructing this new building in 1847, there had been a rather insignificant structure erected in 1839 in the place of the older church of the Holy Virgin that had burnt down in 1813. This latter church, about which little is known, is believed by some to have been built already at the end of the 15th century, at the time of the founding of the little town of Karlî-ova, later Karlovo. In any case, the names of priests serving in the church have been preserved at least from the 18th century on. Although the construction was completed in 1851, the events of the Crimean war and lack of funds delayed the furnishing of the church, and its consecration did not take place until May 20, 1858. Levski's biography is intimately linked with this church because it was here in 1859 that he was ordained as a deacon; here that he sang at all the liturgies in the course of several years; and here again he reappeared after he had cut his hair on Easter 1864.

As used to be the case with the majority of churches built in the Ottoman period, the exterior is simple and modest, the walls of unpolished stone, the joints unfilled, the decoration kept to a minimum. A plain wooden arcade was added later, encircling the western part of the church with the main entrance, and bending to reach the north and south entrances. In 1997, a significant change occurred on the northern wall. A fresco of the Holy Virgin with Child was painted above the entrance. The more dramatic addition was a large fresco covering the northern wall under the arcade. It was commissioned and financed by the Karlovo section of the Committee "Vasil Levski," in agreement with the ecclesiastical Board of Trustees. Again, it had been painted by a local artist—Dechko Todorov—and represents the taking of the holy orders by Vasil Levski. The accompanying inscription explains: "In Anno Domini 1859, in this temple Deacon Ignatii (Vasil Levski) was ordained in the rank of deacons by Metropolitan Paisii of Plovdiv." This fresco was opened and consecrated on July 18, 1997 (Levski's birthday) by the former Metropolitan of Plovdiv, Arsenii. (Plate 16) The main decoration of the interior is the iconostasis separating the nave from the sanctuary. The sanctuary, closed to persons not consecrated, as in all Orthodox churches, contains the altar of the Holy Virgin, as well as an additional one dedicated to Sts. Cyril and Methodius. This we learn from the little guide. What the little guide does not say is that the sanctuary houses the portrait of Levski, hung on the wall above a wooden chest immediately opposite and to the right of the main door of the sanctuary.

Visiting Karlovo in July, 2000, a few days before Levski's birthday, I received the program for the festivities on July 18. They were to open with a Holy Liturgy dedicated to the 2000 anniversary of the birth of Jesus Christ and the 163th anniversary of Levski's birth, and performed by Arsenii, the Metropolitan of Plovdiv. This was to be followed by laying flowers at the grave of Gina Kuncheva, Levski's mother. After this, a poetry performance would take place, followed by a book opening. At the end, there would be the conclusion of the tourist initiative "In the steps of The Apostle," and the awarding of the "Karlovo" prize. Later in the evening, the flag of the Karlovo Revolutionary Committee was to be solemnly taken out, and Patriarch Maxim was to deliver an official address at the monument of Levski. The festivities were to end with a concert by the pop-star Roberta.

Speaking with the young, energetic and dedicated director of the Levski Museum in Karlovo—Dora Chausheva—who was in charge of the festivities, I asked her of her opinion about Levski's canonization. She was against it because "[t]his is a formality. He already is a saint for the nation. The act will only defile and formalize the authentic sanctity." She added some details on the program of the festivities. In the past few years, on July 18 and February 19, the days accepted for the birth and death of the hero, a procession starts from the "Holy Virgin" church and goes to the museum, then to the monument, and back to the church. The procession carries icons, prominent among them the icon of the Virgin who is the patron saint. Lately, among the icons a portrait of Levski is being carried. "Isn't this an informal act of canonization?" I asked. "No," Dora Chausheva replied, "this is not an icon, it is a lay portrait." Where was it kept? She didn't know.

Next morning I was at the church, which is part of the Maxim-led hierarchy. There were no Pimen adherents in Karlovo. The old lady selling candles was friendly and sociable. Is it true they carry Levski's portrait with the icons? Yes. When did they start doing this? Maybe 1997. From where do they bring the portrait? They keep it in the sanctuary. If I wish, I can carefully lift the curtain over the royal gates, and will see it. I did. The portrait of Levski, hung immediately to the right on an inner wall over a wooden chest, looked back at me. I knew I was not allowed to enter. How about, if I didn't enter, but took a photograph? After all, it wouldn't be even my direct gaze; and, besides, right now I was not unclean. The old lady appreciated the casuistry with a grin. I took my photographs from the royal gates, and from the "deacons' door" of the iconostasis (Plates 17, 18, and 18A).

The portrait of Levski, perhaps two feet by one, is an oval shaped image of his bust in civilian attire. It seems to be an oil or watercolor version of one of his earliest portraits by Georgi Danchov, Levski's contemporary and friend, who painted several portraits from memory in the 1880s. True, it is a portrait, and was not painted originally as an icon, but neither was the exact same image of Levski that had been venerated at the canonization ceremony in July, 1996 by the Pimen Church National Council. Subsequently, the Pimen church produced several "real" icons of Levski. One was kept at the metropolitan church "Sv. Paraskeva," and was carried out only during the liturgy or processions on July 18 and February 19. It was, however, for sale as a postcard or a poster, and was the only image of Levski completely consistent with the iconographic tradition. Another icon had been on display between 2001 and 2004 in "Sveta Sofia," the oldest church in Sofia, which had also been part of Pimen's church, and was removed as a result of the disbanding of the alternative Synod. This icon, together with the icon on display in the "Sv. Petka Samardzhiiska" church since 1997, had all the iconographic accoutrements (the nimbus, the inscription, the attire) but both represent a very realistic portrait version of Levski's most popular image. Clearly, it is not the style or genre in which an image is produced but its relational positioning that confers on it the status of an icon, in this case its position within the sanctuary. Levski's portrait/icon is placed almost directly behind the image of Christ Enthroned in the iconostasis, the icon of the first tier—the "local saints"—to the right of the royal gates which is always occupied by the image of the Savior. In any case, the iconography from photograph to portrait to icon has been effectively developed. (Plates 19, 20, and 21)

Both theologians and art historians have emphasized that Orthodox art has a primarily liturgical and, generally speaking, a worshipful purpose, rather than a decorative one. It is evaluated "not from the form, nor from the color, but from the service it renders" (St.John Chrysostom cited Kalokyris 1969: 61). In fact, iconography renders perceptible that which is mystically performed in worship, and it seeks to speak to the faithful by means of symbols, shapes, and forms. It also speaks through placement, and the specific positioning of the Levski icon next to the image of Christ and the Virgin has heroic implications: "The positional meaning of an object derives from its relationship to other symbols in a configuration, a Gestalt, having properties that cannot be derived from its parts or be considered simply as their sum. The object may be part of a cluster of similar or different objects; it may also occupy a central or a marginal position. It may be strikingly contrasted with another object. Position has to do with time as well as space" (Turner 1982: 21).

Compare this to the dispute over the consecration of the newly built chapel of "All Bulgarian Saints." This is a small and pretty white structure adjacent to Levski's museum in Karlovo. In mid-July, 2000, when I visited the place, hectic activities were in place to finish it for the July 18 celebrations. In the neighboring town of Sopot, a wooden iconostasis was being carved out of walnut, and received its finishing touches when we went to the carpenter's shop to inspect its progress. The iconostasis was supposed to hold four icons: of Jesus Christ, of the Holy Virgin, of St. John the Baptist, and of "All Bulgarian Saints." The latter is the chapel's patron icon. The icons had already been painted, and they were all kept in the Levski museum, waiting to be installed in the iconostasis. The icon "All Bulgarian Saints" has a fairly new history. There is only one similar icon in the Rila Monastery but it is not complete. Eye-catching with its bright colors, the icon represents the "Council of all Bulgarian saints." There are more than 40 Bulgarian saints, and the artists were tempted to depict them all but in the limited space they could portray only 28, the rest only hinted at in the background. The icon is crowned by the figure of Christ in heaven held by two angels. I asked one of the artists whether they were tempted to paint Vasil Levski. He laughed: "We can't."

It is in this chapel during my visit on July 14, 2000, that I encountered the artists and workers installing the glass case supposed to house Levski's hair. It had been recently transferred to his museum in Karlovo after passionate debates whether it should be on display in Sofia or in his hometown. It was preserved in a tiny glass box within a glass case as part of the documentary exposition of the museum. The refusal of the museum workers to recognize a reliquary in what they call themselves *khranitelnitsa* (literally reliquary), and their insistence that this was merely a museum display box was understandable in the existing atmosphere of controversy over Levski's canonization. On the other hand, it is difficult to distinguish between disingenuousness and sincere, if somewhat unsophisticated, belief. Only a month before my visit, a group of visitors to the museum from Plovdiv and Asenovgard had suggested that "the holy hair of Hierodeacon the Reverend Martyr Ignatii should be placed in the chapel and in front of them a chandelier should be set." This was a clear reference to the canonized Levski, and it proposed the handling of his hair as a *par excellence* Christian reliquary, exactly what the museum officials were in fact implementing. Here, again, the notion of positional meaning is most helpful, as it was employed above in the analysis of Levski's portrait/icon in the sanctuary of the church. In fact, the chapel of "All Bulgarian Saints" is set to play the role of a classical *martyrium*, a church built over the tomb or relic of a martyr or in honor of a martyr. And in the future it is bound to do that in competition with the Sofia church "Sv. Petka Samardzhiiska."

There had been hopes, Dora Chausheva explained, that Patriarch Maxim would consecrate the chapel but, in the end, he reneged, and the printed program of the festivities omitted the consecration. These hopes had been neither abstract, nor private: they had an important institutional base. The initiative belonged to the Bulgarian Committee "Vasil Levski" (BCVL) with headquarters in Sofia; Levski's museum in Karlovo is its most important partner and member. The committee is an NGO with cultural functions, and was created in 1991. Its self-described goal in its statute is: "to create a broad Bulgarian movement for the study and popularization of the life, ideas and activity of Vasil

Levski, of his associates, of the towns and villages and families, whose destiny has been linked to the struggles for the liberation and unification of the Bulgarians" (*Ustav*, art.2). Its four main spheres of activity include: aiding state institutions in their effort to preserve the legacy of Levski and other revival figures; popularizing Levski's life through different celebrations; encouraging research; broadening contacts with Bulgarians abroad. In the fall of 1991, the Foundation "Vasil Levski" was established, whose main function is to fundraise and support the activities of the committee.

To date, there are 95 local committees as members of the BKVL. They have introduced the celebration of Levski's birthday, and in the case of the Karlovo committee, this has become a popular ritual, of which the festivities of July 18, 2000 were the seventh such celebration. This is clearly a new initiative, and an attempt to move away from the somberness of the previous emphasis on February 19, the day Levski was hanged. In the past few years, the BKVL has organized and sponsored dozens of scholarly conferences and workshops in Sliven, Veliko Tîrnovo, Pleven, Panagiurishte, Kalofer, Ruse, and Sofia around different anniversaries linked to the activities of Levski, Botev, the April Uprising, the Oborishte meeting, the role of the Bulgarian emigration, and so on. It sponsored different publications, among them the guide to the Karlovo museum, but its real pride is the publication of Levski's documentary legacy, a two-volume sumptuous edition. The committee also initiates and supports the building of monuments to Levski and other figures of the Bulgarian revival in the country and abroad "so as to make them a sacral location for sustaining the Bulgarian spirit." Levski's busts have been erected in Razlog, Dzhebel, Blagoevgrad, Strelcha, Vratsa, and a bust of Stambolov in Samovodene. Abroad, Levski's busts have been placed in Washington DC, Buenos Aires, and Bucharest. There are also memorial plaques in Bucharest, Turnu-Mâgurele, Giurgiu (Romania), Tvârdiţa (Moldova), a monument of Rakovski in Bolhrad (Ukraine).

One of the main efforts of the BKVL was the construction of the chapel "All Bulgarian Saints" whose "upcoming consecration and opening was to be carried out on July 18 for the 163rd anniversary of Levski's birth." Professor Doino Doinov, chairman of the BKVL, explains that once the idea crystallized, he visited Metropolitan Arsenii of Plovdiv, within whose diocese Karlovo falls. He told him that the chapel would be constructed as part of the museum complex, but they would like it to be thoroughly canonical and also serve as a church. Arsenii responded that they had to install an iconostasis, and gave them advice what icons to commission. Asked whether it would be acceptable to put Levski's hair in a reliquary, he answered in the affirmative that it was permissible for relics to be placed but in the narthex, not in the sanctuary. In responding this way, Arsenii was representing one of the two current opinions held among prelates of the Maxim-led church which is also supported by the director of the CHAI. The opposing opinion considers the placing of the reliquary as anti-canonical because Levski's hair is part of a human body not a saint's relic.

Whatever the technical motivation that made Patriarch Maxim refrain from officiating in the chapel, his reserve is not surprising: the consecration with Levski's hair in it could be interpreted as an indirect endorsement, as well as a significant step leading to his canonization. The official explanation was that the consecration had to be effectuated on the patron saint's day or another ecclesiastical holiday, not on Levski's birthday. Accordingly, Maxim's address in front of Levski's monument on the evening of July 18, 2000 was highly adulatory but very carefully worded with formulae that invite a secular political rather than canonical analysis. He praised the "great Bulgarian son Vasil Levski, the chief apostle for the whole of Bulgaria, Thrace, and Macedonia" who sacrificed himself for his patriotic ideal, and toward whom Bulgaria feels the duty of unfulfilled legacy. He emphasized his intimate link to the church: "Levski's soul was turned toward God," he was a "worthy son of the church and the nation." Yet, he used exclusively the name Vasil Levski, rather than Deacon Ignatii, and once mentioned the "People's Deacon." The only phrase that could be overinterpreted was the reference to the "godsent Apostle" but this can be easily explained away as a metaphor.

To summarize, despite the present firm stand of Maxim's Holy Synod against canonization, a number of activities point in this direction. Doinov emphasizes that the BKVL "stands only for the national interests, and does not want to interfere in the affairs of the church." Yet, by linking the museum complex to the church, it directly involves the ecclesiastical hierarchy, and presses it to take a stand. Metropolitan Arsenii of Plovdiv, himself an active prelate and ally of Maxim, clearly offered the greatest support to what I have called the orchestration of a grassroots *cultus*. He supported the painting of the fresco on the northern wall of the "Holy Virgin;" he gave his permission for the installment of the reliquary in the chapel; he performed the ceremonial liturgies for Levski in the past few years, and it is unlikely that he is unaware of the location of Levski's portrait/icon in the sanctuary. At the festivities for the 160th anniversary of Levski's birth in Karlovo, at which the former President Stoianov was present, the construction of the chapel had made significant progress although it was not yet covered with a roof. After going through Levski's museum, President Stoianov and his wife Antonina entered the chapel with candles in hand, as if this was an already consecrated temple. In cutting a ritualized posture taken out of the Christian ritual, they added a symbolic religious sacrality to the already existing secular sacrality of the whole museum ensemble.

In the Theological Academy, part of Maxim's church, dissident opinions are tolerated. Professor Petev, careful to express only his personal opinion, thinks Levski should be canonized because he put in practice Christian ideals, especially altruism. He summarizes the objections against in two main rubrics: one asserts he had broken his vows; the other insists he had killed, if only once, a young servant during a raid (interestingly, whenever this objection is voiced, there is never mention of the Turkish soldiers or gendarmes killed by Levski). Petev shows numerous precedents that render these objections invalid. In an otherwise forced passage trying to prove the direct influence of Mt. Athos's ethos on Levski, Konstantinos Nikhoritis (2001: 189) distinguishes between martyrdom for the faith and martyrdom for the nation. He calls Ignatii Starozagorski *prepodobnomîchenik* (holy/reverend martyr), and Levski a *narodnomîchenik* (national martyr). He then muses, implicitly making the case for Levski's sanctification: "Martyrdom [for the faith] and national martyrdom are two terms that are often intertwined in history, and only God, who is cognizant of people's souls, knows who dies *first* for the faith, and *then* for the fatherland, and who does so *first* for the fatherland, and *then* for the faith. But faith and fatherland were so intertwined during the yoke that it is very difficult to distinguish between the two." Petev warns, however, against hastiness. People do not know "the real Levski." They know only the revolutionary, the strategist, the hero. But Levski as Hierodeacon Ignatii remains unknown. People should be prepared with this image before the act is effectuated. Petev works quietly and systematically to bring to the people this "clarified, real image."

Judging from the visitors book at Levski's museum, such a shift is taking place. Levski had always been referred to as a saint, but this was only with a metaphorical connotation. A group of visitors from Troian in June, 1982 quote Vazov's poem—"The simple peasants called him saint"—and add: "Today, we the citizens of the People's Republic of Bulgaria not only call him a saint, but we bow before his deed." It is a secular understanding of sainthood that does not place it at the apex of achievement. In an undated entry in the summer of 1990, one Vîlko Vîlev authored a "Petition from Hierodeacon Ignatii": "The sacred relics should be placed, like the ones of St. Stefan the Serbian king in the "Sv. Nedelia" church in Sofia, in a big temple built on the place of the small church." He was clearly referring to the small "Sv. Petka." This is an example of how the idea of Levski's formal canonization was percolating in the public. On September 6, 1992, a family from Varna (Pancho, Dobrinka and their schoolchildren Ivanka and Dimitîr) explicitly stated: "Our church should canonize as saint the one who proved with his life that he is closest to God, and serves as an example for us with his deeds." A year after the official canonization, someone signed only with the acronym P.I.R. wrote in Church Slavonic, on July 23, 1997: "Lord, in Your grace, pardon and save your servant, the Hierodeacon Vasilii, who died for the Orthodox faith. May his memory live forever!"

5. Commemoration, Ritual, and the Sacred

How do we begin to think about all of this? What is the proper framework of interpretation? One may be tempted to see the phenomenon of Levski's present veneration and canonization fall under the rubric of what Katherine Verdery calls "the political lives of dead bodies" in post-socialist Eastern Europe or, more aptly and wittily, in the first version of her manuscript, as "post-socialist necrophilia." Verdery tried to make sense of the hectic activity around dead bodies (reburials of famous persons returned from abroad, or of famous and anonymous ones at home, as well as the erection and tearing down of statues as icons of dead bodies), and argued that there was something specific to the post-socialist period in this activity: "although corpses can be effective political symbols anywhere, they are pressed into the service of political issues specific to a given polity" (Verdery 1999: 52). For post-socialism, she identifies the main issues as property restitution, political pluralization, religious renewal, and national conflicts tied to building nation-states. What makes the post-socialist context unique is that these issues occur simultaneously. Measured against these criteria, Levski's case does not conform to any: the potential for a national conflict was successfully contained, and Levski as a symbol had little to do with it; nor has he been used as a legitimizing pillar in the process of political pluralization; property restitution can be referred to only if the ecclesiastical split can be read primarily in terms of an intra-church quarrel over prospective property restitution; finally, religious renewal does indeed occur but even there it is not the primary motor behind Levski's case. But Verdery herself admits that this is not the strongest argument for the specificity of post-socialist dead bodies. She further points out that dead bodies "are especially useful and effective symbols for revising the past," or, as in the case of Eastern Europe for "rejecting the immediate past." That is indeed so, and Verdery draws on numerous illustrations to support her contention.

Yet, Levski's example again does not conform to this explanation. If anything, it actually generates the link with the past and effectuates a strong continuity, even if with minor shifts. Verdery stresses that "the specificity of post-socialist corpses lies in the magnitude of the change that has animated them. The *axis mundi* has shifted; whole fields of the past await the plowshare of revisionist pens, as well as the tears of those whose dead lie insufficiently mourned. A change so momentous and far-reaching requires especially heavy, effective symbols, symbols such as dead bodies" (ibid.: 52–3). In the case of Levski, quite apart from the formal difference that we have no body, there is the more substantial one pointing to continuities rather to discontinuities. Verdery is careful to differentiate between sites where dead body politics is rampant (like Hungary), and where it is relatively mute (like Bulgaria). Yet, she makes a systemic claim about Eastern Europe, and attributes the less intensive reburial reflex in Bulgaria to the less extreme political transformation (ibid.: 130). I see the continuities less in the preservation of immediate political structures and political players, than in deeper social structures and longer periods, in the type of nationalism that evolved over the past century and its specific cultural underpinnings. Morbid symbolism never played a central part in the Bulgarian symbolic repertoire (unlike the extreme case among Codreanu's followers in Romania).

Likewise, even though I share Verdery's belief that post-socialist change is much bigger than "shock therapy," writing constitutions, election-management consulting, and the like, I would shy away from the dramatic assertion that "[i]t is a problem of reorganization on a cosmic scale, and it involves the redefinition of virtually everything, including morality, social relations, and basic meanings. It means a reordering of people's entire meaningful worlds" (ibid.: 35). This may be simply a difference in optics but, especially as far as history writing goes, I am more inclined to look for continuities not only between the communist and the post-communist past, but also between the pre-communist and communist one where a much more radical and revolutionary transformation had allegedly taken place. Dichotomies between continuity and rupture are artificial, but the view privileging rupture has been dominant in the literature thus far, although Verdery herself has written perceptively on existing continuities, especially in the realm of nationalism. However, quite apart from the difference in

Commemoration, Ritual, and the Sacred 273

assessment, as far as Levski's case goes, I do not think that his non-existing body (and the plenitude of existing monuments) fit in the parade of Verdery's dead bodies.

On the other hand, I find extremely useful her brilliant treatment of politics, and am thoroughly persuaded by her analytical goal of trying to "animate the study of *politics in general*, energizing it with something more than the opinion polls, surveys, analyses of 'democratization indices,' and game-theoretic formulations that dominate so much of the field of comparative politics." Because she treats politics as "a realm of continual struggles over meaning, over signification" which take place through complex symbolic processes, the "something more" for Verdery includes "meanings, feelings, the sacred, ideas of mortality, the nonrational—all ingredients of 'legitimacy' or 'regime consolidation' (that dry phrase), yet far broader than what analyses employing those terms usually provide" (Verdery 1999: 24–6). It is in this context that I view my own treatment of the Levski case as an attempt to "enchant," "enliven," "enrich," or "animate" (all Verdery's verbs) politics.

I also find convincing her insistence that "authority *always* has a 'sacred' component, even if it is reduced merely to holding 'as sacred' certain secular values." She points out that socialist regimes sought assiduously to sacralize themselves as guardians of secular values. But I do not find that "because their language omitted notions of the sacred, both outsiders and their own populations tended to view them as lacking a sacred dimension." Even a cursory look at the language of socialism can demonstrate the abundance of "sacred" referents: "sacred idea," "sacred republic," "sacred people," "sacred truth," "holy cause," "saints of the revolution," "martyrs for freedom," "martyrs of the revolution," and these at times, in some countries more than in others, were accepted by significant groups in the population. More to the point, however, I do agree that "[p]art of reordering meaningful worlds since 1989, then, is to sacralize authority and politics in new ways" (ibid.: 37).

The sacralization of politics using the symbol of Levski is certainly not unprecedented. There are numerous canonized national figures, of which Joan of Arc is a particularly famous one. The utilization of the iconic genre is also not unprecedented, a striking example being a 1920s icon with the image of the recently deceased Lenin. What is interesting here is that unlike the Lenin case, where the religious form was appropriated by and subordinated to the secular content, in the Levski case it is precisely the reverse: the religious form appropriates and subordinates a secular object (Plate 22).

The sacralization of politics by using Levski's symbol was pioneered already back in the 1870s by the most unorthodox of political configurations—the radical revolutionary alternative—to which Levski himself belonged. This may have been one of the original stumbling blocks on which the resistance of the church to Levski's canonization rested. Botev, without any doubt the greatest revolutionary poet of the 19th century, and a gifted and sarcastic journalist, was himself a revolutionary activist, and became a martyr who perished in the April Uprising of 1876. Alongside his major newspapers *Duma, Budilnik, Zname, Nova Bîlgariia*, that together with Karavelov's *Svoboda* and *Nezavisimost* were the peak of revolutionary journalism, he decided in 1875 to diffuse his message in a subtler though no less subversive way. To this day, the Orthodox church each year prints and sells religious calendars. They include the confession of faith, the commandments, the main holidays, the chief prayers, and detailed entries for the saints celebrated on each day. There is also a wall calendar version arranged around the icon of a saint. Botev published such a wall calendar for the year 1875 which, instead of the icon of a Christian saint, figured the engraving of Khadzhi Dimitîr, the legendary leader of a *cheta* who was killed in battle by the Ottoman troops in the Balkan mountains in 1867. Under the engraving, Botev published the text of his poem, or rather ballad, "Khadzhi Dimitîr." It had been written in 1873, and published first in Karavelov's newspaper *Nezavisimost*. This was the second printing of what in time has arguably become the most recited poem in the Bulgarian language. Under August 5/17, the entry included *Velikomîchenik Khadzhi Dimitîr Asenyov* together with the 15,000 Bulgarian soldiers of Tsar Samuil allegedly blinded by the Byzantine Emperor Basil II in 1014. This was not the only innovation in the calendar. Under March 9/21, the entry read: "+ *40 mîch. I Vasil Levski mîch.*" (SS. Forty Martyrs and Vasil Levski, martyr).

Next year's calendar for 1876 was conceived by Botev to commemorate Levski. An engraving was prepared using his photograph of 1867 as the standard bearer of Panaiot Khitov's *cheta*. It followed the exact same design as the 1875 calendar, with Botev's poem dedicated to Levski printed under the portrait. The poem, Botev's last poetic work, had been completed at the end of 1875, very likely for the purposes of the calendar. We do not know how Levski was entered this time in the daily calendar, simply as *mîchenik* (martyr) or as *velikomîchenik* (magnus martyr) because this calendar has not been preserved or has not yet been discovered. We know, however, that it was printed because one of the books published by Botev—a translation of N. Kostomarov's drama *Kremutsii Kord*—announced that different publications, among them the wall calendar for 1876 with the portrait of Deacon Vasil Levski

Figure 20. Khristo Botev, 1848–1976.

Figure 21. Botev's wall-calendar for 1875.
Source: Bozhidar Raikov, Lidiia Dragolova, eds., *Vestnitsite na Khristo Botev. Duma, Budilnik, Zname, Nova Bîlgariia*, Sofia: Nauka i izkustvo, 1976.

were on sale at the editorial office of *Zname*. The poem itself was published again in August, 1876, and later in edited versions in the 1880s, until it reached its stabilized (but maybe not authentic) popular version of today. The engraved portrait, on the other hand, was preserved by having been reproduced first in Stefan Stambolov's collection of "Songs and Poems" published in Giurgevo (Giurgiu, Romania) in 1877, and again, in Georgi Kirkov's biography of Levski in 1882. Finally, a third and last such calendar was printed for the year 1877, this time dedicated to Khristo Botev himself, who had died a martyr's death the previous year.

Martyrdom appears relatively late in history, around the 4th century BC. Samuel Klausner has elaborated a social theory of martyrdom. A chief prerequisite is the identification of ideology as an independent cultural reality that serves as a symbol of mobilization, and politicizes the relationship between groups. The social function of the martyr is, on the one hand, exemplary, in that he is a model to follow; on the other hand, the deceased martyr is a sacred symbol of an authority around which society rallies. Martyrdom is an unambiguous political act: "the potential martyr is a rival claimant to authority and this political claim may be religiously legitimated" (1995: 231). Klausner differentiates between three types of societies according to the level of their societal independence, and respectively three types of martyrs they produce. These are crescive societies to which early Christian martyrs belong; self-determining societies characterized by missionary martyrs; and, finally, decaying societies, exemplified by pogrom victims. Crescive societies are ones which are politically powerless but beginning to stir, and martyrdom "creates authority, escalates the struggle, unifies the minority, and legitimates the new culture by demonstrating its priority over nature. Furthermore, martyrs propel a politically crescive society toward self-determination, toward social and cultural freedom" (ibid: 233). The exemplar of Christian martyrdom at the crescive stage is the trial and crucifixion on Golgotha. It is clear that both nascent and fairly developed national-revolutionary movements before they have achieved political control fall under the category of crescive societies.

By the middle of the 19th century, both martyrdom and sainthood had achieved wide reception as wholly secularized categories (or sacral categories of a secular religion, like nationalism) but it was

Botev's distinct genius to create a symbiosis between their religious and secular use. His powerful last poem has attracted numerous literary critics, and they have all pointed out that the image he developed of the gallows, without explicitly articulating it, unfailingly evoked the power of the cross. The explicit connection was made by Vazov in his ode to "Levski": "Oh, glorious gallows! In disgrace and in splendor you match the cross!" Botev, on the other hand, did not use direct forms of mythologization and hyperbole, but the biblical reminiscences are undeniable. This could be actually proven after the discovery of his pocketbook in 1940 where earlier, if less poetic, drafts of the poem make the explicit connection. By using the Christ-like imagery in his poem, and by inserting Levski as a martyr in the pantheon of Christian saints, Botev, the radical and pronounced unbeliever, both subverted the traditional veneration of Christian saints and, at the same time, knowingly used the best medium to disseminate his views and reach the widest possible audience. There is no doubt that the sacralization of Levski in Bulgarian collective memory commenced with Botev.

It was already pointed out that the original resistance of the church to Levski's canonization may have rested on the circumstance that his unofficial canonization had been pioneered by what to the church were extreme revolutionaries and unbelievers, Botev certainly at the head of this group. This is no longer the case today. Father Balachev, for example, did not know about Botev's calendar when I spoke to him in the summer of 2000, and was actually happy with the information, ready to use it as further argumentation in favor of Levski's canonization. It takes a good century for even Botev to be accepted symbolically in the fold of the church. In purely formal, typographic terms, the great irony is that when Pimen's church printed its religious calendar, and if/when Maxim's church (or the by now unified church) does the same, they will have closed a circle, and achieved what the non-believer Botev had already done in 1875. Indeed, the alternative Synod, under the chairmanship of Metropolitan Inokentii, published its first synodal calendar for the year 2002, and included the veneration of *Sv. Svshtmchk. Ierod. Ignatii* (St. Holy Martyr, Hierodeacon) Ignatii on February 19. The calendar for 2005 was issued already after the official closure of the alternative church in the fall of 2004 and, for the first time, featured the icon of Levski on its front cover.

278 The National Hero as Secular Saint: The Canonization of Levski

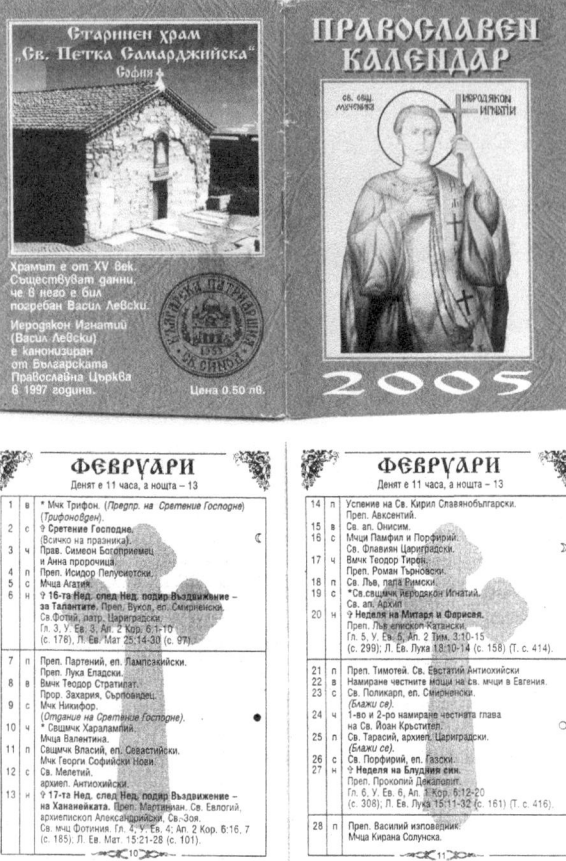

Figure 22. Orthodox calendar for 2005 issued by the secessionist Bulgarian Orthodox church (BOC-P).

Among the numerous journalistic pieces commemorating the 134th anniversary of Levski's hanging in February, 2007, one stood out with its explicit Christological message. Levski is posited to have always lived in two parallel worlds: the saint's and the hero's. The first belongs to "Christianity, the moral world of belief, hope and love (and, for him, this is love for the fatherland)." The other is the world of political and diplomatic struggles for national independence. Throughout, Levski is depicted as consciously playing the role of the Savior moved by Christian compassion. The most curious part of this article is the interpretation it offers of Levski's behavior at the trial. It has been widely (and logically) believed that Levski's testimony was a masterful dissimulation intended to preserve as much of the secret organization intact. Asked about the opinions of Bulgarians he visited, he responded that the educated ones preferred progress through enlightenment, and shunned armed action. Pressed whether he did not take these opinions into consideration, Levski said: "Yes, I too understood that we had been following the wrong road." He then told the prosecutors he had been considering going to Istanbul, meeting the authorities and laying out the peasants' grief, in the hope of soliciting some remedy. Given Levski's actions and writings, no one has taken these words literally. It is, however, the tenure of this article to do so, in order to make the point that at the end of his life Levski embraced Christian humility, and "wanted to be remembered as a preacher of Christ in redemption." Without openly preaching Levski's formal canonization, the article concludes that "Vasil Deacon Levski humbled himself in the face of crude reality, and in his great humility became saint and spiritual victor." The Apostle is depicted as a martyr of his own Christian charity and compassion, and his sacrifice elevates him as a saint of humanity (*Monitor*, IX, February 19, 2007).

Martyrologies, both narrative and cultic, offer a dichotomical moral story: they praise martyrs, and expose evil. By doing so, they prepare martyrs by example. A case in point is the Christian cult of the martyr which exhibits relics (a bone, a lock of hair) on the anniversary of the martyrdom which is celebrated ritualistically as the new birth (*dies natalis*) of the saint. A more contemporary illustration comes from the "training of the kamikadze [which] included worship at a special shrine for those who had died in training or in combat. There the trainees sought spiritual 'intoxication.'" (Klausner 1995: 235). This is heroism induced by mimesis. Relics had become so important in early Christianity, that the VII Ecumenical Council even prohibited the building of churches in the absence of relics. In the Orthodox church they were usually kept in the altar, and exhibited only on the saint's day and the temple's holidays. Unlike ordinary people who celebrate the temporal birth in the manner of the pagan observance, the saint is celebrated on the anniversary day of the martyrdom "which was the day of a Christian's heavenly birth; for this reason the celebrations have the character of a feast and not of a mourning" (Molinari 1965: 112). In Levski's case, while instituting and performing the celebration as strictly secular and separate from the church, the ceremony on February 19 follows this practice.

Can, then, the building of a chapel on the premises of the Levski museum in Karlovo, which houses his hair, be interpreted not merely in rationalist terms as looking for an additional sacral legitimation or as ecclesiastical policy making, but as knee-jerk ritualized behavior? In asking myself this question, I go back to my conversations with the director of the museum, Dora Chausheva, and her firm, even annoyed refusal to recognize that a sanctification is taking place, or that the hair of Levski is treated as a relic. I am struck by the comment that this evokes in my accompanying friend, an anthropologist: "She does it subconsciously or, rather, she does not consciously realize what is happening." It is maybe what Caroline Humphrey and James Laidlaw refer to when they say that "[a]ction is ritualized if the acts of which it is composed are constituted not by the intentions which the actor has in performing them, but by prior stipulation" and further that "[p]eople are inevitably conscious of themselves at some basic level as they engage with the act as something in a sense outside themselves (as elemental or archetypal)" (1994: 97, 162). Indeed, the director of the museum has performed the secular commemorative ritual for years now. But it is not only at the anniversaries of Levski at the time of his birth and death that she is doing this. She performs a sacred ritual every day, especially when she herself is seeing people through the exhibit halls of the small museum.

Turner has lamented that "museums have, traditionally, been at a great disadvantage in terms of conveying to the public the meanings of the objects they exhibit." But this does not hold true for museums dedicated to an individual—a writer, composer, artist, revolutionary, political figure, pop star—where the collected objects are *not* "divorced from their operational and positional contexts" (Turner 1982: 23). Such a museum is a shrine, and the museum guide a cleric who officiates the ritual of commemoration. It need not be an individual museum; it can be a room dedicated to an idea or a person, or even a display box that can take upon itself the role of shrine. The relics, too, need not be *verbatim* relics: objects that have been in close physical contact with the saint are equally worshiped. In Levski's case, these are several objects, apart from his hair, shared by the Karlovo museum and the Military Museum in Sofia: his revolver, his dagger, his tiny printing press, his personal copper bowl. Transferring the hair to the chapel, then, is only an external act. Chausheva is simply extending the space in which she is performing her habitual ritual, and her above quoted words about the futility of an ecclesiastical canonization now acquire truly a new meaning: "This is a formality. He already is a saint for the nation. The act will only defile and formalize the authentic sanctity."

Of the different ways of looking at ritual, I find most useful Renato Rosaldo's view of ritual as a "busy intersection... a place where a number of distinct social processes intersect. The crossroads simply provides a space for distinct trajectories to traverse, rather than containing them in complete encapsulated form" (1993: 17). In the case of the commemorative celebrations around Levski, there is the confluence between several processes. One is a continuing process of nation-building, effectuated by intellectual elites in conjunction with state bureaucracies. In time, they have elaborated different forms, of which the anniversary ceremonies of Levski's death around his monument, have already a century-old tradition. From the outset, these ceremonies introduced a ritual. Ritual is a form that confers meanings to its contents, and "once used in collective ceremony, whether performed for the first time or the thousandth, the circumstance of having been put in the ritual form and mode, has a tradition-like effect" (Moore and Meyerhoff 1977: 8). Today, there is the attempt to broaden this tradition into a biannual ritual ceremony, adding an equal emphasis on Levski's birth date, and have the two rotate between Karlovo and Sofia. This process of nation-building has both the function of socializing the public into a common symbolic language as well as legitimizing political and cultural institutions as bearers and keepers of the "nation's flame." The persistence of Levski as a primary symbol in this process is confirmation both of the power of its content which has survived different appropriations and modifications, and also, and maybe more appropriately, of the essential continuity of the *longue durée* of nationalism, despite the dramatic changes and discontinuities in politics.

Another process is the millennial effort of the church to spread its influence and enlarge its flock. In Bulgaria, the church since the 19th century has been an indelible part of the nation-building process, so it partakes in the celebrations as both national pillar and guardian of the faith. The church, in the pre-1989 period, held liturgical services for Levski as a routine but these were not a central element of its practice. In the post-communist space the church, at least in rhetoric, has been accorded a more prominent place, especially valued by the political class for legitimizing purposes. The abrupt canonization of Levski by the secessionist church gave it a strong legitimation tool but that stopped short of delivering them the Orthodox flock and public support. Instead, it urged Maxim's hierarchy to reconsider quietly its stand, and carefully move in a direction preparing the ground for Levski's sanctification. No doubt, the symbiosis between political and church power in this respect produces public support (or at least broad participation). In both efforts, that of nation-building by the state and church institutions, and that of building a religious community by the church, we are witnessing the importance of ritual's social role in securing and maintaining the unity of the group.

Finally, a third process may be identified, the most basic one of all, consisting of the human need to find meaning in individual and social life, invest the chaos of life with some structure, order it around unifying symbols and events. This is different from positing an ingrained "religious sense" which propels man to express "faith in some god, some mysterious and controlling power outside of himself, a faith accompanied by feelings of awe and reverence and usually attended by external rites and ceremonies" (Hayes 1966: 11). Rather, religion would be seen as a historical epiphenomenon of this urge toward meaningful structure in which ritualized behavior is a prime agent, because it confers stability: "In reproducing ritual acts celebrants are no longer engaged in the constantly renewed compromise of everyday life whereby people endlessly adapt to new circumstances and attempt to turn them into familiar habits" (Humphrey and Laidlaw 1994: 260). As Moore and Meyerhoff have shown, if being "unquestionable" and traditionalizing are the essential attributes of the sacred, then something can be sacred, yet not religious (1977: 20). Such a reading would also overcome the assumed profound difference between Mircea Eliade's *homo religiosus* and modern man.

Anthropologists have been lamenting "the virtual absence of reliable data in anthropologists' accounts of the subjective experiences of those undergoing passage" and that this "failure of anthropology to deal with the experiences of ritual participants—private, subjective, psychological, conscious, and unconscious—is an enormous barrier to our understanding of the subject" (Turner 1982: 25, 118). At first glance, I may be stretching the capacity of anthropological categories in trying to cover commemorative ceremonies or simple museum visits under the rubric of "rites of passage," but there are sufficient accounts that indicate that people in these circumstances feel that they are participating in a sacred activity. In addition, since Durkheim, social anthropologists have paid increasing attention to the social parameters of ceremony and ritual, and have long since expanded their sphere of relevance from the religious and magical to the secular, notably the political.

Visitors books to the Karlovo museum—the so-called "books for impressions" were already discussed at length. The individual entries display genuine and deep-felt emotion, and are equally testaments to the power of the Levski myth as well as commentaries on their writers' worldview and everyday predicament. As Michael Taussig has noted, "[m]onuments create public dream-space in which, through informal and often private rituals, the particularities of one's life make patterns of meaning" (1992: 46). Irena on April 30, 1974 writes that "when I enter the yard, my heart beats as if it is going to fly away. My whole body is excited. I look at everything, and I regret that it is so rarely that one can meet people even with a tiny little bit of His character. I love Levski, and in my most difficult moments he is my guiding star, from him I get strength to overcome difficulties." Not only adulatory statements have been entered. On May 29, 1981 a curly and illegible signature ends the following entry: "I am filled with admiration for Levski's ideals. Bulgaria will be great only if we accept these ideals and make them living. But alas! They do not exist any longer, and we shall be forever slaves of our cowardice." Some six years later, in April, 1987 an unpunctuated sentence by Vildanka and Dodio from Gabrovo states: "We are proud and we are sorry for Levski. Why do we need God when we have Levski!" On April 4, 1990, the Stoianov family from Karnobat adds: "Today our family for the first time visited the home-museum Vasil Levski. Already at the entrance door we felt in another atmosphere, in another time. Our spirit as Bulgarians and humans was lifted. For us Vasil Levski is a symbol of a real Bulgarian and human being. We are leaving with heads high that we have had such a titan, such a great Bulgarian." T. Khubenov from Burgas exclaims on September 5, 1992 that "now Bulgaria is in need of exactly the type of individuals as Levski," and someone from Lom has added in April,

1993 that Levski desired "liberty with discipline and humanity, not the anarchy we Bulgarians have to live in." Under April 19, 1993, immediately following the signature of George and Claudia Wilson from Raleigh, NC, another unreadable signature has contributed the following: "It's nice, after all, that we have Levski; otherwise we wouldn't be proud of being Bulgarians, especially not in the present confused and misconstrued 'democracy.'" A woman from Pernik addresses The Apostle: "I wish you were still alive and could help Bulgaria again" (July 25, 1997). These are widely spread feelings, and Dora Chausheva herself attests that for the inhabitants of Karlovo, in particular, Levski is a special item of pride, "especially now, in these critical times."

And critical times for Karlovo they are, indeed. This small town with a population of ca. 25,000, used to be relatively prosperous thanks to an array of industrial enterprises around. The textile factory produced the famous Karlovo silk chiefly for export, and people would drive specially to Karlovo to buy some of the leftovers in the factory shop. Of the 5,000 workers in the factory, 500 had remained in 1999, but next year there was no production, and it was expected that the factory would close. It was still lingering on in the summer of 2005, but financially ruined after its privatization. The lady who sells tickets at the Levski Museum in Karlovo, used to work as an economist in the silk plant and bemoans the crime of destroying a thriving export industry.

The tractor plant has cut its work force from 6,000 to 600, and seems to be doomed. Most unexpectedly, the industry that had always been profitable, and brought hard currency in the previous decades, was being artificially suffocated. Bulgaria was famous for its attar of roses, the preferred base for French perfumes, and the Rose Valley spans from Kazanlîk to Karlovo, the chief producers of rose oil. Of the formerly 3,700 acres, only 675 were under crop in 2000; of the 2,500 workers, only 500 were employed. In the summer of 2000, only one department at the rose oil plant was open, with 50 workers employed three times a week for four hours. This is unconscionable, the locals were saying, given that the French have to buy their attar of roses from Turkey now, and it is of inferior quality. In the summer of 2005, on a follow-up visit, the situation was more or less the same, but the fields had been privatized, and it was expected that the industry would rebound soon.

The biggest employer for Karlovo used to be the military plant in Sopot, just a few miles from Karlovo. This, too, had been a booming industry but now, with the advent of the unipolar world, there is pressure also for a unipolar arms exporter. The history of the post-communist privatization of Eastern Europe is yet to be written. For now it is still history in the making. Transitologists were focused on significant issues like constitutionalism, civil society and private/public spheres. Problems like the mafia's, a.k.a. new entrepreneurial class's links and/or symbiosis with the state institutions and the organizations of global capital are only beginning to be addressed. The questions that those historians of the future will ask is to what extent was the privatization model imposed from the outside? By whom: organizations, names? To what extent was the process controlled, and how was it correlated to government loans and political support? To what extent was the widely known corruption tolerated or initiated? And for how much? Who were the native agents of the privatization process and how exactly did they fit in the network of international capital?

In the meantime, in the summer of 2000, 2,500 workers from plant had been laid off, and more were expecting to be discharged. They had all been promised a one-time compensation of 1,000 leva (less than $500 at the exchange rate at the time). Bleak as the outlook was, there was still dim hope that things could not get worse. By February, 2001, the situation had become explosive. Since October, 2000, the 7,000 strong work force had not received their salaries. The economic and political globalization is having its very immediate impact on this small provincial Bulgarian town, and people are alert to the challenge. How do they react? In February, 2001, the workers of *VMZ-Sopot* went on strike. Nor were they the only ones in Bulgaria. Another six big enterprises as well as a thousand medical workers in Stara Zagora were also on strike. The workers of the arms industry in Sopot refused to be placated by half-promises and half-measures, and on February 22, 2001, a representative group of 560 workers mounted 8 buses and arrived in Sofia to protest their plight. Their protest march in the afternoon of February 23, 2001 was under the slogan "The Karlovo region wants to live."

Four years later, in the summer of 2005, one small section of the plant was still functioning but with diminished capacity. Another had been privatized and bought by an Austrian enterprise for the production of bearings. In the meantime, two new activities were somewhat alleviating the economic frustration in Karlovo. One was the entry of small, mostly Greek-owned tailoring companies, employing female labor. The other was the newly built barracks for the reformed Bulgarian army, which was transformed from an army of universal male recruitment into a voluntary salaried one. There are significant numbers of local young people, men and women, from Karlovo and the adjacent villages, who have joined the units of the professional army. But there is an enormous number of young people (around a thousand, I am told in the stylish café by the charming waitress) who have little chance to get employment, and have opted to go abroad. Most have ended up in England, of all places. One of them is the son of Gîcho Mitov, a descendant of Levski, and former chairman of the Committee of Relatives. The son now lives in London but it was unclear where and how he was employed. His father obviously did not want to pursue this line of the conversation.

This is not the only link to Levski. February 19, the day of Levski's hanging, is a traditional commemorative day. On February 19, 2001, there were memorial ceremonies all over the country in honor of the 128th anniversary of Levski's death. The government paper *Demokratsiia* reported that the president, the prime minister, the speaker of parliament, the mayor of Sofia as well as cabinet ministers, members of parliament, and representatives of the clergy laid flowers at the Levski monument in the center of Sofia. The paper also reported that visitors to the Levski Museum in Karlovo could see for the first time Levski's hair in the reliquary of chapel "All Bulgarian Saints." It added that "over 5,000 workers of the arms industry marched on foot from Sopot to Karlovo in memory of Levski." What the paper did not mention was that the workers were carrying big slogans: "The portrait of the Apostle has no place in your offices," and "Give us back our work." An elderly worker who was interviewed could barely keep his tears: "We are desperate. We don't believe anybody anymore. If Levski had been canonized, we would have prayed to him as a saint for our salvation." The workers paid their respect to Levski but once the mayor began his speech, they distanced themselves from the official ceremony. Three days later they mounted the buses to Sofia.

It seemed as if the gathering for the ceremony of Levski, his honoring with the 10-kilometer march on foot from Sopot to Karlovo, was like a ceremonial ablution for the workers, a pause at a sacral spot before getting back to the struggle. Alf Lüdtke has remarked that "demonstrations, parades, riots, and other forms of popular 'rough' politics appear, in the academic view, mainly as nonpolitical events," and he draws the attention particularly to strikes which have been treated as a field of activity in which workers make the gradual transition to the "political." In contrast, his approach is "to examine the articulation and expression of both individual and collective needs as forms of political behavior" (in Wilentz 1985: 304, 326). The workers' strike and their march to Levski's monument should be seen as a political act with a carefully chosen symbolic significance.

Looking back at the visitors' entries in the Levski Museum, what is interesting in the quote of the family from Karnobat is the feeling that they have entered "another atmosphere, another time." This is not only the feeling of the museum as temple, but a veritable collapsing of the historical time, a return to and partaking in the time of the hero. Eliade describes this as the human desire to periodically return to "the sacred and strong time [which] is the *time of origins*, the stupendous instant in which reality was created" and which he calls the *illud tempus*. Commenting on the meaning and significance of religious festival, and this can be extended equally to national celebrations, he says: "[H]owever complex a religious festival may be, it always involves a sacred event that took place *ab origine* and that is ritually made present. The participants in the festival become contemporaries of the mythical event. In other words, they emerge from their historical time—that is, from the time constituted by the sum total of profane personal and intrapersonal events—and recover primordial time, which is always the same, which belongs to eternity" (Eliade 1961: 81, 88).

Johannes Fabian (1983) uses the notion of allochronism to describe the original epistemological basis of anthropology as a science of *other* men in an*other* time. In a beautifully argued argument he demonstrates that *geopolitics* has its ideological foundations in *chronopolitics*. Anthropology as a scholarly discipline expunges the Other from our Time although ontologically the subject and the object are synchronous. Allochronism is, of course, at the center of the historical endeavor, a basic principle of historicism, approaching the historical other as inhabiting a foreign country: the past. In the case of Levski, there is a complete reversal of this central principle of dealing with the past; it stands allochronism on its head. What we have is an anthropological experience in which the object (Levski), while ontologically preceding by over a century the present-day individuals who are also the authors of the discourse on Levski, is extracted from his time and treated as coeval precisely because he is not perceived as an *other*. It is as if the space of the nation state has collapsed time so that the present-day nation has left time with only one vector—the present—which could be taken to mean that the temporal dimension is altogether removed. The intellectual framework which allows this is the treatment of the nation not as a fluid and transient process but as a structural entity (no matter whether contingent and finite or else, deterministic and teleological). The psychological framework is also rather simple. Present day individuals who feel inextricably trapped in the geographic and political grid of the nation can freely choose to inhabit a timeless dimension in which they can cohabit with personalities they admire, values they approve of, an atmosphere they feel comfortable in. This redemptive chronopolitics results in the obverse of allochronism, a kind of isochronism that is different from the principle of coevalness recommended by Fabian. This is not the processual and materialist presentism that Fabian calls on to counteract the hegemony of taxonomic and representational approaches. It is a reversal to mythopoetic time.

With a no less metaphysical but less transcendental vocabulary than Eliade, Reinhart Koselleck speaks about the contemporaneity of the noncontemporaneous. This notion expresses the diversity of temporal strata of varying duration. It implies not only the collapse in the present, and subsequent coexistence and comparability, of different strands of time or temporal structures contained in mythical, political, social, or everyday life. It also creates the structural foundations that link the "space of experience" with the "horizon of expectations." Koselleck explains that during the modern period the difference between experience and expectation has increasingly expanded: expectations distanced themselves from all previous experience. Where, in the pre-modern period, expectations exceeded previous experience, they were usually related to the Otherworld. Henceforth, they began serving the idea of improvement on earth, and liberated the future from the constraints of the Final Day. At the same time, the introduction of the concept of "progress" reduced the temporal difference between experience and expectation to a single concept. Not only is modern time distinct from earlier times. There is a definite asymmetry between experience and expectation:

> All concepts of movement share a compensatory effect, which they produce. The lesser the experiential substance, the greater the expectations joined to it. The lesser the experience, the greater the expectation: this is a formula for the temporal structure of the modern, to the degree that it is rendered a concept by "progress." This was plausible for as long as all previous experience was inadequate to the establishment of expectations derivable from the process of a world reforming itself technologically. If corresponding political designs were realized, then, once generated by a revolution, the old expectations worked themselves out on the basis of the new experiences. This is true for republicanism, democracy, and liberalism, to the extent that history permits us to judge. Presumably this will also be true for socialism and also for communism, if its arrival is ever announced (Koselleck 1985: 288).

This, written barely ten years before the collapse of communism has a particularly pungent ring, and tallies with the obverse asymmetry: "the greater the experience, the lesser the expectation." Kosseleck says as much: "the greater the experience, the more cautious one is, but also the more open is the future. If this were the case, then the end of *Neuzeit* as optimizing progress would have arrived" (ibid.: 288). It seems to have arrived in Karlovo. In the case of Bulgaria in general, there is a profound feeling of disappointment, frustration, demoralization, even anomie among the populace occasioned by the economic stagnation and ongoing pauperization, the collapse of state authority and the rise of a political class without credibility, the breakdown of educational and cultural institutions and the complete marginalization of the intelligentsia. With the exception of the several major cities, and especially the capital, where one can cautiously speak of a relative take off, this has not changed in the past years although, if this is any reason for optimism, things are not deteriorating further. In this atmosphere, ceremony is a declaration against indeterminacy. It is, as the culturally determinate, the regulated, the manmade, the named and explained which is celebrated through form and formality. In a similar vein, and emphasizing the psychological basis of myth and ritual,

Clyde Kluckhohn shows how they "promote social solidarity, enhance the integration of society by providing a formalized statement of its ultimate value-attitudes, afford a means for the transmission of much of culture with little loss of content—thus protecting cultural continuity and stabilizing society" (in Segal 2000: 329).

There is a special emotional force, a unique poignancy that characterizes all these processes (the nation-building project, the missionary project, and the grassroots social need for meaning and order) when they traverse the "busy intersection" of the Levski commemorations and worship, especially at this particular intersection of time. In the present circumstances the Levski myth and ritual has the function, in the words of Durkheim, to "perpetually give back to the great ideals a little of the strength that the egoistic passions and daily personal preoccupations tend to take away from them" (cited in Asad 1993: 74). It thus serves not only as a rallying point, a unifying symbol and activity driven by social actors with their distinct perspective and goals, but becomes "a process for social transformation, for catharsis, for embodying social values, for defining the nature of the real" (Bell 1997: 89). Catherine Bell specially emphasizes that ritual is not about unchanging tradition but should be seen as "a particularly effective means of mediating tradition and change, that is, as a medium for appropriating some changes while maintaining a sense of cultural continuity" (ibid.: 251).

6. Heroes and Saints: The Dialectics of Reincarnation

Of the theorists of heroic myth, Lord Raglan insisted most adamantly on the link between myth and ritual, and became the father and chief exponent of myth-ritualism (Segal 2000: 23–6). One does not have to adopt his rejection of the historicity of heroes (particularly his insistence that historical heroes are fundamentally different from mythical ones), nor accept the particular way in which he established the connection between myth and ritual. In the case of Levski, the link is clearly there. What characterized all hero myth theorists in general, despite methodological differences, is that they all base their analysis almost exclusively on examples from antiquity. Yet, hero worship in different forms is central to many historical periods and sites, and it would be useful to try to understand how (or whether) heroes change over time. More specifically, is there anything specific about national heroes, the heroes of the age of nationalism, of whom Levski is a prominent example?

This last section provides a brief survey of the enormous literature on heroes, specifically the link between ancient hero worship and medieval sainthood, and the smaller literature on the relationship between medieval saints and national heroes. Placing the Levski case within this context and comparing it to other national heroes will allow him to "rest" naturally not only within his narrow Bulgarian pantheon but within the international "family" of national heroes or the genus of human heroes at large. Heroes are defined as individuals "real or mythic, whose deeds and sacrifices have come to represent, in the course of time and through narration, the values, ideals and aspirations of a social group, as well as the protection and legitimacy of this group's political and/or territorial position" (Centlivres 1998: 35). They are first and foremost social symbols whose main function is the example they set within the group, and while most authors emphasize the different attributes and roles heroes play in different historical periods, the consensus is that the essential message is the same; as a mythic figure, the hero is perennial. We saw in Part II the extent to which hero worship was at the center of the national project. The period between the mid-18th century and the end of the First World War, the high age of nationalism, saw an unprecedented effort at defining the hero, his taxonomy, and the archeology of his incarnations. Especially after the Second World War, heroes were rarely, if at all, objects of theoretical concern in history or anthropology. This was not because the topic was neglected but because it was treated in a traditional way. Only in the past decade has the problematic again received attention, and this is accompanied by new methods and approaches. These latest works explicitly posit that heroes are constructed socially and culturally, and explore how their significance and meanings vary according to historical periods and political contexts.

In a sweeping overview of the genealogy of the hero, Dean Miller (2000) identifies the origins of the hero cult in ancient Greece, more specifically in the 8th century B.C. Heroism to the Greeks was a multifold concept. In Homer it was used in a generic sense for a free man or for a significant man, a man of status; to Hesiod the hero was a figure of the remote and magnified past set firmly in the mythic Heroic Age; Pindar depicted him as semi-god, hovering between the human and the divine, a beneficial or malignant mediator between the living world and the Otherworld. There are two chief recognizable modes of the ancient hero. The warlike mode in an earlier version expresses the heroic ideal through the exceptional human being, young, physically perfect, valorous individual who attains early death and fame, but is ultimately lonely, solipsistic, extrasocietal, even asocial. Its typical protagonist is Akhilleus. To this version, a later period added the glorious death that is not only individual but is attained for the sake and defense of the *polis*; thus heroism is dying in battle for the mother-city. One of its earliest examples is the veneration of the fallen at the Battle of Marathon. The other mode—the mediating—confers to the hero an essentially social function where he "even anonymously, acts from his postmortem place (the *hêrôon*) to fertilize and protect human society, and especially that important new formation, the city-state." What unified this concept in all its modes was the focus on death, and subsequent immortality that conferred glory on both the individual and his group (the city-state). Greek society not only invented the word hero—*hêrôs*—but transmitted its own and influenced later perceptions of this extraordinary human image and type. Specifically, its heroic model remained practically unchanged with the expansion of Rome and in the Roman world.

In late antiquity a serious challenge and accompanying revision of the warrior hero occurred. This had to do mostly with the new Christian perception of the warrior class as paid servants of the persecuting imperial state. In this configuration, "the original warrior ethic and a new heroism would only be discovered in barbarian Europe beyond the *limes*, in the pullulating impatient Germanic tribes and on the far, equally impatient, Celtic edges of an imploding imperial world." Two concrete historical developments colored the metamorphosis of the European hero in the heartlands. One was the long term technological innovations that gave birth to the heavy cavalry and with it the horsed, armored and noble heroic figure of the *chevalier, cabellero, Ritter, ritsar*, producing figures such as King Arthur, Lancelot, and Galaad. The other development was the expansion of and encounter with Islam that laid the "groundwork for the creation of a whole genus of 'border' epics in which the Christian hero confronted his Moslem counterpart." This latter covers the French *Chanson de Roland*, the Byzantine *Digenes Akrites*, the Spanish *El Cid*, and the Balkan epic songs (Miller 2000: 10–1).

While he speaks of the tension and even open confrontation between the classical and the Christian-chivalric heroic traditions, surprisingly Miller is never tempted to review another medieval type that serves as a social model and has entirely assumed the mediating function of the hero: the saint. For him the saint is totally different from the hero, a different genus. This is an unexpected and curious omission, since the two can be productively subsumed as variations of one type. Granted, Miller is not alone in refusing the focus on the continuity between heroes and saints. Peter Brown, in particular, has been adamant that "to explain the Christian cult of the martyrs as a continuation of the pagan cult of heroes helps as little as to reconstruct the form and function of a late-antique Christian basilica from the few columns and capitals taken from the classical buildings that are occasionally incorporated in the arcades" (1981: 6). He insists on the unique intimacy saints enjoyed with God, which allowed them to intercede for and protect their fellow mortals. The saint was an intercessor "in a way which the hero could never have been." One need not take

Brown's objection too pedantically. His task was different: he wanted to highlight the specificity and uniqueness of late antiquity, while, simultaneously, demonstrating the originality and dynamics of "popular religion" then and in the early middle ages. At the same time, he faithfully documented the lively controversies on the topic (ibid.: 133–4). Also, Brown was writing about Latin Christianity. In his study of the *Panēgiris* of the Byzantine saints, Speros Vryonis emphasizes the strong and organic continuities from antiquity:

> Despite the fact that the Byzantine saints as literary heroes were opposites to the literary heroes of pagan antiquity, they were celebrated in a manner which was, partly, of pagan origin. The *panēgiris*, against which the church fathers declaimed because of its concern with commerce, frivolity, and sin, early became attached to the annual celebration of the saint's cult. Though it included Christian religious ceremony, the *panēgiris* offered Byzantine society that which it has also offered pagan society: recreation and relief from cares; commerce and sex. Thus the Byzantine *panēgiris* represents what anthropologists call cultural adaptation, for it involved the acceptance of a pagan institution re-oriented to the scene of Christian localism; and thus it was passed down into modern times (Hackel 1981: 226).

Most other authors treat sainthood as a variant of heroicism. Czarnowski, in particular, for whom saints are a special subcategory of heroes, establishes the link by means of the function of the hero and the saint as witness. It is his role or, rather, quintessence as witness that makes the hero the incarnation of a social ideal. Just as the ancient hero is the representative, witness and, as a consequence, champion of the group or things whose essence he incarnates, so the Christian martyr is the witness (μάρτυρ) of the faith: "He is venerated not solely as the model of virtues required from the perfect believer. He is glorified above all as a human being who has proven his attachment to the Christian religion and through this has become a shining witness of the faith that inspires his community" (1919: 27). The notion of sainthood is subordinated to a moral and religious ideal fixed in theology. Believing in the correlation between types of heroes and hero worship, Czarnowski insists that sainthood was typical for societies constituted around churches or sects, "because these are the essential conditions in which a theology can be elaborated" (ibid.: 329). This offers a productive opening to the modern period, insofar as any ideological institution or state institutions dominated by ideologies can be structurally seen as identical or analogous to societies organized by churches. The jump from saint to secular hero is, in this understanding, easy to grasp; indeed, it is mandatory.

The models of sanctity, as they developed around the cult of saints, heavily influenced the types of modern heroism. It is widely accepted that the first and most highly valued model of medieval sainthood was martyrdom, although Wolfgang Speyer rightly draws attention to the fact that during the first centuries martyrs were preceded by the apostolic and missionary types (Dinzelbacher 1990: 54). Martyrdom is to be understood both in its grand sacrificial variety, the so-called red martyrdom, as well as in its other forms, especially asceticism that became assimilated into martyrdom. Modern heroism employs a strikingly similar, often indistinguishable, vocabulary, and follows very much the same models: the sacrifice for the collectivity, the voluntary renouncing of the gift of life for the life of the nation, as well as the renunciation of personal happiness, the control of one's body and passions, very much in line with, if not identical to, medieval askesis.

One of the most important types of saints in the middle ages was the figure of the saint king, patron saint of the state or, as they are often called "national saints." Numerically they were never predominant, but their relative proportion was on the rise in the last centuries of the second Christian millennium. These political saints had a disproportional influence, and were easily transformed in a later period into saints/heroes of the nation. We have among this illustrious royal lineage the 4th-century Roman Emperor St. Constantine the Great (venerated as apostolic saint only by the Eastern church), his mother empress St. Helen (venerated by both), the Catholic saints St. Louis, King of France in the 13th century; St. Stephen, the 10th–11th-century Hungarian King (canonized 2000 also by the Orthodox church); Edward the Confessor, the 11th-century English King; St. Ferdinand III, the 13th-century King of Castile and Leon; St. Isabel (Elizabeth), the 13th-century Queen of Portugal; the 11th-century King of Norway St. Olaf; the 11th-century King and Protomartyr of Denmark Canute IV; St. Ludmilla and St. Wenceslas of Bohemia (10th century); the

Orthodox St. Vladimir, Prince of Kiev (10th–11th century) and his grandmother St. Olga; the Russian princely saints of the 11th century Boris and Gleb; the 13th-century Grand Prince of Novgorod, Vladimir and Kiev, Alexander Nevskii; the Serbian Prince Lazar (14th century); the Bulgarian Tsars Boris-Mikhail and Peter, and others. It is the explicit link of these saints with the domain of the political, the state, and the focus on ethnic ties and allegiances, that makes them precursors (and in some opinions pioneers) of early nation-building.

The Renaissance and the Reformation brought a revival of and fascination with the archaic heroic type, while at the same time subverting the heroic model. During this period, Europe's colonial conquests provided a theater for enacting a new heroism. It is in this period that Michael Naumann (1984) locates the shift from sacral to secular heroism, specifically the origins of revolutionary heroism in the baroque veneration of Herculean individualism. There are, however, a couple of telling details that refine the seamless continuity of hero worship. Until the 17th century, the word "hero" was sparingly used and exclusively confined to the pagan demi-gods of antiquity, whereas other notions were employed to denote exemplary individuals: *Held* in German, *personnage illustre* in French, *uomo illustre* in Italian. The semantic broadening of the category "hero" came with the celebratory initiatives of the absolute monarchies' identification with ancient heroism. Even more interesting is the element introduced with the late 16th century ecclesiastical reforms, finalized in 1742 by Pope Benedict XIV's decrees on the rules of canonization and beatification. Heroes with a cult, the saints, were no longer determined through tradition (local, general or corporate) but by means of a minutely detailed and regulated process. Heroic virtues were stipulated by the Sacred Congregation of Rites, and heroism was no longer imposed as a whole, but decomposed in series of virtues scrutinized by judicial rationality, so that "heroic charisma entered the era of suspicion" (Centlivres 1998: 238).

The 18th and especially the 19th century introduced additional shifts and reappraisals of the heroic image that still shape today's perceptions. The romantic enterprise first recovered a host of "authentic" folk heroes, and encouraged the exalted group identity located in the nation; it next underwrote the romantic political vision of the powerful and passionate individual, the voluntaristic leader, the glorious sculptor of human destinies, the Great Man of history. Comparative anthropology allowed for "the construction of patterns of thought and action defining the hero as a cross-cultural, cross-societal, eternally human phenomenon" (Miller 2000: 19). Miller's attention to a region "where imagination and history flowed together" is of particular importance. The 19th-century struggle for Greek independence was nourished, at least in the Philhellenic project, by the prevailing view of the archaic heroic spirit. There was the parallel and locally more widespread popular heroic tradition of the Balkan version of Eric Hobsbawm's social bandit: the Greek *klepht*, the Bulgarian *haidut*, the Serbian *haiduk*. Miller rightly compares these often semi-criminal types generated from social injustices and confrontations, but reinterpreted and heroicized in the popular imagination, with analogous figures in Central and South American rebellions against colonial Spain (ibid.: 22–3).

Again, he precludes the possibility of going into a very fertile realm of inquiry by excluding the revolutionary hero, from the heroes of the national revolution to the heroes of the social revolution. Admitting the existence of a special heroic aspect in relation to the idea of revolution—from the several French revolutions to the practice of the Marxist intellectual legacy—he sidetracks this field of analysis with the facile argument that "in theory, we should not be looking for heroes there" (ibid.: 24). In a rather mechanistic and abrupt fashion, he posits that the national hero is the romantic love child of 19th-century nationalism fertilized by the generic heroic cult: "The European 19th century saw the simultaneous rise and fluorescence, if by no means the original invention, of a cult of heroism and of the wider notion of a reborn 'people' or nation; when these two combine, we suddenly have the image of the national hero, in which various and even conflicting currents may run" (ibid.: 372). This makes neat theory, but neatness is the least validating of arguments. As far as the theoretical framing of the Levski phenomenon goes, these two omissions—saints and revolutionary heroes—provide the most stable vectors for the understanding of Levski's heroicization.

These omissions are all the more strange, since there is a remarkably sophisticated literature on the link between heroes' and saints' worship, as well as on the revolutionary hero. Naumann has convincingly argued that the revolutionary hero is the central literary and visual *topos* of the modern political myth: "He is in a mythical abstraction the real revolutionary" (1984: ix). He follows up the emergence of the modern revolutionary hero in the course of a structural evolution from sacral to secular heroism. What remains the common basis for heroism at every age and stage is the psychological impulse for heroic existence, the impulse for self-deification. The qualitatively new feature in modern heroism is the shift of the justification for political violence from the archaic-mythological past or precedent (for example, the *theogony*) to the *holy future*(ibid.: ix–x, 95–6).

This distinction is evocative but not much different from the apocalyptic, sotirological and millenarian visions of the Second Coming. In the vision of the cherished and holy future, one can easily see the fusion between the sacrifice of saints and modern heroes, revolutionary in general, national in particular. Consciously or subconsciously, the *Imitatio Christi* is one a principal inspiration for many a heroic gesture of the modern hero. It is traceable in the history of the Levski cult, both in the immediate perception and representation and, judging from the scarce if not explicit evidence, also in the self-perception and motivation of the hero. There is an unimaginative insistence in a great part of the literature, on a rupture in the sacred character of the hero with the advent of modernity: "In modern times, the hero has become desacralized... No longer an object of cult worship, he is simply a historical man of mettle, such as George Washington, Horatio Nelson, George Armstrong Custer, Simon Bolivar, Ho Chi Minh, and the like" (Gaster 1995: 304). This stems from a narrow understanding of sanctity as tantamount to organized religion, and disagrees with the presence of secular martyrs, from the ones of the French Revolution to Che Guevara. Philosophers have been aware of the ambiguity of the secular, and Richard Day (1954: 344) aptly formulates the paradox: "If men found that, because there was nothing to die for, life was not worth living, they might choose to die for the continued reign of secularism. That would tend to make it *sacer*. Very likely it would appear sacred in the eyes of those willing to die for it." He documents well not only "the similarity of Christianity to the whole enterprise of the rational ordering of interest, which is the ideal of modern secularism" but also the similarity between heroic paganism and Christianity (ibid.: 511).

Carlyle can be excused for having exclaimed that "the atheistic logic runs off from [the hero] like water," since he was born too early to witness the canonization of atheistic revolutionary figures in the 20th century (1993: 205). No man, however, not even a great man who appreciates great men, should be excused for saying "never" in a grandiloquent manner. When Carlyle pompously pronounced that with the second hypostasis of heroes—the hero as prophet—his divinity had vanished forever, that "in the history of the world there will not again be any man, never so great, whom his fellowmen will take for god" (ibid.: 37) he obviously consciously (and cautiously) overlooked Jesus Christ. But he could not foresee that a century and a half later an atheistic writer in an overwhelmingly atheistic country would pronounce that "Levski is the Bulgarians' God."

Carlton Hayes was wise and convincing when he insisted that only approaching nationalism as religion can we take account of its enormous emotive power, the missionary zeal of its apostles, and the unparalleled readiness to sacrifice one's life. He outlined its commonalities with other great religious systems of the past, primarily Christianity, as nationalism first appeared among peoples that were traditionally Christian and would be influenced by its symbolism. While carefully emphasizing that nationalism as religion was a reaction against the universalism of early historic Christianity, the two main similarities he saw were that the modern nation state, like the medieval church, had an ideal and a mission, the mission of salvation and the ideal of immortality, the eternal nation.

If I am going back to Hayes, despite the questionable work following in his footsteps that equated nationalism with religion in order to stress its irrationality and treat it as false consciousness, it is because first, he was not guilty of the reductionism of his epigones and secondly, his approach allowed him best to highlight the enormous emotive power of nationalism. I stress emphatically that this "return" in no way signals a renewed equivalence between nationalism and religion. The functionalist-evolutionist approach that linked the rise of nationalism in a causal way to secularization, and saw nationalism as a substitute for religion in modernity, has been convincingly criticized. Liah Greenfeld recognizes that the temptation to treat nationalism as religion stems from the fact that as a form of consciousness it sacralizes the secular, but she warns: "The fact that nationalism replaced religion as the order-creating system... implies nothing at all about the historical connection between them and lends no justification to the kind of sociological teleology that is the essence of such reasoning" (1996: 176). Moreover, the correlation between the rise of nationalism and religious decline has been questioned. Quite to the contrary, a number of scholars have highlighted the roots of nationalism in periods of religious fervor. Recent studies demonstrate how variously interrelated the nation and religion are, and how this dynamic relationship cannot be reduced to linear, evolutionist or simplistic functionalist terms, but is instead contingent on the form of the state.

Quite apart from considerations of primacy, causality and correlation, the stress here is on the enormous emotional force of nationalism that is reminiscent only of the power of religion. Few, if any, contest this. As Josep Llobera puts it, "the nation, as a culturally defined community, is the highest symbolic value of modernity; it has been endowed with a quasi-sacred character equaled only by religion" (1994: ix). Benedict Anderson, even as he claimed that nationalism was born both out of and against religious systems, likewise insisted that as a phenomenon it belongs more to "kinship" and "religion" rather than to "liberalism" or "fascism" (1983: 5). And Verdery, stepping on a number of previous anthropologists treats national identities as part of a larger category of social relations, kinship: "Nationalism is thus a kind of ancestor worship, a system of patrilineal kinship, in which national heroes occupy the place of clan elders in defining a nation as a noble lineage" (1999: 41).

In what may seem a leap of imagination, one can compare the rise and function of holy men in late antiquity with the rise and function of national heroes in late modernity. The holy men in Syrian towns and villages followed the "ideal of *Imitatio Christi* which strives for the transcendence of human existence by controlling the most fragile part of it, the body" (Hackel 1981: 33). Nationalism's heroes strove for the transcendence of human existence, which was achieving the national ideal, by not only pledging their own bodies but by controlling and protecting the cherished body politic—the *natio*. The same is true of the revolutionary hero: "imitatio heroica, readiness for sacrifice, courage, moral outrage and enthusiasm are the affective characteristics of the revolutionary." The revolution itself is a heroic enterprise whose aim is, in the words of Kropotkin, "to break violently the thread of history." Revolutionary heroism is a phenomenon that appears at the end of the structural transformation of sacral into secular heroism but precisely because of the dialectical process in which it is involved, one can trace the original religious undertones. Thus, "the fantastic idea of the exemplary heroic death as revolutionary sacrifice for the regeneration of the whole of humanity in line with the revolutionary understanding of the great 19th-century philosophers of history, becomes the residue of initiation rites" (Naumann 1984: 52). Naumann ingeniously argues that the interpretation of the Paris Commune in the theoretical revolutionary tradition may provide a turning point in the history of revolutionary heroism itself. Where for Marx, the workers of 1871 were heroes because they became the precursors of a new society through their sacrifice, fulfilling the laws and direction of history, for Lenin their heroism consisted in trying to fulfill Marx's teaching and prophecy (ibid.: 50–1). We have a new round from the sacral to the secular and again to the quasi-religious.

Revolutionary cults of the French Revolution have aspecifically religious nature: "The cult of the 'patriot saints' illustrates one aspect of the transition from the Catholic religion to the revolutionary cults: it brings together the old religious context and new political elements which are fitted in top traditional forms of worship" (Wilson 1983: 220). And Koselleck, writing about the political death cult, adds that irrespective of whether it occurs on a polytheist, monotheist, deist, pantheist or atheist foundation, the violent death always contains a self-constituting religious element for the community (1994: 9). We have to add here the whole gallery of totalitarian heroes, both on the left and on the right. There is also askesis as a central common attribute of both medieval sainthood and revolutionary heroism. In her study of the ascetic figure in Russian literature, Marcia Morris draws a direct line between the religious strain of apocalypticism and revolutionary apocalypticism, whose adherents also adopted askesis as a way of life (1993: 23). Michael Walzer (1965) and Barrington Moore (1978) have drawn general attention to the psychological and sociological links of asceticism and revolution. In a study of the ideology of political activists in Russia at the end of the 19th century, Dave Pretty has compellingly demonstrated that "the heroic ascetic saint was the role in the Russian cultural vocabulary that best fit the demands of a revolutionary situation." By pointing out the great number of future Bolsheviks who conceded a youthful fascination with sainthood, he concludes that "worldviews anchored in schismatic religion facilitated conversion to social democratic activism and eased adaptation to underground and conspiratorial work" (1995: 296, 303).

There is another circumstance in which modern sanctity and modern heroism parallel each other. While they are still a minority and will remain a minority, an increasing number of saints and heroes of more modest or even humble origins begin to enter the respective pantheons, and this has to do obviously with the processes of democratization and mass politics in the past couple of centuries. Sociological studies on sainthood show that, with the exception of the very first centuries when a number of saints were lowly-born, the overwhelming majority of saints in the Western Church (of whom data has been assembled) came from aristocratic or upper class origins (Delooz 1969). The Eastern Church, where similar quantitative synthetic studies do not exist, still seems to follow the same pattern (Laiou-Thomakides 1980: 87). The "low level" saint in early Byzantium, described so well by Robert Browning as "the counter-hero of the dispossessed and of those to whom the high urban culture of Late Antiquity had nothing to offer" is clearly the exception (Hackel 1981: 127).

The *cause célèbre* is of Joan of Arc, convicted and burnt at the stake for heresy in 1431. This was understood from the outset as a political process, and by 1456 a special commission was appointed by Pope Callistus III, rehabilitating the memory of the Maid of Orléans. Yet, the trial that condemned her has to be understood first and foremost as "the first process undertaken by the 'great minds' from the universities in order to prevent a popular cult from being born and developing... The Fairy Tree, the fountain and the voices of SS Catherine and Margaret, the marks of veneration which had surrounded the Maid in the hour of her success, were all held against her as a result, essentially, of the same rejection: that of a sainthood lived and recognized by simple people" (Vauchez 1997: 539). The greatest irony is that she was finally canonized only in 1920, after almost five centuries in which she was an unofficial saint of the nation but not an official saint of the church. This happened during the high age of nationalism with all the cultural capital it was conferring on its chosen representatives, and the low age of religion. The parallel to the Levski case needs no comment.

It is within this modestly growing egalitarian framework that Levski finds a particularly welcome fit. There is, of course, the circumstance that he is the hero of a relatively egalitarian society but it is also the growing general intellectual acceptance of, and sometimes preference for, heroes of humble origins that is at play; in a word, the "democratization" of hero-worship. As we already saw , Levski's *vita* conforms (in a tongue-in-cheek comparison) to the main incidents in the (ancient) hero pattern. His accordance with the Christian saint, especially as martyr, but also as ascetic, as well as increasingly as intercessor, is amazing. It was demonstrated also that his perception followed closely the Christological ideal. And there is no question of Levski as an archetypal revolutionary hero. We are dealing with a fairly typical hero, in line with numerous others all over the world. He is closer typologically to some heroes than to others, but he belongs to a distinctive universal human genus—the heroic one—and specifically to one of its sub-categories: national revolutionary heroes. In the pantheon of this group, he would probably feel most comfortable in the company of Giuseppe Garibaldi, José Martí and Abraham Lincoln, alongside his Bulgarian friends. So, what does the Levski story tell us in the end? As already said, he is a very attractive and interesting, but not necessarily extraordinary, figure in the general human heroic pantheon. One can say, paraphrasing Campbell (1949), that Levski is one in the gallery of "the hero with a thousand faces." It is not so much what his story tells us, as how we choose to tell his story. Let me end with another "hero of our times" whose life and veneration of Levski encapsulates all the reincarnations of our historical hero.

Dimitîr Chatalbashev is a retired officer from the Bulgarian People's Army in his mid-fifties from the town of Smolian, high up in the Rhodope Mountains. Honest, boisterous, outspoken, a natural contrarian, he was, by all accounts, tremendously popular as a military leader. His grandfather had been opposed to the forceful cooperation of the land by the communists in the 1950s, but this did not get in the way of his army career. He contrasts this with the present absolute party cliquishness, corruption and lawlessness. His memories of his tenure as an officer in one of the most sensitive border regions shed interesting light on episodes from Cold War history. He remembers how, during the Zhivkov era, huge loads of lamb meat were exported through the checkpoint under his control. They were sold to Arab merchants, who directly supplied kitchens of the Sixth American Fleet in the Mediterranean, something well known to his superiors. He also supervised the export of automatic rifles to Arab countries. The usual practice was that Soviet made automatic rifles would be used in the Bulgarian army for a year or so. Then, they were expedited to the military plant near Karlovo, where they were newly oxidized. Their label *Sdelano v SSSR* (Made in the USSR) would be changed to *Napraveno v Bîlgariia* (Made in Bulgaria), and then they would be off to their new destinations.

After 1989, Dimitîr (Mitko) or Chatala, as he is fondly known among friends, was at first happy with the prospect of economic and democratic changes. With the economic stagnation, and concerned about his children (students at the time), he and his wife Annie thought of leaving the country but in the end got cold feet. Smolian was a town of about 60,000–70,000 inhabitants during the socialist period which nowadays has dwindled to about 25,000. It was a mixed town of Christian and Muslim Bulgarians (*Pomaks*) and practically no Turks. The ratio between the two groups was 50:50, but now with so many of the Bulgarians have left, that the percentage of the Pomaks has risen to perhaps 70%. The employment situation is desperate like in most provincial towns. In the past decade, Chatala decided to transform himself into an entrepreneur. Curious and widely read, he had heard that cholesterol-conscious Europeans tended to avoid pork and veal, and preferred organic farming. He also found out that among poultry, the bird with the best nutritional characteristics was the ostrich. Its meat is practically cholesterol-free, it has a low-calorie and high protein content. An ostrich weighs up to 120 kilograms at the age of one, and it yields up to 45 kilograms of meat. The female lays 60 to 80 eggs annually, and young ones hatch and service from 30 to 50 of these.

"Our chance for Europe are the feathered ones," Chatala says, believing that pig- or cow-breeding farms have no chance to withstand competition from the EU. He accordingly transformed the fifty family decares (a little over one acre) on hills above Smolian near the village of Chokmanovo, into an ostrich farm sometime in 2000. He and his wife are now caring for about 15 adult ostriches (male and female) utilized exclusively for breeding purposes. He leaves them to roam freely on the hills during the day, and at night takes the "herd" to its "stable." The ostriches are extremely territorial and one doesn't need dogs to guard the property. The group of fierce male ostriches—Kiro, Mikhal,

Iliia, Boniu, Misho—can scare any trespasser away. Chatala tried to inspire local farmers to start breeding ostriches but by now he has despaired of the lack of entrepreneurship. His hope to be able to export meat for the big restaurant chains in Europe have been dimmed, because he alone and the few other farms in Bulgaria cannot meet the huge demands for regular supply. The local market, on the other hand, is not yet interested in this product. Besides, where one adult ostrich cost around $1,200 a few years ago, in 2005 during our visit it brought no more than 1,000 lev (a little more than $600 at the time). The Chatalbashev farm is, accordingly, specializing exclusively in ostrich breeding. There is a small incubator that Chatala and his son Nikolai have built in the family house in Smolian. Once the young ones hatch, they are taken to the farm, and when they grow a little, they are sold. Chatala sells a young one every three months for around $200.

In the summer of 2005, the Chatalbashev farm became the place for a pilot project. Ten young unemployed people were to be sent to the farm for two months to help out with the daily work, and learn the art of ostrich-breeding. The project is financed by the social ministry according to the European PHARE program for enhancing local communities. The unemployed receive a little over the minimal wage. In an interview he gave to the newspaper *Trud* in June, 2005, Chatala said his greatest satisfaction would be to pass his knowledge and entrepreneurial spirit to the young people. Privately, he voices his skepticism. The money, supposed to promote business initiatives, is usually funneled into supporting the administrative machine. The wages paid to the unemployed are so small that they have no incentive to work. Privately, I am also wondering what exactly Chatala is going to teach these young people. He doesn't hide his opinions on practically anything, politics in particular. When we visited and stayed with him for a few days in June, 2005, the first thing I noticed on the wall of his modest one-room hut at the farm was a portrait of Levski. "Listen" he told me, "let's organize a clandestine National Movement Vasil Levski (*Natsionalno dvizhenie Vasil Levski—NSVL*)." This was a spoof on the then still reigning National Movement Simeon the Second (*Natsionalno dvizhenie Simeon Vtori—NSVD*), the party of the former king and (already former) Prime Minister Simeon Saksoburgkotski. Our movement, Chatala said, would be strictly conspiratorial, and its main ethos would be "Death to the traitors." We discussed some details of its political program over dinner, which consisted of a wonderfully rich omelet prepared for eight people from one single ostrich egg that had to be broken with a drilling machine. The conspiracy is on hold for the moment, but in December, 2005, when we spoke to Chatala from the US, he told me he had just commissioned a large woodcarving of Levski, and intends to venerate it with a perpetually burning candle like an icon.

Conclusion

This book has been an argument for the relevance of microhistory, an attempt to demonstrate the significance of local knowledge in approaching the big issues of the profession and of life in general. It is taken for granted that a narrative, written in a few big languages and using examples from a few big countries, has universal connotations. Other examples in other languages (even languages such as Mandarin, Arabic or Hindi) are, at most, allowed to be footnotes in this universal sweep. It is this book's attempt to demonstrate the general meaning and worth of examples from very small places, even as the language of expression cannot afford challenging the rule of the big.

From this general argument, a number of more specific conclusions may be drawn. Most of these have been made in the course of the analysis, and they are just briefly enumerated here. It is one of this book's larger ambitions to question the posited discontinuities that have dominated East European historiography—especially the bracketing of the communist period—and demonstrate the powerful continuities over the *longue durée*. This was attempted by following the practices and understandings of nationalism during different political regimes, from the newly acquired political independence in the late 19th century to the post-communist adjustments in the early 21st. Insofar as the study focuses on symbols, its aim was to highlight the role of cultural processes and artifacts in the formation of national identity and contribute to a "poetic" understanding of power.

The unusual concentration on one heroic figure—a distinctly Bulgarian particularity—allowed for the diachronic look at the workings of cultural nationalism focused on the same historical personality and its historical peregrinations. The fact that Levski's figure was embroiled in two public scandals—the reburial controversy during the communist period, and his canonization during the post-communist period—permitted to fashion a distinct narrative and to experiment with the style of writing by providing multiple inter-texts, whence the metaphorical use of "archive" in the title.

It also allowed to contribute to the debate about the existence and character of civil society and the public sphere under communism, and to challenge deeply ingrained periodizations and the notions of rupture. The detailed look at the workings of academia in 1980s Bulgaria is not simply a "thick description" of what was happening in one corner behind the Iron Curtain. It is in general about the sites of creation and consumption of historical knowledge, an illustration of the great fight over "who owns history" that is relevant (and pressing) anywhere in the world. Similarly, the canonization of Levski is not only an idiosyncratic glimpse into an exotic space of post-communist Eastern Europe, but provides a theoretical opening at the workings of and relationship between nationalism and religion in general, and during the present regime of globalization in particular. Establishing the link between ancient hero worship and medieval sainthood, and between medieval saints and national heroes, places Levski within a context that compares him to other cases of national heroes and allows him to "rest" naturally not only within his narrow Bulgarian pantheon but, more broadly, within the international "family" of national heroes or the genus of human heroes at large.

Situating Levski's case within the literature on heroism and hero worship, and tracing the genealogy of his worship, allowed to reconstruct in detail how heroes are made, the main receptacles of their cult, the chief mechanisms of transmission, and why and how they become such hot commodities of cultural capital. Throughout, the common waters that provide the space and continuity where all these different ideas are floating, is the sea of nationalism, understood in its most general meaning as a dominant organizational principle and ideology in the past few centuries. Still, what does the Bulgarian case contribute typologically, aside from its (undoubted) narrative value and deepening the knowledge about a region and one of its lesser known aspects?

It was already suggested that Levski is in many ways a typical figure in the general human heroic pantheon, one in Campbell's gallery of "the hero with a thousand faces." Of course, for many Bulgarians he stands out as the purest and holiest but in this he is typical of all national heroes. Even his "bones of contention" are not unique. Although it was shown that his bones are quite distinct from the parade of dead bodies in post-socialist Eastern Europe, obsession with bones and dead bodies is far from an East European particularity. One does not need to go back to the Middle Ages to count the amount of West European saints' bones, additional body parts, pieces of the Holy Cross, and other holy paraphernalia. In 2001, two groups pledged a total of $5 million on an extensive search for the aircraft of Amelia Earhart who disappeared on July 2, 1937. President Roosevelt had authorized $4 million for her search in 1937. Already in the late 1930s, there had been rumors of an aircraft wreckage on the island of Nikumaroro, 2,000 miles southwest of Hawaii. In 1941 bones from an exhumed grave said to be her remains were taken to Fiji. A local doctor pronounced them to be those of a European male. The bones were since lost but experts, studying the doctor's notes, insist that they could have been the remains of a woman (*The International Herald Tribune*, August 7, 2001, 3). In 1961, it was thought that Earhart's and Noonan's bones had been found on Saipan but it turned out to be bones of a native islander. Human folly takes different shapes. It may look funny to the world that a number of people (though decidedly a small number) in a small nation, may be obsessed with the bones of someone revered as the national hero of this small nation. But this costs the world decidedly less than the obsession of (an also decidedly small number of) Americans with their heroine. American interest in bones is not solely nationalistic. Mozart's remains that, as is well known, were buried in an unmarked grave in St. Marx cemetery in Vienna, have taxed the imagination of several generations. In 2005, the University of Innsbruck together with the U.S. Armed Forces DNA Identification Lab in Rockville, Maryland, tested a skull from an Austrian museum, allegedly Mozart's, by using samples from the marked graves of his grandmother and niece. The results were inconclusive. Conclusive or not, this is an excellent alternative way to use the sophisticated facilities of the American armed forces.

Money can afford even quirkier interests than bones. Among the barrage of news getting daily (and nightly) into the newsroom of *The New York Times*, the paper found it worthy to single out one (even if with the proper dosage of tongue-in-cheek) for its op-ed section on May 17, 2007. It concerned the death in Englewood, NJ, of John K. Lattimer, urologist and retired Columbia University professor and collector of military relics, who was the owner of Napoleon's penis.

Before him, the relic was owned by the Philadelphia bookseller and collector A. S. W. Rosenbach who had it on display at the Museum of French Art in New York. And recently *The New York Times* (April 5, 2007) reported that the rib bone supposedly found at the site of Joan of Arc's stake in 1431, and revered as her relic after she was beatified in 1909 and canonized in 1920, turned out to be a fake, coming from an Egyptian mummy dated between the 7th and 3rd centuries B.C.

Still, while there is nothing exceptional about the veneration of Levski—it is typical for any nationalism—there is something unprecedented in his solitary elevation. The preceding analysis demonstrated that his exclusive march to the top was neither an ontological given, nor a foregone conclusion. Instead, it was the result of a gradual historical process that secured his place at the pinnacle of the Bulgarian heroic pantheon only after the First World War, and continues to the present day. What accounts for this unique configuration? Is there something peculiarly Bulgarian about it? It is here that I would like to finally elaborate on the notion of weak nationalism, something promised already in the introduction. It is a melodic suggestion, not a developed musical phrase, as the overall narrative has not been conceived as a four-part piece.

"Weak nationalism" is a syntagm that is part and parcel of the vocabulary of any but especially of strong nationalists. It is usually an accusation or lament for insufficient patriotic feeling, absence of readiness for self-sacrifice or even for banal material sacrifice. As we saw in the preceding text, the absence or weakness of a strong national feeling among the Bulgarians was lamented by writers, scholars, and politicians alike, at different moments of Bulgaria's national development in the past two centuries. Yet, this is a trivial lament: it is typical of any nationalism, at some time or other, in every corner of the earth. The way I would like to approach it here is from a different angle, as an analytical category, complementing the notion of strong, exclusive or messianic nationalism, and thus qualifying the category nationalism in general.

Arguably, weak nationalism is a category more recognizable in a common sense approach than in a strictly analytical and quantifiable one, but I would like to suggest that it can be defined and even measured by the mobilizing ability of an extreme nationalist message in the public sphere. It has received relatively little attention as, naturally, most research concentrates on the cases of powerful and persistent nationalisms, especially the mission of "chosen peoples." It is these "strong" cases that have determined and defined the study of nationalism. The general literature has rightly emphasized its emotive power, intensity, passion and conviction. Jewish, German, and Irish nationalism provide much of the focus for such studies. For Eastern Europe this has meant a concentration on Poland, Serbia, Greece, and Russia.

Elsewhere, I have explored the course and characteristics of Bulgarian nationalism, and have engaged in discussions about the persistent dichotomy in the interpretation of West and East European, civic versus organic, rational versus irrational models of nationalism that I deem heuristically unproductive, although obviously useful for moralizing purposes. A more interesting question for me is what accounts for the different degrees of intensity in separate nationalisms? To go even further, how is it that occasional displays of messianic, exclusive and aggressive nationalism are not even deemed to be characterized as nationalism, as is the present case with the United States? And, on the contrary, how come instances of nationalisms that, even if harshly articulated (as most nationalisms are), have neither become ruling nor mainstream (like, for example, Czech, Slovene, Lithuanian, Bulgarian, Macedonian, Moldavian, and several others) but are still neatly and uncritically subsumed in a model of the virulent, irrational, organic "East European" kind. Focusing on a relatively "weak" case, as in the preceding analysis, helps provide a historical explanation for its causes and manifestations.

Why is Bulgaria—the Balkan country *par excellence*—displaying symptoms of what I call weak nationalism? The chronologically later (by at least a generation) development of Bulgarian nationalism (with a peak on the 1840s–1870s) compared to Greece or Serbia, or to the semi-independent status of the Romanian principalities, complicated its articulation and practical program not only by functioning in an already hotly contested space but also by developing a number of sophisticated and ideologically differentiated alternatives. As a result, at the time of independence, there were contesting visions of the national idea that could not be harmonized, nor did one emerge as an exclusive hegemon. The lack of a messianic claim was coupled by the absence of a strong international patron or movement comparable to philhellenism for the Greeks, the appeal of the Piedmontese analogy for Serbia, the imperial aura of the Turks despite the decline of the Ottoman Empire, or the "Latin" kinship of the Romanians. The proverbial Bulgarian link to Russia has been exaggerated: in reality, the political relationship has been rather ambivalent, while preserving indeed a strong popular cultural affinity.

Above all, and this is the main point, this was a nationalism whose irredentist program was humiliated very early in the attempts at realization, and its consecutive defeats sealed the character of its genuinely *status quo* nationalism. The effects of humiliation were discernible already after the Balkan Wars and the First World War but the Macedonian irredenta (and emigration) continued to fuel passions and actions that resulted in an additional catastrophic revisionist spurt during the Second World War. It is true that, as a rule, practically all European nationalisms after the Second World War have been nationalisms of the *status quo* kind. But there is a psychological difference between, in the end, victorious and humiliated projects, as some postwar comparisons demonstrate: completely devastated Poland versus an also (but less so) devastated Germany; Romania and Hungary; Serbia and Croatia; Italy and Yugoslavia.

In the Bulgarian case, "the three national catastrophes" within the time-span of a single generation secured first, a gloomy and introspective mood in the interwar period, and after the Second World War, a scale of self-mockery and the employment of humor, in what is usually a tradition of solemnity in the articulation of the nationalist discourse, that is quite unique in the Balkan space, and awaits its explorer. Small wonder that Levski was elevated in the 1920s after the series of humiliating defeats that served as a sobering shock to the jingoistic irredentist nationalism. This was the result of a confluence of factors, of which the political impasse was only one, but there is little doubt about the correlation. The principle "victims," as far as the shaping of the heroic pantheon was concerned, were the medieval kings who, up until then, symbolically led the drift toward territorial expansion during the phase of rising and optimistic irredentist nationalism. Now they had to share the lofty position with and even yield to the critical 19th-century national revolutionaries, who were perceived as opponents to the regimes in power. This was reinforced, after the Second World War, both by the political fiasco during the war, as well as by the imposition of an official anti-nationalist rhetoric.

All of this coincided with a general "democratization" of hero-worship, when heroes of humble origins not only began to be increasingly accepted but even started to be preferred. That Levski's cult grew in a relatively egalitarian and relatively anti-intellectual society additionally propelled him to the top. What makes him stand out from among comparable "commoners" in the heroic pantheon of other nations, is his truly broad national appeal (in terms of all citizens, not only of the majority ethnic nation). For someone who gave his life for a specific ethnic cause, he is remarkably popular also among the non-Bulgarian minorities, ethnic Turks inclusive. His unflinching appeal today is not simply a matter of inertia. The Levski myth is at the heart of the political covenant, and in a country that is suffering the syndrome of a "weak society in a weak state," he is both the legitimizing armor of the ones in power, and the protest banner of the powerless.

Aggressive nationalism has been posited to stem from a lack of healthy national self-confidence. The caveat of "healthy" notwithstanding, historical practice hardly supports this view. Where is the line between healthy and excessive? In the Bulgarian case, one can posit that a lack of self-confidence after the two world wars guaranteed what has been described here as non-aggressive, status quo or weak nationalism. This does not mean that the verbal expressions of Bulgarian nationalists have been weaker, or more measured. Quite to the contrary, a list of the harshest and most poisonous invectives can be assembled, that can compete (and probably surpass) the verbal expressions of many a strong nationalism. The point, however, is that the extreme message never managed to effectively mobilize the majority of the population after the 1920s.[1]

While I do think that, in the Bulgarian case, there exists a correlation between national humiliation, the type of hero worship, and

---

[1] The brief outburst over Macedonia during the Second World War, when Bulgaria served as an occupation force and annexed it, has to be seen in the context of an interwar policy that was trying to avoid foreign policy commitments but, in the end, caved in to German pressure. In an unpopular war, the Macedonian venture was the only popular move that can be compared, more properly, to any national unification or reunification, something that can be scrutinized and criticized from a variety of viewpoints, but is not usually attributed to extreme nationalism. The other nationalistic episode—the renaming of the Bulgarian Turks in the 1980s—never had popular support.

weak nationalism (as previously defined), I do not believe that this correlation can be generalized, or that it renders itself to typological conjectures. I propose neither that whenever a singular, non-aristocratic hero is elevated, weak nationalism takes hold, nor that, wherever we notice symptoms of weak nationalism, this would result in a steep heroic pyramid with an exclusive commoner at the top. Nor do I believe that in all cases of national humiliation, sobriety and weak nationalism is the effect, although I wish this were so. All I am saying is that, in the particular case of Bulgaria, there is a conflation of factors that explains the specific phenomenon. However, I would go further with typological disclaimers. While there is now a nearly century-long tradition of what I call weak nationalism, I would stay far away from the now fashionable, in political science circles, category of path dependence. Weak nationalism is not an imminent characteristic of any polity, and there is no guarantee that the most aggressive form would not burgeon in its womb, although I see little structural prerequisites for this in Europe in the near future.

Strong nationalists even in weak states with weak societies characterized by weak nationalism are impatient with nuances: they know the "truth" and the truth can only be one. Bulgarian strong nationalists, in addition, are impatient with knowledge: it adds distorting shades on their one-colored (or colorless) truth. In what for Bulgaria acquired the typical shape of a charade, a recent controversy over a projected scholarly conference centered around a sacred *lieu de mémoire*, unleashed a passionate discussion over the meaning of myth and history. The notion of "myth" provoked and offended nationalist sensibilities: they saw in its use a surreptitious denial of reality. What a pity musical education has so little place in pupils' formation nowadays! Even diehard nationalists would have acquired a different appreciation of myth had they listened in their youth to this diehard nationalist Richard Wagner. For Wagner, myth was "timeless, intuitive, profound, and concerned not with the particular but with the universal," and he made it the subject of his greatest operas. As they make their way to the temple of the Holy Grail in the First Act of "Parsifal," Gurnemanz turns to Parsifal with the words "Do siehst, mein Sohn, zum Raum wird hier die Zeit" (*You see, my son, here time becomes space*). This line Claude Levi-Strauss declared the most profound definition of myth, and pronounced Wagner the father of the structural analysis of myth.

It is this process of time becoming space that was the object of this book. For the rest, let me borrow from Flavius Josephus who wrote 2,000 years ago:

> And here we shall put an end to this our history, wherein we formerly promised to deliver the same with all accuracy, to such as should be desirous of understanding… Of which history, how good the style is, must be left to the determination of the readers, but as for its agreement with the facts, I shall not scruple to say, and that boldly, that truth hath been what I have alone aimed at through its entire composition (Flavius 1928, Book VII, Ch. 11, 5: 481).

References

Anderson, Benedict. 1983. *Imagined Communities: Reflections on the Origins and Spread of Nationalism*. London: Verso.
Angelov, Dimitîr. 2004. *Spomeni*. Sofia: Pradigma.
Arkhimandrit Evtimii, 1942. "Otritsateli na religiiata li sa bîlgarskite poeti i pisateli?," *Godishnik na Sofiiskiia Universitet. Bogoslovski Fakultet/ Annuaire de l'université de Sofia. Faculté de théologie*, XIX, 1941–1942, Sofia: Universitetska pechatnitsa.
Asad, Talal. 1993. *Genealogies of Religion. Discipline and Reasons of Power in Christianity and Islam*. Baltimore and London: The Johns Hopkins University Press.
Ashcraft, Mark H. 1993. *Human Memory and Cognition*. New York: HarperCollins.
Anastasova, Ekaterina. 1993. "Az i drugiiat, mitologiia i identichnost," *Etnicheskata kartina v Bîlgariia. Prouchvaniia 1992 g*. Sofia: Klub 90.
Bailey, Douglas W. 1998. "Bulgarian Archeology. Ideology, sociopolitics and the exotic," in: Lynn Meskell, ed., *Archeology Under Fire. Nationalism, Politics and the Heritage in the Eastern Mediterranean and the Middle East*. London and New York: Routledge.
Bakalov, Georgi. 1934. *Vasil Levski*. Sofia: St. Vasilev.
Bakalov, Georgi. 1938. *Bunt protiv Levski*. Sofia: Radikal.
Bakalova, Elka. 1991. "Zhitiepisno povestvuvanie i izobrazitelna interpretatsiia," *Starobîlgarska literatura*, 25–26.
BAN volume: Nikolai Todorov, ed. 1988. *Arkheologicheski danni po spora za groba na Vasil Levski v tsîrkvata "Sv. Petka Smardzhiiska." Dokumenti i stanovishta*. Sofia: Izdatelstvo na BAN, 1988.
Beissinger, Mark. 2006. "Soviet Empire as 'Family Resemblance,'" *Slavic Review*, 65, 2.
Bell, Catherine. 1997. *Ritual. Perspectives and Dimensions*. New York: Oxford University Press.
Benjamin, Walter. 1060. *Illuminations*, ed. Hanna Arendt, New York.
Blagoev, Dimitîr. *Sîchineniia*, 1957 (vol. I–IV), 1958 (VI), 1959 (X), 1960 (XI), 1964 (XX). Sofia: Izdanie na BKP.
Bloch, Maurice and Jonathan Perry, eds. 1982. *Death and the regeneration of life*. Cambridge: Cambridge University Press.
Bobchev, Sava and Eduard Baltadzhian. 1979. "Kîde e grobît na Levski," *Sofia*, 11.

Bourdieu, Pierre. 1990. *The Logic of Practice*. Cambridge: Polity Press; Stanford: Stanford University Press.
Bozhilov, Ivan. 1995. *Sedem etiuda po srednovekovna istoriia (Seven Essays on Medieval History)*, Sofia: Anubis.
Brown, Peter. 1981. *The Cult of the Saints: Its Rise and Function in Latin Christianity*, Chicago: The University of Chicago Press.
Bruner, Edward. 1986. "Experience and Its Expressions," in Victor W. Turner and Edward M. Bruner, eds., *The Anthropology of Experience*. Urbana: University of Illinois Press.
Bruner, Jerome. 1993. "The Autobiographical Process," in Robert Folkenflik, ed., *The Culture of Autobiography. Constructions of Self-Representation*, Stanford, CA: Stanford University Press.
Campbell, Joseph. 1949. *The Hero with a Thousand Faces*. Bollingen Series XVII. Princeton, NJ: Princeton University Press.
"Canonization of Saints in the Orthodox Church." 1931. *The Christian East*, XII.
Carlyle, Thomas. 1993. *On Heroes, Hero-Worship, and the Heroic in History*. Introduction and notes by Michael K. Goldberg. Berkeley: University of California Press.
Centlivres, Pierre, Daniel Fabre and Françoise Zonabend. 1998. *La fabrique des héros*. Paris: Éditions de la Maison des sciences de l'homme.
Challis, Natalia. 1980. "Glorification of Saints in the Orthodox Church," *Russian History/ Histoire Russe*, 7, parts 1–2.
Chudomir. 1994. *Dnevnik, 1947–1967*. Kazanlîk: Fondatsiia Chudomir, IKK Slavika.
Cohen, Jean L and Andrew Arato. 1992. *Civil Society and Political Theory*. Cambridge, MA and London: MIT Press.
Colocotronis, Vassilis. 1918. L Ame bulgare et l âme greque d après la poésie populaire, *Revue de Grèce* 1(1).
Czarnowski, Stefan. 1919 *Le culte des héros et ses conditions sociales. Saint Patrick, héros national de l'Irlandie*. Paris: Librarie Félix Alcan, 1919.
Dafinov, Zdravko. 2006. *Priiatelstva i sîpernichestva mezhdu bîlgarskite poeti, pisateli i krititsi: Dokumentalna khronika 1845–1945*. Sofia, Iztok-Zapad.
Davis, Natalie Zemon. 1996. "Who Owns History? History in the Profession," *Perspectivesr*, vol. 34, n. 8.
Day, Richard. 1954. *Heroic Death: A Study from a Christian Point of View*. Unpublished dissertation. New York: Columbia University.
Delooz, Pierre. 1969. *Sociologie et canonisation*. Liège: Faculté de droit, La Haye: Nartinus Nijhoff.
Dinzelbacher, Peter and Dieter R. Bauer. 1990. *Heiligenverehrung in Geschichte und Gegenwart*. Ostfildern: Schwabenverlag.
Eisenstadt, Shmuel.2006. "Multiple modernities, public spheres and social movements in the contemporary era," *Jahrbuch 2004/2005*, Berlin: Wissenschaftskolleg zu Berlin.
Eliade, Mircea. 1961. *The Sacred and the Profane. The Nature of Religion*. New York: Harper & Brothers.

Fabian, Johannes. 1983. *Time and the Other. How Anthropology Makes Its Object*. New York: Columbia University Press.
Falk, Barbara J. 2003. *The Dilemmas of Dissidence in East-Central Europe: Citizen Intellectuals and Philosopher Kings*. Budapest – New York: Central European University Press.
Feierman, Steven Feierman, "The Creation of Invisible Histories," in Victoria E. Bonnell and Lynn Hunt, eds., *Beyond the Cultural Turn*. Berkeley, Los Angeles, London: University of California Press, 1999, 206.
Flavius Josephus. 1928. *The War of the Jews*. Translated by William Whinston, London and Toronto: J. M. Dent, New York: E. P. Dutton.
Fraser, Nancy. 1996. *Justice Interruptus. Critical Reflections on the "Postsocialist" Condition*. New York: Routledge.
Gaster, Theodor. 1995. "Heroes" in *The Encyclopedia of Religion*. Ed. Mircea Eliade. Vol. 5 & 6. New York: Simon & Schuster, MacMillan.
Geertz, Clifford. 1973. *The Interpretation of Cultures*. New York: Basic Books.
Geertz, Clifford. 1980. *Negara. The Theatre State in Nineteenth-Century Bali*. Princeton, NJ: Princeton University Press.
Gellner, Ernest. 1983. *Nations and Nationalism*. Ithaca: Cornell University Press.
Genchev, Nikolai. 1973. *Levski, revoliutsiiata i bîdeshtiiat sviat*. Sofia: Izdatelstvo na Otechestveniia Front.
Genchev, Nikolai. 1987. *Vasil Levski*. Sofia: Voenno izdatelstvo.
Genchev, Nikolai. 2005. *Izbrani proizvedeiia*, Tom 5 *Spomeni*, Sofia: Izdatelstvo "Gutenberg."
Giaurov, Khristo. 1959. "Grobît na V. Levski," *Dukhovna kultura*, XXXIX, N.2, 30–31.
Greenfeld, Liah. 1996. "Is Nationalism the Modern Religion?," *Critical Review* 10 (2).
Hackel, Sergei ed. 1981. *The Byzantine Saint. University of Birmingham Fourteenth Spring Symposium of Byzantine Studies*. London, Chester: Fellowship of St. Alban and St. Sergius, The Bemprose Press.
Hann, Chris and Elizabeth Dunn, eds. 1996. *Civil Society: Challenging Western Models*. London and New York: Routledge.
Haraszti, Miklós.1987. *The Velvet Prison: Artists Under State Socialism*, trans. Katalin and Stephen Landesmann, New York: Basic Books.
Haskell, Thomas. 1998. *Objectivity is not Neutrality: Explanatory Schemes in History*. Baltimore and London: The Johns Hopkins University Press.
Hayes, Carlton. 1966. *Essays on Nationalism*. New York: Russell & Russell.
Holmes, Leslie. 1997. *Post-Communism: An Introduction*. Durham: Duke University Press.
Humphrey, Caroline and James Laidlaw. 1994. *The Archetypal Actions of Ritual. A Theory of Ritual Illustrated by the Jain Rite of Worship*. Oxford: Clarendon Press, 1994.
"Ierodiakon Ignatii ili Vasil Levski bezbozhnik li e bil?" 1898. In D. Marinov, ed., *Religiozni razkazi*, III, 1–2, Sofia: Pechatnitsa "Prosveshtenie."
In Quest of the Hero 1990. Princeton, NJ: Princeton University Press.

Jay, Martin. 1998. *Cultural Semantics: Keywords of Our Time*. Amherst: University of Massachusetts Press.
Jireček, Konstanitn. 1876. *Geschichte der Bulgaren*. Prag: Verlag von F. Tempsky.
Kalokyris, Constantine. 1969. "The Essence of Orthodox Iconography," *Greek Orthodox Theological Review*, 14, 1.
Karakostov, Stefan. 1943. "Predgovor," in *Vasil Levski (Diakonît). Cherti iz zhivota mu ot Zakhari Stoianov. Kritichno izdanie pod redaktsiiata na Stefan Karakostov*. Sofia: Pechatnitsa V. Ivanov.
Kaviraj, Sudipta and Sunil Khilani, eds. 2001. *Civil Society: History and Possibilities*. Cambridge University Press.
Khaitov, Nikolai. 1985. *Poslednite migove i grobît na Vasil*. Plovdiv: Khristo G. Danov.
Khaitov, Nikolai. 1987. *Grobît na Vasil Levski*. Plovdiv: Khristo G. Danov.
Khaitov, Nikolai. 1989. *Izbrani proizvedeniia*. Sofia: Bîlgarski pisatel.
Khaitov, Nikolai. 1997. *Aferata s groba na Levski*. Sofia: Bîlgarski pisatel.
Khaitov, Nikolai. 2001. *Koito ima ukho, da chue*...Sofia: s.p.
Khaitov, Nikolai. 2002. *Grobît na Vasil Levski: Sbornik s istoricheski i arkheologicheski dokumenti i svidetelstva*. Sofia: Goreks Press.
Khaitov, Nikolai. 2003. *Prez sito i resheto. Zhivotoopisanie*. Sofia: Slîntse.
Klausner, Samuel. 1995. "Martyrdom," in Mircea Eliade, ed., *The Encyclopedia of Religion*, 9, New York: MacMillan.
Kohl, Philip and Clare Fawcett, eds. 1995. *Nationalism, Politics, and the Practice of Archeology*. Cambridge University Press.
Konrád, György. 1984. *Antipolitics: An Essay*. trans. Richard E. Allen, San Diego: Harcourt, Brace, Jovanovich.
Koselleck, Reinhart. 1985. *Futures Past. On the Semantics of Historical Time*. Cambridge, Massachusetts and London: The MIT Press.
Koselleck, Reinhart, Michale Jeismann, eds. 1994. *Der politische Totenkult: Kriegerdenkmäler in der Moderne*. Munich: Wilhelm Fink Verlag.
Krîstev, Krîstio. 1898, "Velikiiat apostol. Psikhologicheski eskiz," *Misîl*, VIII, No. 2.
Laiou-Thomakides, Angeliki, ed. 1980. *Charanis Studies. Essays in Honor of Peter Charanis*. New Brunswick, NJ: Rutgers University Press.
Levin, Eve. 1989. *Sex and Society in the World of the Orthodox Slavs, 900–1700*. Ithaca and London: Cornell University Press.
Lewin, Moshe. 1988. *The Gorbachev Phenomenon: A Historical Interpretation*. Berkeley, Los Angeles: University of California Press.
Lincoln, Bruce. 1989. *Discourse and the Construction of Society. Comparative Studies of Myth, Ritual and Classification*. New York: Oxford University Press.
Lipcheva-Prandzheva, Liubka. 2001. *Levski: Bukvi ot imeto*. Sofia: Primaprint.
Llobera, Josep. 1994. *The God of Modernity: The Development of Nationalism in Western Europe* Oxford: Berg, 1994.
Lowenthal, David. 1985. *The Past is a Foreign Country*. Cambridge: Cambridge University Press.

Manchov, D.V. 1880. *Kratîk izvod ot bîlgarska istoriia. Knizhka za uchenik v osnovno uchilishte*. Plovdiv, Svishtov, Solun, 1880: Pechatnitsa i knizharnitsa na D. V. Manchov.
MacDermott, Mercia. 1967. *The Apostle of Freedom. A Portrait of Vasil Levsky Against the Background of Nineteenth Century Bulgaria*, London: George Allen and Unwin Ltd.
Meinardus, Otto. 1970. "A Study of the Relics of Saints of the Greek Orthodox Church," in *Oriens Christianus. Hefte für die Kunde des christlichen Orients*, Band 54.
Moore, Sally, Barbara Meyerhoff, eds. 1977. *Secular Ritual*. Assen/Amsterdam: Van Gorcum.
Morris, Marcia. 1993. *Saints and Revolutionaries: The Ascetic Hero in Russian Literature*. New York: State University of New York Press.
Mikhailov, Stamen. 1959. "Stenopisite na tsîrkvata Sv. Petka Samardzhiiska v Sofia," *Izvestiia na arkheologicheskiia institut*, XXII, 291–327.
Mikhailov, Stamen. 1961. "Tsîrkvata 'Sv. Petka Samardzhiiska' v Sofia", in *Izsledvaniia v chest na Karel Shkorpil*. Otdelen otpechatîk. Sofia: Arkheologicheski institut i muzei, BAN, 167–178.
Miller, Dean. 2000. *The Epic Hero*. Baltimore and London: The Johns Hopkins University Press.
Mitchell, Timothy. 1991. "The Limits of the State: Beyond Statist Approaches and Their Critics," *The American Political Science Review*, 85, 1, 77–96.
Mitev, Plamen. 1999. *Bîlgarskoto vîzrazhdane. Lekstionen kurs*. Sofia: Polis.
Molinari, Paul. 1965. *Saints. Their Place in the Church*. New York: Sheed and Ward.
Moore, Barrington. 1978. *Injustice: The Social Bases of Obedience and Revolt*. White Plains: M. E. Sharpe.
Naumann, Michael. 1984. *Strukturwandel des Heroismus. Vom sakralen zum revolutionären Heldentum*. Königstein/Ts., Athenäum.
Nabokov, Vladimir. 1959. *The Real Life of Sebastian Knight*. New York: New Directions.
New Catholic Encyclopedia. 1967. New York: McGraw-Hill.
Nikhoritis, Konstantinos. 2001. *Sveta Gora – Aton i bîlgarskoto novomîchenichestvo*. Sofia: Akademichno izdatelstvo "Prof. Marin Drinov."
Odermatt, Peter. 1996. "Built heritage and the politics of representation. Local reactions to the appropriation of the monumental past in Sardinia," *Archeological Dialogues: Dutch Perspectives on Current Issues in Archeology*, vol. 3, n. 2.
Petev, Ivan. 1993. *Po-vazhni momenti ot zhivota i deloto na ierodiakon Ignatii – Vasil Levski*. Sofia: Voennoizdatelski kompleks "Sv. Georgi Pobedonosets".
Popov, Zhechko. 1976. *Vasil Levski v bîlgarskoto izobrazitelno izkustvo*. Sofia: Bîlgarski khudozhnik.
Poptodorov, Radko. 1970. "Pravoslavno-khristiianskata viara i bîlgarskata narodna tsîrkva kato faktori za zapazvaneto na bîlgarskiia narod, za formirane na natsionalno-revoliutsionnoto mu sîznanie i za kulturnoto mu razvitie

prez vreme na petvekovnoto osmansko robstvo," *Godishnik na dukhovnata akademiia "Sv.Kliment Okhridski,"* XX (XLI), 1970/1971, Sofia.

Portelli, Alessandro. 1998. "What makes oral history different," in Robert Perks and Alistair Thomson, eds., *The Oral History Reader*, London and New York: Routledge (reproduced from *History Workshop*, 1981, no. 12, 96–107).

Pretty, Dave. 1995. "The Saints of the Revolution: Political Activists in 1890s Ivanovo-Voznesensk and the Path of Most Resistance," *Slavic Review* 54, 2.

Radevski, Khristo. 2000. *Razgovor sîs sebe si. Nepublikuvan dnevnik*. Sofia: Zakharii Stoianov.

Raikin, Spas. 1993. "Schism in the Bulgarian Orthodox Church," *Religion in Eastern Europe*. ed. Paul Mojzes, XIII, N.1.

Randeria, Shalini. 2002. "Entangled Histories of Uneven Modernities: Civil Society, Caste Solidarites and Legal Pluralism in Post-Colonial India," in Yehuda Elkana, Ivan Krastev, Elisio Macamo, Shalini Randeria, eds., *Unraveling Ties—From Social Cohesion to New Practices of Connectedness*. Frankfurt: Campus Verlag.

Revel, Jacques Revel and Lynn Hunt, eds. 1995. *Histories. French Constructions of the Past*. New York: The New Press.

Rosaldo, Renato. 1993. *Culture and Truth. The Remaking of Social Analysis*. Boston: Beacon Press.

Schmitt, Carl. 1976. *The Concept of the Political*, transl. George Schwab, with comments by Leo Strauss, New Brunswick, New Jersey: Rutgers University Press.

SGODA: Sofia City District State Archives.

Segal, Robert. 2000. *Hero Myths: A Reader*. Oxford; Malden, Mass.: Blackwell.

Seligman, Adam. 2002. "Civil Society as Idea and Ideal," in: Simone Chambers and Will Kymlicka, eds., *Alternative Conceptions of Civil Society*, Princeton.

Sharova, Krumka. 1991. "Krizisni iavleniia v BRCK prez liatoto i esenta na 1872 g.," *Istoricheski pregled*, 3.

Sharova, Krumka. 1993. "Istoricheskoto znachenie na politicheskite razkritiia v Bîlgariia prez esenta na 1872 i nachaloto na 1873 g." *Po pîtia na bezsmîrtieto. Ot Kîkrina do Sofia. Sbornik ot dokladi posvetena na 120-ta godishnina ot gibelta na Apostola*, Veliko Tîrnovo: IK "Vital."

Sharova, Krumka. 1997. "Osnovopolozhnitsite na nauchnite znaniia za Levski," *Istoriia*, 5.

Shishmanov, Ivan. 1976. *Ivan Vazov. Spomeni i dokumenti. S predgovor, dobavki i belezhki ot Mikhail Arnaudov*. Sofia: Bîlgarski pisatel.

Simeonov, Khristo. 1999. *Bîlgarski natsionalni legioni. Minalo i nastoiashte*. Sofia: n.p.

Smith, Anthony. 1999. *Myths and Memories of the Nation*. Oxford: Oxford University Press.

Stanchev, Nikola. 1937 "De sa kostite na Levski," *Mir*, No.10987, March 6 (also in *BAN volume*, 242).

Stanilov, Stanislav. 1985. "Knigata na Nikolai Khaitov 'Poseldnite migive i grobît na Vasil Levski' v sektsiiata za srednovekovna arkheolgiia na Arkheologicheskiia institute pri BAN," *Vekove*, 6.
Stavrianos, Leften. 2000. *The Balkans since 1453.* New York: New York University Press.
Stoianov, Maniu. 1981. "Bîlgarski svetii i mîchenitsi ot epokhata na turskoto vladichestvo," in *Tsîrkvata i sîprotivata na bîlgarskiia narod sreshtu osmanskoto igo. Iubileen sbornik po sluchai 100 godini ot Osvobozhdenieto*, Sofia: Sinodalno izdatelstvo.
Stoianov, Zakhari. 1883. *Vasil Levski (Diakonît). Cherti iz zhivota mu ot Zakhari Stoianov.* Plovdiv.
Stoianov, Zakhari. 1990. *Vasil Levski. Chetite v Bîlgariia. Khristo Botyov.* Sofia: Idatelstvo na BZNS.
Strashimirov, Dimitîr. 1927. *Levski pred kîkrinskata golgota.* Sofia: Fakel.
Strashimirov, Dimitîr. 1929. *Vasil Levski: Zhivot, dela, izvori*, vol.1. *Izvori*, Sofia: Narodniiat komitet "Vasil Levski."
Sviatye iuzhnykh slavian. 1865. *Opyt opisaniia zhizni ikh. Sochinenie Filareta, arckhiepiskopa chernigovskago.* Chernigov: V tipografii Il'inskago monastyria.
Talbot, Alice-Mary, ed. 1996. *Holy Women of Byzantium. Ten Saints' Lives in English Translation.* Washington, D.C.: Dumbarton Oaks Research Library and Collection, 1996.
Taussig, Michael. 1992. *The Nervous System.* New York, London: Routledge.
Tonkin, Elizabeth. 1992. *Narrating Our Pasts. The Social Construction of Oral History.* Cambridge University Press.
Trouillot, Michel-Rolph. 1995. *Silencing the Past. Power and the Production of History.* Boston: Beacon Press.
Tsankov, Stefan. 1939. "Bîlgarskata pravoslavna tsîrkva ot Osvobozhdenieto do nastoiashte vreme," *Godishnik na Sofiiskiia universitet. Bogoslovski fakultet*, XVI, 6, 1938–1939. Sofia: Pridvorna pechatnitsa.
TsDA: Central State Archives.
Turner, Victor. 1974. *Dramas, Fields, and Metaphors. Symbolic Action in Human Society.* Ithaca and London: Cornell University Press.
Turner, Victor. 1981. "Social Dramas and Stories About Them," in W.J.T. Mitchell, ed., *On Narrative*, Chicago: University of Chicago Press.
Turner, Victor, ed. 1982. *Celebration. Studies in Festivity and Ritual.* Washington, D.C.: Smithsonian Institution Press.
Undzhiev, Ivan. 1947. *Vasil Levski. Biografiia.* Sofia: Direktsiia na izkustvata pri ministerstvo na informatsiiata i izkustvata.
Undzhiev, Ivan, Nikola Kondarev, 1971. *Sviata i chista republika. Pisma i dokumenti.* Sofia: Nauka i izkustvo.
Ustav na fondatsiia "Vasil Levski". 1991. Sofia.
Vasil Levski 1837–1987. Bio-bibliografiia. 1987. Sofia: Natsionalna biblioteka. "Kiril i Metodii."
Vasil Levski i negovite spodvizhnitsi pred turskiia sîd. 1952. Sofia: NBKM, 1952.
Vasil Levski 1941. *Pisma, Statii, Pesni.* Ed. Stefan Karakostov. Sofia: Nov svet, 1941.

Vauchez. André. 1997. *Sainthood in the Later Middle Ages.* Transl. by Jean Birrell. Cambridge: Cambridge University Press.
Vazov, Ivan. 1996. *Nemili-nedragi.* Sofia: Bîlgarski pisatel.
Vazov, Ivan. 1950. *Sîbrani sîchineniia. Pîlno izdanie,* Sofia: Nauka i izkustvo.
Verdery, Katherine. 1999. *The Political Lives of Dead Bodies. Reburial and Postsocialist Change.* New York: Columbia University Press.
Walzer, Michael. 1965. *The Revolution of the Saints: A Study in the Origins of Radical Politics.* New York: Atheneum.
Wilentz, Sean ed. 1985. *Rites of Power. Symbolism, Ritual, and Politics Since the Middle Ages.* Philadelphia: University of Pennsylvania Press.
Wilson, Stephen, ed. 1983. *Saints and their Cults: Studies in Religious Sociology, Folklore and History.* Cambridge: Cambridge University Press.
Vîzpomenatelna kniga Vasil Levski. 1837–1873–1937. Plovdiv: Izdava Karlovskoto sdruzhenie "V.Levski," 1937
Weber, Claudia. 1999. "'Opiti za sîzhiviavane' – kîm nachalata na bîlgarskata kultura na pametta," *Balkanistichen forum*, 1-2-3.
Zhelev, Zheliu. 1982. *Fashizmît: dokumentalno izsledvane na germanskiia, italianskiia i ispanskiia fashizîm.* Sofia: Narodna mladezh.
Zhelev, Zheliu. 1995. *Inteligentsiia i politika (Intellectuals and Politics).* Sofia: Literaturen forum.
Zhitiia na svetiite, 1974. Sofia: Sinodalno izdatelstvo.
Zhivov, V.M. 1994. *Sviatost'. Kratkii slovar' agiograficheskikh terminov.* Moscow: Gnosis.

Index

11th Party Congress, 30
168 chasa, 177

Aegina, 236
Akhilleus, 292
Alabin, P.V., 15
Albanians, xii, 106, 142
Aleksii II, 221
Alexander from Thessaloniki, 237
allochronism, 287, 288
Altînchair, 254
Anastasios, 221
Andrić, Ivo, 179
Angelov, Dimitîr, 8, 43, 61, 81–83, 91
Apostolus, 235
Archeological Institute, 3, 79
archeology, *see* historical profession
archive, xi, xix, 64n1, 84, 85, 152, 175, 182, 244, 308
Arendt, Hanna, 69
Asen I, 150
Asparukh, 54, 150, 201

Bakalov, Georgi, 157, 162, 163, 173–75
Bakîrdzhiev, Vasil, 154
Balachev, Anatolii, 226–29, 231, 245, 277
Balevski, Angel, 8, 39, 42, 43, 65, 66, 92, 93
Balkan nationalism, xi, xv, 115
Balkan Wars, 54, 149, 160, 312
Balkani, 180
Baltadzhian, Eduard, 30
BAN, *see* Bulgarian Academy of Sciences
Bartholomew I, 221

Bauer, Adolf, 120
Baum, Paul Franklin, 120
Bebel, August, 161
Beissinger, Mark, 72
Belgrade legion, 121
Benchev, Mikhail, 9, 93
Benedict XIV, 230, 296
Benhabib, Seyla, 69
Benjamin, Walter, 131
Berlin Treaty, 55
Bernstein, Eduard, 161
Beshevliev, Veselin,
biography, 11, 123, 124, 129, 145, 152, 16, 179, 188, 189, 201, 241, 243–45, 249, 252, 254, 256, 257, 261, 276
Biolchev, Boian, 105
Bitolski, Angel, 237
Bizet, Georges, xix
Blagoev, Dimitîr, 157–63, 165, 167
Blagoevgrad, 266
Bobchev, Sava, 27–31, 34, 36, 37, 49, 59, 85, 86, 164
Bobchev, Stefan, 129, 130, 140, 141
Boev, Petîr, 25, 29, 34, 35, 37, 41, 50
Boiadzhiev, Stefan, 8, 41, 42, 79, 84
Boian-Enravota, 240
Bokova, Anastasiia Ilieva (*also* Anastasiia Bokova), 17, 23, 83
Bolhrad, 266
Boris III, 153
Botev, Hristo, 16, 54, 55, 67, 112, 124, 126, 127, 130, 135, 136, 138, 144, 154, 156–65, 168, 176, 187, 188, 198, 201, 237, 246, 248, 249, 266, 274–77
"Botev-Levski" Institute, 23

Bourdieu, Pierre, 6, 225, 226
Bozhilov, Vasil, 19
Bozveliev, Kosta, 175
Brown, Peter, 293, 294
Buchinski, Dimitîr, 49
Bulgaria, xii, xiv, xvi, 13, 33, 40, 53–56, 104–07, 113–15, 121–28, 132, 135, 138, 140, 142, 150, 153–56, 163, 164, 167, 170, 172, 175, 177, 188–90, 192–96, 204, 206, 207, 221–23, 239, 240, 267, 269, 272, 281, 283–85, 289, 304, 305, 308, 311, 313n1, 314
Bulgarian Academy of Sciences (BAN), 3, 7, 8, 9, 14, 25, 36, 39, 40, 41, 43, 49, 51, 52, 60, 61, 63–66, 68, 75, 79–82, 91–93, 96, 98, 238
1986 debate, 7, 8, 40, 44, 60–64, 68, 79, 81, 83, 91, 93, 96
Bulgarian Committee "Vasil Levski," 185, 265
Bulgarian National Television, 34, 102, 203
Bulgarian Orthodox Church, xvii, 97, 99, 211, 221, 223, 238, 251
split, xv, 99, 211, 212, 214, 217, 220, 221, 251, 272
BOC under Maxim, 99, 211, 212, 217–23, 225, 227, 228, 240, 263, 265, 267, 268, 277, 282
BOC under Pimen, 211, 212, 217–22, 225–28, 240, 277
Bulgarian Revolutionary Central Committee (BRCC), 123, 168
Bulgarian Turks, 4, 313n1
Bulgarians, xii, 10, 11, 13–15, 44, 51, 56, 59, 93, 97, 102, 103, 105, 107, 112–14, 122, 127, 132–34, 136, 142, 145, 149, 154, 161, 163, 167, 170, 171, 176, 177, 180, 181, 185, 192, 203–05, 242, 266, 279, 283, 284, 299, 304, 308, 310

Callistus III, 302
Campbell, Joseph, 120, 303, 308
canonization, xv, xvii, xx, 68, 127, 151, 207, 208, 211–14, 225–40, 251, 262, 263, 265, 267, 269, 271, 274, 277, 279, 281, 282, 296, 299, 307, 308
Canute IV, 295
Carlyle, Thomas, 117–19, 298, 299
Central Committee (also Central Committee of the Bulgarian Communist Party), 35, 57, 82, 84, 91, 92, 94, 123, 189, 191, 193, 197
Central Historical-Archeological Museum of the St. Synod, 49
Chatalbashev, Dimitîr, 303, 305
Chatarjee, Partha, xvii
Chausheva, Dora, 262, 263, 265, 280, 281, 284
Chervenkov, Vîlko, 57
Chorbadzhiiski, Dimitîr Khristov (Chudomir), 175, 176
Christodoulos, 221
Church Historical and Archival Institute of the Bulgarian Patriarchate (CHAI), 212, 228, 267
Church of St. Eusthatios, 235
civil society, *see* communism
Codreanu, Corneliu Zelea, 155, 272
Colocotronis, Vassilis, xiii
Commission of the Committee of Art and Culture, 31
Committee for Art and Culture, 31
Committee for Friendship and Cultural Ties with Foreign Countries, 33
Committee for State and People's Control, 50, 84
communism, xi, xvi, 4, 6, 59, 68–73, 76, 84, 85, 111, 221, 285, 289, 308
Cosquin, Emmanuel, 120
Council of Serdica, 221

Danov, Khristo, 140
Davis, Natalie Zemon, xvii, 5

Delchev, Gotse, 54–56
Demokratsiia, 217, 286
Department of History (University of Sofia), 189
Department of Museums and Monuments, 15
Deutsche Welle, 177
Dichev, Stefan, 179–81, 183
Dimitîr, Khadzhi, 101, 134, 141, 274
Dimitrov, Borislav, 88–90
Dimitrov, Georgi, 101, 187, 188, 197, 198, 219
Dimitrov, Ilcho, 189–91
Dimitrov, Philip, 219
Dimitrova, Blaga, 180
Dimkov, Petîr, 18, 19
Dochev, Ivan, 156
Doinov, Doino, 30, 31, 92, 266, 267
Donchev, Anton, 179
Douglas, Mary, 212
Dundes, Alan, 120, 121
Dzhebel, 266
Dzhingov, Georgi, 8, 24, 37, 48, 79, 83–86

Eastern Europe, xvi, 68, 70, 76, 271, 272, 285, 308, 309, 311
Eastern European communism, xvi, 76
Eco, Umberto, 181
Edward the Confessor, 295
Eliade, Mircea, 282, 287, 288
Engels, Friedrich, 161
Evangelistria, 236
Evtimov, Evtim, 65

Father Paisii, *see* Paisii of Khilander
Fehér, Géza, 53
Feierman, Steven, 5
Ferdinand, 150
Feuchtwanger, Lion, 179
Filaret, Cherinigov, 237
Filov, Bogdan, 53
First World War, xii, 54, 123, 127, 128, 131, 147, 149, 150, 160, 292, 310, 312

Fol, Alexander, 193
Foucault, Michel, 69
Fraser, Nancy, 69, 71
Free Europe, 177

Gabrovo, 206, 283
Ganovski, Sava, 25
Garibaldi, Guiseppe, xiii, 203, 303
Geertz, Clifford, xvii, 151, 212, 213
Gellner, Ernest, 71, 127
Genchev, Nikolai, 10, 88, 89, 118, 124, 125, 127, 130, 131, 149, 150, 156–58, 160, 162–65, 170, 175, 188–200
Genovich, Nikola, 169
George of Neapolis, 235
Georgiev, Evlogi, 129, 167
Georgiev, Khristo, 129, 167–69
Gerasimos the Younger, 233
Gergova, Diana, 3, 8, 61, 83
Gerov, Naiden, 167, 168
Giaurov, Khristo, 17, 18, 22–25, 27, 28, 31, 48–52, 68, 83
Ginzburg, Carlo, xvii, 5
Giurgiu, 266, 276
globalization, xvii, 5, 59, 203, 285, 308
Goshev, Ivan, 48
Gramsci, Antonio, 69
Greeks, xii, 55, 142, 292, 311
Gregory IX, 230, 232, 235

Habermas, Jürgen, 69, 71, 72
Hagias Laurentios, 235
Hagioi Pantes, 236
haidouts, xii
hajduks, xii
Haraszti, Miklós, 73
Hayes, Carlton, 242, 299
Hegel, Georg Wilhelm Friedrich, 69
heroes, xii, xiii, xiv, xv, xx, 54–56, 112, 115, 117–20, 122, 128, 135, 150, 157, 158, 160, 169, 177, 187, 195, 198, 199, 201–03, 215, 291–302, 308, 313
historical profession, 9, 15, 214, 156

Hugo, Victor, 134, 135, 137
Humphrey, Caroline, 280
Huxley, T.H., 117

Iambol, 206
Ianeva, Atanasa, 21
Iazova, Iana, 180–82
iconography, 264
Ignatius IV, 221
Ilinden Uprising, 55
Institute for History, 30
Institute for the Preservation of Cultural Monuments, 30
Institute of Culture, 29n1
Interior Ministry, 44
Iordanov, Georgi, 36, 39
Iotov, Iordan, 35, 47, 92
Ipati, 235
Iribadzhakov, Nikolai, 191
Isusov, Mito, 91–93
Ivanov, Khristo, 168
Ivanov, Vicho, 159

Jamestown, 33
Joan of Arc, 11, 203, 273, 302, 310
John XV, 230
Juhász, Péter, 35

Kalofer, 112, 206, 266
Kaloian, 51
Kalymnos, 236
Kapudaliev, Emil, 218
Karan Vîrbovka, 66–67
Karavelov, Liuben, 54, 113, 123–27, 141, 158–63, 168–72, 174, 248, 274
Karavelov, Petko, 161
Karlovo, 112, 122, 130, 152, 153, 167, 184, 185, 200, 203–05, 207, 211, 241, 243, 254, 261–66, 268, 280, 281, 283–856, 289, 304
Karnobat, 283, 287
Kautski, Karl, 161
Kazanlîk, 175, 284
Khaitov, Nikolai, xvi, 3, 4, 8, 13, 14, 17, 19, 20, 28, 35, 37–43, 47, 48, 50–54, 56, 58, 59, 61–68, 75, 77–87, 91–94, 96, 100–05, 107
Khalacha, Dencho, 171
Khambarkov-Gîskata, Khristo, 17, 18
Khitov, Panaiot, 122, 124, 141, 142, 274
Khristov, Georgi Pop, 254
Kîkrina, 244
Kirkov, Georgi, 276
Kirova, Zlatka, 31
klefts, 10
Kluckhohn, Clyde, 290
Kolev, Georgi, 8–9
Konstantin, Archimandrite, 255
Koselleck, Reinhart, 69, 288, 301
Kosev Commission, 37, 48–50
Kosev, Dimitîr, 8, 37, 50, 86, 92, 193
Krappe, Alexander, 120
Kretschmer, Ernst, 154
Krîstev, T., 136–38, 165
Krîstiu, Pop, 9, 12, 14, 18, 20, 126, 172, 180, 205, 244–46
Krum (Khan), 177
Kuncheva, Gina, 262

Laidlaw, James, 280
Lamia, 235
Lasal, Ferdinand, 161
Lazarov, Iliia, 16, 17
Le Monde, 193
Legion of Archangel Michael, 155
Lessmann, Heinrich, 120
Levin, Eve, 238
Levski, Vasil
  betrayal controversy, 12, 77, 126, 172, 244, 245, 247
  biography, 11, 123, 124, 129, 145, 152, 169, 179, 188, 201, 241, 243, 244, 252, 256, 257, 261, 276
  and Botev, 55, 111–112, 124, 126, 127, 130, 135, 136, 138, 154, 156–65, 168, 176, 187, 188, 198, 201, 248, 266, 274, 276, 277
  burial versions, xvi, xvii, xix, 11, 12, 14, 16, 18, 20, 21, 23, 30, 34–36,

38, 41, 42, 44, 47, 51, 52, 59, 61,
  81–85, 93, 97, 102, 228, 307
canonization, xvii, xx, 68, 127, 151,
  207, 208, 211–14, 226–36, 240,
  251, 262, 263, 265, 267, 269, 271,
  274, 277, 279, 282, 307, 308
commemoration, 123n2, 144, 146,
  153, 188, 274, 290
and contemporary assessments,
  124–29, 142, 168–74, 214
and fascists, 150–57, 187
and the Orthodox church, xvii, 97,
  99, 229, 241, 242, 262, 279, 280
political appropriations, 111–16,
  149–67, 174–78
reception of, 168, 176, 187, 199,
  201–08
religiosity, 164, 243, 248, 250, 256
and socialists, 157–60, 164, 173,
  204
in historiography, xvi, 138, 142,
  175, 182, 187, 199, 212, 214,
  244, 257
in textbooks, 9, 54, 139–42, 150,
  198, 199, 201, 202
in literature, 124, 130, 132–39,
  151, 152, 179–86
visual representations, 111, 113,
  179–86, 220, 262–65, 268, 275,
  276, 286, 305
Lewin, Moshe, 71
Liebknecht, Karl, 161
Liebknecht, Wilhelm, 161
Lincoln, Abraham, 11, 303
Lincoln, Bruce, 151
Literaturen front, 64
Lokorsko, 17
Lom, 283
Lord Raglan (FitzRoy Richard
  Somerset, 4th Baron Raglan),
  120, 121, 291
Lovech, 9, 123, 169, 173, 205, 219,
  244
Lucaris, Cyril, 233
Luhmann, Niklas, 69
Luxemburg, Rosa, 161

Macaulay, Thomas, 117
MacDermott, Mercia, 243, 257–59
Madara horseman, 51
Magdalene, 236
Malakope, 235
Manchev, Dragan, 237
Manchov, Dragan, 140
Mann, Heinrich, 179
Maritsa, 172
martyrdom, 133, 141, 227, 235, 238,
  239, 268, 276, 279, 295
Marx, Karl, 69, 161, 301
Mazhar Pasha, 14
McCartney, Eugene, 120
Medieval Section (of the
  Archaeological Institute), 8, 30,
  39, 57, 78, 79, 96, 102
memoirs, xx, 9–12, 14–17, 21, 22,
  67, 81, 89, 124, 130, 131, 135,
  152, 158, 168, 175, 179, 188,
  189, 194, 196, 197, 214, 252,
  253, 314
memory, xv–xx, 11, 18, 19, 34, 56,
  63, 67, 73, 93, 98, 101, 115, 126,
  130, 145, 149, 151, 162, 177,
  204, 207, 227, 231, 237, 239, 252,
  254, 256, 263, 269, 277, 286, 302
Metaxas, Ioannis, 153
Meyerhoff, Barbara, 282
microhistory, 5, 307
Midhat Pasha, 171, 179
Mîglenska, Zlata, 240
Mikhailov, Andrei, 97, 98
Mikhailov, Apostol, 227
Mikhailov, Stamen, 8, 19, 22, 25, 27,
  28, 35, 36, 42, 43, 47–53, 61, 66,
  67, 79, 80, 85, 86, 88, 97
Mikhailov, Stoian, 91, 92, 93
Milev, Gancho, 114
Miller, Dean, 292, 293, 297
Milushev, Mikhail, 97, 228
Mir, 22, 83
Misîl, 136, 137
Mitov, Gîcho, 286
Mladezh, 192, 193
Mostich, Chîrgubil, 51

Mount Athos, 235, 236, 241, 268
Museum of the City of Sofia, 8, 31, 48–50, 52
Mushanov, Nikola, 9, 30–32
Mutafchieva, Vera, 182
Myron, 232, 233
myth, xv, 117, 119, 120, 139, 145, 149, 150, 151, 283, 289–91, 297, 313, 314

Nabokov, Vladimir, 15
Nai-Novi, Georgi Sofiiski, 240
Napoleon, Bonaparte, 119, 309
"Narodna kultura" (publishing house), 180
National Humanities Center, 18
National Library, xix, 238, 252
nationalism, xi–xiii, xv, 56, 59, 76, 101, 103, 114, 115, 117, 118, 127, 134, 145, 150, 155, 182, 192, 195, 259, 272, 297, 299, 307, 308, 310–13
 Balkan, xi, xv, 115
 Bulgarian, xiii, xix, 59, 67, 115, 178, 193, 311
 and religion, xv, 214, 242, 276, 299, 300, 308
 symbols, xii, xiv, 12, 112, 212, 242, 307
 weak, xx, 19, 101, 115, 310, 311, 313, 314
Nektarios of Jerusalem, 231, 232
Nevrokop, 68
Nevskii, Alexander, 296
Neznakomov, Petîr, 90
Nicephoras of Chios, 235
Nikolov, Khristo, 9–10
Nikolova, Dora, 64–66
Nordic, 34
Novi Pazar, 51

Office of Religious Affairs (ORA), 217–21
Open Society Institute, 104
Orozov, Nikola, 228
Otechestvo, 217

Ovcharov, Dimitîr, 8, 41–43, 48, 50, 66,
Ovcharov, Nikolai, 95

Paisii of Khilendar, 226, 239, 240
Panagiurishte, 266
Patlagean, Evelyne, 231
Patmos, 236
Patriarch Evtimii, 240
Patriarch Gregory V., 235
Patriarch Kiril, 226
Patriarch Maxim, 99, 211, 212, 217, 219, 220, 222, 262, 265, 267
Patriarch Nikon, 236
Patriach Philotheos, 232
Patriarch Pimen (Metropolitan of Nevrokop), 68
Pavlov, Todor, 51–57, 191
Pelin, Elin, 54
Pernik, 284
Peter VII, 227
Petev, Ivan, 12–17, 19, 20, 268, 269
Plekhanov, Georgi, 161
Pleven, 266
Pliska, 51
Plovdiv, 133, 134, 145, 155, 167, 172, 201, 202, 219, 265
Pogled, 88, 89, 93
Popova-Mutafova, Fani, 179
Poppavlova, Maria, 16, 17, 19, 22, 83
Poptodorov, Radko, 217, 218, 222, 227, 251
Pravets, 96
Prince Lazar, 296
Propp, Vladimir, 120
Puls, 27, 93

Rabotnichesko delo, 27, 30, 35, 47, 85
Rabotnik, 135
Radeva, Rumiana, 112
Radevski, Khristo, 175
Radichkov, Iordan, 38, 104
Radkov, Radko, 182
Rainov, Theofan, 167, 168

Rakovski, Georgi Sava, 54, 101, 121, 122, 136, 141, 142, 156, 159, 162, 179, 243, 248, 266
Randeria, Shalini, 71
Rank, Otto, 120, 121
Razboinikov, Spas, 9
Razgrad, 207
Razlog, 266
Real Life of Sebastian Knight, The, 15
relics, 32, 229, 231, 234–36, 240, 267, 269, 279, 280, 309
Research Institute of Criminology, 44
Revel, Jacques, 5
Revival Period, 30, 31, 174, 184, 194
Rila Monastery, 55, 264
Rilski, Kamen, 66
ritual, xvii, xx, 120, 130, 150, 213, 214, 226, 235, 236, 266, 268, 281–83, 289–91
Rizov, Dimitîr, 48
Roberta, 262
Romanians, xii, 142, 312
Ruse, 101, 169, 207
Ruse District, 67
Russo-Turkish (Liberation) War, 54, 129, 145, 235, 237
Ryle, Gilbert, 213

Sahlins, Marshall, 212
Samokov, 238
San Stefano Treaty, 54–55
Sandanski, Iane, 188
Saras of Kalymnos, 236
Sava (Polish Archbishop), 221
Schmeing, Karl, 126
Schmitt, Carl, 69, 86
Second Bulgarian Legion, 122
Second World War, 6, 55, 120, 127, 130, 139, 157, 163, 175, 184, 189, 196, 212, 220, 243, 292, 312, 313n1
Sendov, Blagovest, 80
Serbs, xii, 55, 106, 142, 170
Serdica Fortress, 51
Shakespeare, 3, 118, 188
Sharova, Krumka, 170, 171, 174
Shishman, Ivan, 237
Sîbev, Khristofor, 217–19
Simeon (Czech Archbishop), 221
Simeon I, 54, 150, 201
Simeon II, *see* Simeon Sakskoburggotski
Simeon Sakskoburggotski, 222, 305
Skanderbeg, Georgi Kastrioti, 185
Skete of St. Anne, 236
Slaveikov, Pencho, 137
Slaveikov, Petko, 171, 237
Sliven, 134, 266
social drama, xvi, 7, 9, 20–22, 27, 37, 60, 88, 97
Sofia, 3, 4, 9, 14–18, 39, 40, 47, 49, 51, 53, 57, 94, 107, 123, 124n3, 126, 128, 130, 140, 143, 145, 153, 155, 170, 183, 189, 196–202, 206, 218–21, 223, 238, 252, 263, 265, 266, 269, 281, 285, 286
Sofia, 28, 34, 47
Sopot, 264, 285, 286
Soros, George, 104, 105
Sotirov, Ivan, 8
South Slavs, xii, 237
Spencer, Herbert, 117
St. Agathon Monastery, 235
St. Cecilia, 67
St. Constantine the Great, 295
St. Ferdinand, 295
St. Georgi Novi Sofiiski, 238, 240
St. Helen, 295
St. Hieronimus, 211
St. Isabel (Elizabeth), 295
St. John of Rila, 188
St. Louis, 295
St. Ludmilla, 295
"St. Paraskeva" church (*also* "Sv. Parashkeva"), 18, 22, 212, 220, 263
St. Petersburg Slavic Committee, 15
St. Sofronii Vrachanski, 226, 239
St. Stephen, 295
St. Vladimir, 296
St. Wenceslas, 295

Stambolov, Stefan, 161, 201, 266, 276
Stancheva, Magdalina, 8, 30–32, 43, 49–51, 53, 61, 84
Stanev, Emiliian, 179
Stanilov, Stanislav, 66, 67, 80, 96–98
Stara Zagora, 48, 144, 241, 285
Stari, Georgi Sofiiski, 238
Stoev, Gencho, 179
Stoianov, Maniu, 238
Stoianov, Peter, 220, 221, 268
Stoianov, Zakhari, 118, 124, 129, 130, 135, 136, 138, 145, 158, 159, 163–65, 168, 179, 181, 241, 242, 244, 245, 249, 252, 263
Stoianova, Velichko, 169
Strashimirov, Dimitîr, 130, 152, 188, 252
Strelcha, 266
Strumishki, Anastasii, 238
"Sv. Parashkeva" church, see "St. Paraskeva" church
"Sv. Petka" church, see "Sv. Petka Samardzhiiska" church
"Sv. Petka Samardzhiiska" church (also "Sv. Petka"), 4, 18, 22, 25, 30, 36, 44, 57, 78, 94, 97, 98, 226, 228, 263, 265
Svoboda, 113, 274

Takiia, Nikolov Pop Khristo, 10
Talbot, Alice-Mary, 229
Talev, Dimitîr, 179
Teteven, 172
"The Grey Horse" pub, 18
Theoctist, 221
Theological Academy, 12, 22, 23, 48, 52, 217, 218, 227, 228, 251, 268
Thracian, 34, 99, 154
Tîrnovo, 32, 172, 189, 219, 266
Tito, Josip Broz, 55, 56
Todorov, Dechko, 261
Todorov, Nikolai, 7, 8, 43, 44, 60–62, 64n1, 68, 91–93, 96
Tolbukhin (Dobrich), 204

Totiu, Philip, 142
Trifonov, Slavi, 102
Troian, 269
Trouillot, Michel-Rolph, 5, 87
Trud, 22, 24, 52, 83, 305
Tsankov, Vili, 183
Tsar Alexei Mikhailovich, 236
Tsar Boris, 54
Tsar Boris-Mikhail, 226, 240
Tsar Ivan Asen II, 150, 237
Tsar Peter, 240
Tsar Samuil, 274
Tsar Simeon, 54, 150, 201
Tsarevets, 32, 33
Tsonev, Todor, 111
Turks, xii, 4, 81, 114, 132, 140, 180, 181, 207, 237, 238, 304, 312, 313
Turner, Victor, xvi, 7, 39, 75, 91, 99, 280
Turnu-Mâgurele, 266
Turtsiia, 124, 169, 170

Ulrich (Bishop of Augsburg), 230
Undzhiev, Ivan, 10, 11, 13, 19, 23, 88, 89, 102, 152, 168, 169, 179, 183, 188, 242–44, 251–59
University of Sofia, 3, 219, 251
Urban VIII, 230

Varlaam (Archbishop of Okhrid), 238
Varna, 64, 68, 204, 219
"Vasil Levski" People's Committee, 152
Vasilev, Iordan, 180–82
Vasilii, Khadzhi, 241
Vazov, Ivan, 54, 118, 132–39, 144, 151, 154, 177, 179, 181, 183, 185, 201, 245–47, 252, 269, 277
Velichkov, Konstantin, 246
Velkov, Velizar, 8, 78, 79
Videnov, Zhan, 219, 220
Vienna, 18, 79, 107, 309
Vodenicharov, Todor, 66, 67
von Hahn, Johann Georg, 120
Vrachanski, Sofronii, 226

Vrana, 192
Vratsa, 144, 255, 266
Vryonis, Jr., Speros, 294

Weber, Claudia, 144, 145
Williamsburg, 33

Young, Iris Marion, 69

Zagorchinov, Stoian, 179
Zaimov, Stoian, 164, 253

Zhelev, Zheliu, 29n1, 103, 118, 130, 197, 200, 219
Zhirov, Iuri, 34
Zhivkov, Georgi, 249
Zhivkov, Todor, 33, 57, 81, 82, 94–96, 104, 111, 177, 183, 191–93, 217, 303
Zhivkova, Liudmila, 30, 31, 36, 59, 93, 104, 193, 194
Zograf, Zakharii, 238
Zographou Monastery, 235

Plates

▲ **Plate 1** Levski monument in Karlovo. Bronze statue by Marin Vasilev (1905)
Source: author's photograph

Plates

▲ **Plate 2** Photograph of Levski from 1870, probably made in Bulgaria during his third organizational visit. This is arguably Levski's most popular image today

▲ **Plate 3** Photograph of Levski in Bucharest from 1872. This is the image distributed to the Ottoman police

▲ **Plate 4** Vasil Levski as a standard bearer in the *cheta* of Panaiot Khitov, 1867

Plates

▲ **Plate 5** Levski in the uniform of the First Bulgarian Legion, Belgrade
Source for Plates 2–5: These images of Levski are ubiquitous, but the best reproductions are in Khristo Ionkov and Stoianka Ionkova. *Vasil Levski i bîlgarskata natsionalna revoliutsiia*. Sofia: Izdatelstvo na BAN, 1987, p. 21: plate 1, p. 20: plate 5, p. 56, plate 10, p. 168, plate 19.

Plates

◀◀ **Plate 6** Levski's portrait by Georgi Danchov, 1880s
Source: Zhechko Popov, *Vasil Levski v bîlgarskoto izobrazitelno izkustvo*, Sofia: Bîlgarski khudozhnik, 1976, Reproduction 2.

◀ **Plate 7** Levski's bronze high relief at the Sofia monument by Rudolf Weir (1895)
Source: Zhechko Popov, *Vasil Levski v bîlgarskoto izobrazitelno izkustvo*, Sofia: Bîlgarski khudozhnik, 1976, Reproduction 4.

◤ **Plate 8** Nikola Kozhukharov. The capture of Levski, 1952
Source: Zhechko Popov, *Vasil Levski v bîlgarskoto izobrazitelno izkustvo*, Reproduction 42.

▶ **Plate 8a** Levski tatoo

▼ **Plate 9** Levski Street, Sofia
Source: author's photograph

◂ **Plate 10** The chapel "All Bulgarian Saints" as part of the Levski museum ensemble in Karlovo
Source: author's photograph

◂ **Plate 11** Mounting the reliquary
Source: author's photograph

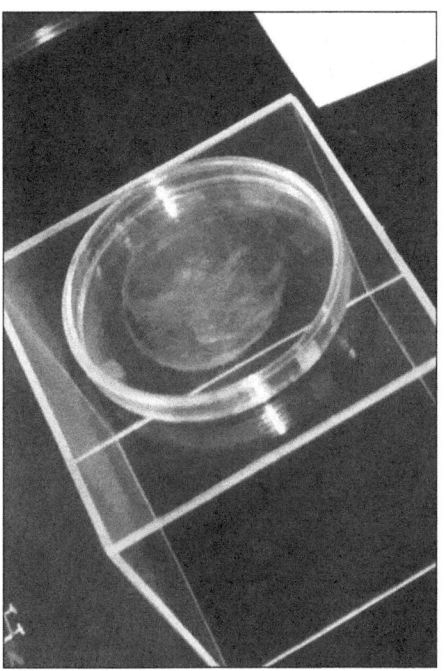

◀ **Plate 12** Levski's hair, kept at the chapel "All Bulgarian Saints"
Source: author's photograph

▼ **Plate 13** Commemorative plaque exhibited on the exterior of the "Sv. Petka Samardzhiiska" church, 1999.
Source: author's photograph

Plates

◄ **Plate 14** Plaque: close-up.
Source: author's photograph

▶ **Plate 15A** Levski's icon: blow-up
Source: author's photograph

◤ **Plate 15** Levski's icon in the interior of the "Sv. Petka" church
Source: author's photograph

▼ **Plate 16** Fresco on northern wall of the Holy Virgin church in Karlovo, 1997
Source: author's photograph

▲ **Plate 17** Iconostasis of the Holy Virgin church in Karlovo
Source: author's photograph

▲ **Plate 18** Levski's portrait-icon in the altar space
Source: author's photograph

▲ **Plate 18A** Levski's portrait-icon: blow-up
Source: author's photograph

▲ **Plate 19** Levski's icon in the "Sv. Sofia" church
Source: author's photograph

▲ **Plate 20** A poster of Levski's icon
Source: author's photograph

▲ **Plate 21** From photograph to icon

Plates

▲ **Plate 22** Icon of Lenin, 1920s
Source: Miltiades Papanikolaou, ed., *Licht und Farbe in der russischen Avantgarde: die Sammlung Costakis aus dem Staatlichen Museum für Zeitgenössische Kunst Thessaloniki* Köln: DuMont, 2004.

For Product Safety Concerns and Information please contact
our EU representative GPSR@taylorandfrancis.com Taylor & Francis
Verlag GmbH, Kaufingerstraße 24, 80331 München, Germany

T - #0009 - 220426 - C0 - 229/152/21 - PB - 9786155053092 - Matt Lamination